Gainsborough

Frontispiece:
Detail from *Mary, Countess Howe* (1732–1800).
Canvas, 96 × 60 in. About 1763–4.
London, Iveagh Bequest, Kenwood
(Note 55)

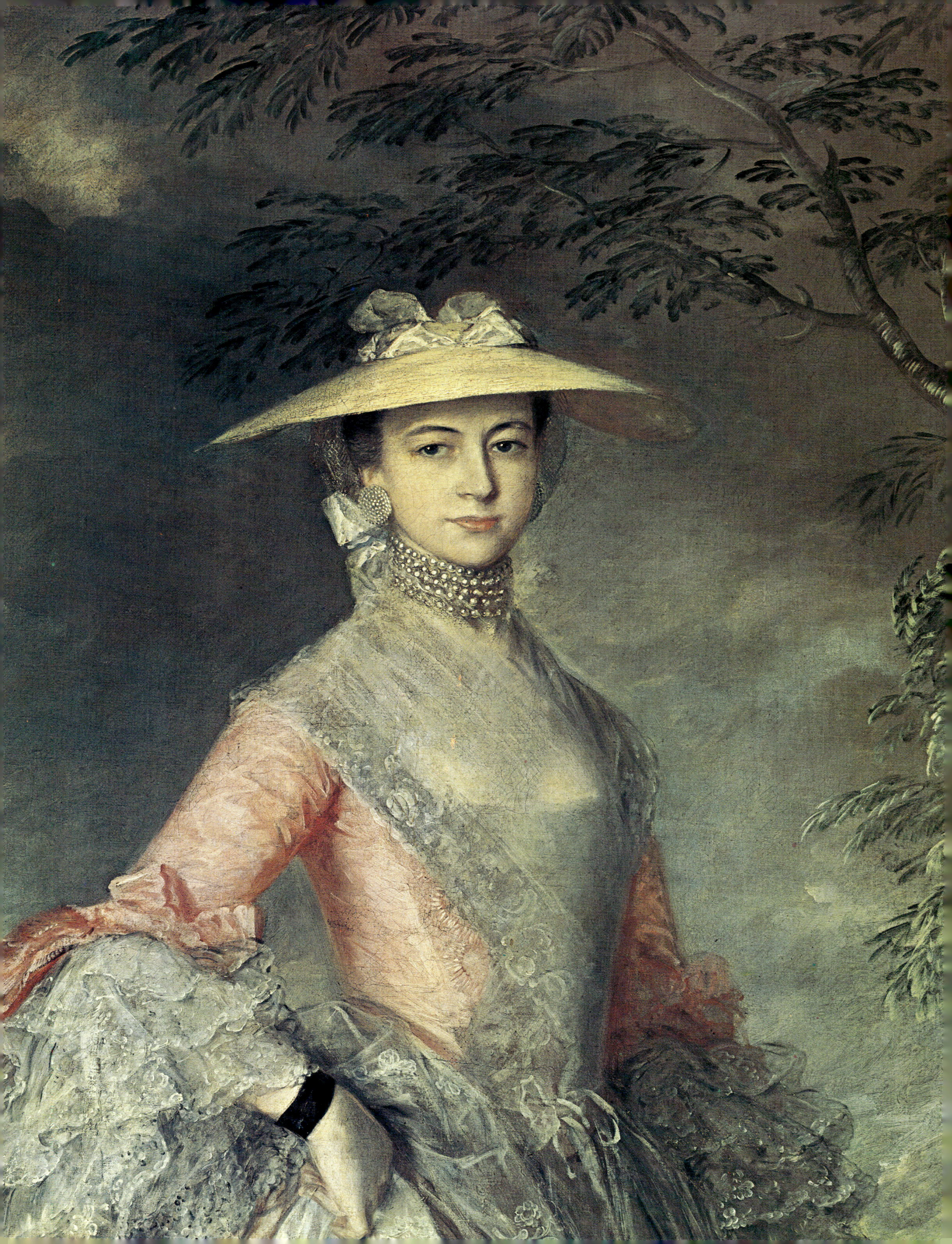

John Hayes

Gainsborough

Paintings and drawings

Phaidon

Phaidon Press Limited, 5 Cromwell Place, London SW7 2JL

Distributed in the United States of America
by Praeger Publishers Inc., 111 Fourth Avenue, New York, N.Y. 10003

First published 1975

ISBN 0 7148 1639 6
Library of Congress Catalog Card Number 75–721

Text printed in Great Britain by Westerham Press, Kent
and illustrations by Well Hall Press, Kent

CONTENTS

For my parents

PREFACE

THOMAS GAINSBOROUGH is by general consent one of the most delightful, spontaneous and naturally gifted of all English painters and draughtsmen. Any book devoted to his art must depend upon the quality and choice of illustrations, the more especially since his work is scattered in galleries and private collections the world over, and not concentrated, as with Constable and Turner, in any one place. Much care, therefore, has been given to the plates in this book, which have been selected partly to demonstrate his range and originality and partly to emphasize the perennial nature of his appeal – his extraordinary technical accomplishment and the sensuous beauty of his handling. A number of comparisons have been made between works of different periods, and the arrangement of the illustrations is only broadly chronological; but the notes, which include a full analysis of each composition, are arranged in strict chronological order, and are intended to form, if read in sequence, a sustained art-historical account of Gainsborough's development.

In the introductory essay, which is less concerned with the direct visual impact of his art, I have sought to bring into focus, from the various detailed studies of aspects of his work I have made over the last twenty years, my feelings about Gainsborough, both as man and artist, and my view of his achievement, not only in terms of the eighteenth century but in the wider context of European art as a whole. Gainsborough was as inspired when he set pen to paper in his personal correspondence as he was in his painting and, wherever possible, I have tried to let him speak in his own words, often idiosyncratic but vividly descriptive and wholly to the point. Those who wish to go beyond this book to discover more about this remarkable and very lovable person will find a bibliographical note at the back; most to be recommended, both for understanding of the man and for sheer enjoyment, are the *Letters* and Reynolds's warm appreciation, contained in his *Discourses*. Ample reproductions of the paintings will be found in Ellis Waterhouse's *Gainsborough*, 1958, and of the drawings in my own book on that subject, published in 1970.

Robert Wark has kindly read the typescript of my introduction, and I owe him a special debt of gratitude, not only for his valuable criticisms of this essay, but for the many happy hours I have spent with him discussing an artist for whom we share a particular affection. I must also acknowledge the courtesy of Ronald Paulson in allowing me to read the chapter on Gainsborough from his new book well in advance of publication. Particular thanks are due to Keith Roberts, of Phaidon Press, for the pleasures of creative collaboration, to Miss Mollie Luther for her impeccable typing and to Mrs Jenny Haviland for her care in reading proofs. Mrs Jenny Wright has been the most efficient and helpful of editors.

Her Majesty The Queen has granted gracious permission for pictures in the royal collection to be illustrated, and owners and curators have almost unfailingly been kind in allowing the reproduction of works in their possession or charge and in providing facilities for special photography when this was needed. A book of this kind depends upon such kindness and forbearance, and it is a pleasure for me to acknowledge the help so freely given. Some of Gainsborough's letters survive only in later transcripts but wherever the originals are known to exist excerpts have been quoted from the manuscripts themselves.

December 1974 J.H.

BIOGRAPHICAL OUTLINE

1727 Baptized on 14 May at the Independent meeting house in Friars Street, Sudbury, Suffolk, the fifth son of John Gainsborough, clothier, and Mary Burroughs

1739 Ramsay (1713–84) settled in London

*c.*1740 Sent up to London and became a pupil of Hubert François Gravelot, the French draughtsman and engraver. Hogarth presented his full-length of *Thomas Coram* to the Foundling Hospital

*c.*1745 Established his own studio in London

1746 Married Margaret Burr on 15 July at Dr Keith's Mayfair Chapel, London

1748 Returned to Sudbury to practise. Birth of his elder daughter, Mary

1752 Birth of his younger daughter, Margaret. Moved to Ipswich

1753 Reynolds (1723–92) settled in London as a portraitist after his return from three years study in Italy. Painted his *Admiral Keppel*, inspired by the Apollo Belvedere

1757–8 Wilson (1712/14–82) settled in London as a landscape painter after spending six or seven years in Italy

1758 Worked as a travelling portrait painter in the Midlands

1759 Moved from Ipswich to Bath

1760 First exhibited at the Society of Artists

1764 Death of Hogarth at the age of sixty-seven

1766 Moved to a house in The Circus, Bath

1768 Invited to become a founder-member of the Royal Academy, of which Reynolds had been appointed President

1769 First exhibited at the Royal Academy

1772 Took as an apprentice his nephew, Gainsborough Dupont (1754–97). Dupont was his only recorded pupil and assistant

1773 Quarrelled with the Royal Academy over the hanging of his pictures, which resulted in his not contributing to the annual exhibition again until 1777

1774 Settled in London, taking a tenancy of the west wing of Schomberg House, Pall Mall

*c.*1782 Made a tour in the West Country with Gainsborough Dupont. Death of Wilson

*c.*1783 Constructed his peep-show box in which he displayed his transparencies

1783 Made a tour of the Lakes with Samuel Kilderbee

1784 Again quarrelled with the Royal Academy over the hanging of his pictures, which he withdrew. Never again exhibited at the Academy, and started a series of annual exhibitions in his own studio at Schomberg House. Death of Ramsay, and appointment of Reynolds as Principal Painter to the King

1788 Died on 2 August, buried in Kew Churchyard

1789 Private sale of his pictures and drawings held at Schomberg House. Further sales were held at Christie's in 1792, 1797 (following the death of Gainsborough Dupont) and 1799 (after Mrs Gainsborough's death)

1792 Death of Reynolds. Lawrence (1769–1830) appointed Principal Painter to the King

INTRODUCTION

Gainsborough's Personality and Methods of Work

GAINSBOROUGH'S lifetime spanned an age of profound change in British painting and in the public's attitude towards British artists. He was born in 1727, when Hogarth was painting his first genre scenes and conversation pieces, and died in 1788, when Boydell's commissions for the Shakespeare Gallery in Pall Mall were giving a new impetus to British history painting. At his death, this modest and lovable man was the subject of one of the most thoughtful and beautifully written obituaries accorded to an English painter. 'If ever this nation should produce genius sufficient to acquire to us the honourable distinction of an English School, the name of Gainsborough will be transmitted to posterity, in the history of the Art, among the very first of that rising name.'[1] Such was the generous tribute of his great rival as a portraitist, Sir Joshua Reynolds. The celebrated Fourteenth Discourse was the only one of Reynolds's Christmas end-of-term addresses to the students of the Royal Academy, when it was his custom to develop his ideas about the philosophy and practice of the fine arts, which he illustrated by reference to a single painter – and that, moreover, a contemporary English painter, not Raphael or Michelangelo.

What moved Reynolds to devote an entire discourse to Gainsborough? For Gainsborough was an artist who had never been to Italy, who cared little about the Grand Manner, and whose heart lay in what was then considered the lesser genre of landscape painting: in short, who was as chalk to cheese as far as the President of the Academy was concerned. The answer is that, though an intellectual, Reynolds was less a theorist than a pragmatist, a man of great common sense in an age of common sense. 'I confess', he said, 'I take more interest in, and am more captivated with, the powerful impression of nature, which Gainsborough exhibited in his portraits and in his landskips, and the interesting simplicity and elegance of his little ordinary beggar-children, than with any of the works of that [the Roman] School, since the time of Andrea Sacchi, or perhaps, we may say Carlo Maratti . . . I am well aware how much I lay myself open to the censure and ridicule of the academical professors of other nations, in preferring the humble attempts of Gainsborough to the works of those regular graduates in the great historical style. But we have the sanction of all mankind in preferring genius in a lower rank of art, to feebleness and insipidity in the highest.'[2] Nature, simplicity and genius: these are the significant words in this passage. Nature was a concept beloved of the eighteenth century – though much abused by it, since it was susceptible of a variety of different interpretations; Reynolds was surely using it here literally, in the sense of 'naturalism', as we might apply that term to the works of Monet. Simplicity implied a Rousseauistic approach to country life and the inhabitants of the countryside, in which Gainsborough was at one with his age. But genius: this was a far less common word of approbation before the romantic era. The truth was that Reynolds was forced to acknowledge something extraordinary about Gainsborough's painting, something beyond the limits of academical training or of his own considerable powers, which compelled his admiration and aroused his intellectual curiosity. He was keenly aware that his great contemporary was both of, and not of, the eighteenth century; that he was a conformist, even a traditionalist, in some respects, but an original in others. In what, however, did this originality consist? Let Reynolds continue, this time on Gainsborough as a companion.

'He had a habit of continually remarking to those who happened to be about him, whatever peculiarity of countenance, whatever accidental combination of figures, or happy effects of light and shadow, occurred in prospects, in the sky, in walking the streets, or in company. . . . He neglected nothing which could keep his faculties in exercise, and derived hints from every sort of combination.'[3] Gainsborough had an eye as sharp as Rembrandt's, but he had more than just a perceptive eye; he possessed an extraordinary capacity to translate what he observed into the medium of oil paint which puts him firmly, along with Rembrandt, and with artists such as Velazquez, Manet, Renoir and Picasso, into the top flight of 'born painters'. Such dexterity of hand, such sensitivity of touch, so exquisite a feeling for the possibilities of the medium, do not, alas, always attend upon sharpness of vision or upon unusual powers of imagination. Constable fought bitterly hard to master these qualities, Reynolds never fully possessed them, and it was probably this miraculous combination of hand and eye that the latter most envied in Gainsborough. 'It is certain', he said, 'that all those odd scratches and marks, which, on a close examination, are so observable in Gainsborough's pictures, and which even to experienced painters appear rather the effect of accident than design; this chaos, this uncouth and shapeless appearance, by a kind of magick, at a certain distance assumes form, and all the parts seem to drop into their proper places.'[4] Gainsborough's close friend Philip Thicknesse remarked that it was possible to judge a Gainsborough portrait as though it were the living person,[5] and tells a revealing story of how 'after returning from the Concert at Bath, near twenty years ago, where we had been charmed by Miss Linley's voice, I went home to supper with my friend, who sent his servant for a bit of clay from the small beer barrel, with which he first modelled, and then coloured her head, and that too in a quarter of an hour, in such a manner that I protest it appeared to me even superior to his paintings!'[6]

Gainsborough never worked much, if at all, on the head of one of his portraits without the sitter before him, a luxury denied to most society portraitists by force of circumstance, and which, with the aid of the photograph, painters now feel they can reasonably neglect. This practice of Gainsborough's we may fairly deduce from a letter he wrote in 1771 about a portrait of Lady Dartmouth (Pl. 89) with which her husband was (justifiably) disappointed: 'I shall be extreemly willing to make any alterations your Lordship shall require, when Her Ladyship comes to Bath for that purpose, as I cannot (without taking away the likeness) touch it unless from the Life.'[7] Likeness, not composition or grandeur or self-advertisement, was always his first consideration, 'the principal beauty & intention of a Portrait', as he put it. And this, he maintained, was hard to achieve if one subscribed to Reynolds's view (and Lady Dartmouth's wish in the case of this particular commission) that, if a portrait was to retain a timeless quality, the costume and accessories should not be painted in the fashion of the day, necessarily evanescent, but either in the manner of the Antique or else in sufficiently generalized a way to defy the vagaries of fashion and thus any possibility of the picture's rapidly taking on the dismal appearance of last year's cast-off dress. Again to Lord Dartmouth: 'Had a picture Voice, Action, &c to make itself known, as Actors have upon the Stage, no disguise would be sufficient to conceal a person; but only a face, confined to one View, and not a muscle to move to say here I am, falls very hard upon the poor Painter who perhaps is not within a mile of the truth in painting the Face only . . . A Tune may be so confused by a false Bass, that if it is ever so plain simple and full of meaning it shall become a jumble of nonsense, and just so shall a handsom Face be overset by a fictitious bundle of trumpery of the foolish Painters own inventing . . . I only for the present beg your Lordship will give me leave to try an Experiment upon that Picture to prove the amazing Effect of dress – I mean to treat it as a cast off Picture and dress it (contrary I know to Lady Dartmouths taste) in the modern Way; the worst consequence that can attend it will be Her Ladyships being angry with me for a time – I am vastly out in my notion of the thing if the Face does not immediatly look like; but I must know if Lady Dartmouth Powders or not in common: I only beg to know that, and to have the Picture sent down to me . . .'[8] What is interesting about the whole episode is that when Gainsborough did produce a fresh portrait of the Countess he painted her in Van Dyck costume (Pl. 90) which, although fashionable and certainly the reverse of generalized, was also open to his own criticism, that of being 'a fictitious bundle of trumpery'. In fact,

Gainsborough was perfectly capable of producing a vivid likeness without the help of fashion – the dress worn by Mrs Lowndes-Stone (Pl. 103) is scarcely less generalized than the one in Lady Dartmouth's portrait – and one suspects him of making an issue of the matter because he had not been given sufficient freedom of choice and was aware that he had produced an indifferent result.

Of course, Gainsborough's ability to achieve a likeness that still carries imaginative conviction was, at least to some extent, restricted by his range of sympathies. He 'maintained an importance with his sitters, such as neither Beechy [sic] or Hoppner can preserve',[9] and was impervious to the claims of rank: 'now damn Gentlemen, there is not such a set of Enemies, to a real Artist, in the world as they are . . . *They* think . . . that they reward your merit by their Company & notice; but I, who blow away all the chaff & by G—in their Eyes too if they dont stand clear, know that they have but one part worth looking at, and that is their Purse . . . If any Gentleman comes to my House, my Man asks them if they want me . . . and then he askes *what* they would please to want with me; if they say a Picture Sir please to walk this way and my Master will speak to you; but if they only want me to bow & compliment Sir my Master is walk'd out.' But, he went on, 'If a *Lady* a handsome Lady comes 'tis as much as his Life is worth [to] send them away so . . .'[10] Gainsborough – married to a wife whom he certainly loved (Fig. 6), and who was unquestionably devoted to him, but was frugal and mean and 'never much formed to humour my Happiness'[11] – adored the opposite sex, and his most captivating portraits are of attractive girls of both the nobility and the *demi-monde* (Pls 99 and 149), and of older women of character and distinction (Pl. 65). 'Had I been blessed with your penetration and blind eye towards fool's pleasures', he wrote to his Methodist sister Mary Gibbon, 'I had steer'd my course better, but we are born with different Passions and gifts . . .'[12] And more pungently, signing a letter to his straitlaced friend William Jackson, 'I could say a deal more but what can a Man say pent up in a corner thus; if you was a Lady I would say what I have often said in a corner by way of making the most of the last Inch, yours up to the hilt.'[13] Jackson was a composer of some merit who subsequently became organist of Exeter Cathedral, and it was among musicians, actors and men of the theatre rather than scholars and literary people, let alone politicians, that Gainsborough always felt most at home. He was an intimate of Abel, Johann Christian Bach, Garrick, Giardini, the Linleys and de Loutherbourg, gave advice to Henderson, the actor, became father-in-law to Fischer, the distinguished oboeist, and knew the 'cellist Crosdill and the instrument maker Merlin, one of whose harpsichord-cum-pianos features in the full-length of Fischer (Pl. 127). Portraits of these friends – such as have come down to us – are among his finest and most original works (Figs 10 and 11, and Pls 126 and 127).

Gainsborough was not only 'passionately fond of music',[14] but himself performed on several instruments, taking lessons from Jackson in return for instruction in painting and drawing. Jackson, who declared that Gainsborough never had application enough to learn his notes, readily acknowledged that he was 'possessed of ear, taste, and genius',[15] and Rimbault, the organist of St Giles-in-the-Fields, who was an enthusiastic collector of the artist's drawings, said precisely the same: he may have been 'too capricious to study music scientifically' but 'his ear was so good, and his natural taste so refined, that these important adjuncts led him far beyond the mechanical skill of the mere performer who relies only upon technical knowledge . . . his chief forte consisted in modulating upon the harpsichord.'[16] 'His performance on the Viol de Gamba', so Bate-Dudley pronounced, 'was, in some movements, equal to the touch of Abel. He always played to the feelings.'[17]

Gainsborough's intuitive approach to music was paralleled in the idiosyncrasy of his talk and correspondence, so similar in character to the inconsequence and sensitivity of his brilliant contemporary Sterne, 'that if it were not for an originality that could be copied from no one, it might be supposed that he had formed his style upon a close imitation of that author';[18] 'he had, and used, a nomenclature purely his own, for everybody and everything';[19] 'his conversation was sprightly, but licentious – his favourite subjects were music and painting; which he treated in a manner peculiarly his own. The common topics, or any of a superior cast, he thoroughly hated, and always interrupted by some stroke of wit or humour . . . so far from writing, [he] scarcely ever read a book – but, for a letter to an intimate friend, he had few equals, and no superior. It was like his conversation, gay, lively – fluttering round subjects which he just touched, and away to another';[20] 'I question', wrote Gainsborough himself with typical modesty, for, when one gets down to it, there was a shrewdness and depth of understanding in everything he said which served as a ground-bass to his wit, 'I question if you could splice all my Letters together whether you would find more connection & sense in them than in many Landskips joind where half a Tree was to meet half a Church to make a principal Object.'[21]

As we examine his sympathies and his attitudes the character of the man begins to emerge. What did he look like physically? Apart from Gainsborough's own self-portraits (Figs 1, 2 and 5), a rapid sketch in chalks by de Loutherbourg, now in the Mellon collection, and a rather staid likeness, perhaps by the Bath artist William Hoare (Fig. 3), Zoffany's tiny sketch

(Fig. 4) is the only portrait that has come down to us. Fortunately this is a most sensitive study and leaves a clear impression of his personality; the sharp turn of the head, the quivering nostrils, the half-parted lips, the searching eyes, all these add up to an image of someone vibrantly alive – alert, observant, excitable, highly strung. Garrick is reported to have said that 'his cranium is so crammed with genius of every kind that it is in danger of bursting upon you, like a steam-engine overcharged';[22] and indeed his enthusiasms usually carried the day with him, whether it was 'a Moments Gratification' with his 'Friends . . . towards the City'[23] which he would afterwards regret, a musical instrument he coveted, a picture (not always a good one) he was determined to buy, or a new technique with which he would experiment far into the night. 'I am the most inconsistent, changable being', he declared, 'so full of fitts & starts.'[24] Inconsistent, impulsive and, of course, easily touched. Such was his natural generosity of heart that, one evening on the way to the theatre, moved by a tale of misfortune he heard from his friend Thicknesse, he promptly returned home: 'I could not go to the play till I had relieved my mind by sending you the inclosed bank note, which I beg you to transmit to the poor woman by tomorrow's post.'[25] Another story tells of his painting the portrait of a child just off to boarding school, in an effort to comfort the sick father, and having the picture set at the foot of his bed as a surprise.[26] If he constantly took thought for others, he was also a hedonist himself. 'Do but recollect', he once wrote, 'how many hard featured fellows there are in the world that frown in the midst of enjoyment, chew with unthankfulness, and seem to swallow with pain instead of pleasure.'[27] Such was not his own practice; though unlike his contemporary Rowlandson, his constitution and nervous system were by no means robust. 'I have done nothing but fiddle since I came from London,' he wrote from Bath in 1774, 'so much was I unsettled by the continual run of Pleasure which my Friend Giardini and the rest of you engaged me in.'[28] Gainsborough's daughter Margaret told Farington that her father had 'often exceeded the bounds of temperance & his Health suffered from it, being occasionally unable to work for a week afterwards',[29] and, in his last illness, Gainsborough confided to his old friend Samuel Kilderbee that he regretted the dissolute life he had led, adding, however: 'They must take me altogether, liberal, thoughtless, and dissipated.'[30]

But there was another side to the coin, as his daughter was careful to indicate: 'He had two faces, his studious & Domestic' as well as 'His Convivial one.'[31] He thought and acted like a gentleman, was elegant in person, unpretentious in deportment and 'of a modest, shy, reserved disposition, which continued with him till his death;'[32] Thicknesse, whose view this was, said that he had once told Lord Bateman, who had asked Gainsborough to his house in the country for the purpose of executing a pair of portraits, that though the painter had a high personal regard for his patron he was yet, 'as he might see, a shy bashful man, that he should have *opened him* with a bottle of Champaigne at dinner, and another at supper.'[33] Nevertheless Gainsborough's reserve was not only a matter of diffidence; he could be serious-minded when he needed to be, cared passionately for 'truth and Day light' in all things,[34] and was capable of offering considered and excellent advice. He was not irreligious; coming of Dissenting stock, he had a brother, Humphrey, who was a Methodist minister, and though he joked with his pious eldest sister, Sarah, about her Methodist beliefs, was himself, perhaps surprisingly, a chapel man. Unlike Reynolds, he did not work on the Sabbath: 'I generally view my Works of a Sunday, tho: I never touch.'[35] He also admired modesty, simplicity and quiet distinction in others, as we know from his description of the great lawyer, Dunning: 'Besides this neatness in outward appearance, his Store-Room seems cleared of all french Ornaments and gingerbread Work . . . He seems the only Man who talks as Giardini plays, if you know what I mean; He puts no more motion than what goes to the real performance, which constitutes that ease & gentility peculiar to damn'd clever Fellows, each in their way.'[36]

The same combination of excitability and bohemianism on the one hand, seriousness and practical good sense on the other, is apparent in Gainsborough's approach to the practice of his craft. 'He was irregular in his application, sometimes not working for 3 or 4 weeks together, and then for a month wd. apply with great diligence. He often wondered at Sir Joshua Reynolds *equal* application.'[37] 'I wish you would recollect', he wrote to a long-suffering patron, 'that Painting & Punctuality mix like Oil & Vinegar, & that Genius & regularity are utter Enemies, & must be to the end of Time.'[38] Not that he did not sometimes repent the disorder of his life, as we may guess from a note to Garrick: 'with this sensible scull of mine I have order'd my Business so as to have three sitters one after another to-morrow, besides having caught a d—m'd cold by riding in the rain this afternoon.'[39] There are several stories on record of unfinished canvases, and clients being kept waiting, and doubtless these represent a not unusual state of affairs. But he was a rapid worker. Indeed he was as impetuous in the way he tackled a picture as in his relations with his 'Friends . . . towards the City'. He preferred to work directly on the canvas, rather than make careful studies beforehand, and this accounts for the numerous *pentimenti* in his paintings; in a letter to Garrick concerning his portrait of the great actor standing beside a bust of Shakespeare, he describes this process as it must often have worked out in practice, complaining that he had been 'several days rubbing in & rubbing out my design for Shakespeare.'[40]

Of course, he must have made more studies in his earlier years – the three sketches for the portrait of *Miss Lloyd*[41] are a case in point – but in his maturity, and setting aside his landscapes, which were often executed direct from drawings he had done independently, for his own pleasure, as relaxation in the evenings, and little changed in the translation except for the addition of *staffage*, he normally only made composition drawings for his more complex pictures, subject pieces like the *Diana and Actaeon* (Pls 165–6) and portraits such as the *Duke and Duchess of Cumberland with Lady Elizabeth Luttrell* (Pls 158–9) or the *Prince of Wales on horseback*. Occasional studies of detail exist, drawings of plants (Pl. 18) or animals (Pl. 31) which were incorporated in the foregrounds of his landscapes, sketches of some element of costume, a coat or cuff, one lone drawing of hands; there are also a good many studies of ladies' costume, most of which date from the 1760s, when he was first painting full-lengths, and these were evidently done with the purpose of studying the fall of the elaborate folds and flounces of the fashions of the day as they occurred in different attitudes; for his first equestrian portrait he was equally careful, as we know from a letter in which he wrote that he had been on a visit to Wilton, 'partly for my amusement, and partly to make a Drawing from a fine Horse of L^d^. Pembroke's, on which I am going to set General Honeywood, as large as life.'[42] But, generally speaking, remarkably few of Gainsborough's drawings relate to his paintings; drawing, for him, was more an act of love than a preparatory process. Gainsborough's impetuosity as a printmaker is documented: he was a superb etcher but, in the case of his most beautiful and subtle early etching, of which only one impression is now known, we are told that 'he spoilt the plate by impatiently attempting to apply the aqua fortis before his friend, Mr. Grignion, could assist him, as was agreed.'[43] Angelo supports this view of Gainsborough when he says that 'he was as impatient as a spoiled child waiting for a new toy'[44] whilst working on his 'moppings', or experimental drawings. He also found it hard to contain himself when he was in pursuit of some new material or pigment he had found effective (but then this is so with any good artist). Gainsborough cared passionately for the quality of his materials, and for excellence of technique; and where his pictures have suffered in the course of time it has usually been from the ignorance of restorers, who have swept away his scumbles and glazes along with his easily soluble varnish, rather than from any deficiency in his own technique (though deficiences there were, of course, understandably, in his earlier work). The business of painting meant everything to Gainsborough, as it did

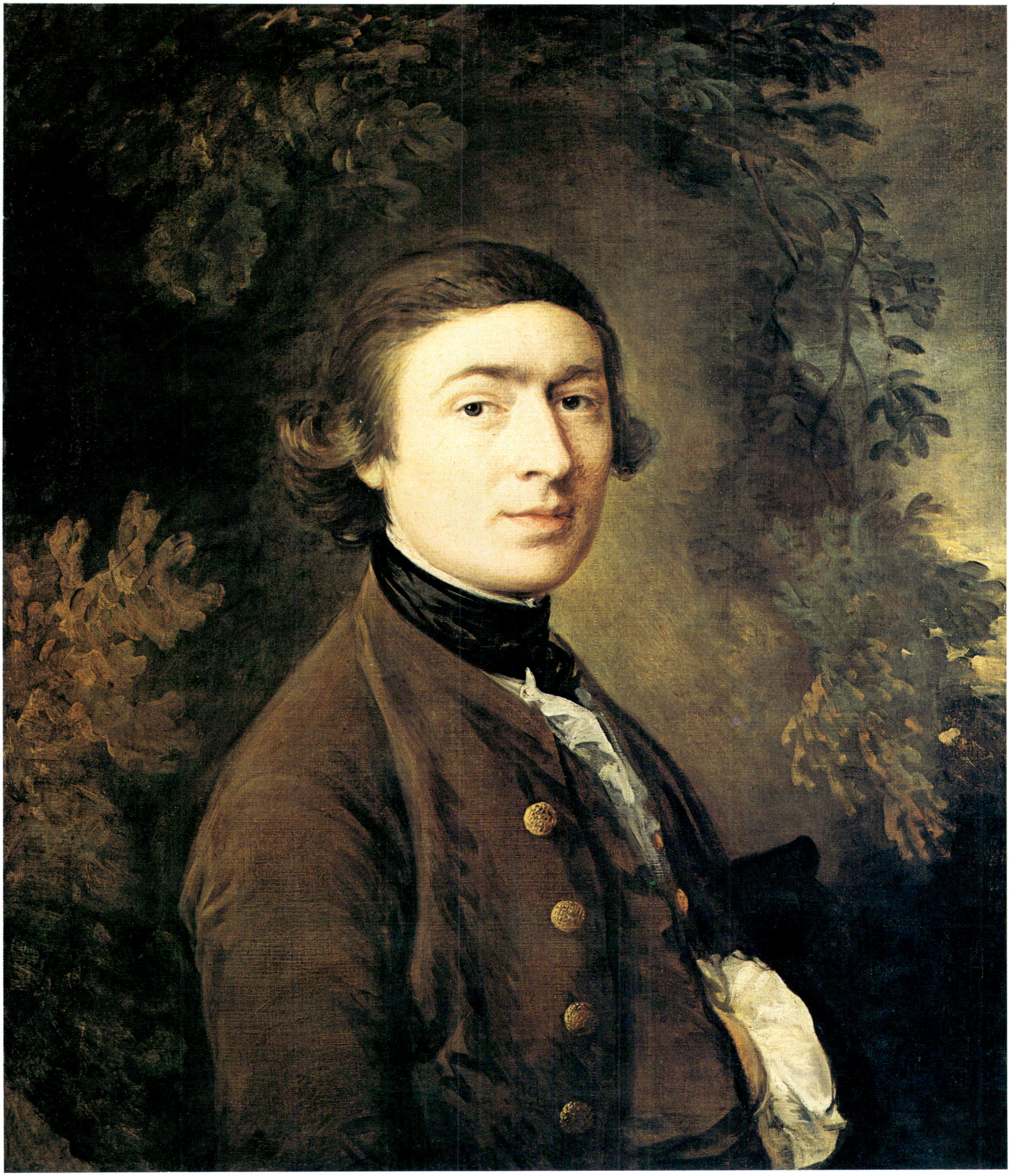

Fig. 1. *Self-portrait in his early thirties*. Canvas, 30 × 25 in. About 1758–9. London, National Portrait Gallery

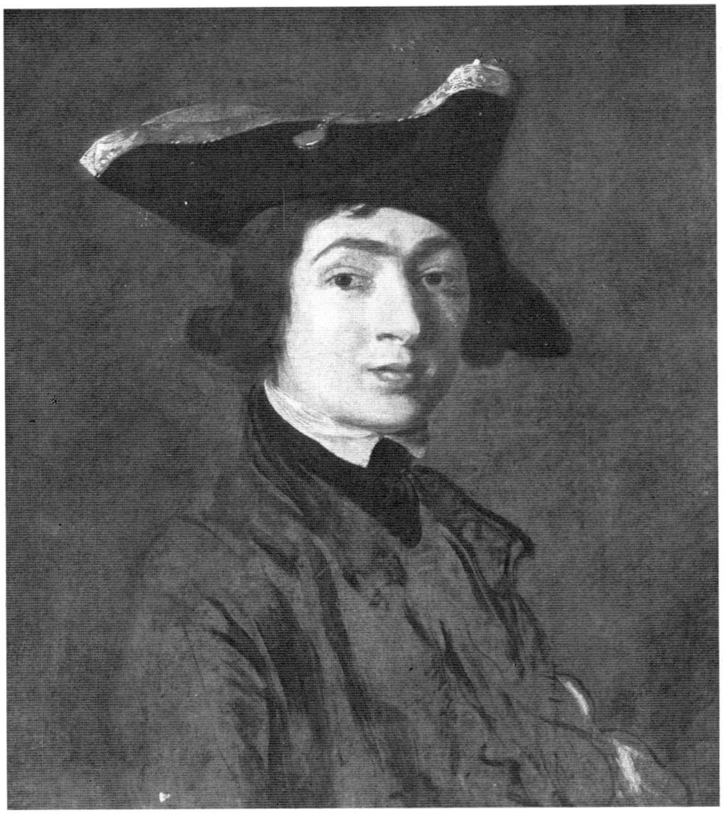

Fig. 2. *Self-portrait in his late twenties*. Canvas, 23 × 19½ in. (unfinished). Dated on the back 1754. Marquis of Cholmondeley

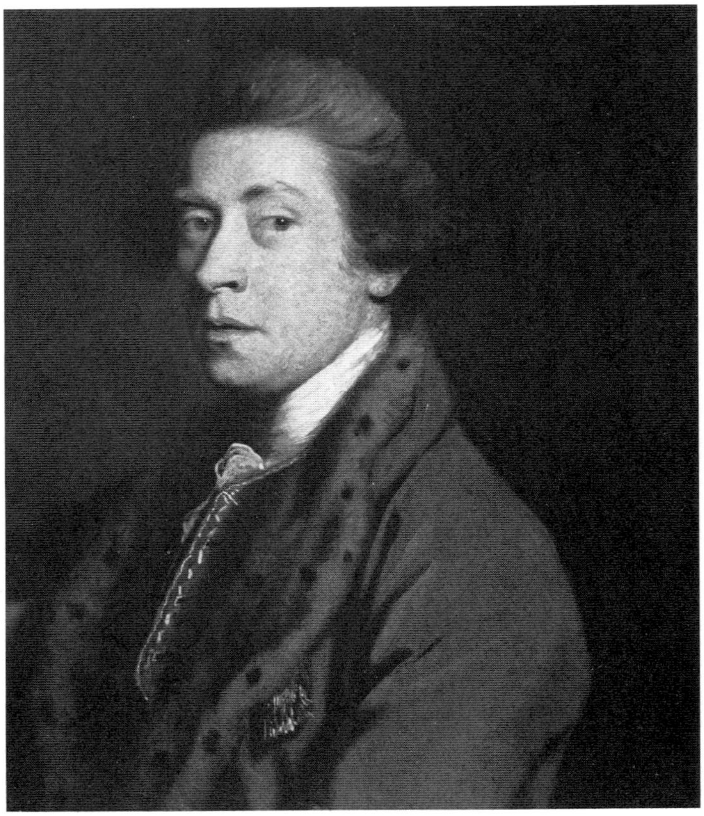

Fig. 3. Attributed to William Hoare (1707–92): *Gainsborough at about forty*. Detail. Canvas, 49 × 39¾ in. About mid 1760s. Santa Barbara, California, Museum of Art

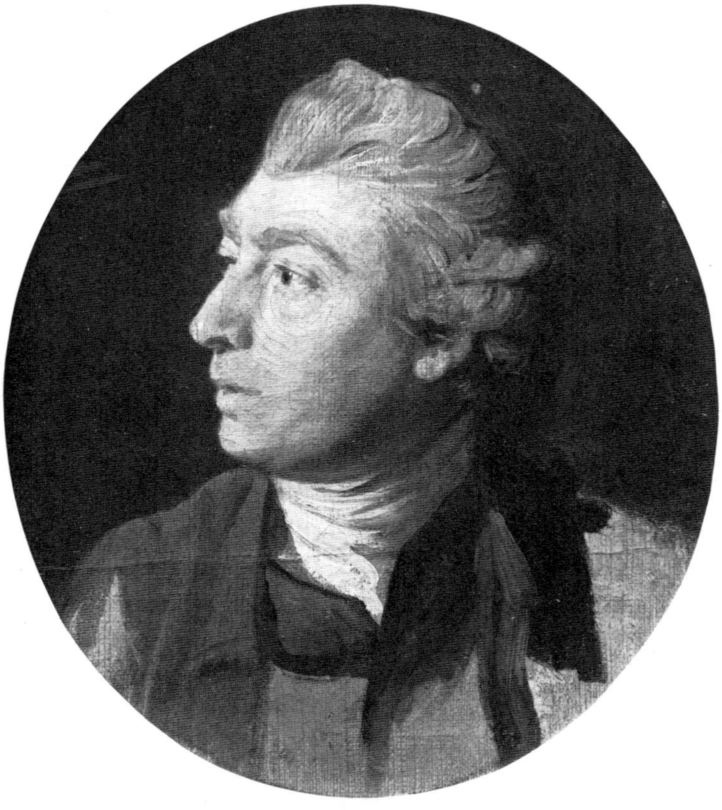

Fig. 4. Johann Zoffany (1734/5–1810): *Gainsborough in his early to mid forties*. Canvas, 7⅝ × 6⅝ in. About 1771–2. London, Tate Gallery (on permanent loan to the National Portrait Gallery)

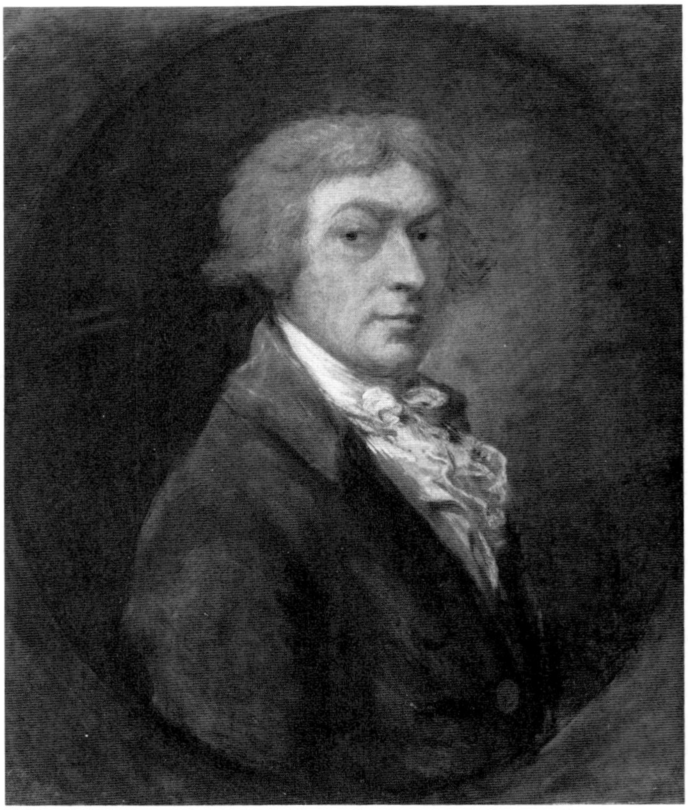

Fig. 5. *Self-portrait at the age of sixty*. Canvas, 29½ × 24 in. About 1787. London, Royal Academy of Arts

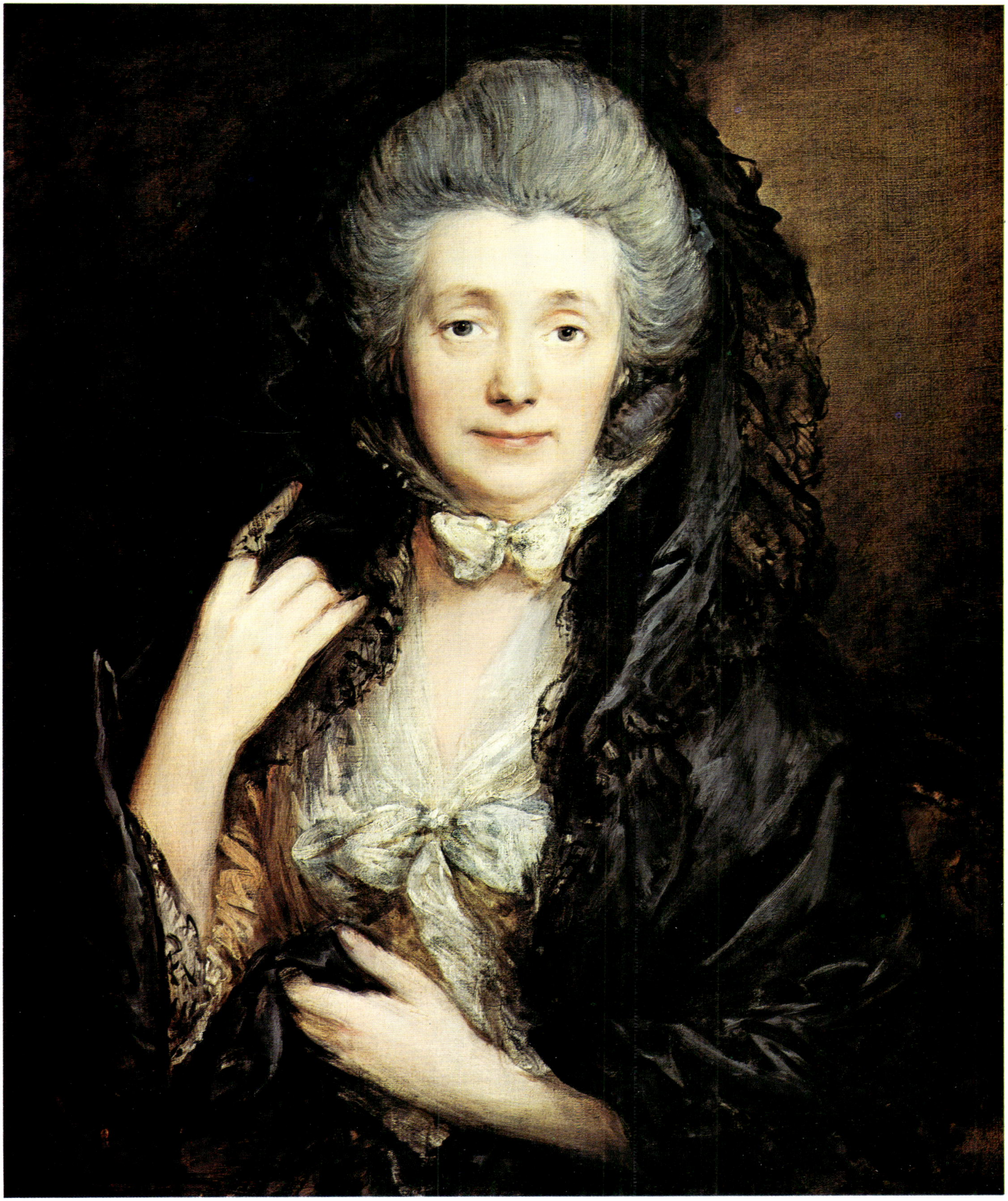

Fig. 6. *Mrs Thomas Gainsborough, née Margaret Burr* (1728–98). Canvas, 30¼ × 25¼ in. About 1778. London, Courtauld Institute Galleries (Note 93)

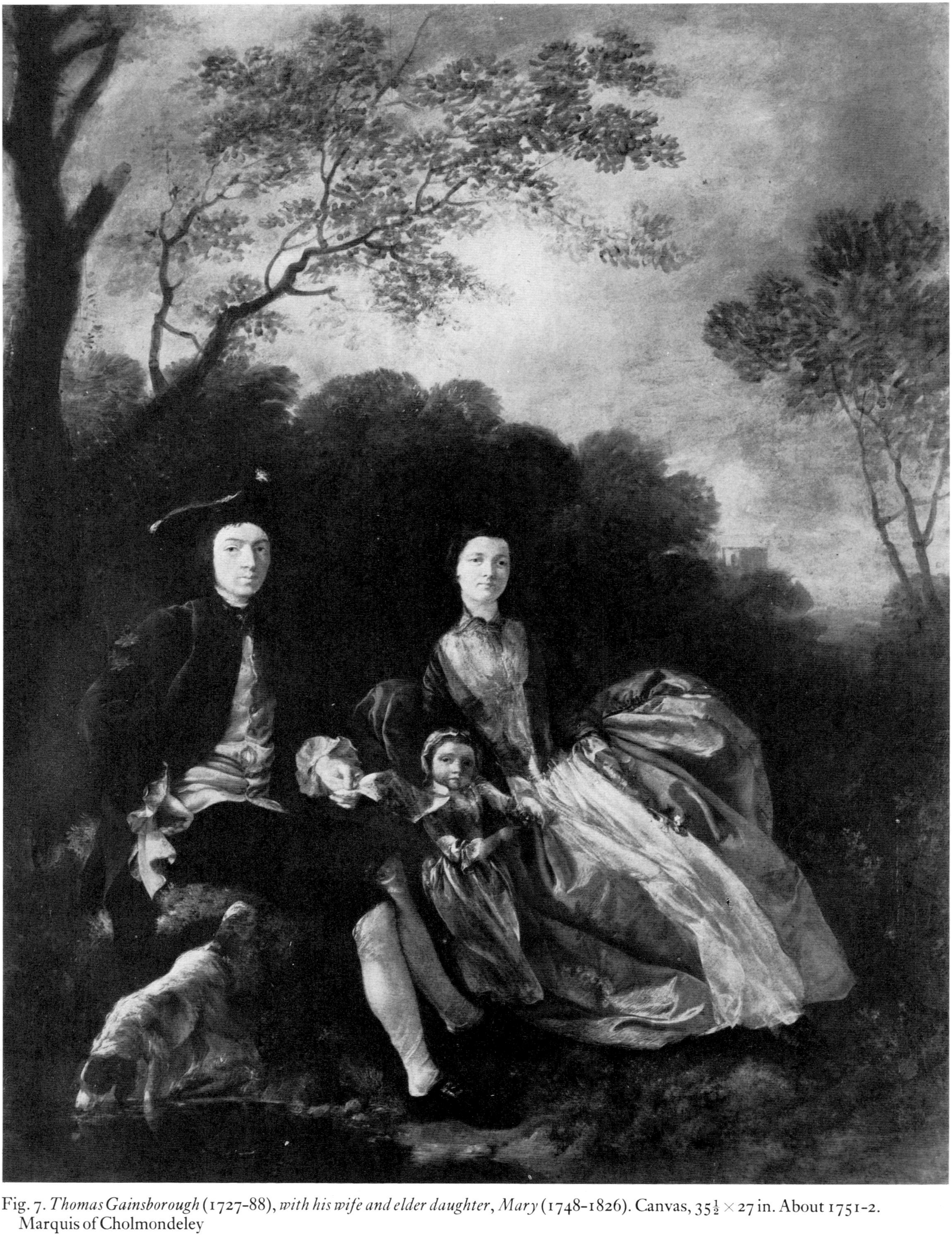

Fig. 7. *Thomas Gainsborough* (1727–88), *with his wife and elder daughter, Mary* (1748–1826). Canvas, $35\frac{1}{2} \times 27$ in. About 1751–2. Marquis of Cholmondeley

not to Reynolds, and fortunately we know a good deal about his studio practice from contemporary and near-contemporary sources.

The only useful information about the actual rooms in which he worked concerns Schomberg House, Pall Mall, where he lived from 1774, after leaving Bath. Here he added a separate studio and exhibition room at the back of the house: two large rooms, an upper and a lower, each fifteen feet high, with single large windows overlooking the gardens of Marlborough House,[45] a south-easterly not a northern aspect, the latter being of little consequence to Gainsborough, since he controlled his own light. Ozias Humphry, writing in the early 1760s, said that Gainsborough's 'Painting Room even by Day (a kind of darkened Twilight) had scarcely any Light; and our young Friend has seen him, whilst his Subjects have been sitting to him, when neither they or their pictures were scarcely discernible'; the image was 'so placed upon the Eisel as to be close to the Subject he was painting, which gave him an Opportunity (as he commonly painted standing) of comparing the Dimensions and Effect of the Copy, with the original both near and at a distance; and by this method (with incessant study and exertion) he acquired the power of giving the Masses, and general Forms of his models with the utmost exactness. Having thus settled the Ground Work of his Portraits, he let in (of necessity) more light, for the finishing of them; but his correct preparation was of the last Importance, and enabled him to secure the proportions of his Features as well as the general Contours of Objects with uncommon Truth.'[46] Gainsborough's practice of painting by subdued light in order to establish the basic tonal relationships is amply attested; Thicknesse confirms 'that he stood, not *sat* at his Palate, and consequently, of late years at least, five or six hours work every morning, tired him exceedingly',[47] a point substantiated by Margaret Gainsborough, who told Farington that 'her father always dined at 3 oClock, began to paint abt. eleven oClock and was generally exhausted by dinner time.'[48] This constant drain on his reserves, both physical and nervous, certainly accounts in part for his ambivalent attitude towards portraiture and for his devotion to landscape, which he indulged in the summer months after he had sent off his pictures to the annual Exhibition: 'If the People with their damnd Faces could but let me alone a little,' he wrote to James Unwin at the end of May 1768, 'Thank God I shall now shut myself up for the summer and not appear til september comes in.'[49]

John Thomas Smith also supports Humphry's account and elaborates on Gainsborough's concern with verisimilitude: 'Mr. Gainsborough . . . allowed me frequently to stand behind him to see him paint, even when he had sitters before him. I was much surprised to see him paint portraits with pencils on sticks full six feet in length, and his method of using them was this: he placed himself and his canvases at a right angle with the sitter, so that he stood still, and touched the features of his picture exactly at the same distance at which he viewed his sitter.'[50] In his earlier years, when he was inexperienced, and his work less generalized, Gainsborough tended to work piecemeal, as may be seen in the unfinished canvas of *The Gipsies*;[51] but his mature practice was to form 'all the parts of his picture together; the whole going on at the same time,'[52] though the head was usually finished first, as Thicknesse remarks of his own picture: 'he soon finished the head, rubbed in the dead colouring, of the full length, painted my Newfoundland dog at my feet.'[53] Gainsborough's fluency of effect was achieved by diluting his paints with turpentine; his daughter Margaret said 'his colours were very liquid, and if he did not hold the palette right would run over.'[54] But expedition did not imply carelessness; his technique was extremely sound. He generally employed fine-grained canvases in order to achieve a smooth surface, using hog's-hair brushes for his broad effects and camel's-hair for his detailed work;[55] he began with a light priming, usually of a greyish-yellow or pinkish tint, an initial layer which provided a luminous basis and was frequently left to break through and enrich the texture of his paint; sketched out his design, often using a mauve outline for his portraits and hints of local colour; took infinite trouble over the quality of his pigments; built up his paint structure solidly, the outer film being firmly resistant to possible solvents; finished with elaborate scumbles and glazes, the chief beauty of his handling; and, in order to protect these, used an easily soluble spirit-of-wine varnish of his own preparation.[56] He took equal care over the framing of his pictures and, where he could influence the matter, over their hanging; once he was constrained to write to Garrick: 'If you let your Portrait hang up so high, only to consult your Room, and to insinnuate somthing over the other Door, it can never look without a hardness of Countenance and the Painting flat: it was calculated for breast high & will never have its Effect or likeness otherwise.'[57] It was differences over the placing of his pictures that led to quarrels with the Academy hanging committee, and to his final withdrawal, in 1784, from the annual exhibitions: 'as he has painted the Picture of the Princesses, in so tender a light, that notwithstanding he approves very much of the established Line for strong Effects, he cannot possibly consent to have it placed higher than five feet & a half, because the likenesses & Work of the Picture will not be seen any higher; therefore at a word, he will not trouble the Gentlemen against their Inclination, but will beg the rest of his Pictures back again.'[58] Thereafter he exhibited in his own rooms at Schomberg House.

Sir Martin Archer Shee, who succeeded Lawrence as President of the Academy, said that he believed 'all the painters of any eminence were very dissatisfied with their own productions in the *Exhibition-room*' and that Gainsborough 'often painted higher for the room, and afterwards brought his pictures down.'[59] We can see at once from his exhibited canvases that Gainsborough did take into account the conditions under which pictures were to be seen in public, and a letter to a sitter makes his concern clear: 'I think we could still finish a little higher, to great advantage, if it would not be intruding too much upon your good nature, to bestow one more little sitting of about half an hour . . . I am fired with the thoughts of M^rs. Pulteney's giving me leave to send you to the Royal Exhibition, and of making a good Portrait of you.'[60] Though he disliked forced effects, 'the abuse of Natures *lights*',[61] and complained in 1766 that there was 'a false taste & an impudent stile prevailing, which if Vandyke was living would put him out of countenance',[62] there is no doubt that, under the influence of Rubens, he came to develop, principally in his landscapes, increasingly dramatic and brilliant effects, and that, for a period in the early 1770s, he did 'force' both his tones and his colours. In 1772 he exhibited at the Academy 'Two landscapes, drawings, in imitation of oil painting', upon which Horace Walpole commented: 'very great effect, but neat, like needlework.'[63] The landscapes in question cannot be identified, but a number of works of this description do exist – datable to the early 1770s on stylistic grounds – and in nearly all of them the tonal balance is so disturbing as to raise doubts about authenticity: the plain fact is that Gainsborough was trying to achieve precisely what was described in the Academy catalogue, and failed. Significantly, he was criticized in the very same year for excesses in his portraiture, otherwise much admired: a reporter of *The Middlesex Journal*, writing of *The Linley Sisters* (Pl. 102), said that 'his colours are too glaring. It would be well for him if he would borrow a little of the modest colouring of Sir Joshua Reynolds'[64], and *The Westminster Magazine* claimed that he threw 'a dash of purple into every colour.'[65] Yet at the same time Gainsborough was advising Garrick to 'spare the poor abused Colors, til the Eye rests & recovers' and to 'steal back into the mild Evening gleam and quiet middle term.'[66] It was as though he was only too aware of the temptations which beset them both, in their respective professions. As we know from Ozias Humphry, Gainsborough had already learnt the advantages of working by candlelight, chiefly in relation to highlighting and dramatizing his subject-matter, and 'in the latter part of his life [he] painted chiefly by candlelight, which became his inclination.'[67] His transparencies, which were designed for insertion in a specially constructed show-box and were lit from behind by candles diffused through a semi-transparent silk screen, were the ultimate extension of his candlelight painting: Rubens finally outdone.

Especially in his later work Gainsborough's brushwork, and the application of wash in his drawings, was rough and indeterminate, hatching round, or loosely suggesting, rather than describing, forms or features, much like Sterne. As *The Morning Chronicle* obituarist put it: 'His portraits are calculated to give effect at a distance, and that effect is produced in so eminent a degree, that the picture may almost be mistaken for the original, but closely inspected, we wonder at the delusion, and find scumbling scratches that have no appearance of eyebrows or nostrils.'[68] The extraordinary, and increasing, mastery of his handling from a purely naturalistic point of view is underlined by the fact that, in spite of this impressionistic and seemingly haphazard technique, he continued to work as much as he could direct from the living model. Though his final intentions in his landscapes and figure paintings were far from being naturalistic, he drew constantly from nature, making summertime sketching trips in the company of his friends; in 1782 it was the West Country he visited,[69] in 1783 the Lakes.[70] 'If, in his walks, he found a character that he liked, and whose attendance was to be obtained, he ordered him to his house: and from the fields he brought into his painting-room, stumps of trees, weeds, and animals of various kinds; and designed them, not from memory, but immediately from the objects. He even framed a kind of model of landskips, on his table; composed of broken stones, dried herbs, and pieces of looking glass, which he magnified and improved into rocks, trees, and water.'[71] This latter stimulus to his imagination he seems to have used over a long period, and right up to his last years drawing was a source of relaxation to him in the evenings, compensating for the day's grind at portraiture. Margaret Gainsborough said 'her Father had drawn much by Candle Light towards the latter part of his life when He thought he did not sleep so well after having applied to drawing in the evening not being able to divest himself of the ideas which occupied his mind, He therefore amused himself with Music.'[72]

Other studio properties Gainsborough is known to have had in his possession included a number of jointed dolls, each no doubt with its own wardrobe of clothes, from which he made studies of ladies' costumes and which he used for his painting of *The Mall* (Pl. 148);[73] laymen 'most ingeniously constructed with brass-work joints,'[74] which he must constantly have used for his portraits; 'a lamp with the sides painted with vermillion, which illuminated the shadows of his figures, and made them like the splendid impositions of Rubens';[75] and suits of Van Dyck costume, for those who wished to be painted in this form of fancy dress (which had been fashionable since the 1730s).[76] It would be wrong to say that Gainsborough never employed assistants; payments exist to Peter Toms, the well-known drapery painter,[77] and his nephew, Gainsborough Dupont, who was employed in the studio from 1772 onwards, assisted with repetitions, the mezzotints after his portraits, and probably much else besides.[78] We know from a letter that Gainsborough was prepared to entrust to Dupont such commissions as a 'Dog painted separate'[79] and we are told that in the case of one of his most important works, the full-length of *Queen Charlotte*, now at Windsor, 'the drapery was done in one night by Gainsborough and his nephew, Gainsborough Dupont; they sat up all night, and painted it by lamp-light.'[80] But, generally speaking, and in total contrast to most of his contemporaries, Gainsborough executed the whole of a picture with his own hand;[81] for an artist as passionately absorbed in the business of painting as he, drapery, accessories and background all involved exciting passages he had no wish to delegate. Nor was he able to switch off entirely from the business in hand. 'Before going to rest He would often go into his painting room & mark with chalk on his pictures such alterations as he proposed to make in them.'[82] His dedication to his art was absolute.

In spite of his impulsiveness, and occasional aberrations of judgement – such as his idea of painting the tragedy of the wrecked East Indiaman, the *Halswelle*, a subject more fitted to the pencil of Copley or Joseph Wright, and actually painted by Northcote[83] – he kept firmly within his range of experience, and was praised for this by Reynolds. He declared that he 'never could have patience to read Poetical impossibilities'[84] and candidly confessed, when he saw the Raphael Cartoons (then at Hampton Court) 'that their excellence, whatever it might be, had not fallen within his line of study.'[85] This is not at all to say that he was unadventurous; indeed in the last few years of his life he was striking out in several new directions. But the point was that these new developments in his painting, none of which could have been attempted with equal conviction by any of his contemporaries, sprang from the very depths of his being. A few weeks before he died he wrote to Reynolds asking him to call. 'Without entering into a detail of what passed at this last interview,' Sir Joshua recalled, 'the impression of it upon my mind was, that his regret at losing life, was principally the regret of leaving his art; and more especially as he now began, he said, to see what his deficiencies were; which, he said, he flattered himself in his last works were in some measure supplied.'[86]

Gainsborough's Art

MILIEU

OBVIOUSLY it is impossible to understand, or measure, an artist's genius – even that of giants like Michelangelo or Rembrandt – without knowing a good deal about the circumstances of the time, the point in the history of art in which a particular artist had the good, or the bad, fortune to study and to develop his powers. What, then, was the artistic situation in which Gainsborough found himself in England in the second quarter of the eighteenth century?

First of all he was severely restricted, in common with his contemporaries, by the canons and requirements of the patrons who counted for most. The academic theory of the hierarchy of painting, in which subjects drawn from the Bible or from ancient history ranked highest because they conveyed eternal truths, was accepted dogma with the cultivated connoisseur; until the close of the century, in spite of every effort, first by Hogarth then by Reynolds, it was *de rigueur* for collectors to acquire Old Master, or at least foreign, examples of the 'higher' branches of art,[87] and the only compensation for this state of affairs was the richness of material in English private collections available for artists to study. Gainsborough's simple comment on one of Reynolds's discourses was only too true, that 'betwixt Friends Sir Joshua either forgets, or does not chuse see that his Instruction is all adapted to form the History Painter, which he must know there is no call for in this country.'[88] Lower down the hierarchy, pastiches of Claude or Gaspard Dughet might be commissioned, chiefly for decorative purposes, but otherwise landscape had to be closely associated with topography if it was to prove acceptable, and a steady income could only be made from executing views, whether in oils, watercolour or for engraving; decorative work, such as flower painting, was certainly in request, but the insatiable demand was for likenesses, not only of people but of dogs and horses, and portraiture was almost the only branch of painting in which it was possible for an eighteenth-century English painter to achieve prosperity. In other words, the native painter lacked both patronage of a serious nature and the status generally accorded to, say, poets and writers; the Royal Academy, set up in 1768, alleviated the situation, but had not done very much to change it in Gainsborough's lifetime.

On the other hand, Gainsborough had the luck to be born at precisely that moment in the eighteenth century which Professor Waterhouse has so rightly called 'the most drab in the history of British painting'[89] and to grow up amongst lively and talented men – the so-called 'St Martin's Lane set'[90] – who changed the whole artistic scene in London; anti-establishment, anti-Palladian, anti-academic, they obliterated the remnants of outworn tradition, especially in portraiture, where Kneller's contemporary, Michael Dahl, was still the most busily employed practitioner as late as the 1730s, and poured out a wealth of new and exciting ideas, inventions and forms, which transformed not only painting but architecture, gardening, sculpture, the decorative arts and book illustration. To be alive, and training to be an artist, in the London of the 1740s must have been an exhilarating experience, and Gainsborough owed just about everything to those formative years. Hubert François Gravelot had settled in London in 1732 and, through the medium of his drawings for every possible branch of artistic activity, but mainly for book illustration, was chiefly responsible for introducing and disseminating the rococo; and Gravelot was Gainsborough's master.[91] But the genius of the age was, of course, Hogarth. He had taken up the conversation piece and the portrait-in-little with landscape setting from Mercier, and evolved the idea of morality paintings, for which he is best known, from the example of the contemporary stage; he started the St Martin's Lane Academy; he promoted, at the Foundling Hospital, a scheme of decoration for the Court Room, including history paintings, which, since the room was a fashionable meeting place, would serve as an advertisement for contemporary painters; he had painted, in the *Captain Coram*, the first great middle-class portrait, a taunt to the Frenchman, Van Loo, who had taken fashionable London by storm in 1737; and was producing, in the 1740s, a series of portraits as informal and direct as any character in his friend Fielding's novels. Ramsay, who was painting in a similarly direct manner in these same years, had settled in London in 1739 and was boasting the following year that he had 'put all your Vanlois and Soldis and Ruscas to flight and now play the first fiddle myself.'[92] In sculpture, the portrait busts of Roubiliac, informally posed and sharply characterized, were the exact stylistic counterpart of Hogarth and Ramsay; and it was Roubiliac who provided the great figure of Handel for the adornment of Vauxhall Gardens in 1738.

Now Vauxhall, the most fashionable and the most lively of all the London pleasure gardens of the eighteenth century and the *locus classicus* of the rococo style in England, was, as Mark Girouard aptly puts it, 'a St Martin's Lane design-job'.[93] Hogarth was a close friend of the proprietor, Jonathan Tyers, who was a collector of *avant-garde* art, one of the earliest patrons of Richard Wilson and said to have 'laid out more money in the encouragement of English art, than any man of his time';[94] and it was Hogarth who must have procured for Hayman the commission to paint a series of large-scale paintings of traditional games and pastimes for the decoration of the supper-boxes there. Gainsborough would have known Hayman through Gravelot, and may have been asked to assist on the Vauxhall paintings, as one of the figures in *Building Houses with Cards* has been convincingly attributed to him.[95] Popular art of this description was something quite novel in England and, like the subject paintings of Hogarth, teeming with motifs and characters observed at first hand in the streets of the metropolis, and the informality and naturalism of the new portraiture, it depended on the patronage of a lower stratum in English society – the independent middle class – tradesmen and professional men who wanted to improve themselves and to acquire knowledge about every aspect of life and society and who were uncomfortable with the pretentiousness of the baroque, whether in art or in music. It was they who subscribed to the periodicals which had sprung into a vigorous existence, *The Tatler*, *The Spectator*, *The Gentleman's Magazine*, and others; they who applauded Lillo's *London Merchant* (the source for the *Harlot's Progress*), and they who provided a responsive audience for *The Beggar's Opera*, a work based on popular melodies and performed in English, not the fashionable Italian.[96] Simplicity and naturalism were in the air. Even Horace Walpole admitted the virtues of the ordinary Dutch genre painters of the seventeenth century and, in the 1740s, demand awakening supply, pictures by the more naturalistic Dutch landscape painters, Hobbema, Ruisdael and Wijnants, began to appear in the London auction rooms for the first time,[97] side by side with Roman and Bolognese history paintings, Poussin and Claude, and the Dutch Italianates. Such was the scene that Gainsborough knew as a student and for the three years he had a studio on his own in London; then, in 1748, having 'not formed any high ideas of his own powers, but rather considered himself as one, among a crowd of young Artists, who might be able in a country town (by turning his hand to every kind of painting) pick up a decent livelihood,'[98] he returned to his native Sudbury with his wife Margaret, to whom he had now been married a couple of years, to set up a practice.

RESPONSE

QUITE unlike Hogarth, Gainsborough was not a deliberate innovator, nor was he in the least polemical or politically inclined; it is unimaginable that he would have been so piqued by foreign competition as to sign a portrait 'T. Gainsborough *Anglus*.' He cared deeply for the welfare of his friends but was bored by general causes, hardly ever bothered to attend council meetings at the Academy, and had no pretensions about the status of artists in general or about his own art in particular. His attitude towards history painting makes this clear. Jackson said that he 'either wanted conception or taste, to relish historical painting, which he always considered as out of his way, and thought he should make himself ridiculous by attempting it.'[99] 'Do you consider', Gainsborough had written to Jackson in 1767, 'what a deal of work history Pictures require to what little dirty subjects of coal horses & Jack asses and such figures as I fill up with.'[100] In fact, during the last decade of his life, Gainsborough was distinctly more preoccupied with this problem of subject-matter, and the nature of its emotional appeal; but, at first, instead of following the normal course, resort to Biblical, historical or literary themes, for which he possessed neither the learning nor the inventive capacity, he devised his own reply to the grand manner – the 'fancy picture'.

In these fancy paintings the figures in his landscapes took on the scale of life and were treated as idealized representations of country simplicity and virtue; judging by several fine late drawings and the celebrated painting of *The Woodman*, destroyed by fire in 1810, which he regarded as his most important composition, the woodcutter was his favourite image, and the expressiveness of the heads in this series of works suggests that, by the late 1780s, he was coming to regard this particular labourer as the embodiment of the eternal peasant, much as Wordsworth saw him. Gainsborough was inclined to joke about the new developments in his painting, but the badinage betrays not only his diffidence but an underlying seriousness and intensity of feeling. The letter to Sir William Chambers, written just before the opening of the Academy of 1783, is the most important document that has come down to us about Gainsborough's thoughts and intentions at this period: 'I sent my fighting Dogs to divert you, I believe next Exhibition I shall make the Boys fighting and the Dogs looking on – you know my cunning way of avoiding great subjects in painting and of concealing my Ignorance with a flash in the pan; if I can do this, whilst I pick pockets in the Portraits two or three years longer I intend to sneak into a Cot and turn a serious fellow.'[101] Such pictures as *The Woodman* and the *Two shepherd boys with dogs fighting* (Pl. 154) were one, highly personal, manifestation of this new, but entirely unacademic, seriousness; the ravishing *Diana and Actaeon* (Pl.166), his only mythological painting, for which three careful preparatory drawings survive, is another. Bate-Dudley tells us that he was also contemplating Shakespearean subjects, the grave-diggers in *Hamlet* and Timon in solitude,[102] which would presumably have developed the strain of melancholy apparent in *The Country Churchyard* (Pl. 117); and other evidence that Gainsborough was entering a new phase in his last years can be drawn from his work both in landscape and in portraiture.

Landscape was always his chief love. It had been his boyhood obsession for sketching in the country round his home in Sudbury, 'not a Picturesque clump of Trees, nor even a single Tree of beauty' in which he did not hold 'perfectly in his *mind's eye*,'[103] that had persuaded his father to send him up to London for training in the first place; when he set up on his own in 1745 'his first efforts were small landscapes . . .';[104] and his *cri de coeur* to Jackson, written in his mid forties, is well known: 'I'm sick of Portraits and . . . hate . . . being confined *in Harness* to follow the track, whilst others ride in the Waggon, under cover, stretching their Legs in the straw at Ease, and gazing at Green Trees & Blue skies without half my *Taste* That's d—mn'd hard.'[105]

His earliest landscapes were hybrid in character, a combination of Watteauesque freshness of handling, rococo rhythms, Dutch naturalism and *staffage*, Dutch crispness of touch and compositional construction, and a wholly English feeling for light; they were immature and often diffuse – but they were charming, they contained passages of sensitive observation and great beauty of touch, and they were totally without precedent in British painting. For twenty years and more landscape business had been in the hands of Wootton and Lambert, who were fundamentally decorators and *pasticheurs* of Claude and Gaspard Poussin, ready to turn their hands to imitations of Ruisdael and Hobbema when these artists became fashionable but – though it would be wrong to forget Lambert's occasional and delightfully fresh views of the English countryside – clearly unprepared to treat landscape as a serious genre or to develop an original landscape style. The revolutionary nature of Gainsborough's style – his early appreciation of the importance of light as a unifying factor in landscape, his exploration of the problems of landscape construction – is nowhere more apparent than in the Court Room of the Foundling Hospital, where his only surviving topographical painting, *The Charterhouse* (Pl. 19), hangs as one of a series of eight identical-sized views of London hospitals by contemporary artists. Though the strong perspective lines and the notion of taking the building 'on the angle', common to several of the set, derive from Hogarth, Gainsborough used these ideas in a wholly personal and original way, emphasizing the principal subject of his painting – the gateway to the Charterhouse, casually and unconventionally left in shadow – by means of the sunlit path, and concentrated his attention upon purely pictorial qualities, the evocation of a summer's day in London and the shafts of sunlight playing over the town and flagstones; for all its debt to Hogarth, the result is more like a Jan van der Heyden or a Van Goyen, and the picture remained a unique phenomenon in British eighteenth-century topography. Gainsborough did not repeat his experiment; if he had, he might well have anticipated Constable's *Wivenhoe Park*.

For, though he continued all his life to paint dazzling detail and his creativity depended on the stimulus of nature, the depiction of actual scenery was a hindrance to what he wished to achieve in landscape painting. When, some fifteen years after the completion of *The Charterhouse*, he was asked to paint a view, he passed the job on: 'Paul Sanby is the only Man of Genius, he believes, who has employ'd his Pencil that Way – Mr G. hopes Lord Hardwicke will not mistake his meaning, but if His Lordship wishes to have anything tollerable of the name of G. the Subject altogether, as well as figures &c must be of his own Brain.'[106] It may seem a paradox that a painter so passionately concerned about likeness in portraiture should not be so in landscape. In fact, the two genres satisfied totally different sides of his nature: his warm response to individual human beings, and his yearning for an arcadian order of things, under which people could continue to lead their lives contentedly and undisturbed by change.

Gainsborough's arcadianism dictated the course of his stylistic development. He made an exceptionally intelligent use of everything that was available for him to study in the London of the 1740s, and these years were crucial to the direction of his art but, although there is no doubt (and *The Charterhouse* demonstrates it) that he was capable of making use of the history of art in precisely the way that Constable did, that is to say, as lessons in the solution of particular artistic problems from which to proceed to yet more accurate representations of natural appearances, he was so completely in tune with the outlook of the eighteenth century, and sufficiently pragmatic, not to have the slightest inclination to take naturalism beyond a certain point. Effect and poetic, rather than scientific, truth – picture-making, not what Constable called 'natural philosophy' – were what mattered to him in the last analysis. This orthodox eighteenth-century attitude towards landscape was still common currency, indeed, in Constable's day, and the latter's disrespect for 'the old ways of doing things', keystone of the English way of life, helps to explain, what seems so inexplicable to art lovers today, his almost life-long unpopularity; Constable's devoted friend and patron, Sir George Beaumont, himself expressed this attitude as late as 1801: 'The old masters rarely painted views I believe never, unless commissioned – like poets they did not confine themselves to matter of fact, they chose rather to exhibit what a country suggested than what it really consisted of, & took as it were the essence of things.'[107]

Nothing makes Gainsborough's philosophy of landscape clearer than the difference between his work in London in the late 1740s and his output when he was back in East Anglia. One might reasonably suppose that the latter would be closer to nature; in fact, the reverse is the case. His Suffolk style, a blend of the Dutch and the rococo, became increasingly mannered and generalized, even frivolous, the English counterpart to the pastoral artificiality of Zuccarelli on the one hand and the rustic idylls of Boucher on the other. It is true that the local demand was principally for decorative work, overdoors or overmantels – but then *The Charterhouse* was just a topographical commission; true also that he was away from the stimulus of London – but he was now in the countryside he loved, and sketching avidly. The truth is that the Suffolk pastorals, distillations of his London learning, in which peasant lovers, the anglicized equivalent of Boucher's elegantly dressed shepherds and shepherdesses, became the predominant *staffage*, represent the real beginnings of his mature style, the inner soul of the man.

As Gainsborough was quick to learn from the work of the Dutch naturalists who first became popular with collectors in the 1740s, so he responded, with equal enthusiasm, twenty years later, to the work of Cuyp, and to the landscapes of Claude, Gaspard Poussin, Teniers, Rubens and other masters he was able to see in the collections of his West Country patrons. Never in any sense a chameleon, he took from his predecessors in the art of landscape whatever he needed to enrich his style, and his work now increased in breadth and scale, and matured in effect, though changing little in its pastoral subject-matter. In the event it was Rubens who proved, in the mid 1760s, the principal catalyst and the most enduring influence on his later style. He did not adopt the complicated constructional patterns of Rubens's landscapes, nor the enormous variety of figures and motifs with which he filled his canvases; the ground-plan of a mature Gainsborough is usually simple, generalized, even nebulous, and he developed steadily towards a point in which a single figure or group of figures established the mood he wished to create. Rather it was the virility of Rubens's imagination that excited him, the vigorous rhythms of his compositions, the dynamic character of his trees and rock-forms, the boldness of his drawing, the richness of his colouring and brushwork, and above all, the drama of his effects: glowing dawns and sunsets, sunlight breaking through trees, massive shadows, spotlit animals and figures, and brilliant reflections in water. All these elements are to be found, in greater or lesser degree, in Gainsborough's later landscapes; and, as we have seen, it was a desire to outdo even Rubens that led him towards transparency painting – a technique the importance of which in contemporary stage production has yet to be studied – and, under the spell of his friend de Loutherbourg's moving picture exhibition, the *Eidophusikon*, to the invention of his peep-show box. But the extraordinary brilliance and fluency which Gainsborough displayed in much of his later work did not deflect him from his fundamental purpose, to use landscape as an organ of sentiment. A peasant and his girl-friend riding home from market (Pl. 73), a herdsman driving cattle to a secluded watering-place, a family gathered at a cottage door (Pl. 114); these were the themes he loved to vary and develop. It was a nostalgic vision of a rural England that was even then rapidly changing under the impact of the industrial and agrarian revolutions not to mention the fashion for landscaping – a prefiguration of the 'sweet Village' where he wanted to 'enjoy the fag End of Life in quietness & ease.'[108]

Too much should not be made of Gainsborough's well-known statement, part of the excuse he offered to Lord Hardwicke, that 'with regard to *real Views* from Nature in this Country, he has never seen any Place that affords a Subject equal to the poorest imitations of Gaspar or Claude.'[109] This could not have been true even in 1764, and in 1783 he went on a sketching tour of the Lake District, with the avowed intention of demonstrating that the popular travel writers of the day were 'tawdry fan-Painters' in their descriptions; 'I purpose', he declared, 'to mount all the Lakes at the next Exhibition, in the great stile.'[110] During this last decade of his career, Gainsborough made a determined and successful effort both to widen the range and to intensify the drama of his landscapes and, right at the end of his life, his art flowered into a new heroic style: the *Peasant smoking at a cottage door* (Pl. 164), the last large-scale landscape he ever painted, is the Huntington picture (Pl. 116) done over, while in tranquillity of mood, as well as nobility of design, *The Market Cart* (Pl. 162) comes astonishingly close to such masterpieces by Constable as *The Cornfield* or the late *Dedham Vale*. Unquestionably he had turned a 'serious fellow' in the genre which came closest to his heart. But what of portraiture, the branch of painting by which he earned his living, and acquired a coach, a house in Richmond and a not inconsiderable fortune in stocks and shares?

When he first went back to Suffolk, after those exciting 'prentice years in London, Gainsborough found the going hard, and as a practical (and modest) professional man with a wife and daughter to care for he was obviously prepared to fit in, where necessary, with the wishes of his patrons. Most of his early portraits are simple head-and-shoulders images, set against a plain background or within a decorative feigned oval – much in the traditional manner of, say, Cornelius Johnson, and perpetuated by painters such as David Heins, who dominated portraiture in East Anglia in the second quarter of the eighteenth century. On the other hand, naturalistic portraiture influenced by Hogarth, portraiture more concerned with likeness and character than with status, was not unfamiliar in the Suffolk of the 1740s, so that there is no reason to suppose that Gainsborough had much, if any, local prejudice to overcome in superimposing upon the conventional patterns of English provincial portraiture the direct, informal approach to taking likenesses which he had learnt from the example of Hogarth and Roubiliac and that suited to perfection his own straightforward attitude towards life. He introduced the fresh tonality and soft, smooth modelling of the flesh characteristic of Van Loo and Ramsay and, later, under the influence of the French pastellists, La Tour and Perroneau, developed first a nervous, flickering, then a hatching, touch in his brushwork which immeasurably enhanced the vitality of his heads – a touch which, in its turn, gave way to a broader modelling in light and shade comparable to that of Reynolds. 'You please me much', he wrote to a client in Colchester at this time, 'by saying that no other fault is found in your picture than the roughness of the surface . . . being of use in giving force to the effect at a proper distance, and what a judge of painting knows an original from a copy by; in short being the touch of the pencil, which is harder to preserve than smoothness.'[111] By the late 1750s no other painter, not even his mentor Hogarth, surpassed Gainsborough in the ability to capture a living presence.

Within the limits of his range Gainsborough's invention, also, went beyond that of his contemporaries. Though some of his few more elaborate designs for portraits on the scale of life dating from the Suffolk period look decidedly gauche beside the accomplished elegance of Ramsay, portraits like that of William Wollaston (Pl. 49), not to mention the entrancing little canvas of his daughters chasing a butterfly (Fig. 12), excel Ramsay – excel Hogarth for that matter – not only in vividness of detail but in inspired informality. What would one not give to discover his sketch of a convivial evening at the Ipswich musical club, still extant in the middle of the last century?[112] The *Wollaston*, with its sharp changes of axis and sinuous highlighting of the lining of the coat, is one of the finest examples of the specifically English transmutation of the principles of rococo portraiture; and it leads on directly to the flowing, serpentine conception of *Mrs Thicknesse* (Pl. 54), a design of such rhythmic power that it transcended the intentions of rococo art and of such startling originality as to assail the sensibilities of the fashionable world. 'A most extraordinary figure, handsome and bold', wrote Mrs Delany, half in admiration, 'but I should be very sorry to have any one I loved set forth in such a manner.'[113] Yet the roots of that magnificent invention lay in the work of Van Dyck himself, and it was Van Dyck, upon coming to Bath, whom Gainsborough principally studied and came increasingly to admire.

Van Dyck's assurance, sophistication and exquisite beauty of handling were the touchstone for Gainsborough's mature style in portraiture: *Lady Molyneux* (Pl. 92) and *Mrs Graham* (Pl. 108) would be unimaginable without his example, while *Lady Howe* (Pl. 61) represents Gainsborough's personal translation of Van Dyck into his own more direct idiom, with the background landscape, vigorous and stormy, playing a role in the emotional impact of the picture no less important than the beautifully rendered head. Gainsborough's backgrounds were always far less formalized than those of Reynolds, but in his late works they ceased merely to be backgrounds, however lively, and became part of the landscape in which the sitters breathed and moved, the sitters themselves very often ceasing to be represented in a purely static pose. This was a wholly new concept of portraiture. *The Morning Walk* (Pl. 157), where the sitters are shown strolling through an arcadian landscape with which they are clearly linked compositionally, in touch and in colour, was recognized at the time to have been painted 'in a nouvelle stile';[114] and it is a tragedy that *The Richmond Water-walk*, in which five or six figures, for some of whom superb studies happily survive (Pl. 151), were to be shown promenading in a romantic landscape, was never completed, for this might well have proved Gainsborough's supreme achievement in painting.[115] By far the largest canvas Gainsborough executed, a painting ten feet by twelve, perished in a fire a hundred years ago. This was his portrait of Sir Francis Sykes with his groom, two horses and a dog, painted in 1787,[116] another extension of his normal range, and which one could wish to compare with Wootton and Stubbs. One of his late masterpieces, the *Lady Sheffield* (Pl. 100), followed precisely the same pose as one of the figures intended for *The Richmond Water-walk*, and *Lady Petre*, the last female full-length he ever painted, is in the same genre.

It has been argued that these late portraits, and some of the fancy pictures executed at the same time, represent an equivalent to the contemporary fashion in gardening, which required prospects to be animated with incident; and it is true that Daines Barrington, in a paper on gardening read before the Society of Antiquaries as early as 1782, selected Gainsborough as the most fit designer for an English garden in the contemporary taste.[117] But the analogy should not be pushed too far. Gainsborough may have satisfied the same taste, but it is doubtful if he was aware of the connection, any more than in his late picturesque drawings he was likely to have been aware that he was reproducing the imagery of Gilpin – whom he would certainly not have read for the purpose; he seems rather to have been proceeding on the same lines as certain of his contemporaries because of his own inner compulsion and an identity of feeling. In fact, the late portraits, in which the figures

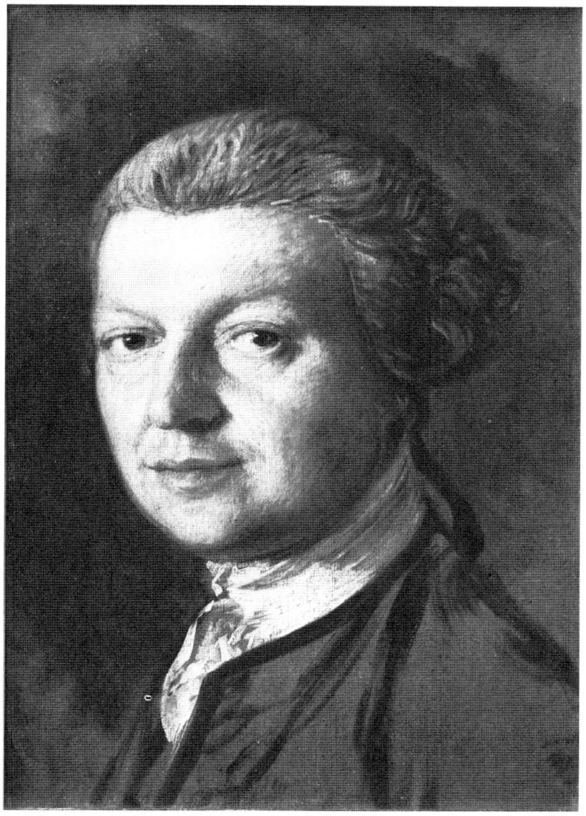

Fig. 8. *Joshua Kirby* (1716-74). Canvas, $16\frac{1}{2} \times 11\frac{1}{2}$ in. (unfinished). About 1757-8. London, Victoria and Albert Museum (Note 37)

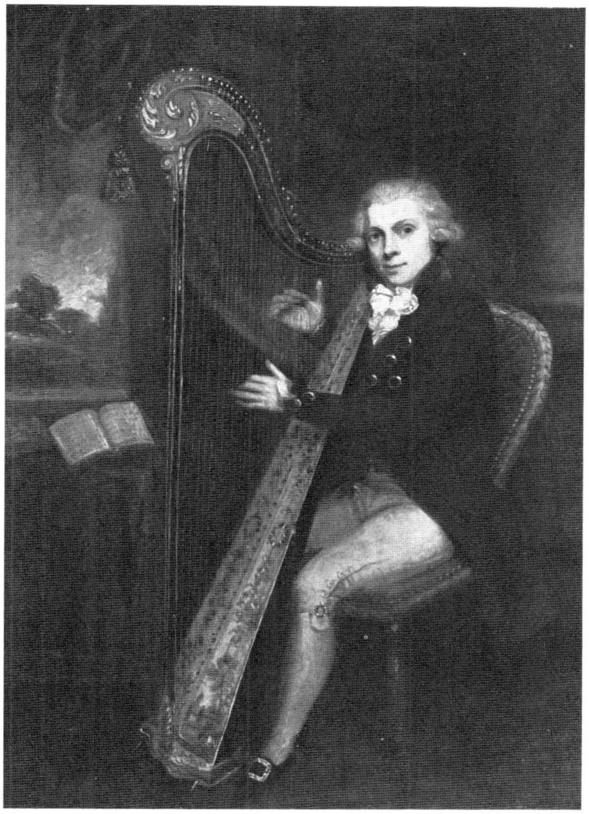

Fig. 9. John Downman (1750-1824): *William Jackson* (1730-1803). Canvas, $24 \times 17\frac{1}{2}$ in. Private Collection

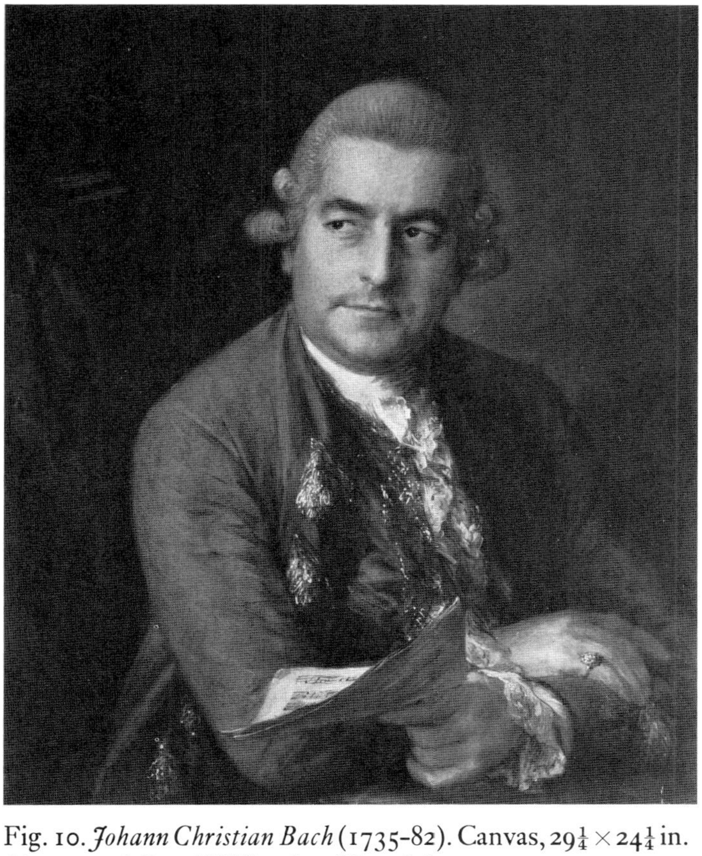

Fig. 10. *Johann Christian Bach* (1735-82). Canvas, $29\frac{1}{4} \times 24\frac{1}{4}$ in. About 1776. Lord Hillingdon (Note 85)

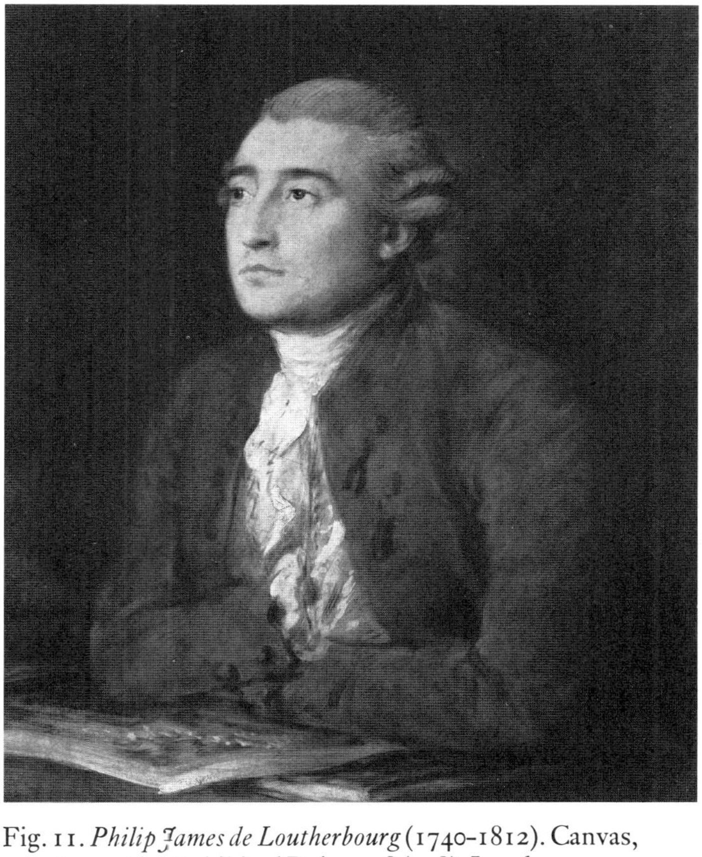

Fig. 11. *Philip James de Loutherbourg* (1740-1812). Canvas, $30\frac{1}{8} \times 24\frac{3}{4}$ in. Exhibited R.A. 1778 (408). London, Dulwich College Picture Gallery (Note 91)

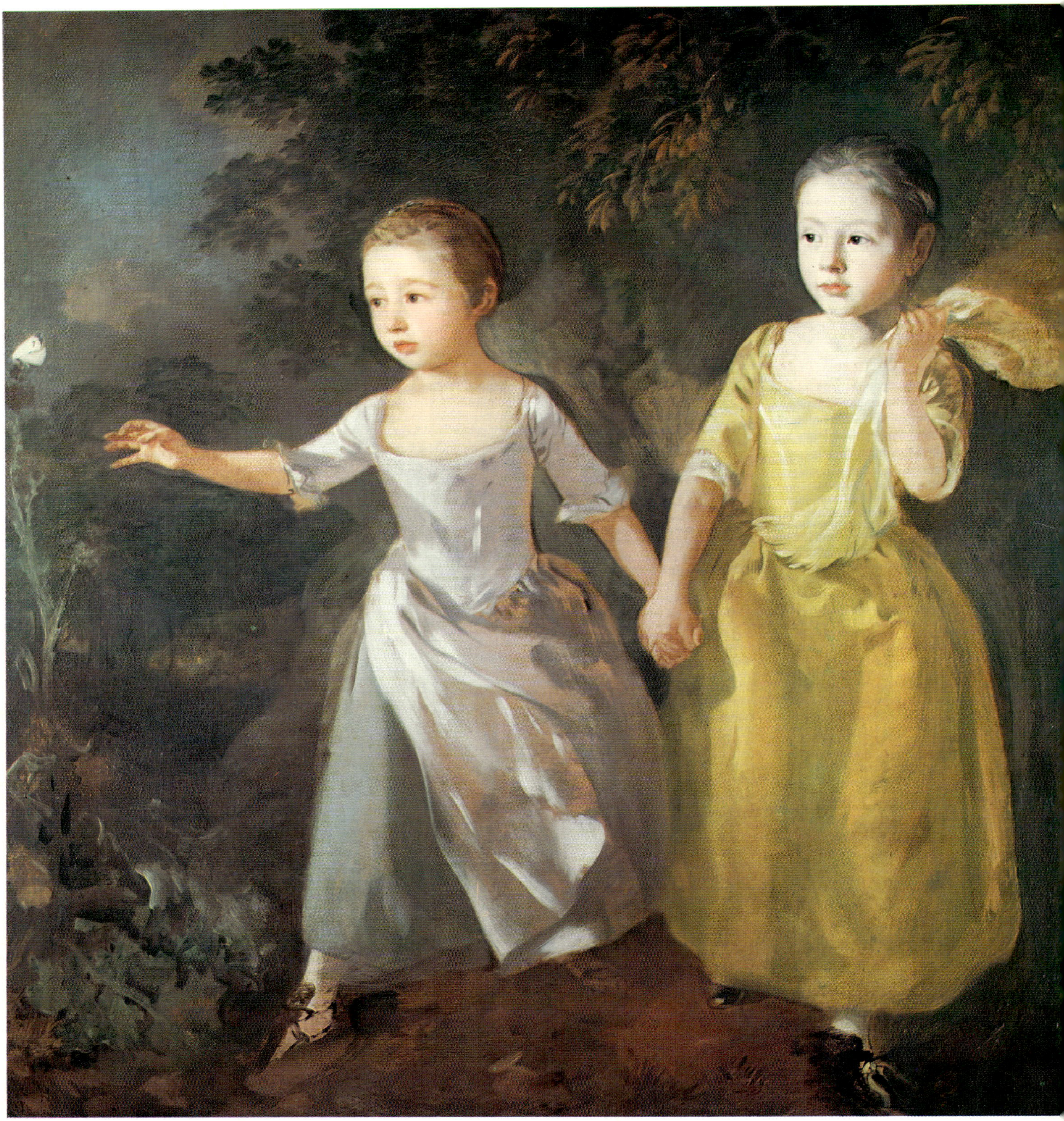

Fig. 12. *The painter's daughters, Margaret* (1752–1820) *and Mary* (1748–1826), *chasing a butterfly*. Canvas, $44\frac{3}{4} \times 41\frac{1}{4}$ in. About 1756. London, National Gallery (Note 31)

merge into, and become part of, the landscape, derive ultimately from Gainsborough's earliest work in a slightly different genre, the portrait-in-little with landscape background popularized by Mercier, Hogarth and Devis. For where, in the portraits and groups by the latter painters, the landscape was usually pure backdrop, Gainsborough closely involved figures and landscape one with the other. The classic example is, of course, *Mr and Mrs Robert Andrews* (Pl. 21), where the sitters are set in their own parkland, which occupies fully half the composition and is as beautifully constructed and as atmospherically painted as an early Gainsborough landscape; but one should also mention *John Plampin* (Pl. 55), in which figure and landscape are integrated by means of a highly developed rococo design. When, in later life, Gainsborough was commissioned to paint a group containing the Duke and Duchess of Cumberland, he turned first for inspiration to the conversation pieces of Zoffany, then at the height of fashion; but, rejecting this concept, reverted to his earliest love, Watteau. In 1747 Watteau had inspired the enchanting *scène galante* of a young couple, probably the painter and his wife, seated on a park bench in a landscape dominated by a garden temple (Pl. 10). For his second design for the *Cumberlands* (Pls 158–9), Gainsborough took up, but revolutionized, this early idea, placing a simple garden prop – an urn on a pedestal – amongst the trees which soar above the promenading figures, spreading over the scene an extraordinary pattern of brilliantly handled foliage with a vigorous life of its own – an outpouring of romantic feeling which one finds also in those incomparable late landscape drawings that were amongst his most remarkable creations.

In portraiture, as well as in landscape and his own type of subject picture, Gainsborough enthusiastically studied the work of his own contemporaries as well as the great masters of the past but, unlike so many artists of his day, was able to use what he learnt, not slavishly, but to nourish and enrich his own painting – which developed, in the 1780s, and in all the genres he pursued, into a highly individual style that fully expressed his own personal predilections and scale of values. But, if he gradually satisfied himself, to what extent did he satisfy his patrons, the public, the critics and the taste of succeeding generations? And where does he stand as a creative artist, not just in relation to British painting, but *sub specie aeternitatis*?

ACHIEVEMENT

THE most obvious clue to Gainsborough's standing in his own day is supplied by the prices he was able to charge. When he started his practice in London in about 1745, at the age of eighteen, 'his first efforts were small landscapes, which he frequently sold to the dealers at trifling prices, and when he afterwards engaged in portraits, his price was from three to five guineas.'[118] It seems likely that the latter were portraits-in-little, rather than portraits on the scale of life, since nothing but works in this genre can now be dated to these early years. He appears never to have been able to secure enough commissions for himself when he was living in Suffolk, though he kept his charges down to eight guineas for a head and fifteen for a half-length, and he was often in debt;[119] in 1758 we find him writing to a client in Colchester, apologizing for not being able to make a promised visit, 'but business comes in, and being chiefly in the Face way, I'm afraid to put people off when they are in the mind to sit.'[120] It was this situation, unlikely ever to improve in a provincial town, that led him to move to Bath in 1759. There he was an instant success, and 'business came in so fast'[121] that he soon raised his prices from eight to twenty guineas for a head, and from fifteen to forty guineas for a half-length; his fee for a full-length was sixty guineas, and this remained the case until 1769.[122]

By the beginning of the 1770s he was charging thirty, sixty and a hundred guineas respectively. Though he did not touch Reynolds, who had been charging a hundred guineas for a full-length more than a decade earlier and had already raised his fee to one hundred and fifty in 1764, he was well ahead of any other rival, and in a letter to Jackson he exclaimed: 'I might add perhaps in my red hot way that damn me Exeter is no more a place for a Jackson, than Sudbury in Suffolk is for a G—.'[123] Gainsborough kept to this scale of charges for most of the rest of his career; a double portrait, such as *The Morning Walk* (Pl. 157), or a full-length with a horse, cost one hundred and twenty guineas.[124] Though he was constantly criticized for his raw colour and impressionistic touch, which may have been the reason he did not risk higher charges, he never suffered from lack of clients; a year after settling in London he was able to reassure his sister that 'my present situation with regard to encouragement is all that heart can wish',[125] and he was soon the firm favourite of the royal family, only failing to secure appointment as Principal Painter to the King, on Ramsay's death in 1784, because 'Reynold's Friends stood in the way'.[126] Not until 1787 did he raise his fees again, this time to forty, eighty and one hundred and sixty guineas; this was closer to Reynolds's scale which, since 1782, had been fifty, one hundred and two hundred guineas. It is significant that the standards set by Reynolds and Gainsborough, and the demand which they satisfied, enabled Lawrence to equal Gainsborough's scale by 1793, when he was only twenty-four, and Reynolds's in 1807; by 1811 he was charging no less than three hundred guineas for a full-length.

Though Gainsborough's landscapes received critical acclaim from the beginning, on the whole they sold badly: in view of the nature of their appeal and the success of Zuccarelli's pastorals, which were far from the accepted classical idiom of Claude, Gaspard and Wilson, this is difficult to understand. Vertue tells us that, of the roundels done for the Foundling Hospital, *The Charterhouse* (Pl. 19) was 'tho't the best & masterly manner';[127] but many of the Ipswich pastorals were left on Gainsborough's hands[128] and, according to Prince Hoare, he was 'so disgusted at the blind preference paid to his powers of portraiture, that, for many years of his residence at Bath, he regularly shut up all his landscapes in the back apartments of his house, to which no common visitors were admitted.'[129] At this time Wilson was thought to hold 'the first Rank among the landskip Painters,'[130] and it was he who was most imitated. *The Watering Place* (Pl. 111), exhibited in 1777, may have been considered by Horace Walpole to be 'by far the finest Landscape ever painted in England, & equal to the great Masters,'[131] and, of the six major landscapes Gainsborough sent to the Academy in 1780, the critic of *The Morning Chronicle*, voicing the general chorus of approval, wrote that 'everyone . . . beggars description';[132] yet Gainsborough's influence on the course of contemporary landscape painting was no greater now than it had been earlier, and Beechey recalled that his landscapes 'stood ranged in long lines from his hall to his painting-room, and they who came to sit to him for their portraits, for which he was chiefly employed, rarely deigned to honor them with a look as they passed them.'[133] It is true that the Prince of Wales bought two, and that Lord Shelburne and the young Duke of Rutland were among contemporary picture lovers who acquired landscapes, but masterpieces such as *The Harvest Waggon* (Pl. 77), *The Watering Place* (Pl. 111), and *The Mall* (Pl. 148) failed to find purchasers, and the Huntington *Cottage Door* (Pl. 116) was not sold until six years after it was exhibited.

The prices Gainsborough charged for his landscapes are not easy to establish; indeed he kept them a secret even from his wife[134] – who accounted for his finances rather too closely. For the two overmantels he painted for the Duke of Bedford in 1755 (Pls 27 and 45) he charged fifteen and twenty-one guineas respectively; for the larger picture bought by Sir William St Quintin in 1766 (Pl. 71) he charged forty guineas, inch for inch much less expensive than his fees for a portrait at this time. By the 1770s his scale had certainly risen, since the Duke of Rutland paid eighty pounds apiece for landscapes of the same size as the St Quintin picture (Pl. 114); and by 1785 it had risen further, for the Prince of Wales was charged one hundred guineas for a landscape of this size (Pl. 78). It is clear, however, that Gainsborough regarded some of his landscapes as far more important than others, and by the later 1780s, at any rate, his landscape prices do not conform to any kind of scale: *The Market Cart* (Pl. 162), painted in 1787, was sold to Sir Peter Burrell for three hundred and fifty guineas,[135] and for the *Peasant smoking at a cottage door* (Pl. 164) he seems to have wanted five hundred guineas.[136] These are the kind of prices he was charging for his fancy pictures, to which in sentiment some of these late landscapes were closely akin; and with the fancy pictures, 'those little simple subjects . . . that awakened in the heart the most pathetic sensations',[137] and which were so wholly in tune with the mood of the time, he had no problems. *The Girl with Pigs* (Pl. 146) he sold to Reynolds in 1782 for one hundred guineas,[138] a price exactly commensurate with the landscape for the Prince of Wales; three years later *The Cottage Girl with Dog and Pitcher* (Pl. 147), intended for the Prince of Wales, was sold to Sir Francis Basset for two hundred guineas,[139] while in 1787 *The Cottage Children with an Ass* was bought by the Earl of Gainsborough for three hundred guineas,[140] and in 1788 *The Cottage Girl with a Bowl of Milk* and *Young Hobbinol and Ganderetta* (Pl. 140), both smaller canvases, were sold to Thomas Macklin for three hundred and three hundred and fifty pounds respectively.[141] For *The Woodman* he refused an offer of four hundred guineas from Desenfans because he hoped it might be purchased by George III; Macklin offered Mrs Gainsborough five hundred guineas shortly after the painter's death, but in the event it was purchased by Lord Gainsborough at the same price.[142] For a large Shakespearean scene, to contain twelve figures, he expected Boydell to pay one thousand pounds;[143] this work was never begun.

There was a considerable vogue for Gainsborough's work, notably his drawings, in the years immediately following his death, but by 1794 the dealer, Vandergucht, was telling Farington that 'the pictures of Gainsborough are decreasing in value. The raging fashion of collecting them subsiding fast.'[144] Certainly Gainsborough's wife and daughter were unable to obtain the prices they expected for the works left in the studio. Though Dupont continued to paint in Gainsborough's style until his own death in 1797, Gainsborough's portraiture was almost totally eclipsed by Lawrence, and it was the landscapes and fancy pictures that retained their popularity; when a commemorative exhibition was held at the British Institution in 1814, forty-five landscapes and almost all the fancy pictures were included, but only fourteen of the portraits. Thomas Green, writing in 1820, said that 'it is on the merits of his landscapes, beyond all doubt, that his fame as an artist will ultimately rest';[145] and Constable's deeply felt words still sum up Gainsborough's whole achievement in this field: 'With particulars he had nothing to do; his object was to deliver a fine sentiment, and he has fully accomplished it.'[146] Hazlitt, who believed that it was the fancy pictures 'on which Gainsborough's fame chiefly rests', was more critical about Gainsborough's sentiment, and wrote that it was his 'general fault . . . that he presents us with an ideal common life, of which we have had a surfeit in poetry and romance', finding in a characteristic example 'a consciousness in the turn of the head, and a sentimental pensiveness in the expression, which is not taken from nature';[147] *pari passu* he considered the principal defects of the late landscapes were that they 'neither presented the spectator with a faithful delineation of nature, nor possessed any just pretensions to be classed with the epic works of art'.[148] Fidelity to appearances was one of the touchstones of Victorian appreciation, especially in landscape, and when Gainsborough's popularity revived in the later nineteenth century, it was through the medium of his most glamorous portraits; the 'millionaire taste' fostered by Duveen was anticipated by Millais in his later work, and a whole spate of books on the artist appeared between 1894 and 1910. Since then, Gainsborough's achievement has been subjected to a more careful scrutiny, and it is possible to venture something more closely approaching a balanced judgement.

If Gainsborough is taken on his own ground, his ability to translate what he saw before him into terms of oil paint – paint that sings from the canvas with the magnetic quality of a Garrick's voice – he is equalled by the merest handful of artists, whether he was concerned with the delineation of a plant, the suggestion of silks or satins, the characterization of a head, or the portrayal of the face in movement; and to achieve such living presence he was forced far beyond the conventions of the age and developed a technique increasingly impressionistic in character, so that, except for the arbitrary nature of the colour in his 'pencilling' touch, one may fairly compare him with the Impressionists of a hundred years later, notably with Renoir.

He presents us with a magnificent gallery of eighteenth-century faces, drawn particularly from fashionable society, the *demi-monde*, and the world of music and the stage. But he depended upon the living model. One recalls his reluctance to finish except with the sitter before him, and his search for suitable beggar children whom he could employ to pose for his fancy pictures. Admirable as this characteristic was when verisimilitude was the aim (and not every portrait painter has possessed Gainsborough's integrity), it reveals his most fundamental weakness: his lack, in ordinary circumstances, when his imagination was not fired by some instinctively powerful image, of inventive power, of the 'variety' of adequate responses to an artistic problem which he envied in Reynolds. The point is illustrated by his landscape models, by the 'blots' he used to assist his landscape invention, by the banality of some of his grander portrait designs, the *Berkeley* for example, and by the weakness of others, such as the *Argyll* (Pl. 75), the *Burrell*, the *Rodney*. In the case of the *Garrick standing beside a bust of Shakespeare* we know his feelings: 'G-damn it I can make nothing of my Ideas . . . I have been several days rubbing in & rubbing out my design for Shakespeare . . . I was willing like an Ass as I am, to expose myself a little, out of the simple Portrait way.'[149] On the other hand, when what he was about sprang from the depths of his being, his designs could be as inspired as the movement of his brush; his feeling for certain of his sitters generated striking and original poses which captured their character and personalities to an extraordinary degree. Works like *The Morning Walk* (Pl. 157) or the Huntington *Cottage Door* (Pl. 116) evoked a particular mood with equal genius, and in that one incomparable mythological canvas, the *Diana and Actaeon* (Pl. 166), he took up, with apparently effortless ease, the *poesie* of Giorgione and Titian, or of Van Dyck's *Cupid and Psyche*, and produced a masterpiece in this genre which can stand beside Watteau's consummate *L'Embarquement pour Cythère*.

It is, above all, in the evocation of mood that Gainsborough is supreme. What he sought to do, and splendidly accomplished, in the late portraits, the *Mrs Sheridan* (Pl. 153), the *Cumberlands* (Pl. 159) or the *Lady Bate-Dudley* (Pl. 130), was unique; and there is no unfinished work in Gainsborough's oeuvre one misses more than *The Richmond Water-walk*, in which five or six magnificent figures were to be set in the most romantic of landscapes. The height of Gainsborough's achievement lay in this relationship of figures to an expressive background, where the unity of mood was held in perfect balance, and where it is shape and colour and handling, rather than subject or resonance down the images of past time, that awaken our emotional responses. The evocation of mood, usually an arcadian view of country life, but sometimes one tinged with melancholy, was the primary intention of his landscapes, and most obvious in the drawings, which were his most personal works; and it was this preoccupation, in addition to his life-long concern for, and use of, precisely those motifs and qualities soon to be classified as 'Picturesque' that must have led Daines Barrington, in 1782, to relate his landscape art to the needs of contemporary gardening.[150]

Arcadianism, the nostalgia for a golden age, the notion that simple country folk were somehow innately superior to, and more worthy than, those who lived in towns – these attitudes of mind were part of the climate of the age, in France as well as in England;[151] but there is no doubt also, that if Gainsborough reflected fashionable taste, he was genuinely moved by the everyday simplicities of country life. Uvedale Price, who, as a young man, used to ride out in the country with Gainsborough, recalled that 'when we came to cottage or village scenes, to groups of children, or to any objects of that kind which struck his fancy, I have often remarked in his countenance an expression of particular gentleness and complacency'.[152] It is this simplicity and utter genuineness of feeling that raises his fancy pictures – as remote to the disenchanted eye of the twentieth century as the moralities and saccharine quality of his popular contemporary, Greuze – far above the commonplaces of Wheatley, Bigg and Thomson, which filled the Academy at the turn of the eighteenth century and the beginning of the nineteenth. His feelings about the countryside, nostalgic if not escapist, have had as perennial an appeal as the dark moods of Constable or the apocalyptic vision of Turner, and were expressed in language at least as eloquent as either; some of his images may indeed verge on the banal, as some in Wordsworth do, but masterpieces such as *The Cottage Girl with Dog and Pitcher* (Pl. 147), where the pensive turn of the head may take the mind back to a fifteenth-century Madonna but does not disturb us in the comparison, the Huntington *Cottage Door* (Pl. 116), the Toronto *Harvest Waggon* (Pl. 78) or *The Market Cart* (Pl. 162), can stand beside the best of Murillo, Rubens, Claude or Constable. It is again this intensity of feeling, albeit within a limited range, that informs the general run of his landscapes, and where these delight our senses through the fluency or rich brokenness of touch, the loveliness of colour, the brilliance and assurance of pen or chalk, or the atmospheric suggestiveness of stump or wash, should one rate them below a landscape by Renoir or a watercolour by Cézanne because they are framed within an eighteenth-century convention? They are different, but no less examples of that harmony of mind, heart and touch which results in the alchemy we call great art.

REFERENCES

1. Sir Joshua Reynolds, *Discourses on Art*, ed. Robert R. Wark, San Marino, 1959, p. 248. A paperback re-issue of this edition, but with only a brief introduction, was published by Collier Books, 1966. The most important earlier edition of the *Discourses* printed in English is that of Roger Fry, published in 1905; this is now most valuable for its introduction. A cheap edition was published in Everyman's Library (No. 118) in 1906.
2. Ibid., p. 249.
3. Ibid., p. 250.
4. Ibid., pp. 257–8.
5. Anon. (= Philip Thicknesse), *Sketches and Characters of the most Eminent and most Singular Persons now living,* Bristol, 1770, p. 96.
6. Philip Thicknesse, *A Sketch of the Life and Paintings of Thomas Gainsborough, Esq.*, London, 1788, p. 39.
7. Gainsborough to the Earl of Dartmouth, Bath, 8 April 1771 (ed. Mary Woodall, *The Letters of Thomas Gainsborough*, London, 2nd edn revised, 1963, No. 16, p. 49).
8. Gainsborough to the Earl of Dartmouth, 18 April (1771) (Woodall, op. cit., No. 18, pp. 51–3) and Bath, 13 April 1771 (ibid., No. 17, p. 51).
9. *The Farington Diary*, 6 January 1799 (from the typescript in the British Museum Print Room, p. 1419).
10. Gainsborough to William Jackson, Bath, 2 September 1767 (Woodall, op. cit., No. 50, p. 101).
11. Gainsborough to Mrs Mary Gibbon, 26 December 1775 (Woodall, op. cit., No. 36, p. 79).
12. Ibid.
13. Gainsborough to William Jackson, Bath, 14 September (1767) (Woodall, op. cit., No. 51, p. 103).
14. *The Farington Diary*, 29 January 1799, p. 1454.
15. William Jackson, *The Four Ages; together with Essays on Various Subjects,* London, 1798, p. 154.
16. Edward F. Rimbault, 'Gainsborough as a Musician', *Notes and Queries*, 13 January 1871, p. 39.
17. *The Morning Herald*, 11 August 1788.
18. Jackson, op. cit., p. 160.
19. Anon. (= W.H. Pyne), 'The Greater and Lesser Stars of Pall Mall', Ch. 2, *Fraser's Magazine*, November 1840, p. 551.
20. Jackson, op. cit., pp. 160 and 183.
21. Gainsborough to William Jackson, Bath, 14 September (1767) (Woodall, op. cit., No. 51, p. 101).
22. Ephraim Hardcastle (= W.H. Pyne), *Wine and Walnuts*, London, 1824, Vol. 2, p. 215.
23. Gainsborough to James Unwin, Bath, 25 October 1763 (Woodall, op. cit., No. 83, p. 149) and to Giovanni Battista Cipriani, Bath, 14 February 1774 (Woodall, op. cit., No. 13, p. 45).
24. Gainsborough to William Jackson, Bath, 14 September (1767) (Woodall, op. cit., No. 51, p. 103).
25. Thicknesse, op. cit., p. 41, and Gainsborough to Philip Thicknesse, n.d. (Woodall, op. cit., No. 81, p. 145).
26. The source for this story was Wordsworth (ed. Tom Taylor, *Life of Benjamin Robert Haydon*, 2nd ed., London, 1853, Vol. 3, p. 221).
27. Gainsborough to John Henderson, Bath, 18 July 1773 (Woodall, op. cit., No. 45, p. 93).
28. Gainsborough to Giovanni Battista Cipriani, Bath, 14 February 1774 (Woodall, op. cit., No. 13, p. 45).
29. *The Farington Diary*, 29 January 1799, p. 1454.
30. Anon. (= Thomas Green), 'The Diary of a Lover of Literature', 12 May 1809, *The Gentleman's Magazine*, February 1835, p. 130.
31. *The Farington Diary*, 15 February 1799, p. 1458.
32. *Sketches and Characters*, op. cit., p. 97, and Thicknesse, op. cit., p. 8. Northcote described him as 'a natural gentleman' (William Hazlitt, *Conversations of James Northcote, Esq., R.A.*, London, 1830, p. 260).
33. Philip Thicknesse to John Cooke, October (1773), R.R. Wark, 'Thicknesse and Gainsborough: Some New Documents', *Art Bulletin*, December 1958, p. 332.
34. Gainsborough to Mary Gibbon, n.d. (collection of Mr and Mrs Paul Mellon, Upperville, Virginia).
35. Gainsborough to William Johnstone Pulteney, Bath, n.d. (Woodall, op. cit., No. 66, p. 127).
36. Gainsborough to William Jackson, Bath, 2 September (year unknown) (Woodall, op. cit., No. 55, p. 111).
37. *The Farington Diary*, 29 January 1799, p. 1454.
38. Gainsborough to the Hon. Edward Stratford, Bath, 1 May 1772 (Woodall, op. cit., No. 77, p. 141).
39. Gainsborough to David Garrick, n.d. (Woodall, op. cit., No. 30, p. 71).
40. Gainsborough to David Garrick, Bath, 22 August 1768 (Woodall, op. cit., No. 28, p. 67).
41. John Hayes, *The Drawings of Thomas Gainsborough*, London, 1970, Vol. 1, Nos 5–7, pp. 110–11, and Vol. 2, pls 309–11.
42. Gainsborough to James Unwin, n.d. (Woodall, op. cit., No. 86, p. 155).
43. John Hayes, *Gainsborough as Printmaker*, London, 1971, No. 21, p. 105. An impression of this subject has come to light since the publication of this book.
44. Henry Angelo, *Reminiscences,* London, Vol. 1, 1828, p. 219.
45. *Survey of London*, Vol. 29, 1960, p. 377 and ground-plan on p. 370.
46. Ozias Humphry, 'Biographical Memoir', MSS., *c.* 1802 (*Original Correspondence of Ozias Humphry, R.A.*, Vol. 1: Royal Academy Library).
47. Thicknesse, op. cit., p. 35.
48. *The Farington Diary*, 15 February 1799, p. 1458.
49. Gainsborough to James Unwin, Bath, 25 May 1768 (Woodall, op. cit., No. 90, p. 165).
50. John Thomas Smith, *Nollekens and his Times*, London, 1828, Vol. 1, p. 186.

51. Tate Gallery No. 5845; Ellis Waterhouse, *Gainsborough*, London, 1958, No. 864, p. 110.
52. Reynolds, op. cit., p. 251.
53. Thicknesse, op. cit., p. 23.
54. Walter Thornbury. *The Life of J.M.W.Turner, R.A.*, London, 1862, Vol. 2, p. 62.
55. William T.Whitley, *Thomas Gainsborough*, London, 1915, p. 247.
56. Gainsborough to an unknown recipient, Bath, 28 July 1763 (Woodall, op. cit., No. 100, p. 173), and to Thomas Harvey, London, 22 May 1788 (Woodall, op. cit., No. 43, p. 91).
57. Gainsborough to David Garrick, n.d. (Woodall, op. cit., No. 34, p. 77).
58. Gainsborough to the Royal Academy Hanging Committee (10 April 1784) (Woodall, op. cit., No. 3, p. 29).
59. Anon. (= Thomas Green), 'The Diary of a Lover of Literature', *The Gentleman's Magazine*, March 1834, p. 252.
60. Gainsborough to William Johnstone Pulteney, n.d. (Woodall, op. cit., No. 66, p. 127).
61. Gainsborough to David Garrick, n.d. (Woodall, op. cit., No. 34, p. 75).
62. Gainsborough to David Garrick (Bath, 1766) (Woodall, op. cit., No. 26, p. 63).
63. Annotation in Royal Academy catalogue (Mentmore Library).
64. *The Middlesex Journal*, 23–25 April 1772.
65. Whitley, op. cit., p. 87.
66. Gainsborough to David Garrick, n.d. (Woodall, op. cit., No. 34, p. 75).
67. *The Farington Diary*, 29 October 1794, p. 238.
68. *The Morning Chronicle*, 8 August 1788.
69. *The Morning Herald*, 19 September 1789.
70. Gainsborough to William Pearce, n.d. (Woodall, op. cit., No. 64, p. 125).
71. Reynolds, op. cit., p. 250.
72. *The Farington Diary*, 30 January 1799, p. 1455.
73. Jackson, op. cit., p. 167 (footnote). Gravelot and Roubiliac are both known to have had similar dolls. Those belonging to the former were described in the catalogue of his sale (Basan, 19 May 1773 (Lugt 2169), Lots 11 and 12), and one of the latter's (with full wardrobe) survives in the London Museum. William Collins, the painter, who acquired Gainsborough's palette, owned a 'little model of an old woman, dressed by the same great painter's hand' (W.Wilkie Collins, *Memoirs of the Life of William Collins, Esq., R.A.*, London, 1848, Vol. 2, p. 244).
74. Mrs Gainsborough sale, Christie's, 11 May 1799 (Lugt 5917), Lots 91–2.
75. Jackson, op. cit., p. 168.
76. On this fashion see J.L.Nevinson, 'Vogue of the Vandyke Dress', *Country Life Annual*, 1959, pp. 25–7.
77. Recorded in Gainsborough's account with Hoare's Bank, 17 August 1776.
78. On Gainsborough Dupont generally, see my article, 'The Drawings of Gainsborough Dupont', *Master Drawings*, Vol. 3, No. 3, 1965.
79. Gainsborough to the Hon. Edward Stratford, n.d. (Woodall, op. cit., No. 78, p. 143).
80. ed. Ernest Fletcher, *Conversations of James Northcote R.A. with James Ward on Art and Artists*, London, 1901, p. 161.
81. *Sketches and Characters*, op. cit., p. 96.
82. *The Farington Diary*, 30 January 1799, p. 1455.
83. Whitley, op. cit., p. 254. It is perhaps significant that Bate-Dudley was horrified at the idea of representing such a subject: 'A shocking choice! which carries with it proof of a callous heart! – Painting should never seize upon subjects of calamity, so likely to affect the feeling!' (*The Morning Herald*, 1 March 1786).
84. Gainsborough to the Earl of Dartmouth, 18 April (1771) (Woodall, op. cit., No. 18, p. 53).
85. *The Library of the Fine Arts*, Vol. 3, June 1832, p. 461.
86. Reynolds, op. cit., p. 252.
87. See, for example, John Pye, *Patronage of British Art*, London, 1845. The situation as regards landscape is discussed in my article, 'British Patrons and Landscape Painting: 2. Eighteenth-century collecting', *Apollo*, March 1966, pp. 188–97.
88. Gainsborough to William Hoare (1773) (Woodall, op. cit., No. 46, p. 95).
89. Ellis Waterhouse, *Painting in Britain 1530 to 1790*, London, 1953, p. 104.
90. Mark Girouard, 'English Art and the Rococo – 1', *Country Life*, 13 January 1966, p. 59.
91. On Gravelot see H.A.Hammelmann, 'A French Master of English Illustration: Gravelot's Years in London', *Country Life*, 3 December 1959.
92. Waterhouse, *Painting in Britain*, op. cit., p. 152.
93. Girouard, op. cit., p. 60.
94. Angelo, op. cit., Vol. 1, p. 151.
95. Lawrence Gowing, 'Hogarth, Hayman and the Vauxhall Decorations', *The Burlington Magazine*, January 1953, p. 11.
96. For the development of this middle-class ethos, and the relationships between artists, writers and dramatists at this period, see Frederick Antal, *Hogarth and his Place in European Art*, London [1962], especially Ch. 1: 'Hogarth's World of Ideas'.
97. John Hayes, 'British Patrons and Landscape Painting: 2. Eighteenth-century collecting', *Apollo*, March 1966, p. 190.
98. Thicknesse, op. cit., p. 8.
99. Jackson, op. cit., p. 179.
100. Gainsborough to William Jackson, Bath, 23 August (1767) (Woodall, op. cit., No. 49, p. 99).
101. Gainsborough to Sir William Chambers, London, 27 April 1783 (Woodall, op. cit., No. 11, p. 43).
102. *The Morning Herald*, 5 May 1789.
103. Thicknesse, op. cit., p. 6.

104. *The Morning Chronicle*, 8 August 1788.
105. Gainsborough to William Jackson, Bath, 4 June (1772) (Woodall, op. cit., No. 56, p. 115).
106. Gainsborough to Lord Hardwicke, n.d. (Woodall, op. cit., No. 42, pp. 87 and 91).
107. Sir George Beaumont to William Gilpin, 15 June 1801 (quoted in Carl Paul Barbier, *William Gilpin*, Oxford, 1963, p. 107). Contemporaries were quite aware that this was precisely the attitude taken by Gainsborough: a critic said of a landscape painted after his return from the Lakes (see p. 36) that 'though not a portrait of any particular spot, the picture is highly characteristic of that country. Another landscape, painted on his return, from a town in *Wales*, has also such evident marks of *locality*, that whoever has been west of the *Severn*, will be struck with this mimic scene' (*The Morning Post*, 6 April 1789).
108. Gainsborough to William Jackson, Bath, 4 June (1772) (Woodall, op. cit., No. 56, p. 115). For the contemporary attitude of nostalgia towards landscape, and the desire to shut out the realities of change, see Leslie Parris's perceptive remarks in the catalogue of the Tate Gallery exhibition, 'Landscape in Britain *c.* 1750–1850', 1973, p. 58.
109. Gainsborough to Lord Hardwicke, n.d. (Woodall, op. cit., No. 42, p. 87).
110. Gainsborough to William Pearce, n.d. (Woodall, op. cit., No. 64, p. 125).
111. Gainsborough to (probably) William Mayhew, Ipswich, 13 March 1758 (Woodall, op. cit., No. 25, p. 61).
112. George Williams Fulcher, *Life of Thomas Gainsborough, R.A.*, London, 1856, 2nd edn, pp. 54–7.
113. Mrs Delany to Mrs Dewes, Bath, 23 October 1760 (ed. Lady Llanover, *The Autobiography and Correspondence of Mary Granville, Mrs Delany*, London, 1861, Vol. 3, p. 605).
114. *The Morning Herald*, 28 March 1786.
115. See my article, 'Gainsborough's "Richmond Water-walk"', *The Burlington Magazine*, January 1969, pp. 28–31.
116. Waterhouse, *Gainsborough*, op. cit., No. 648, p. 91.
117. The Hon. Daines Barrington, 'On the Progress of Gardening', *Archaeologia*, Vol. VII., 1785, p. 130 (paper read before the Society of Antiquaries, 13 June 1782).
118. *The Morning Chronicle*, 8 August 1788.
119. See his letter to his landlady, Mrs Rasse, n.d. (Woodall, op. cit., No. 104, p. 179); in February 1755 he borrowed three hundred pounds from James Unwin, which he repaid two years later out of his wife's annuity (Sydney E. Harrison, 'New Light on a Gainsborough Mystery', *The Connoisseur*, January 1922, p. 5).
120. Gainsborough to (probably) William Mayhew, Ipswich, 13 March 1758 (Woodall, op. cit., No. 25, p. 61).
121. Thicknesse, op. cit., p. 17.
122. The evidence for Gainsborough's scale of prices derives largely from the bills and receipts for payments recorded in private archives and (to a lesser extent) transactions in the artist's account with Hoare's Bank; see also Waterhouse, *Gainsborough*, op. cit., p. 19.
123. Gainsborough to William Jackson, Bath, 14 September (1767) (Woodall, op. cit., No. 51, p. 103).
124. See my article, 'A Note on Gainsborough's "The Morning Walk"', *The Burlington Magazine*, August 1963, p. 370.
125. Gainsborough to Mary Gibbon, 26 December 1775 (Woodall, op. cit., No. 36, p. 79).
126. Gainsborough to the Earl of Sandwich, 29 November 1784 (Woodall, op. cit., No. 71, p. 133).
127. Vertue Note Books, Vol. III., *Walpole Society*, Vol. XXII, 1934, p. 157.
128. *The Ipswich Journal*, 20 October 1759.
129. Prince Hoare, *Epochs of the Arts*, London, 1813, pp. 76–7.
130. *The Public Advertiser*, 1 May 1767.
131. Annotation in R.A. catalogue (Mentmore Library).
132. *The Morning Chronicle*, 2 May 1780.
133. Fulcher, op. cit., p. 116.
134. Gainsborough to Mrs Mary Gibbon, 22 September 1777 (collection of Mr and Mrs Paul Mellon, Upperville, Va.).
135. Whitley, op. cit., p. 273.
136. This was the price put on it at the Schomberg House sale in 1789 (Ibid., p. 323).
137. *The Morning Herald*, 2 May 1786.
138. Ibid., 1 May 1782.
139. Ibid., 6 June 1785.
140. Ibid., 7 May 1787.
141. *The Monthly Magazine*, February 1801, p. 63.
142. Whitley, op. cit., p. 330; *The Morning Herald*, 29 February 1788, and 18 August 1788, and Ellis Waterhouse, 'The Sale at Schomberg House, 1789', *The Burlington Magazine*, March 1945, p. 77.
143. *The Morning Herald*, 5 January 1787.
144. *The Farington Diary*, 15 July 1794, p. 196.
145. Henry Reveley, *Notices Illustrative of the Drawings and Sketches of some of the most Distinguished Masters in all the Principal Schools of Design*, London, 1820 (ed. and revised by Thomas Green), p. 261.
146. Constable to C.R.Leslie, n.d. (= 1834) (ed. R.B.Beckett, 'John Constable's Correspondence III', *Suffolk Records Society*, Vol. 8, 1965, p. 116).
147. William Hazlitt, *Criticisms on Art*, London, 1843, pp. 194–5.
148. *Quarterly Review*, May 1809, p. 48.
149. Gainsborough to David Garrick, Bath, 22 August 1768 (Woodall, op. cit., No. 28, p. 67).
150. Barrington, op. cit., p. 130.
151. Anita Brookner, *Greuze*, London, 1972, p. 23. Dr Brookner's detailed analysis, in the first three chapters of her book, of the cult of *sensibilité* in eighteenth-century France is highly relevant to our understanding of late Gainsborough and of the attitudes of his contemporaries.
152. Uvedale Price, *Essays on the Picturesque*, London, 1810, Vol. 2, p. 368.

BIBLIOGRAPHICAL NOTE

GAINSBOROUGH'S career and work are most inadequately documented until about 1780, chiefly due to the fact that he was not a methodical person; he never kept letters, and such account or sitter books as he may have used have not come down to us. Receipts for payments are to be found in various archives; a number of drafts exist on his account with James Unwin 1754–60, and his accounts with Hoare's Bank 1762–85 and Drummond's Bank 1782–8 can be studied in those firms' ledgers; his will is preserved at Somerset House. But the main source for our knowledge and understanding of Gainsborough is his correspondence, which has a place beside Sterne in eighteenth-century English literature. Of his letters, original, lively and entertaining – in addition to being instructive – about a hundred survive, and these have been collected together by Mary Woodall (The Cupid Press, 1963); probably they are the merest fraction of those he actually sent, since we know, for example, that Margaret Gainsborough 'regretted much having lost many letters which He wrote to her and her Sister while they were at Blacklands School, containing instructions for drawing', while Farington noted that 'Mrs. Downman has in her possession a large collection of letters written by Gainsborough to Jackson, in a truly original & singular stile' (these are not the series now in the Royal Academy) and Thomas Green records the existence in 1816 of 'the brilliant but eccentric letters of Gainsborough to Mr. Kilderbee: too licentious to be published' (there is no letter to Kilderbee in the Woodall edition).

The catalogue of the sale of Gainsborough's pictures held at Schomberg House in 1789 was reprinted in *The Burlington Magazine* for May 1944, prefaced by an article by Tancred Borenius on Gainsborough's collection of old masters, and a list of purchasers and prices at the studio sale, drawn from an annotated catalogue, was published in *The Burlington Magazine* for March 1945; the Gainsborough and Gainsborough Dupont sale, held after the latter's death in 1797, was reprinted, with prices and buyers' names, in the *Walpole Society* volume for 1915–17. Neither of the sales held at Christie's on 2 June 1792 (Lugt 4926) and 10–11 May 1799 (Lugt 5917), the latter of which contained Gainsborough's books, have been published.

There are innumerable useful references to Gainsborough in the contemporary press, chiefly covering the last decade of his life, and notably in *The Morning Herald*, of which Bate-Dudley was both editor and proprietor; conversations with Margaret Gainsborough, Gainsborough Dupont and others close to Gainsborough are recorded in the pages of *The Farington Diary* (partially published 1922–8: complete typescript available in the British Museum Print Room) and the other most valuable early sources are the obituaries in *The Morning Herald* for 4 August 1788 (written by Bate-Dudley) and *The Morning Chronicle* for 8 August 1788, and the memoirs of Reynolds (*Fourteenth Discourse*, 10 December 1788), Thicknesse (*A Sketch of the Life and Paintings of Thomas Gainsborough, Esq.*, 1788, but see also his *Sketches and Characters of the most Eminent and most Singular Persons now living*, 1770, and the references to Gainsborough in the letters he wrote to John Cooke, transcribed in *The Art Bulletin* for December 1958), Jackson (*The Four Ages*, 1798) and Humphry (autobiographical fragment contained in Vol. 1 of his *Correspondence*, preserved at the Royal Academy, which includes an account of Gainsborough's methods: partially published in Whitley); Cunningham (*The lives of the most eminent British Painters . . .*, 1829–33) is largely derivative. Information, criticism and anecdotes from other sources, some of which, by gossip-writers such as Henry Angelo and W.H.Pyne, have to be treated with caution, are scattered in early and mid nineteenth-century books and periodicals (many references can be unearthed by consulting the Whitley Papers in the British Museum Print Room).

The first biographical study of any length, which also contains the beginnings of a catalogue of Gainsborough's work, is G.W.Fulcher, *Life of Thomas Gainsborough, R.A.*, 1856; this was written by a native of Sudbury and drew upon local sources of information. The spate of books which appeared between 1894 and 1910 adds nothing to our knowledge, and the standard biography, based on years of patient research and incorporating a vast amount of new material derived from eighteenth-century newspapers, is William T.Whitley's *Thomas Gainsborough*, 1915; Sir Walter Armstrong's uncritical catalogue of the paintings (in *Gainsborough and his Place in English Art*, 1904) has been superseded by Ellis Waterhouse's *Gainsborough*, 1958, which also contains a useful bibliography and the best corpus of plates, and is the most important general study of the artist. Recent short accounts are Mary Woodall, *Thomas Gainsborough: His Life and Work*, 1949, Oliver Millar, *Thomas Gainsborough*, 1949, Ellis Waterhouse's chapter in his *Painting in Britain 1530 to 1790*, 1953, 3rd edn, 1969, and John Hayes, 'Gainsborough' (lecture reprinted in the *Journal of the Royal Society of Arts*, April 1965).

Useful specialized studies of different aspects of Gainsborough's work have only begun to appear in the last forty years. Ronald Paulson's essay on form versus representation in Gainsborough, which relates his evocative imprecision to Sterne, will be published in his *Emblem and Expression: Meaning in English Art of the Eighteenth Century*, 1975. John Hayes's 'Gainsborough and the Bedfords' in *The Connoisseur* for April 1968 contains an account of Gainsborough's relationship with an important patron. The pioneer study of the landscape drawings, with a catalogue listing nearly five hundred examples, was produced by Mary Woodall in 1939; a new book on the drawings in general, with full bibliography, a *catalogue raisonné* comprising 878 entries, and illustrated by 462 plates, was published by John Hayes in 1970, followed by a study and *catalogue raisonné* of the prints in 1971. The fancy pictures were first discussed, in relation to the literature of the period, in C.B.Tinker's *Painter and Poet*, 1938, and an article containing a chronological catalogue of them was published by Ellis Waterhouse in *The Burlington Magazine* for June 1946. The same author's 'Preliminary Check List of Portraits by Thomas Gainsborough', which appeared in the *Walpole Society* volume for 1953, contains a certain amount of material which could not be included in his 1958 catalogue; there is a detailed analysis of the Suffolk style in John Hayes's 'Some Unknown Early Gainsborough Portraits', *The Burlington Magazine*, February 1965, and the *Richmond Water-walk* is discussed by the same writer in *The Burlington Magazine* for January 1969; Emilie Buchwald's penetrating study of the relationships between Gainsborough's portrait backgrounds and the changing ideals of eighteenth-century gardening appeared in *Studies in Criticism and Aesthetics*, ed. Howard Anderson and John S.Shea, 1967. Fresh insights into Gainsborough's style are also to be found in Robert Wark's essays on '*The Blue Boy*' and *The Cottage Door* in his *Ten British Pictures*, 1971, and in David Manning's 'Gainsborough's Duke and Duchess of Cumberland with Lady Luttrell' in *The Connoisseur* for June 1973. John Hayes's 'Gainsborough and Rubens' formed the second of a series of articles on Gainsborough's landscapes which appeared in *Apollo* for November 1962, August 1963 and July 1964; the most recent account of Gainsborough's development as a landscape painter is by Luke Herrmann, in his *British Landscape Painting of the 18th Century*, 1973. John Hayes's *catalogue raisonné* of the landscape paintings will be published shortly. A new, fully annotated, edition of Gainsborough's letters is in course of preparation by the same author.

PLATES

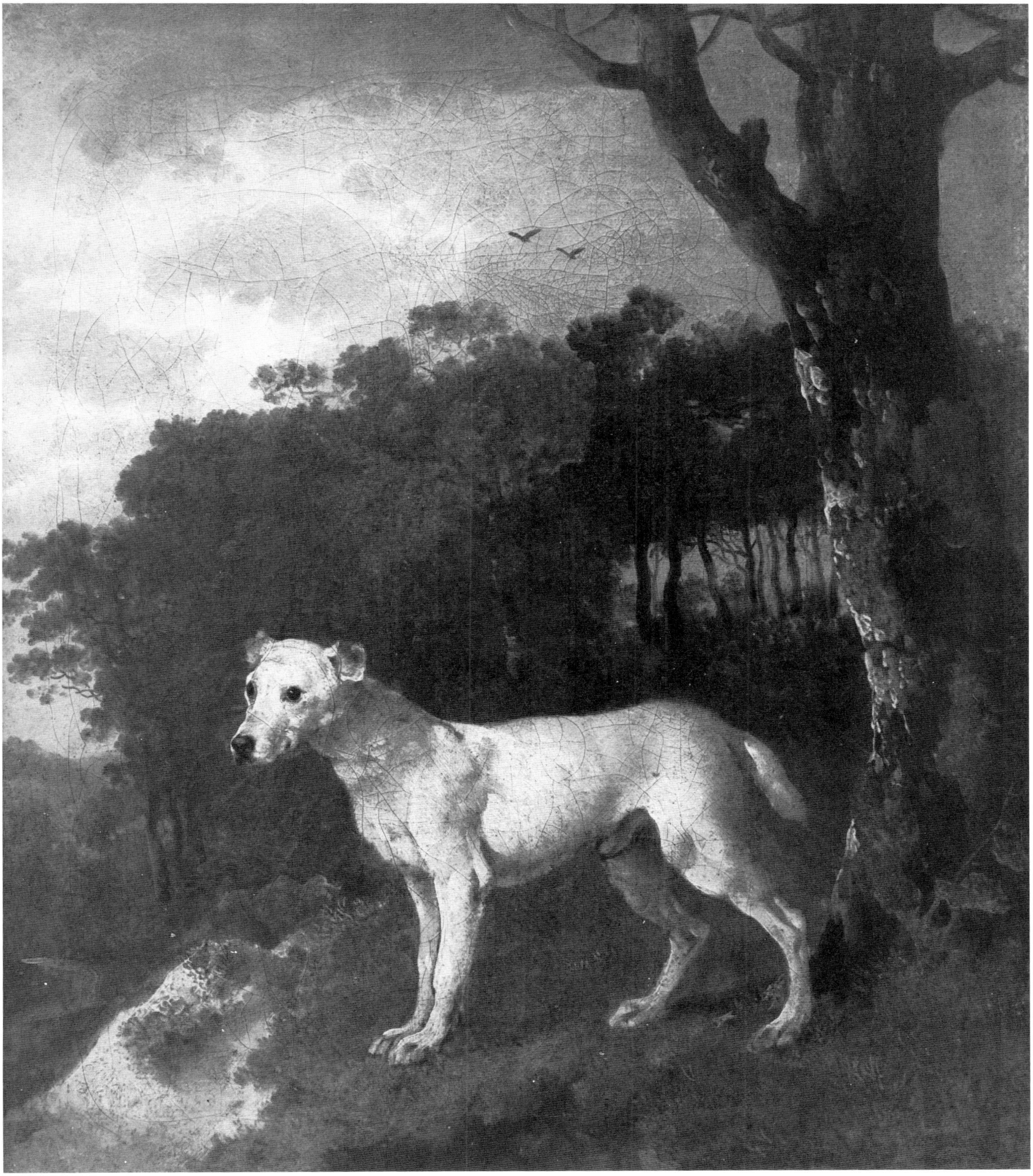

1. '*Bumper*', *bull-terrier owned by Mrs Henry Hill*. Canvas, $13\frac{3}{4} \times 11\frac{3}{4}$ in. Signature and date 1745 copied onto the relining canvas. Raveningham, Sir Edmund Bacon, Bt (Note 1)

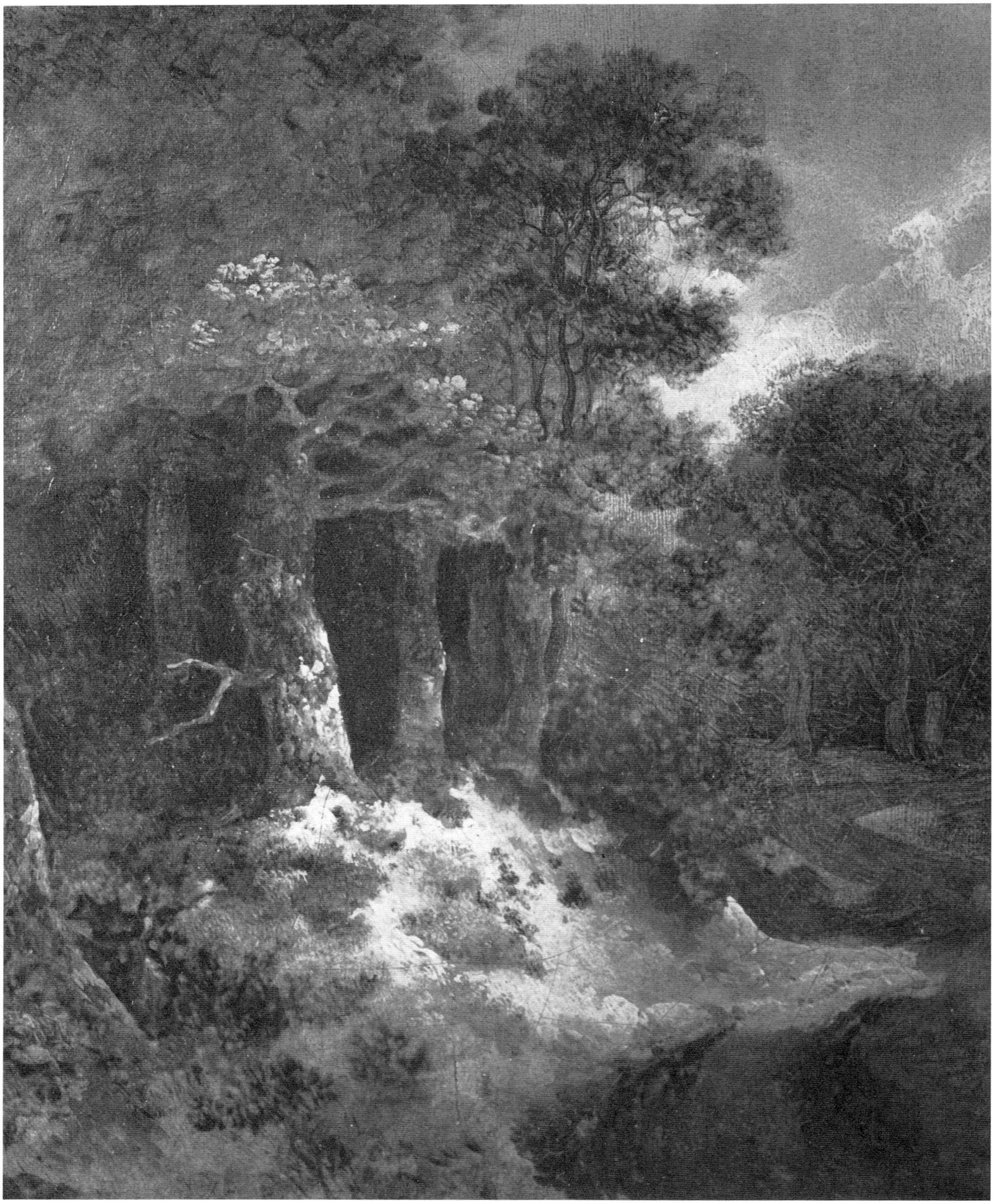

2. '*The Path through the Woods*'. Canvas (unfinished), $13\frac{1}{2} \times 10\frac{1}{4}$ in. About 1744–6. Russborough, Sir Alfred Beit, Bt (Note 2)

3. Antoine Watteau (1684–1721): detail from '*Le Mezzetin*'. Canvas, $21\frac{3}{4} \times 17$ in. New York, Metropolitan Museum of Art

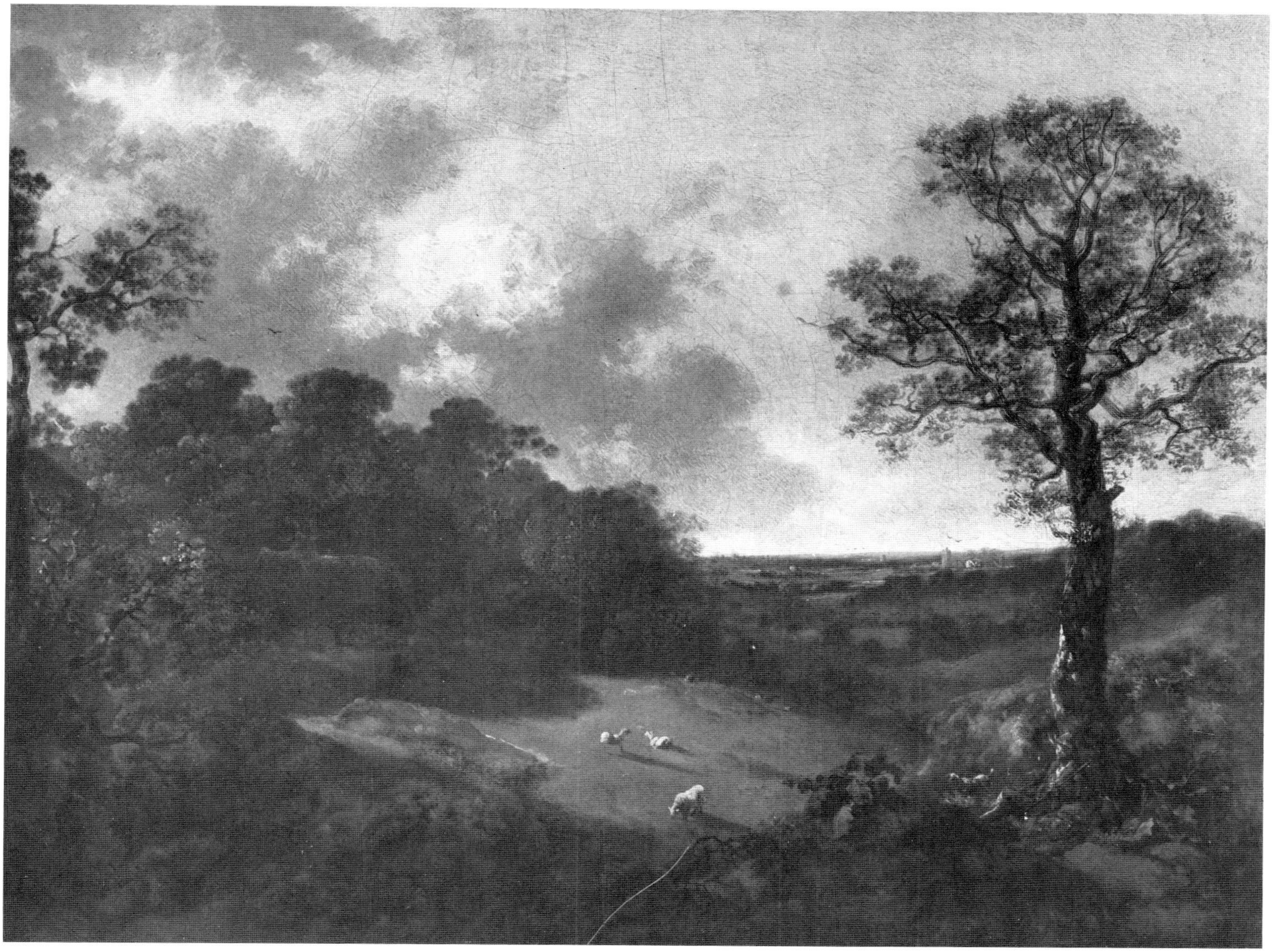

4. *Wooded landscape with shepherd and sheep and distant village*. Canvas, $17\frac{1}{4} \times 21\frac{1}{4}$ in. About 1746–7. Private Collection (Note 5)

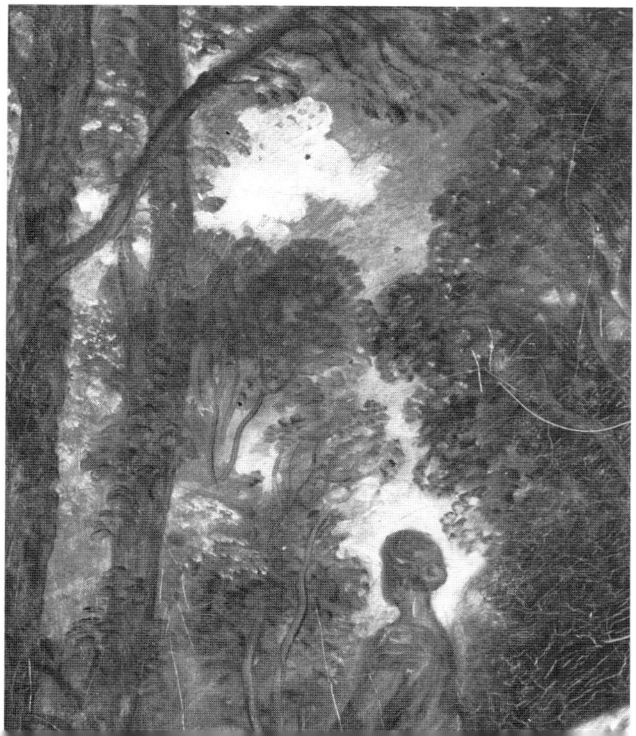

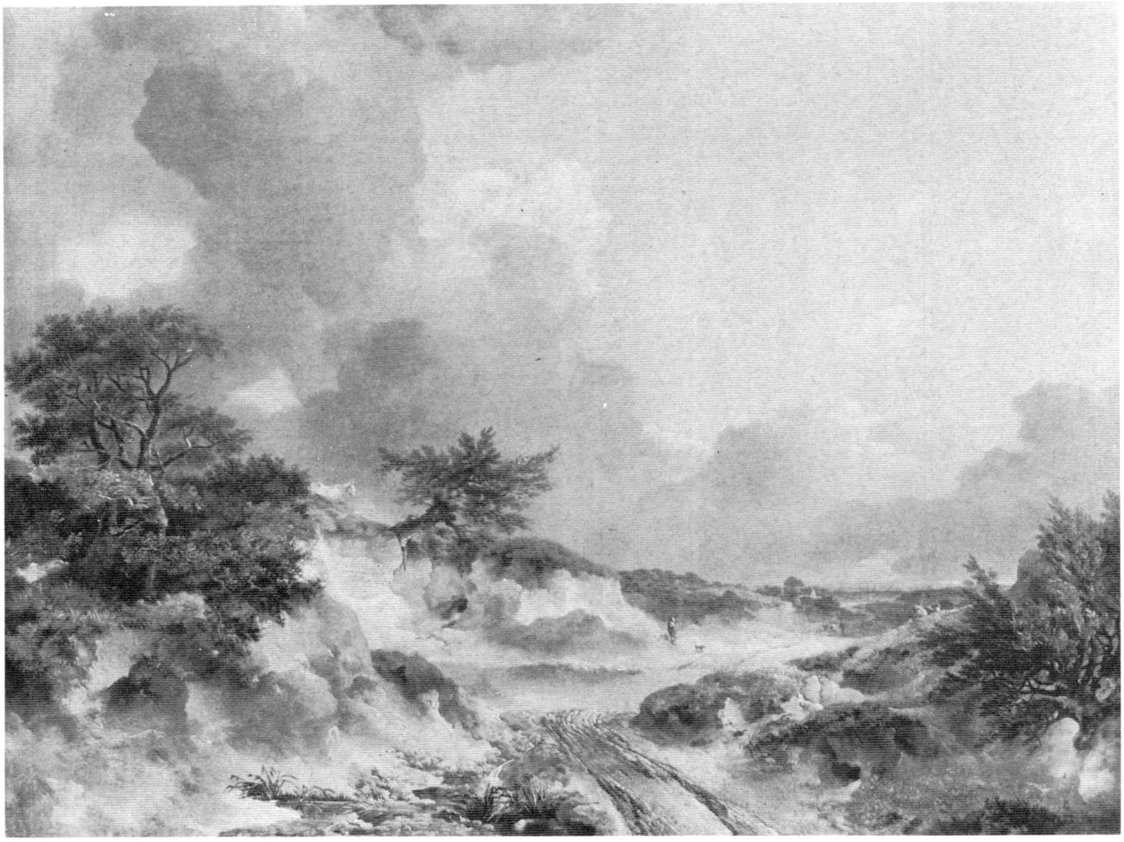

5. *Sand pit by a sandy road : village in distance.* Canvas, $18\frac{1}{2} \times 24$ in. About 1746–7. Dublin, National Gallery of Ireland (Note 4)

6. *Wooded landscape with herdsman, cow and cottage.* Pencil, $5\frac{3}{8} \times 7\frac{7}{8}$ in. About 1746–7. New York, Pierpont Morgan Library (Note 3)

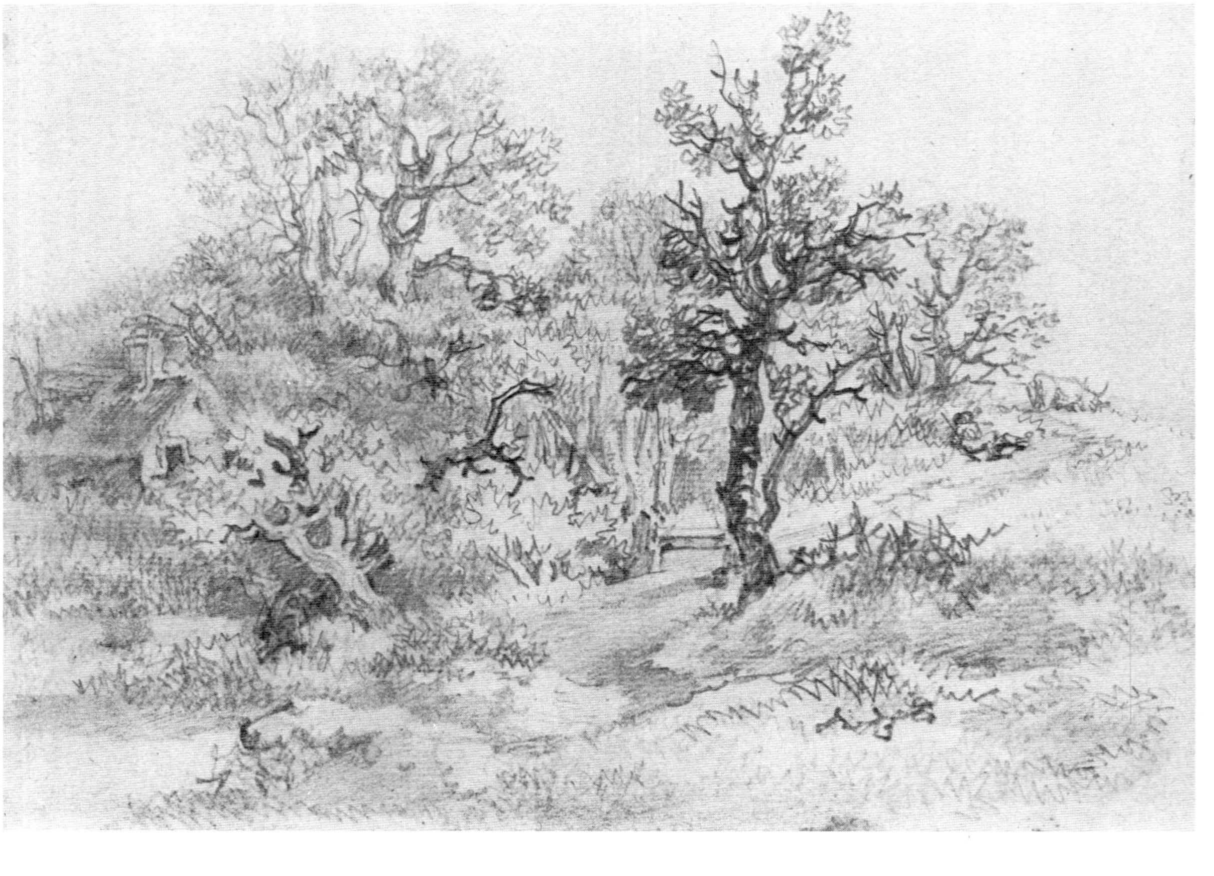

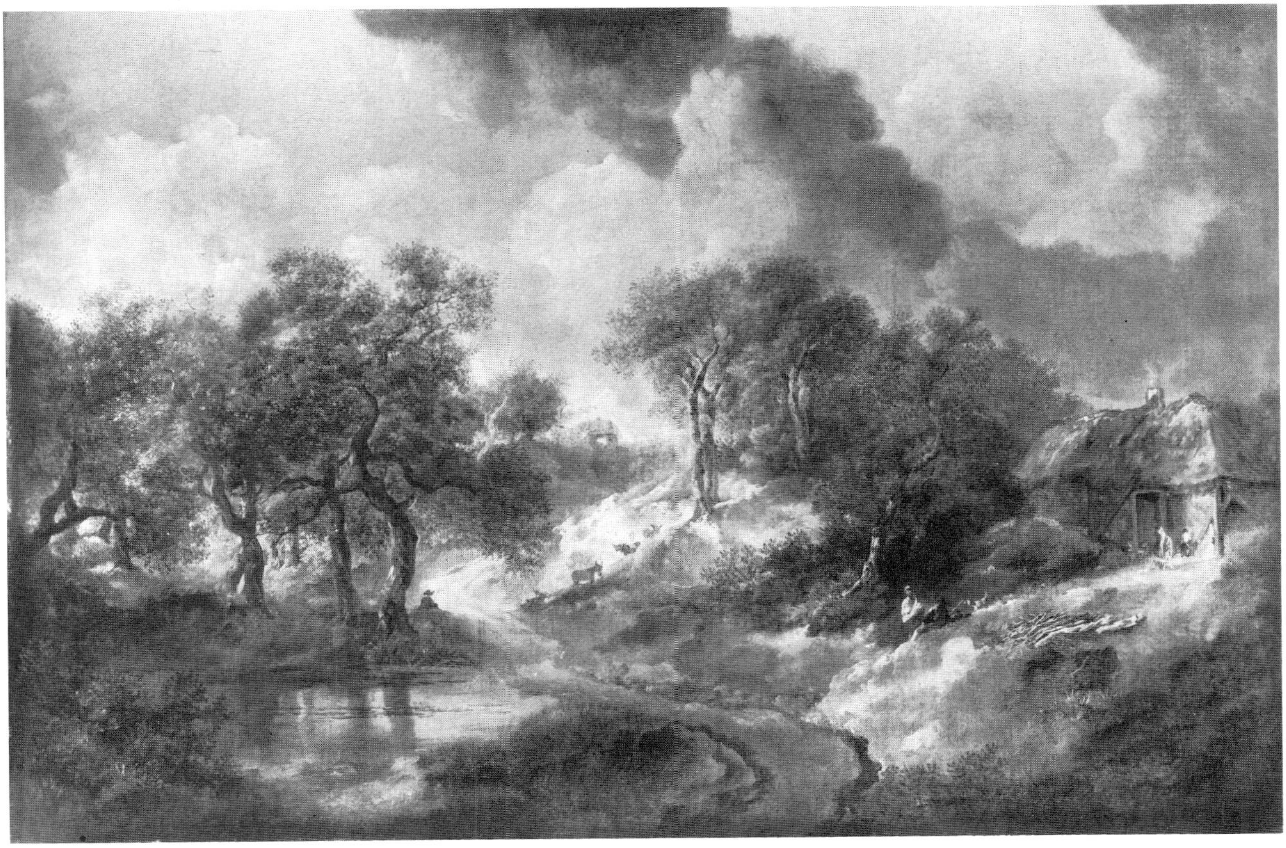

7. *Sandy lane through woods with cottage and donkeys*. Canvas, 26 × 37⅜ in. About 1748. Vienna, Kunsthistorisches Museum (Note 13)

8. *Wooded landscape with seated figure*. Canvas, 24⅝ × 30¾ in. About 1747. London, Tate Gallery (Note 7)

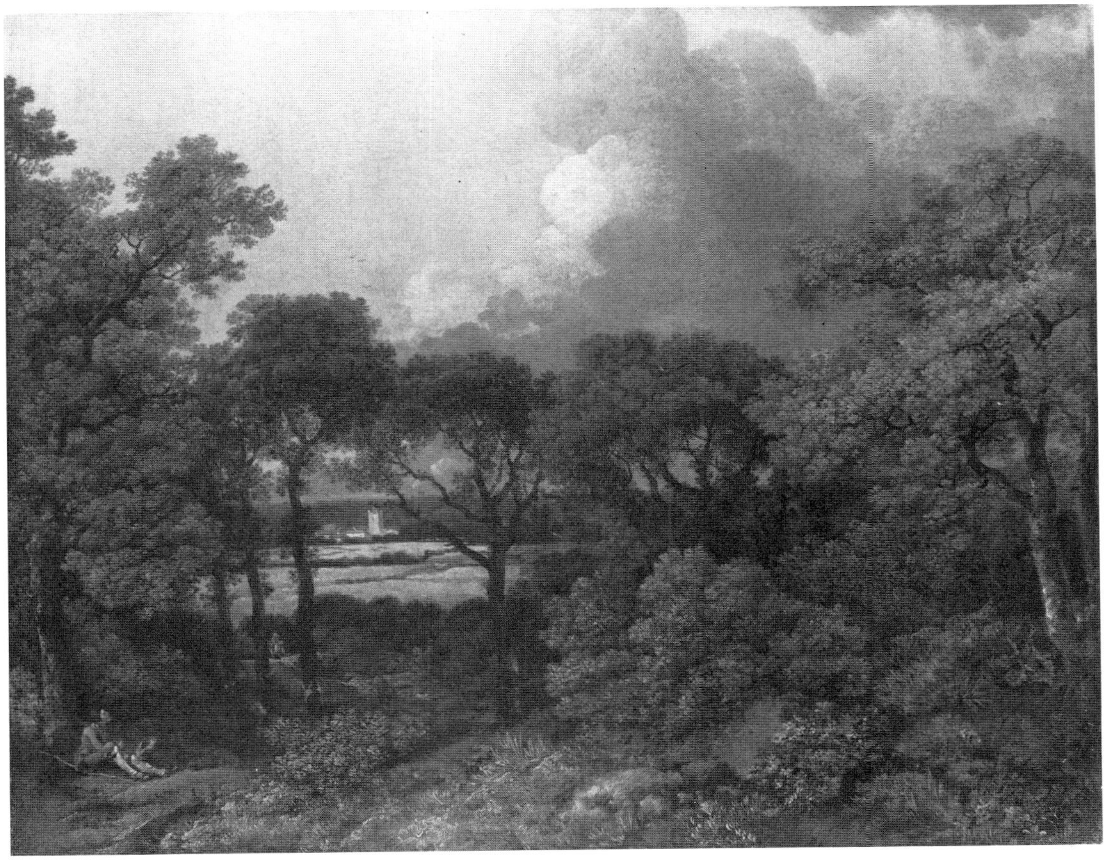

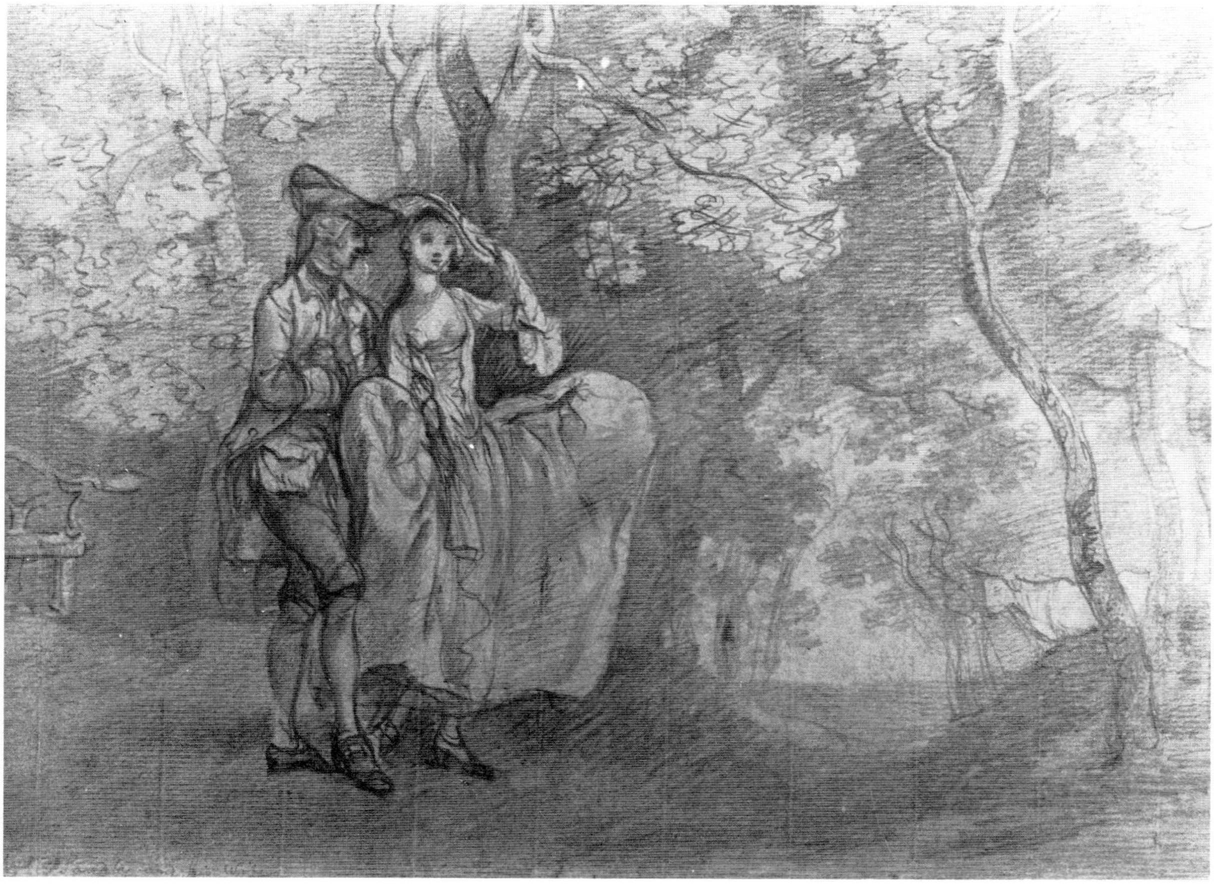

9. *Self-portrait with his wife, Margaret* (probably). Pencil, $7\frac{15}{16} \times 10\frac{9}{16}$ in. About 1746-7. Paris, Private Collection (Note 9)

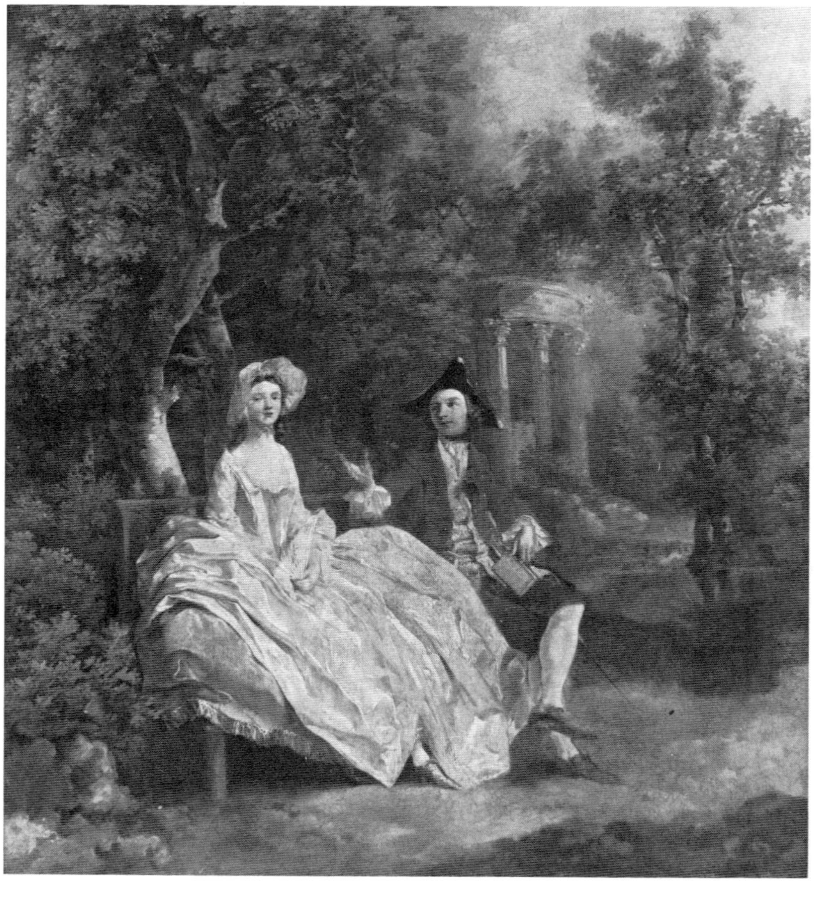

10. *Self-portrait with his wife, Margaret* (probably). Canvas, $30 \times 26\frac{1}{2}$ in. About 1746-7. Paris, Louvre (Note 10)

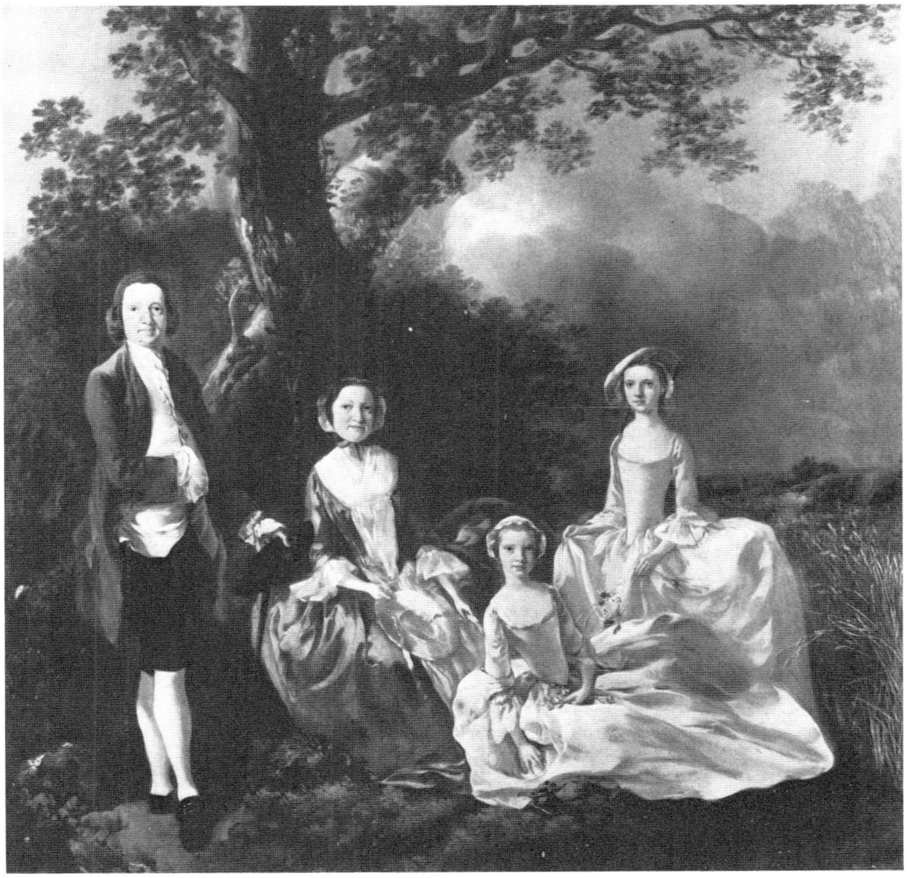

11. *The Gravenor family*. Canvas, $35\frac{1}{2} \times 35\frac{1}{2}$ in. About 1747. London, Private Collection (Note 11)

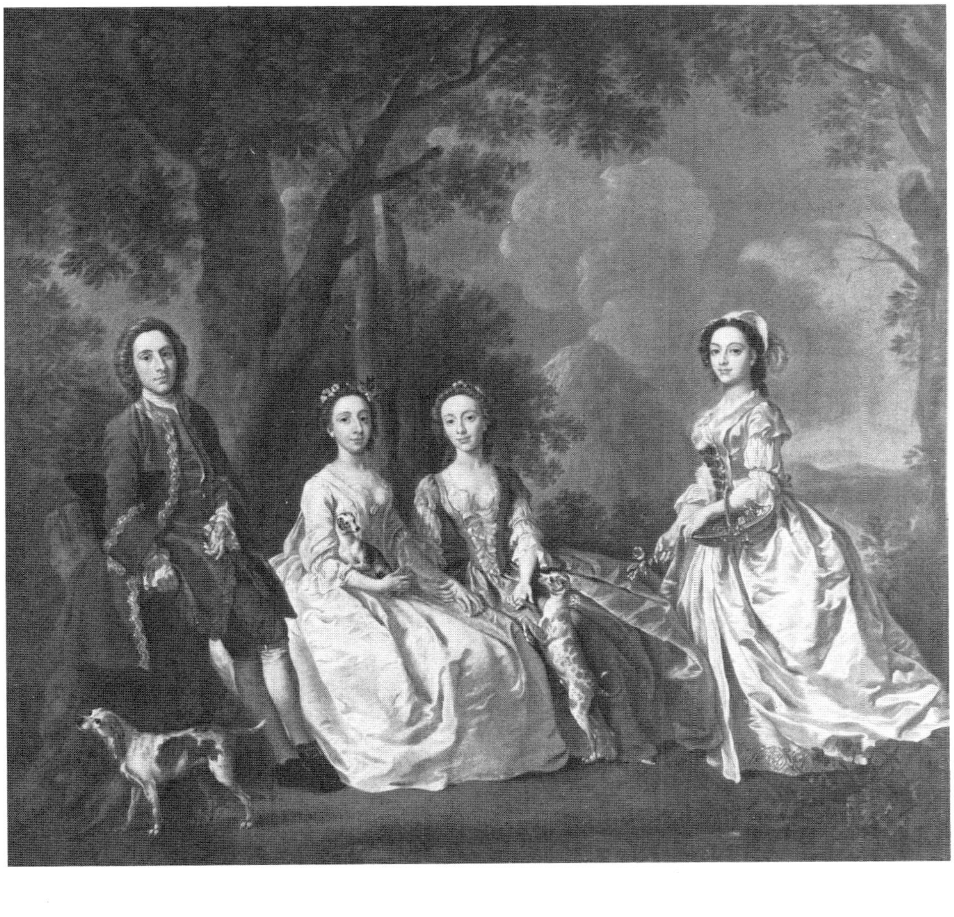

12. Francis Hayman (1708–76): *The Jacob family*. Canvas, $40 \times 42\frac{1}{2}$ in. About 1745. Private Collection

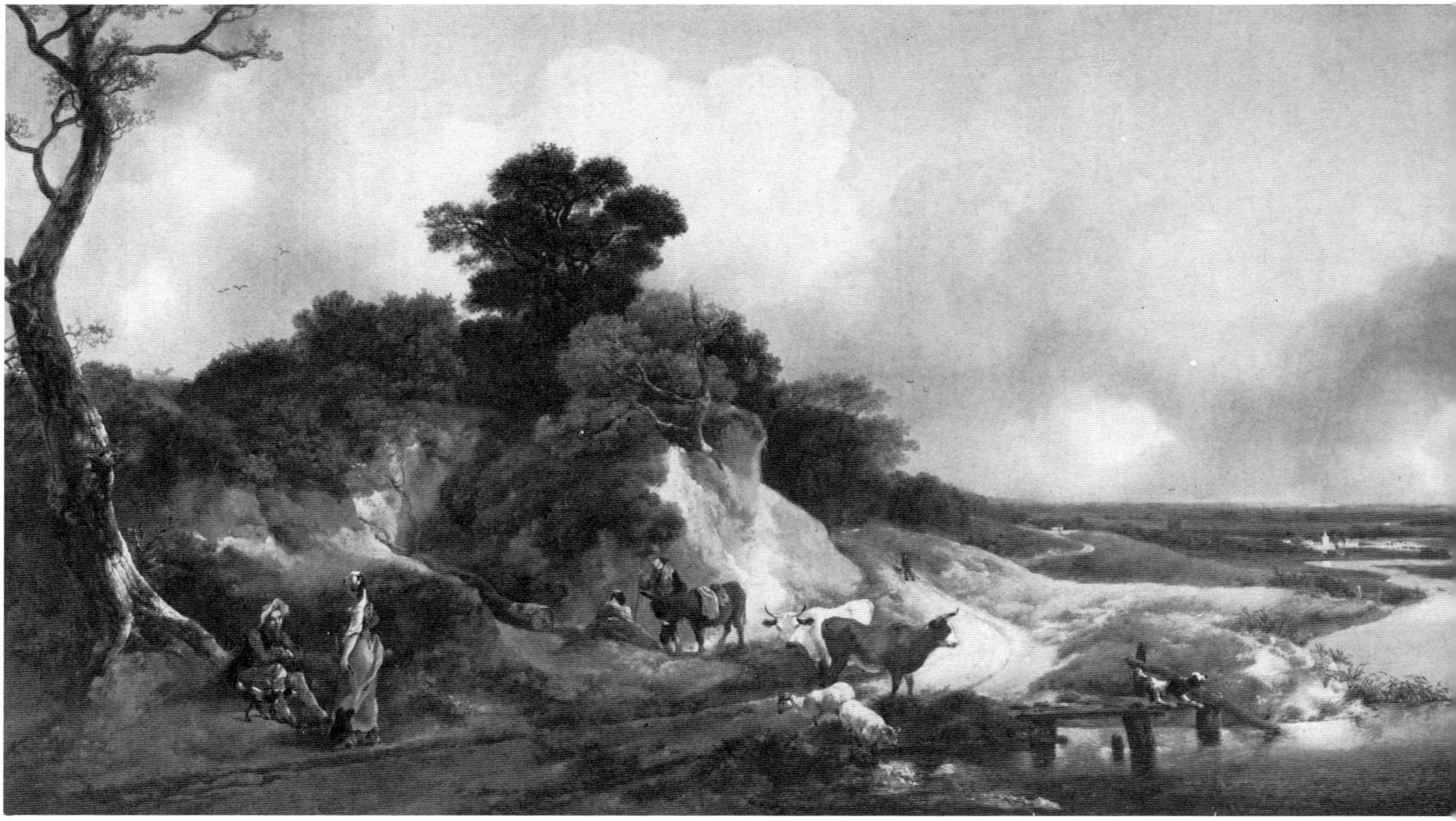

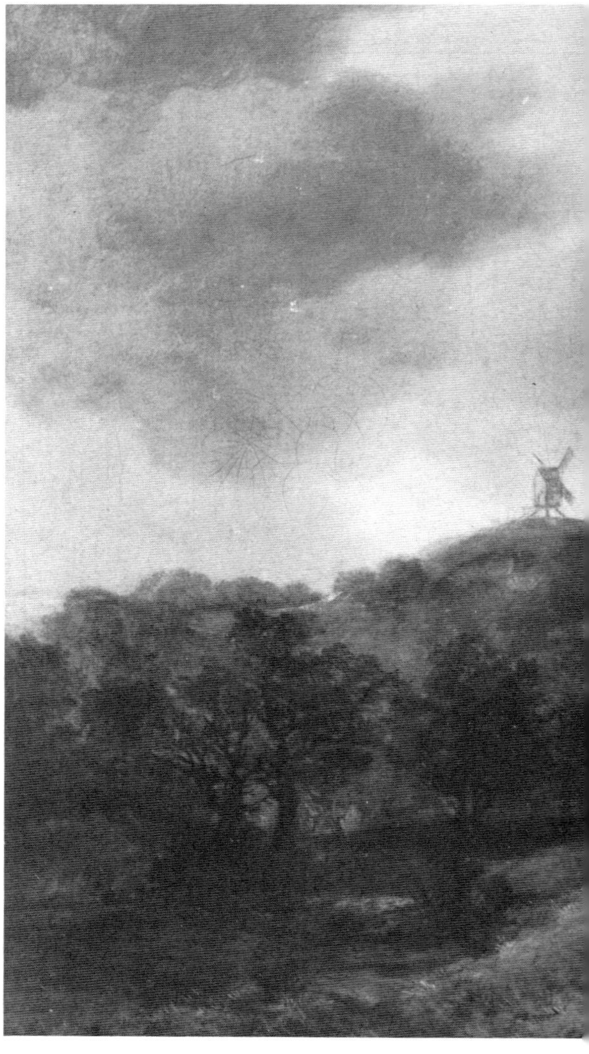

14. *Figures and donkeys on a road, distant windmill.* Canvas, 24 × 42 in. About 1754–5. Arundel Castle, Duke of Norfolk (Note 25)

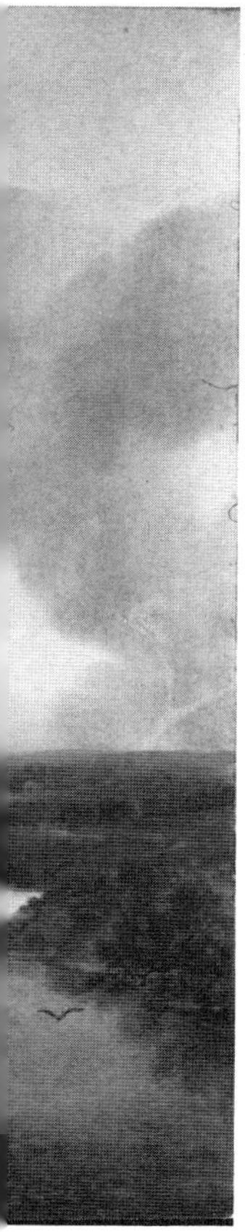

13. *River scene with figures and dog barking at a swallow*. Canvas, 30 × 59½ in. About 1747. Edinburgh, National Gallery of Scotland (Note 6)

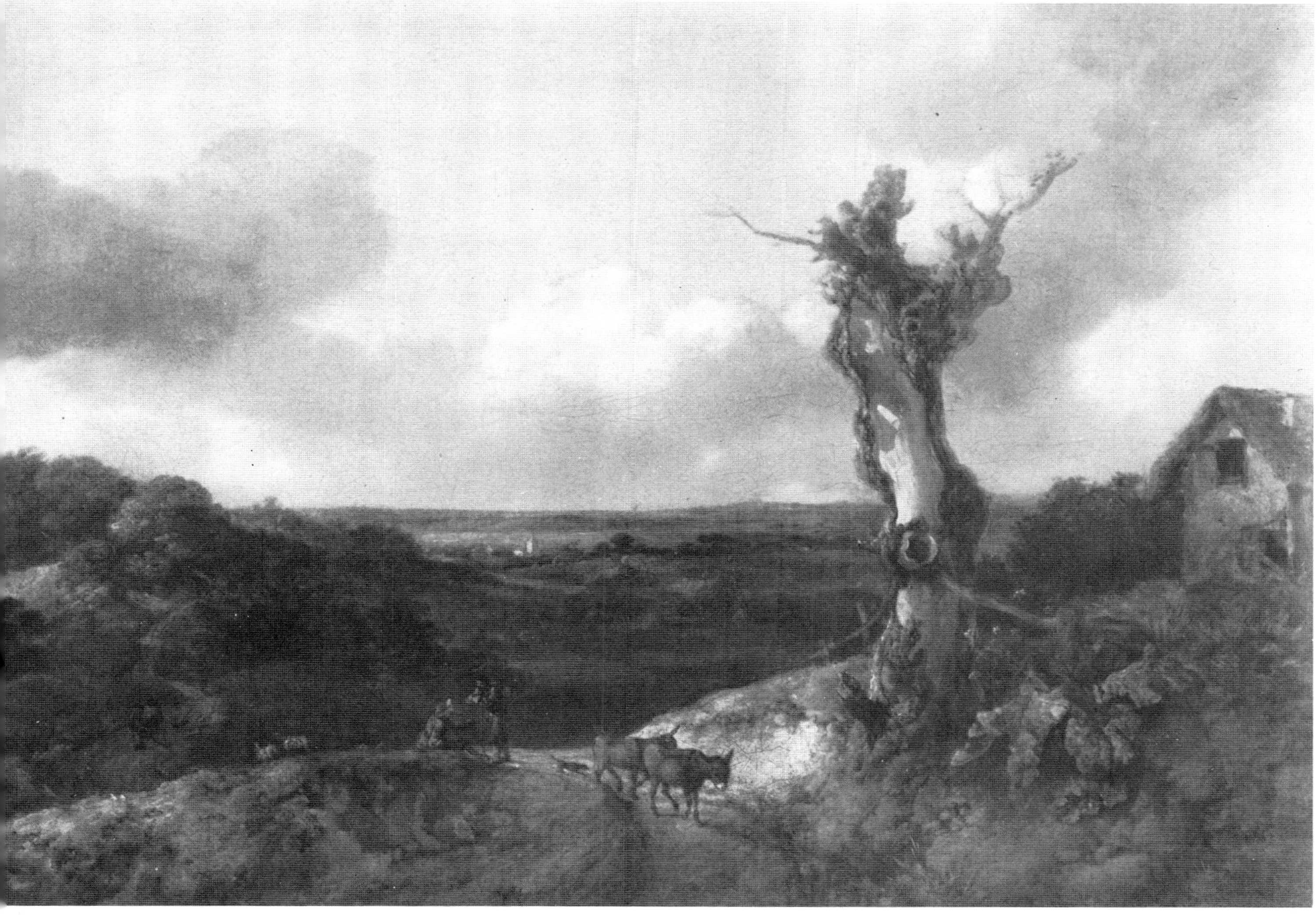

15. *Wooded landscape with river, cattle and figures* (after Ruisdael). Black and white chalks on buff paper, $16\frac{1}{16} \times 16\frac{5}{8}$ in. About 1747. Manchester, Whitworth Art Gallery (Note 8)

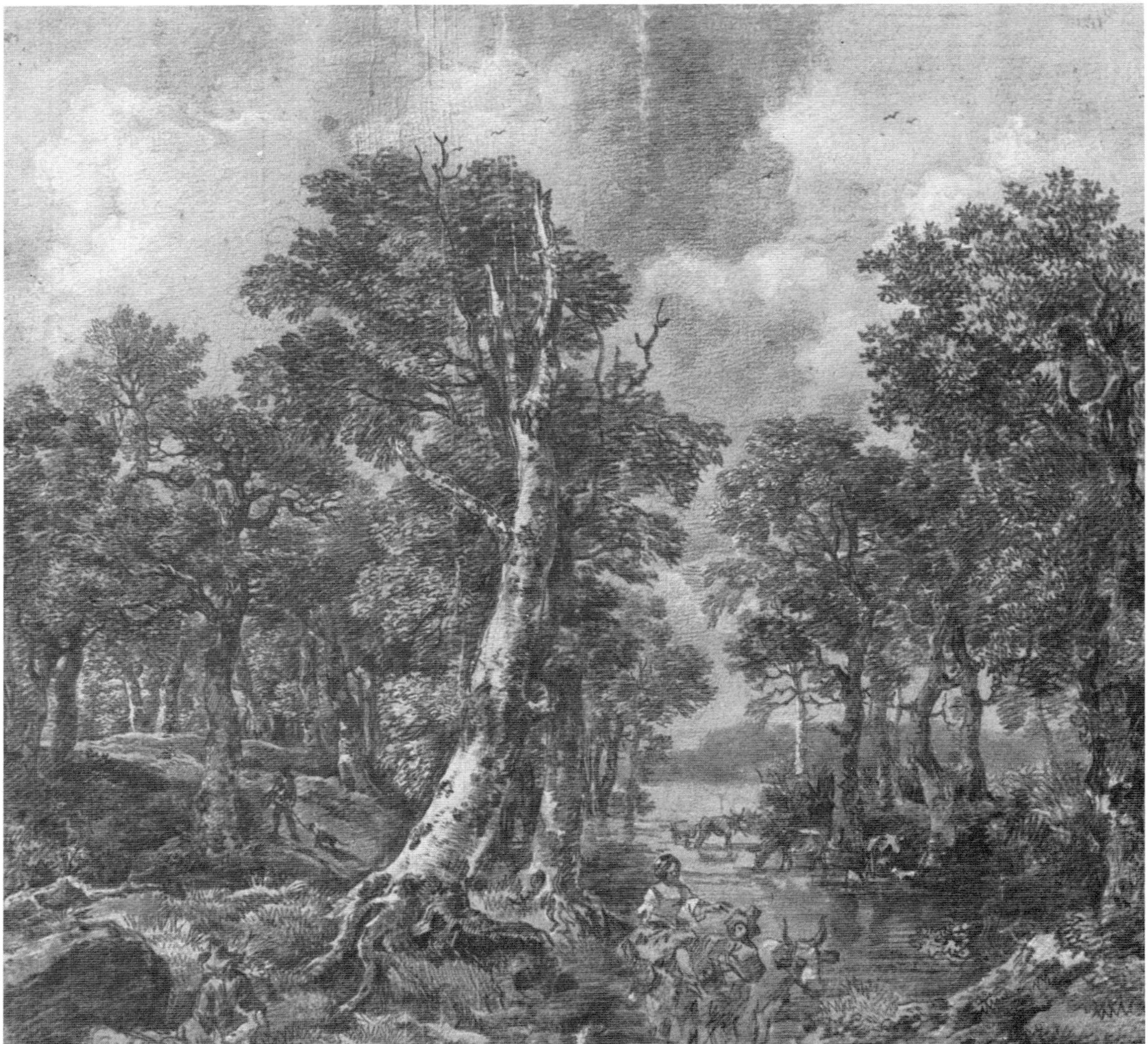

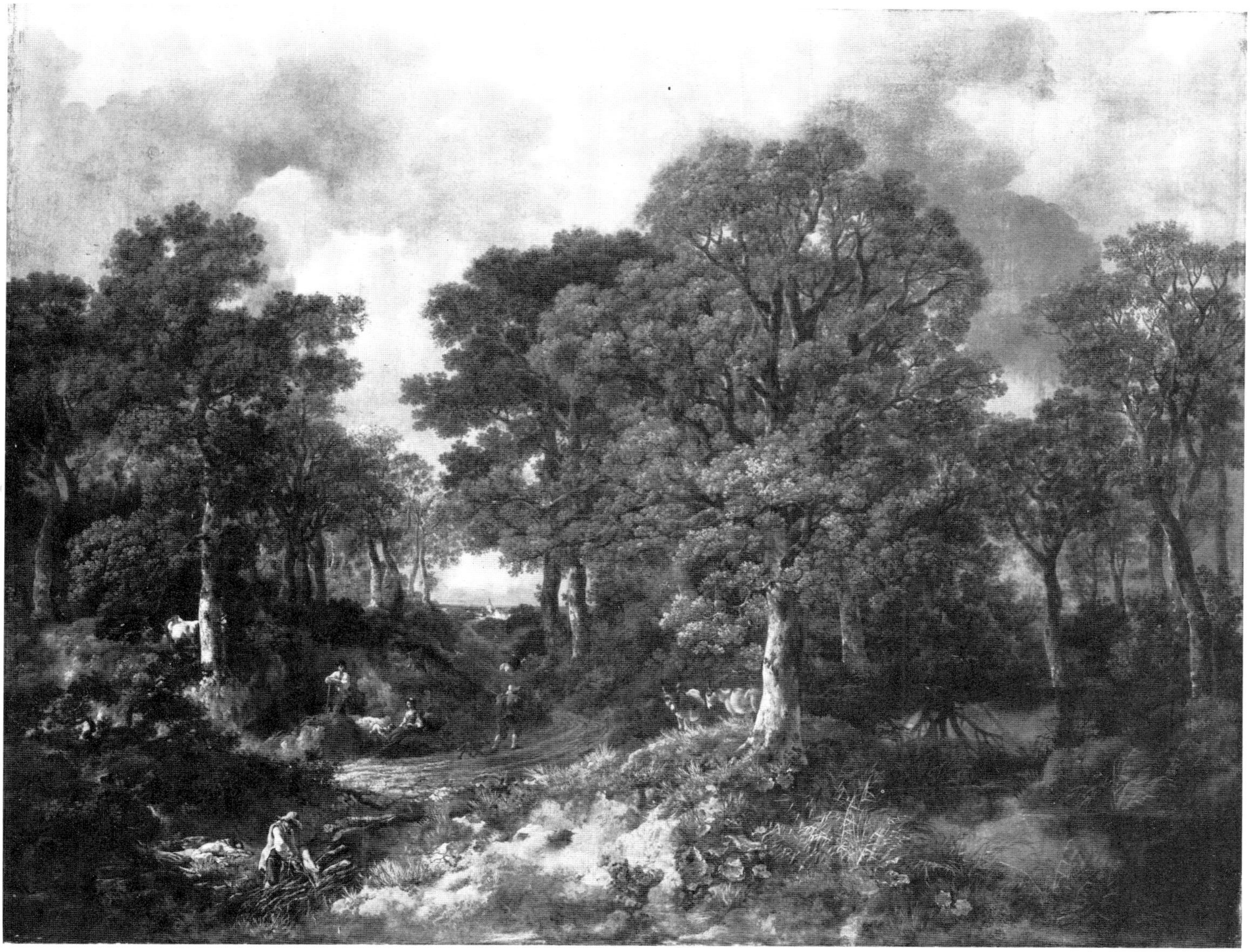

16. *Wooded landscape with figures, animals and distant village*. Known as '*Gainsborough's Forest*'. Canvas, 48 × 61 in. Painted 1748 (engraved 1790). London, National Gallery (Note 15)

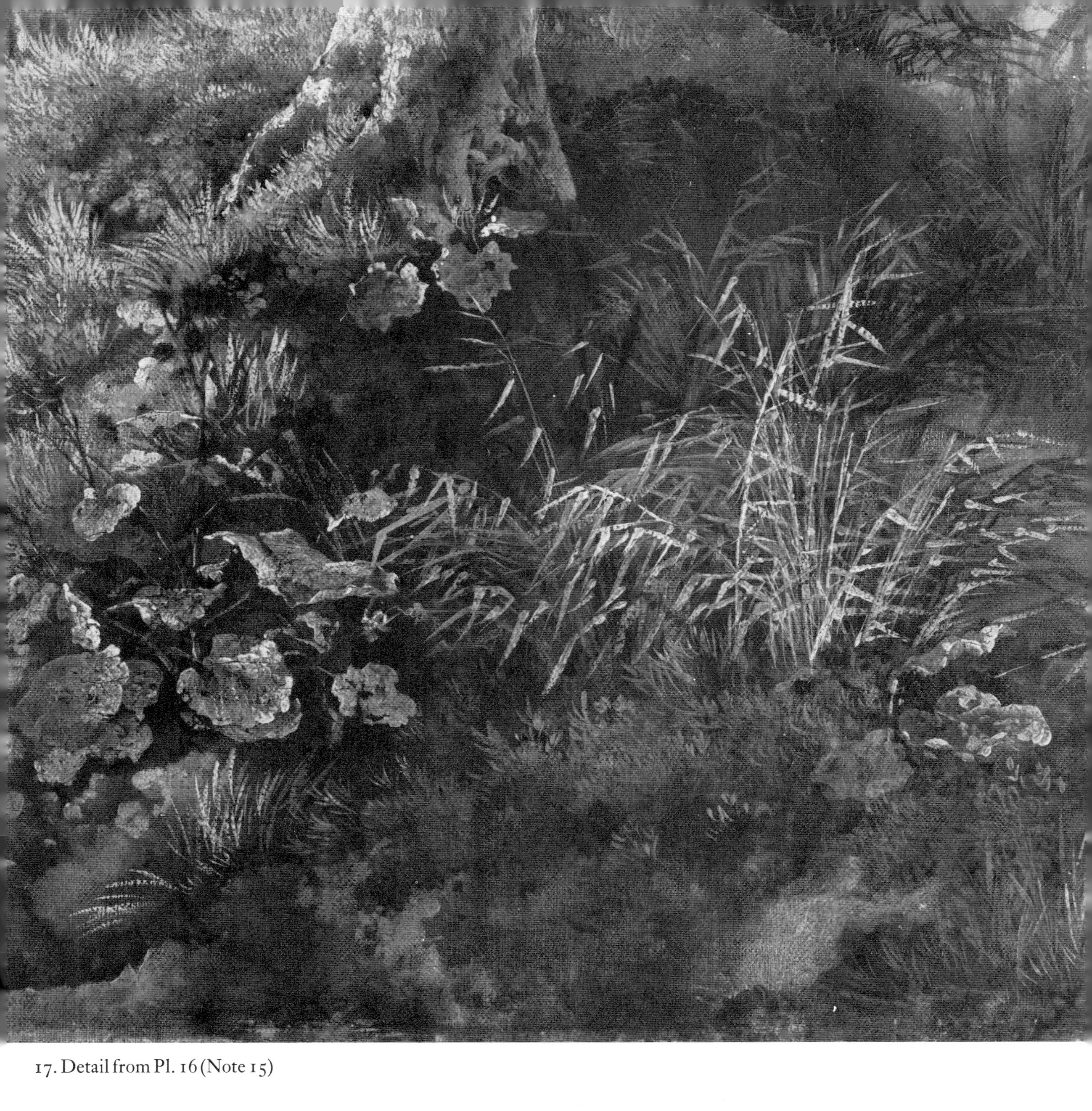

17. Detail from Pl. 16 (Note 15)

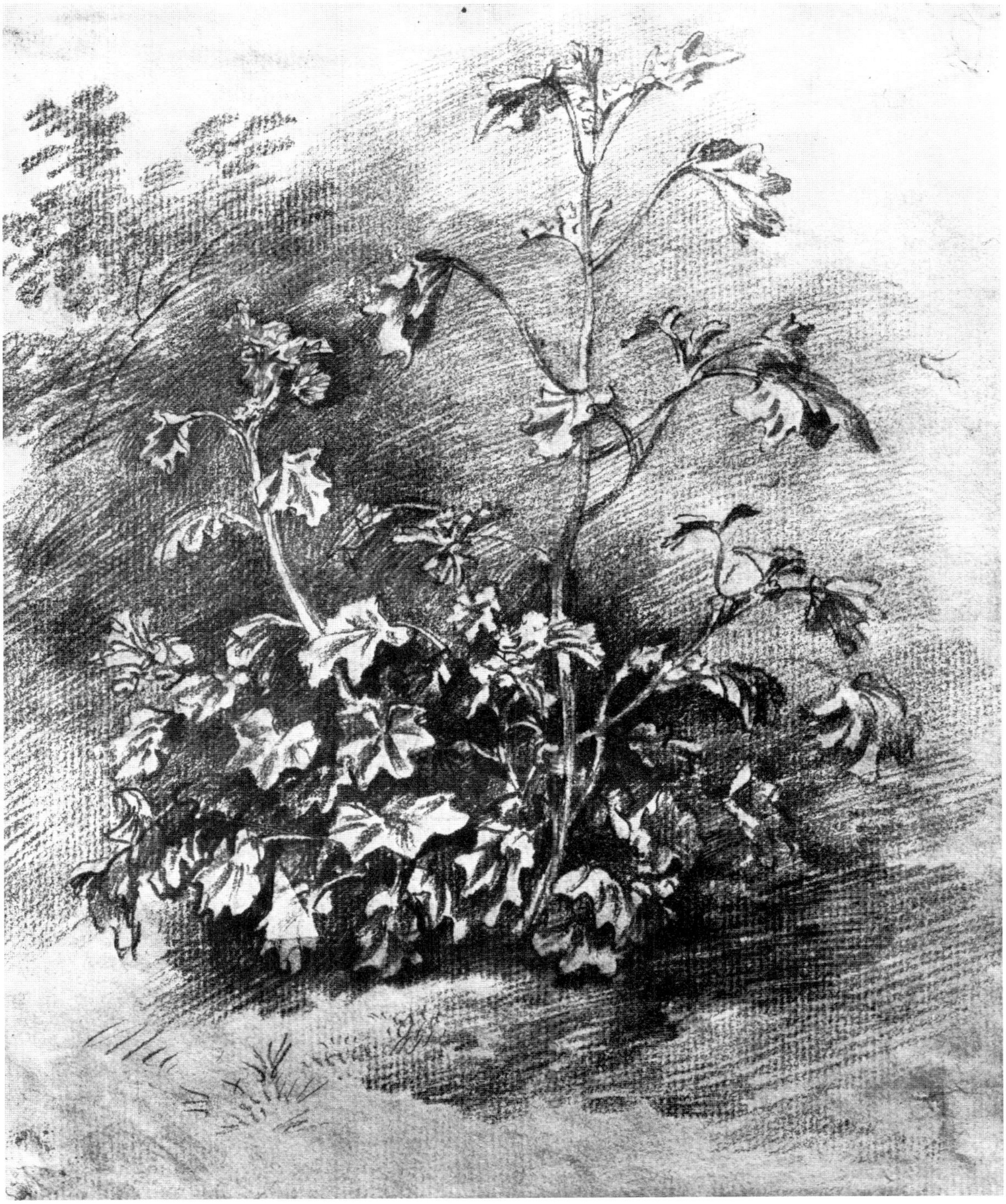

18. *Study of mallows*. Pencil, $7\frac{1}{2} \times 6\frac{1}{8}$ in. Later 1750s. Private Collection (Note 44)

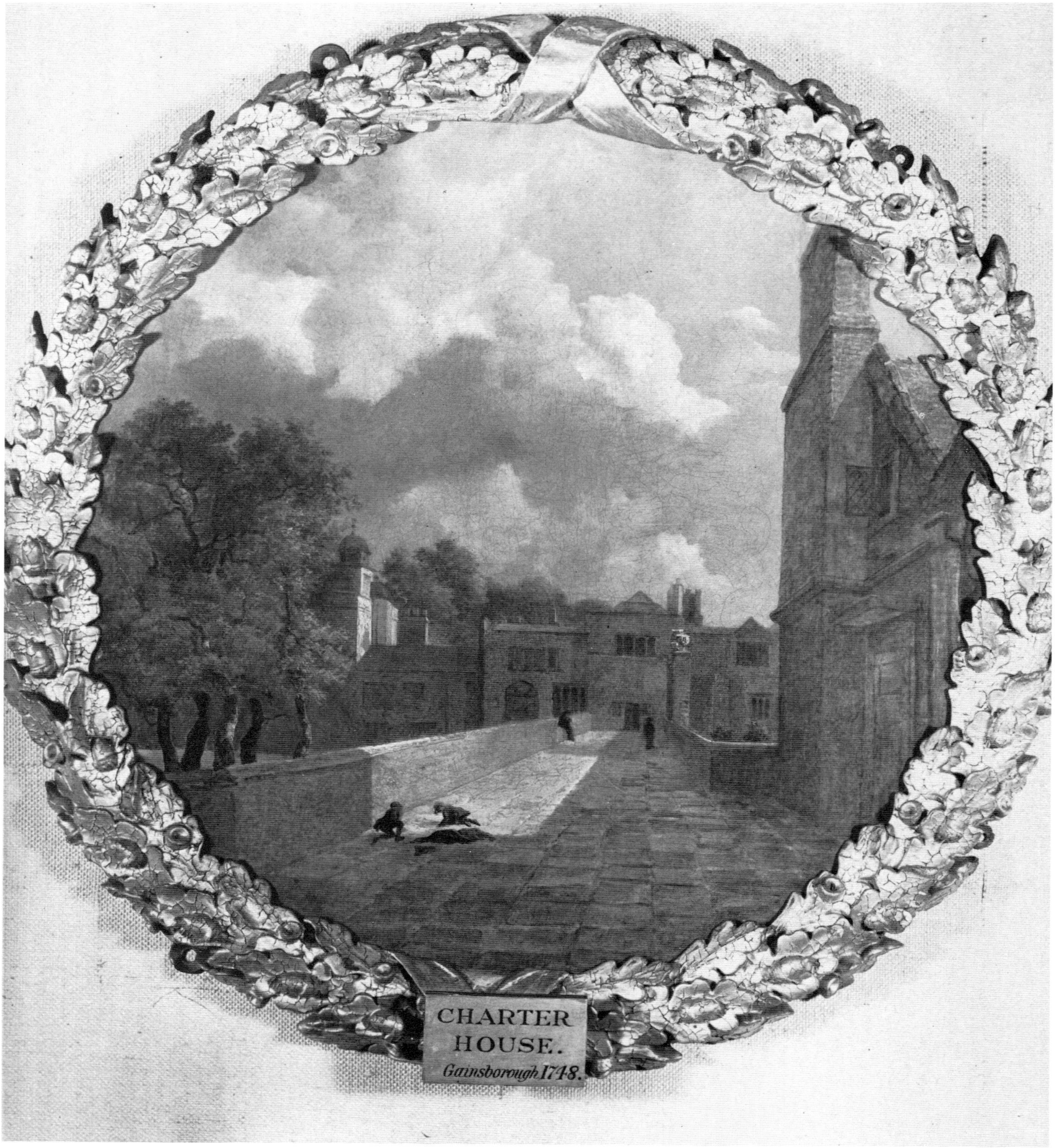

19. *The Charterhouse*. Canvas, 22 in. diameter. Presented to the Foundling Hospital by the artist, 1748. London, Thomas Coram Foundation (Note 14)

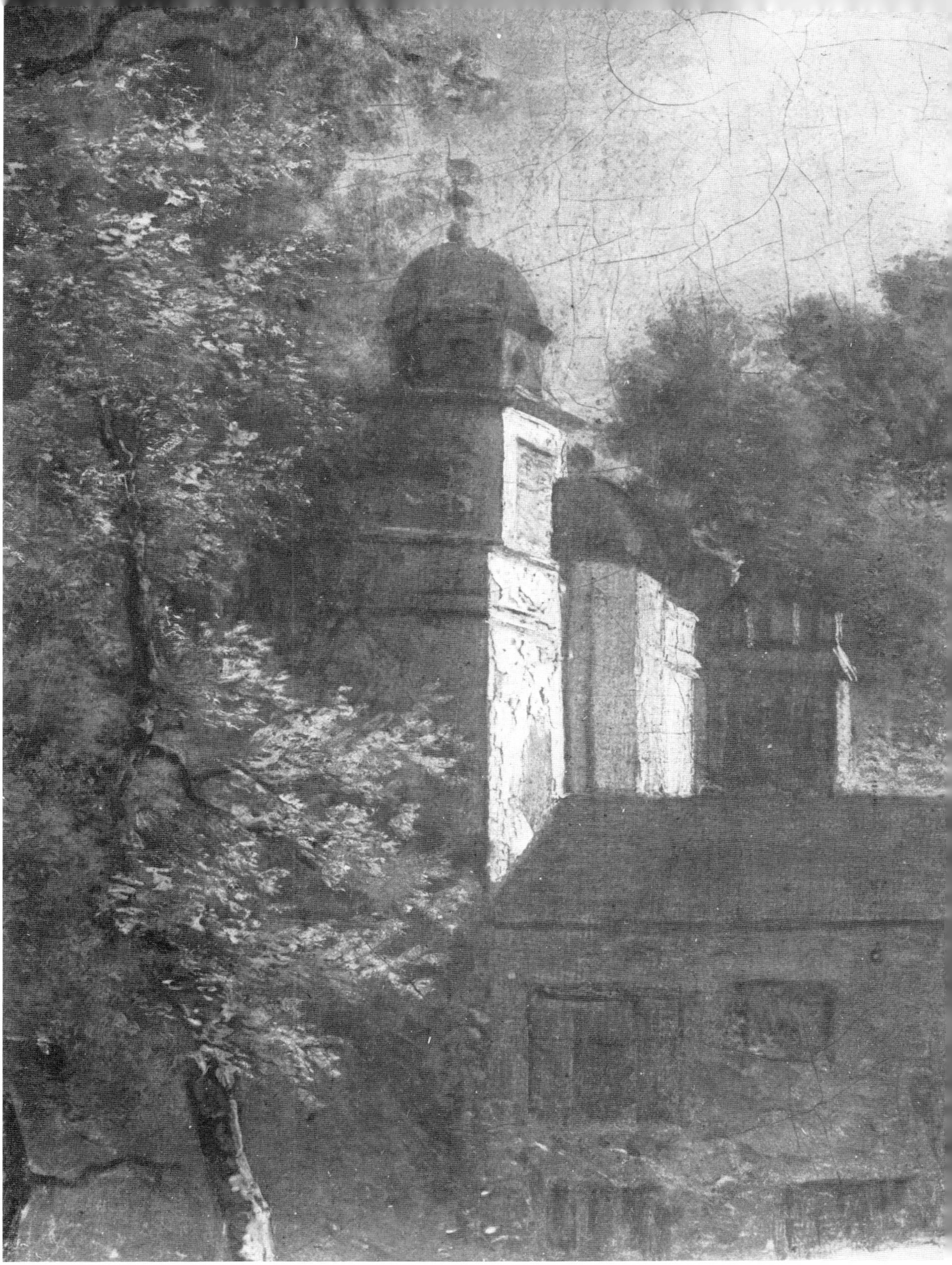

20. Detail from Pl. 19 (Note 14)

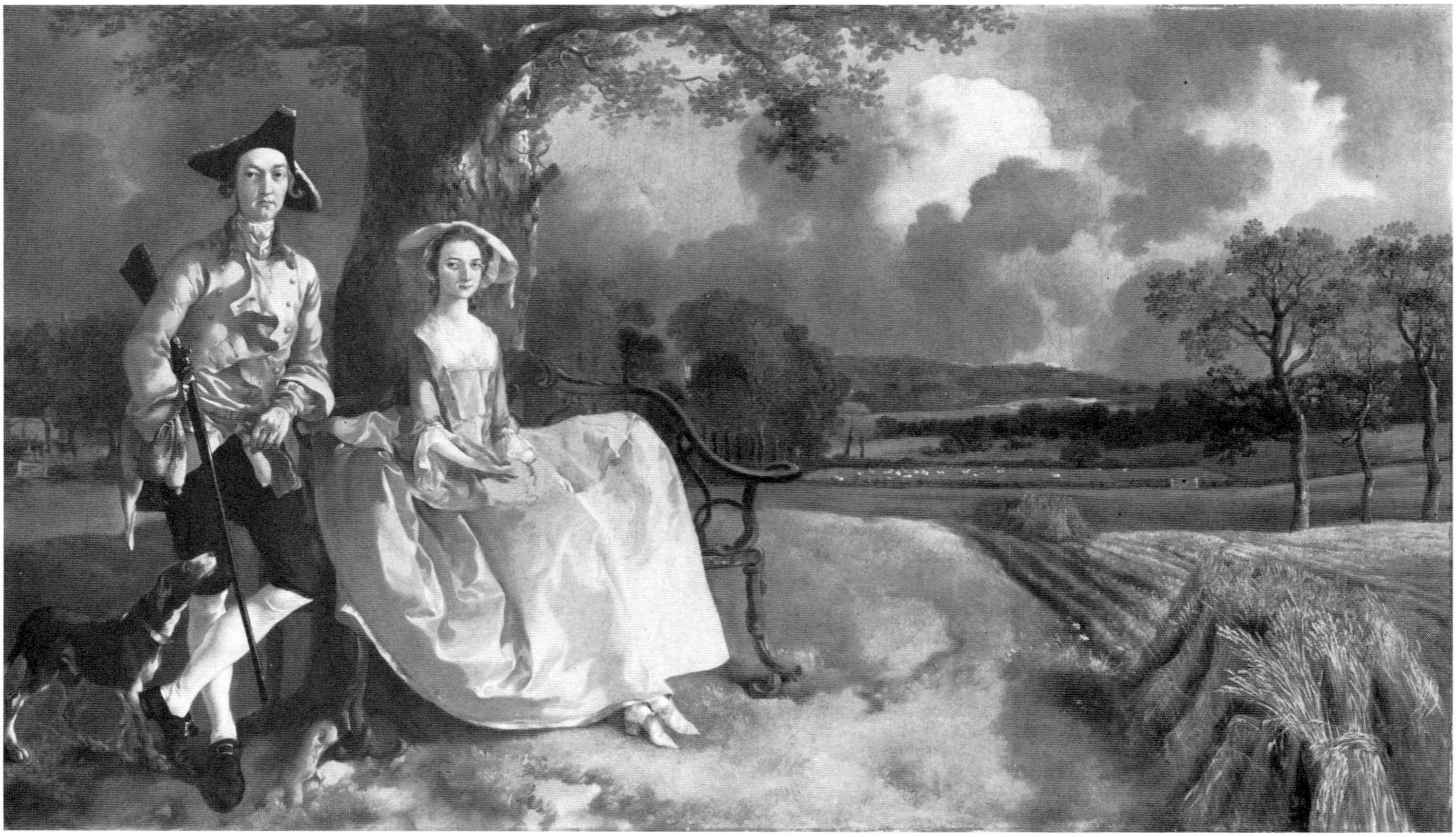

21. *Robert Andrews* (1726 ?–1806) *and his wife Frances* (*c.* 1732–80). Canvas, $27\frac{1}{2} \times 47$ in. About 1748–9. London, National Gallery (Note 12)

22. Arthur Devis (1711–87): *Sir George and Lady Strickland in the grounds of Boynton Hall, Bridlington*. Canvas, 35×44 in. Painted 1751. Kingston upon Hull, Ferens Art Gallery

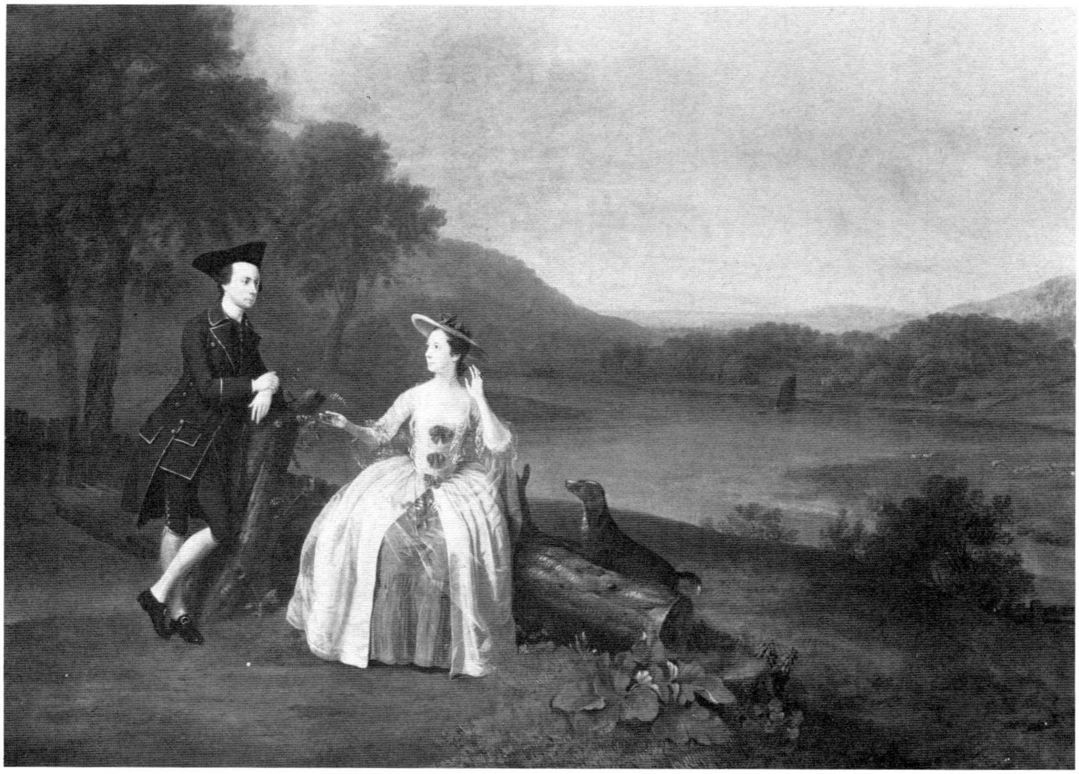

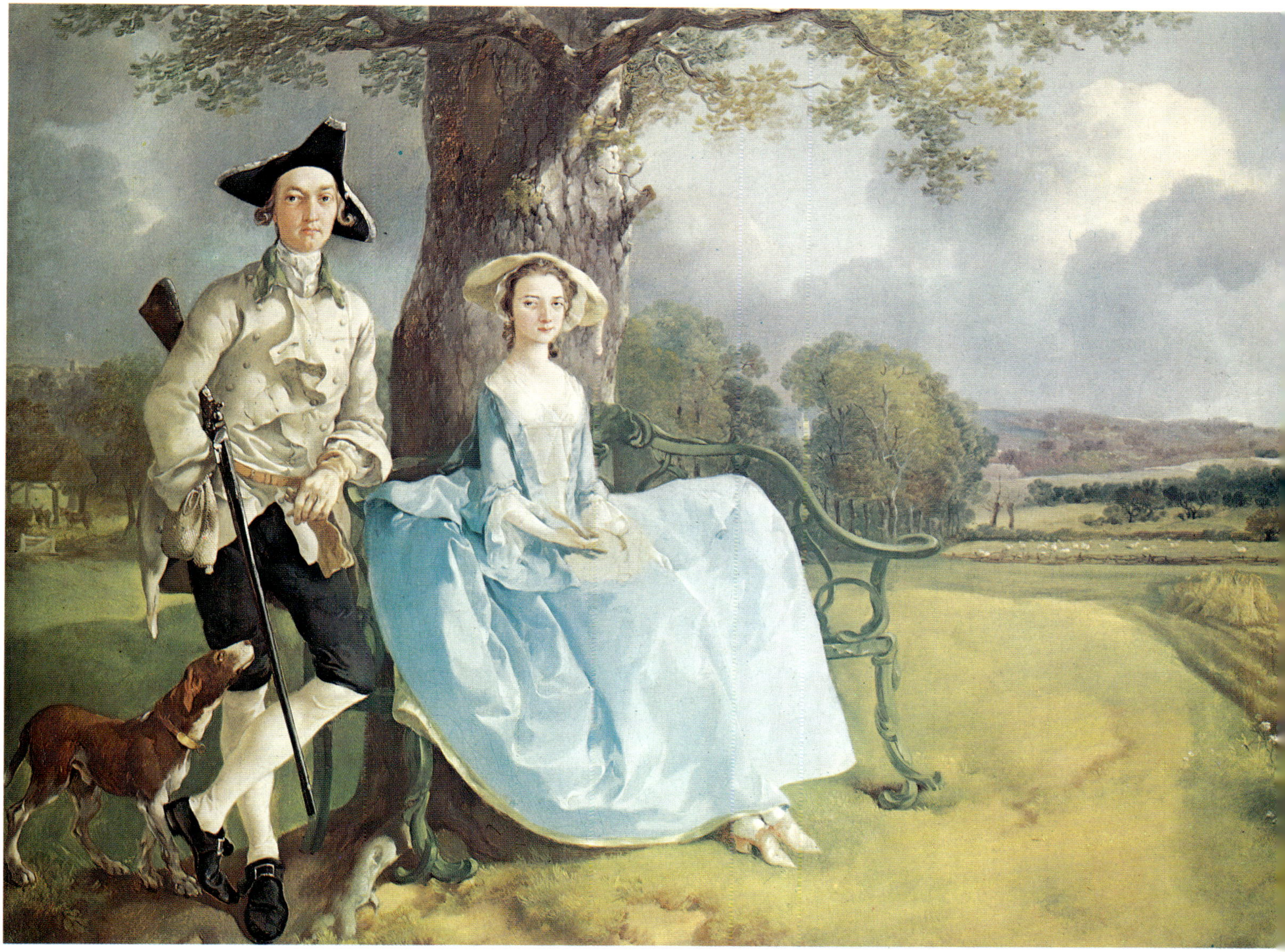

23. Detail from Pl. 21 (Note 12)

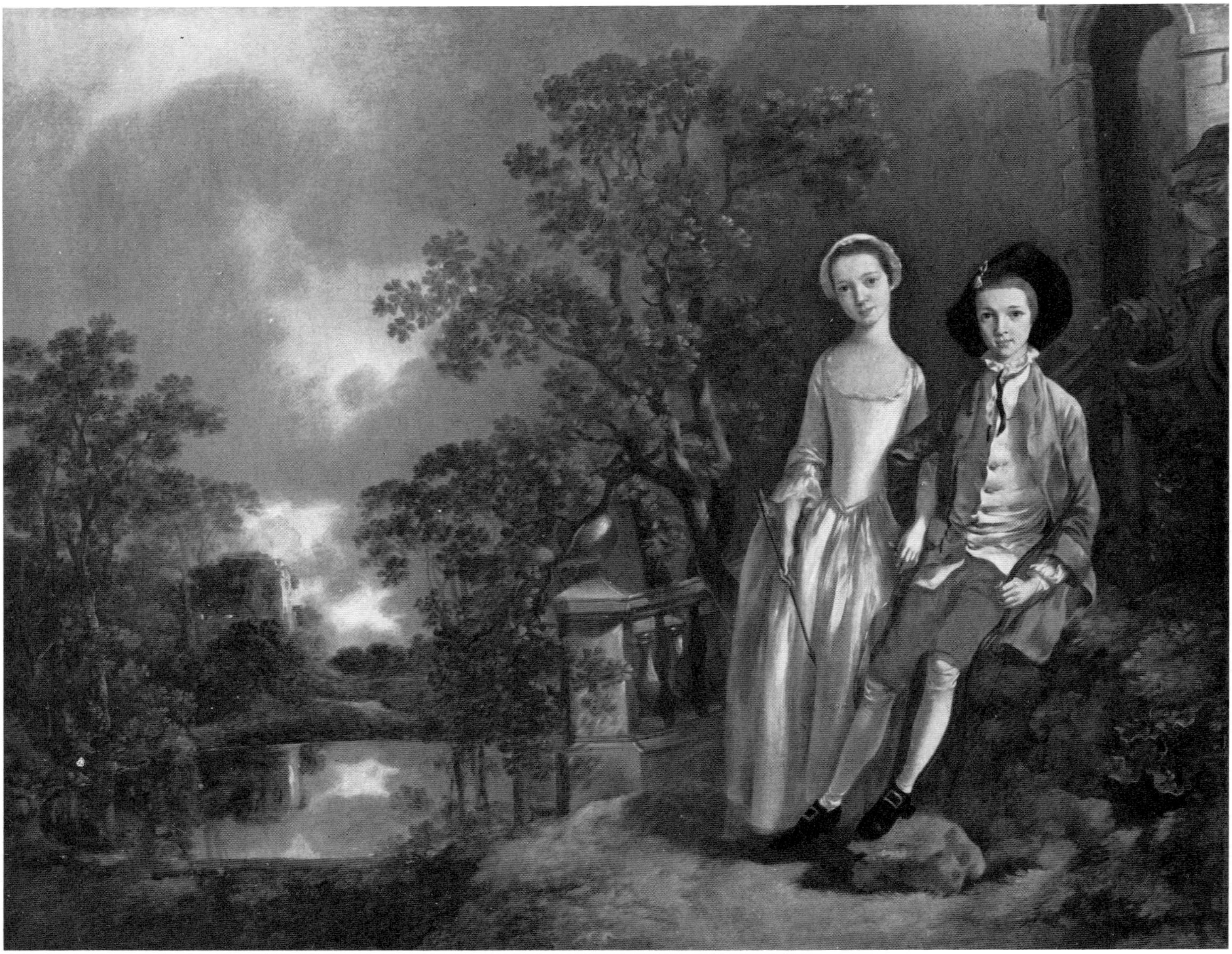

24. *Heneage Lloyd* (1742/3–76) *and his sister* (probably). Canvas, $25\frac{1}{4} \times 31\frac{7}{8}$ in. Signed. Early 1750s. Cambridge, Fitzwilliam Museum (Note 21)

25. Detail from Pl. 24 (Note 21)

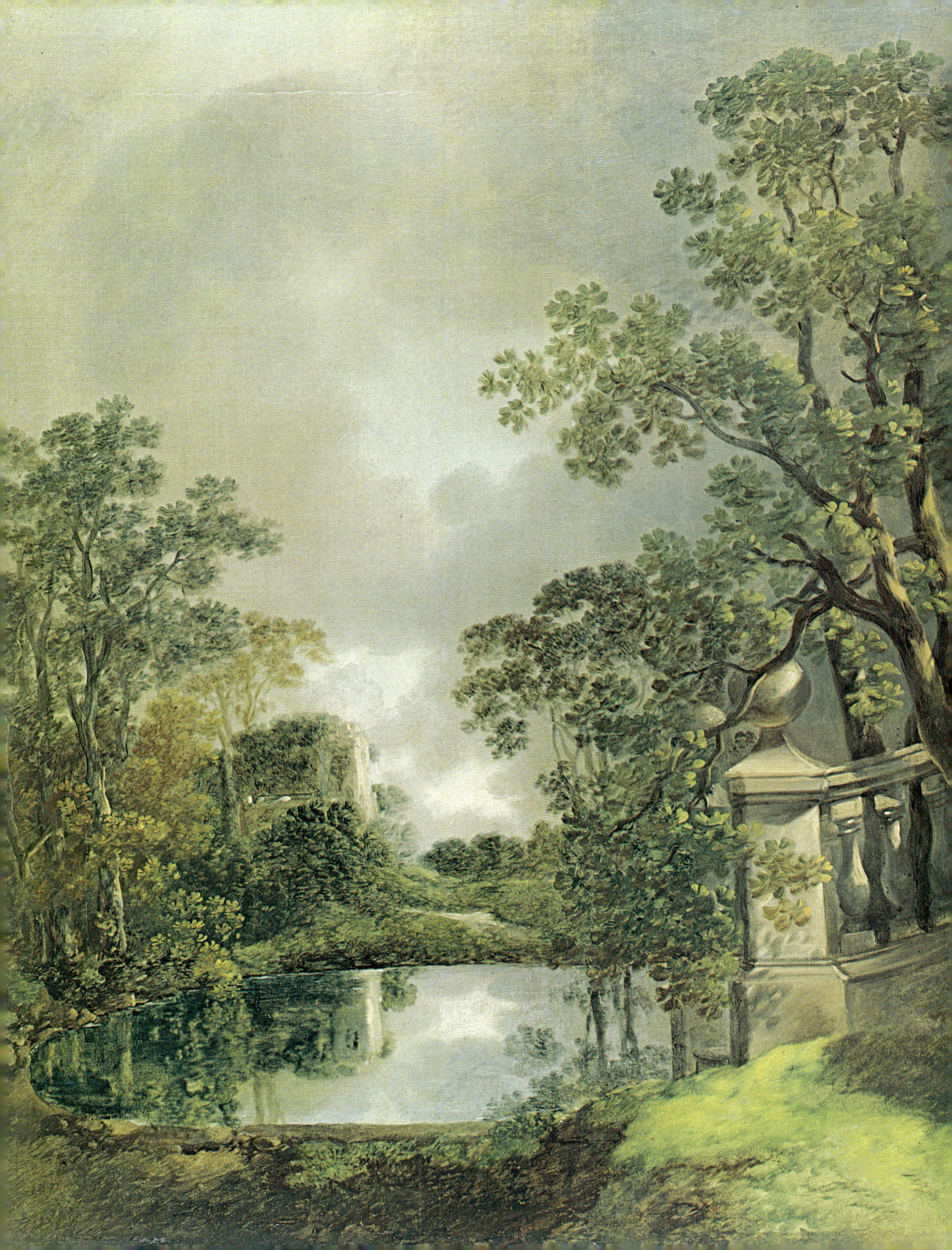

26. Detail from '*Wooded slope with cattle and felled timber*'. Canvas, 40 × 36 in. About 1748–50. Minneapolis, Institute of Arts (Note 16)

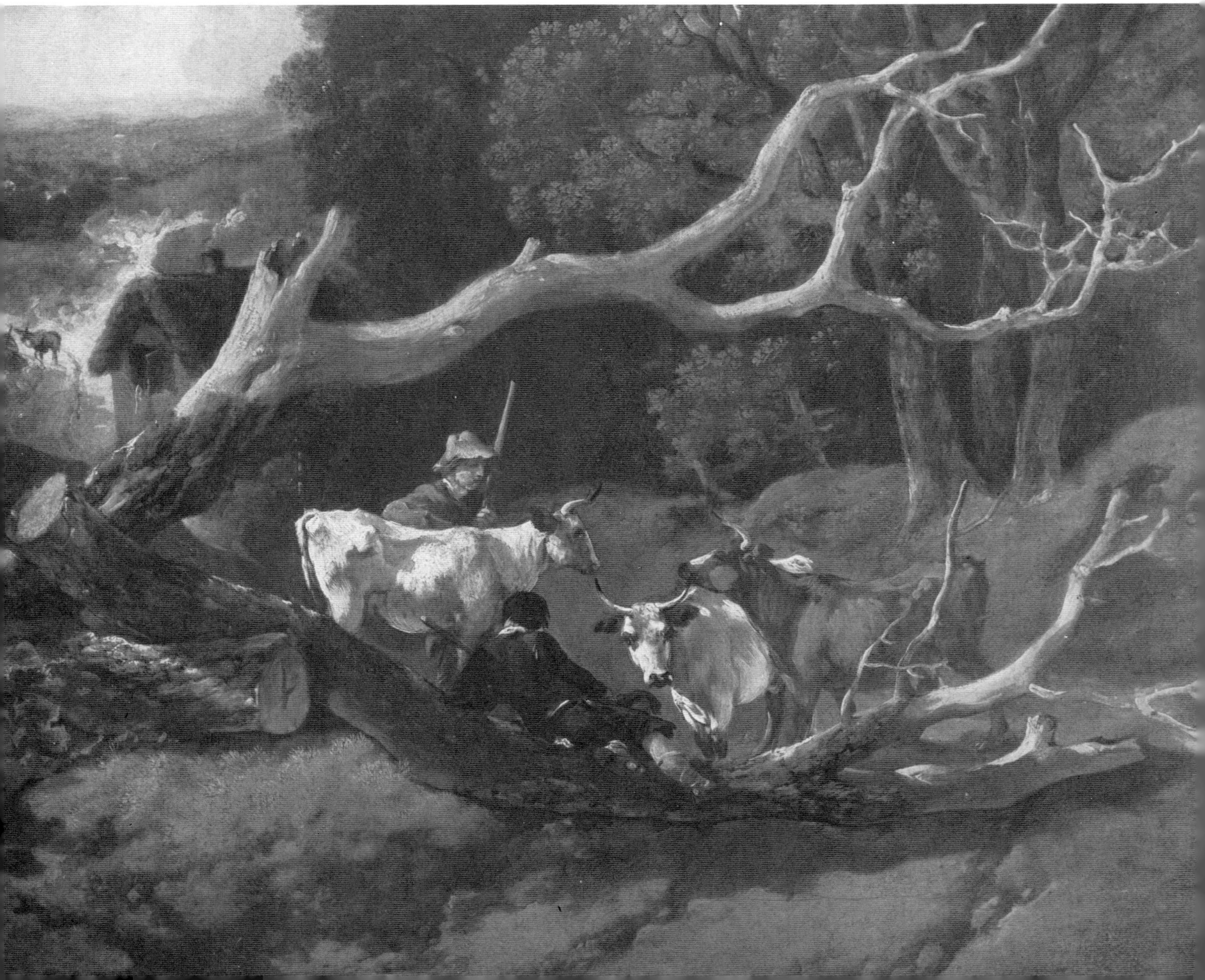

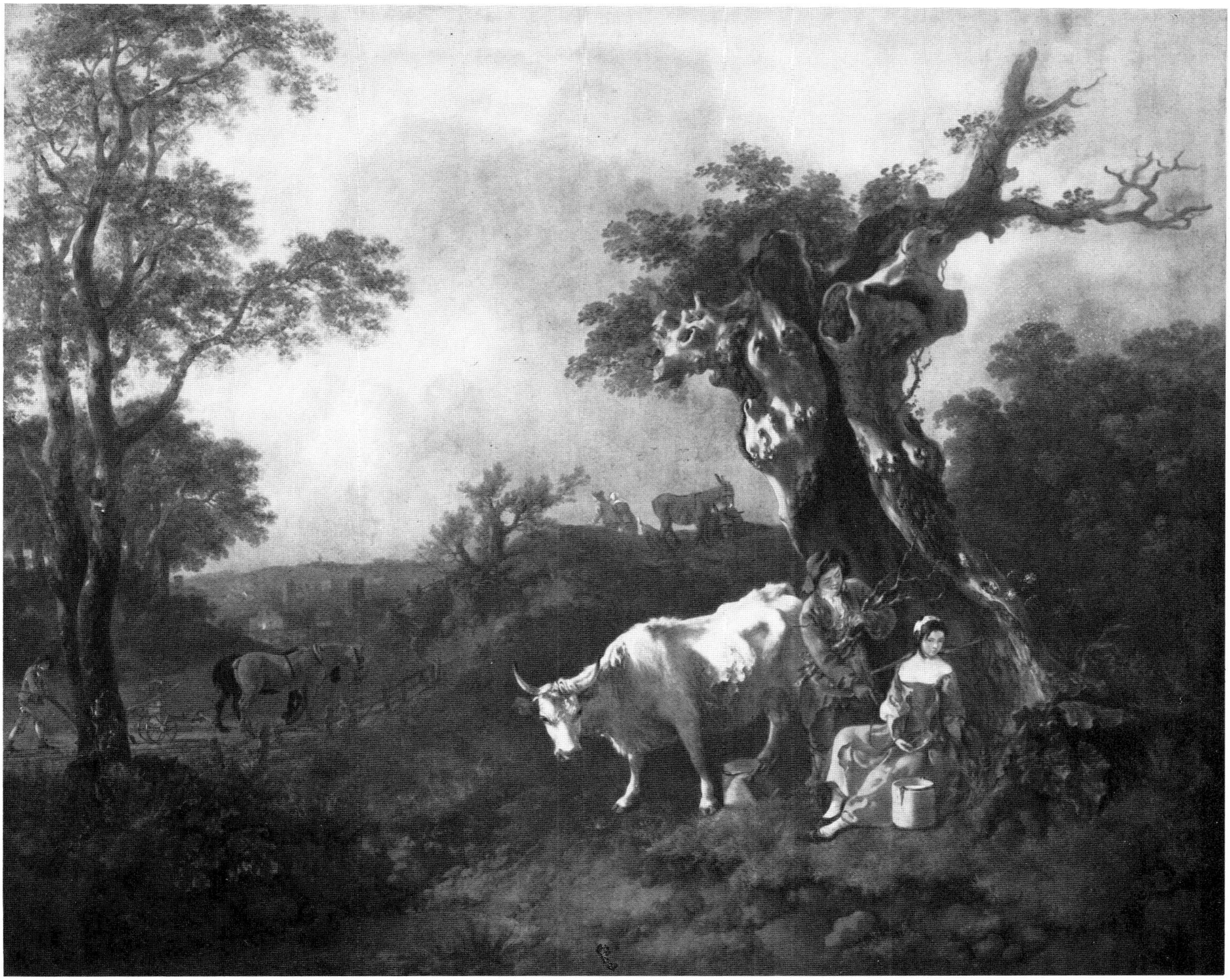

27. *Woodcutter courting a milkmaid*. Canvas, $43\frac{3}{4} \times 51$ in. Signed. Payment dated May 1755. London, Duke of Bedford (Note 26)

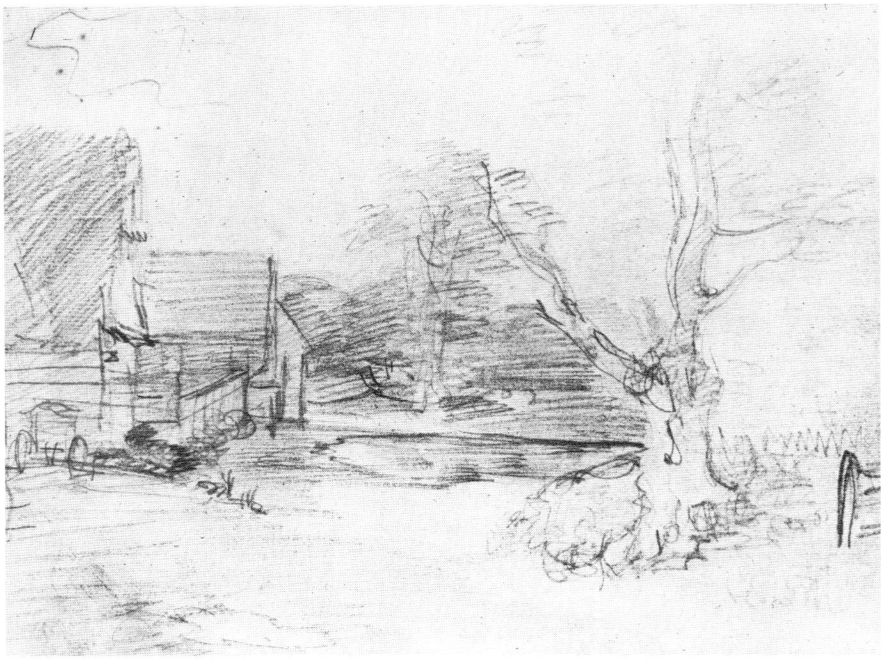

28. *Study of farm buildings near a pond.* Pencil, $5\frac{13}{16} \times 7\frac{5}{8}$ in. About 1755. London, British Museum (Note 28)

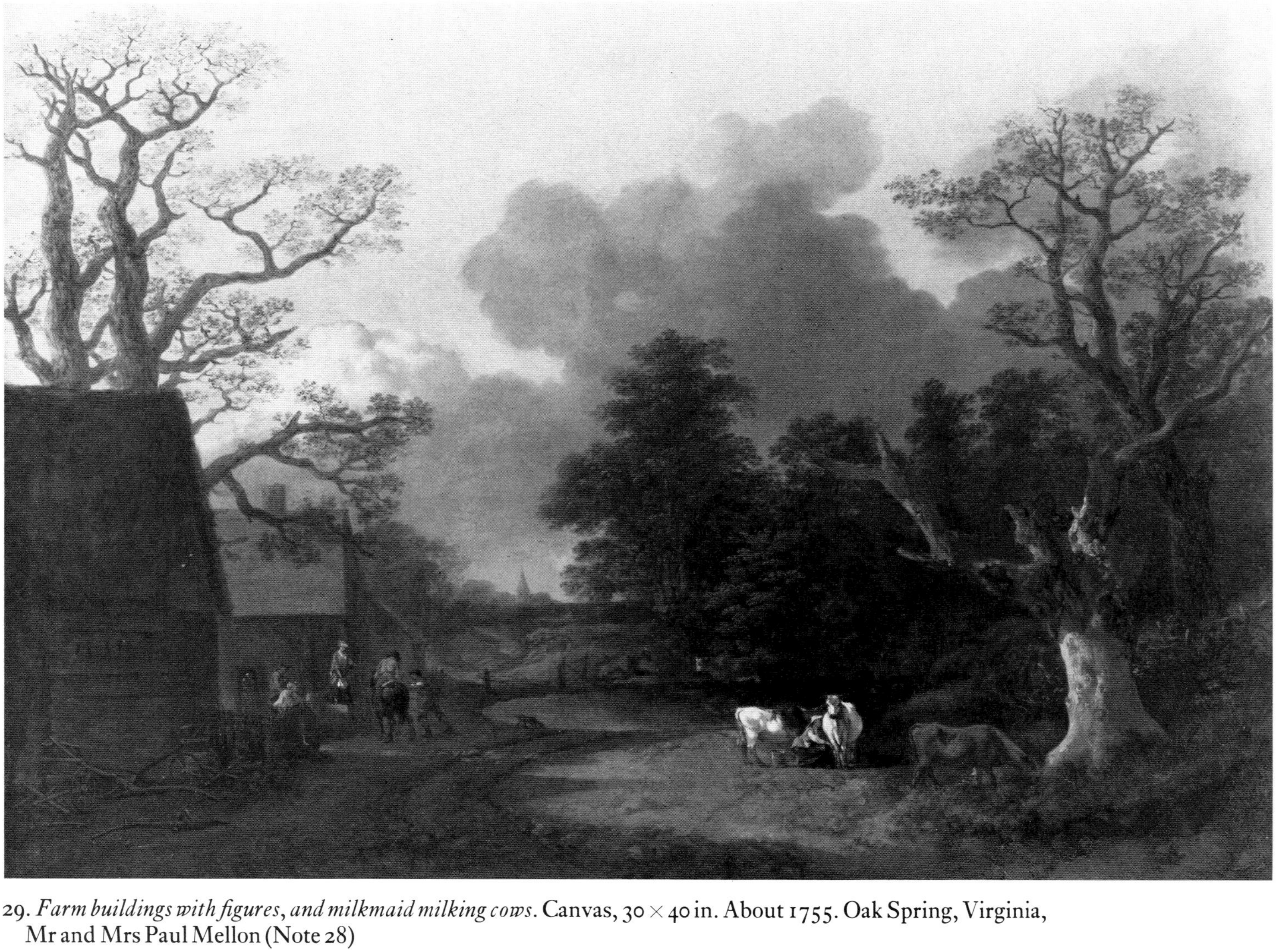

29. *Farm buildings with figures, and milkmaid milking cows.* Canvas, 30×40 in. About 1755. Oak Spring, Virginia, Mr and Mrs Paul Mellon (Note 28)

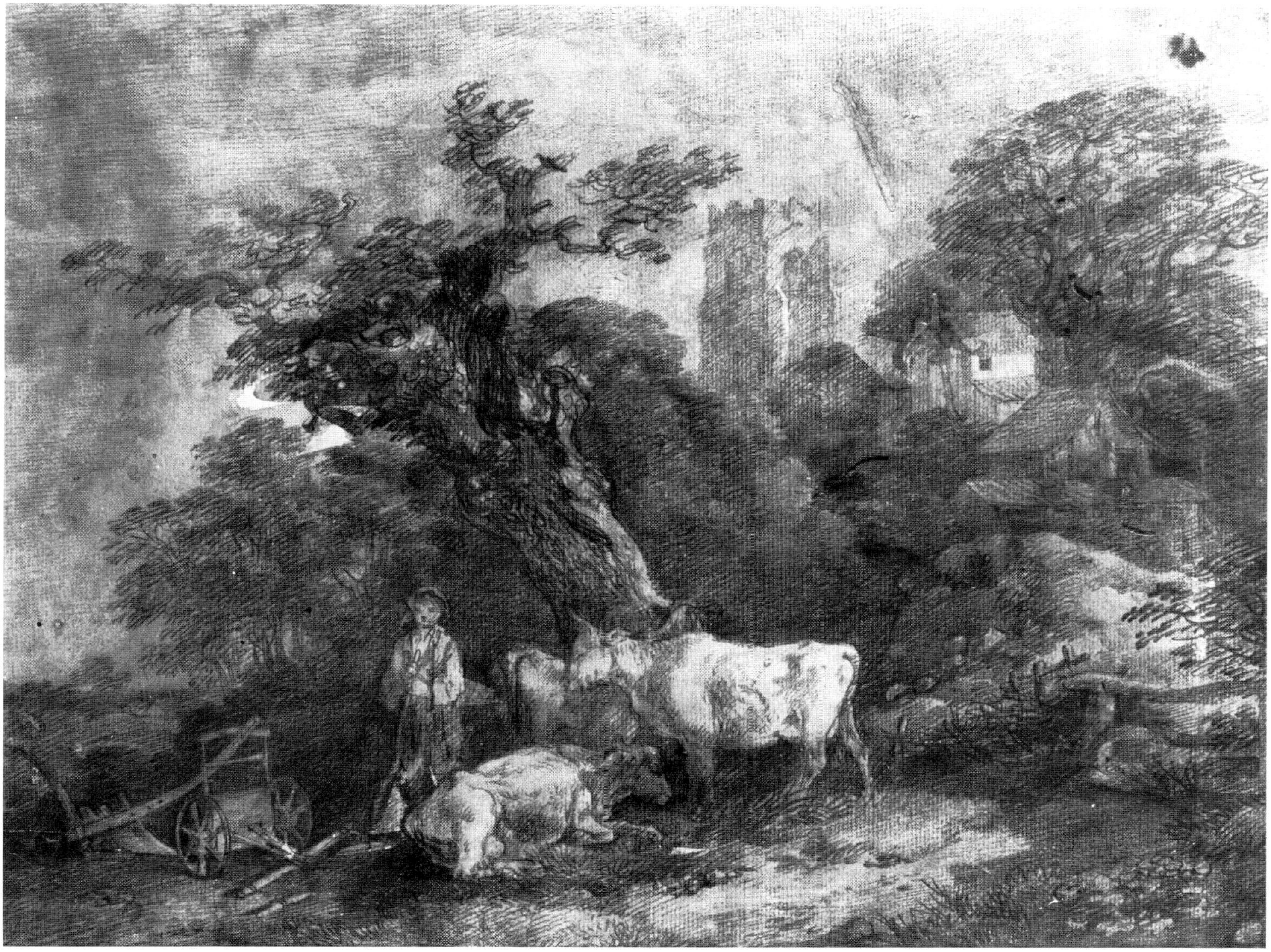

30. *Wooded landscape with herdsman, cows and buildings.* Pencil, varnished, $11\frac{1}{8} \times 14\frac{1}{2}$ in. About 1755-7. Hamden, Connecticut, F. Bulkeley Smith (Note 29)

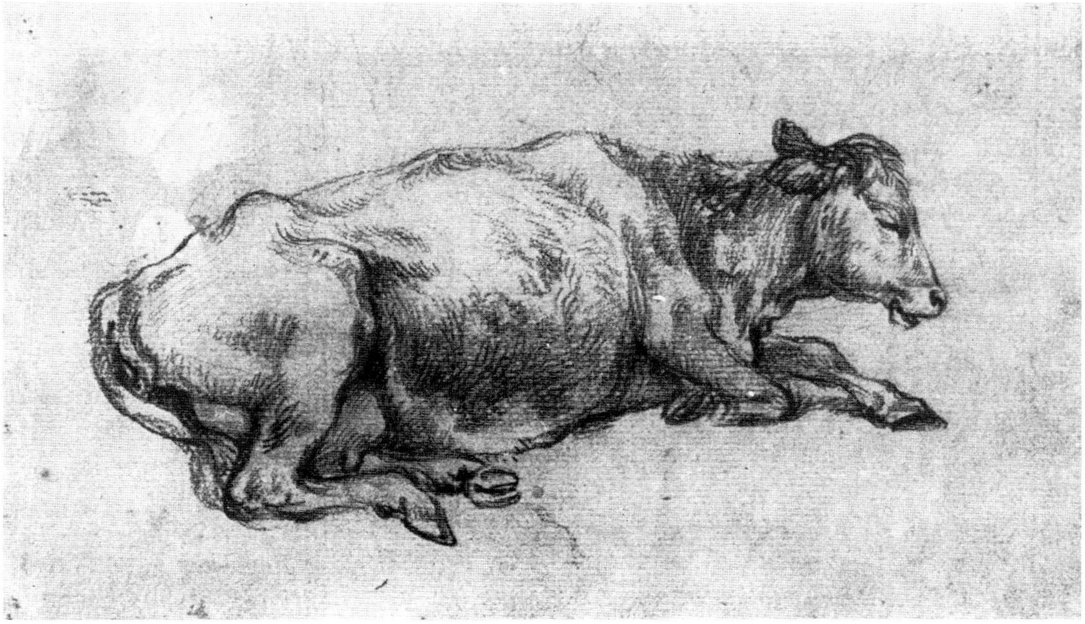

31. *Study of a cow.* Pencil on brown-toned paper, $6 \times 7\frac{7}{16}$ in. (Upper part of sheet not reproduced.) About 1755-7. London, D.L.T. Oppé (Note 29)

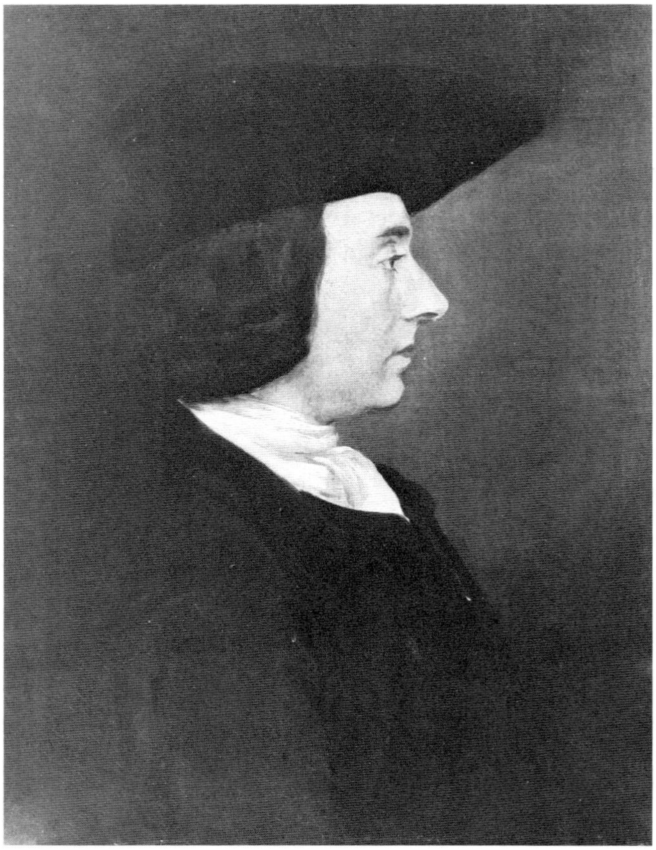

32. *John Gainsborough* (1711-85). Canvas, $22\frac{7}{8} \times 18\frac{7}{8}$ in. Early 1750s. Dublin, National Gallery of Ireland (Note 18)

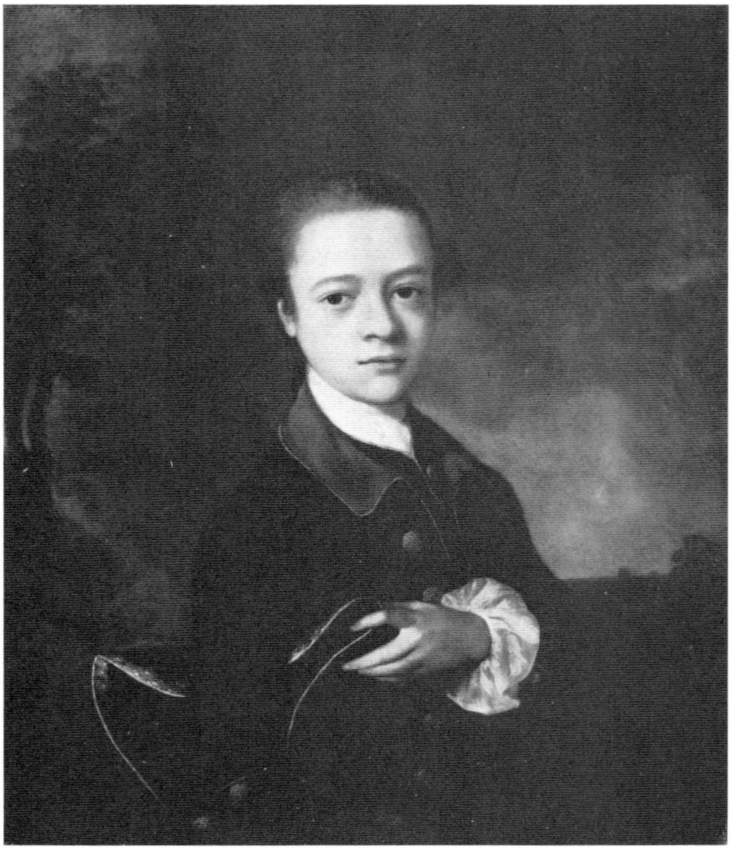

33. *Philip Bowes Broke* (?). Canvas, $29\frac{1}{4} \times 24\frac{1}{4}$ in. About 1753-5. New Bern, North Carolina, Tryon Palace Commission (Note 20)

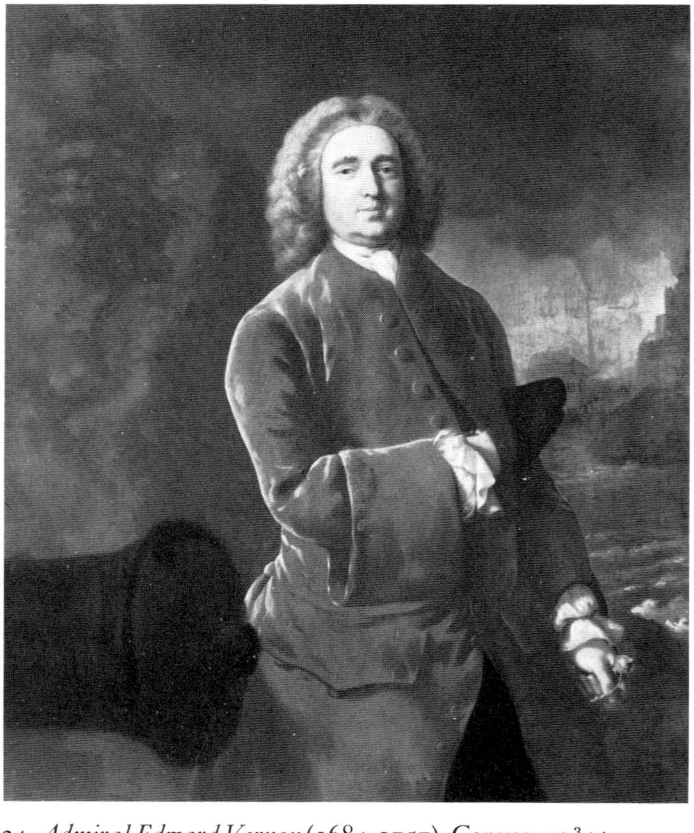

34. *Admiral Edward Vernon* (1684-1757). Canvas, $49\frac{3}{4} \times 40\frac{7}{8}$ in. About 1753 (engraved). London, National Portrait Gallery (Note 19)

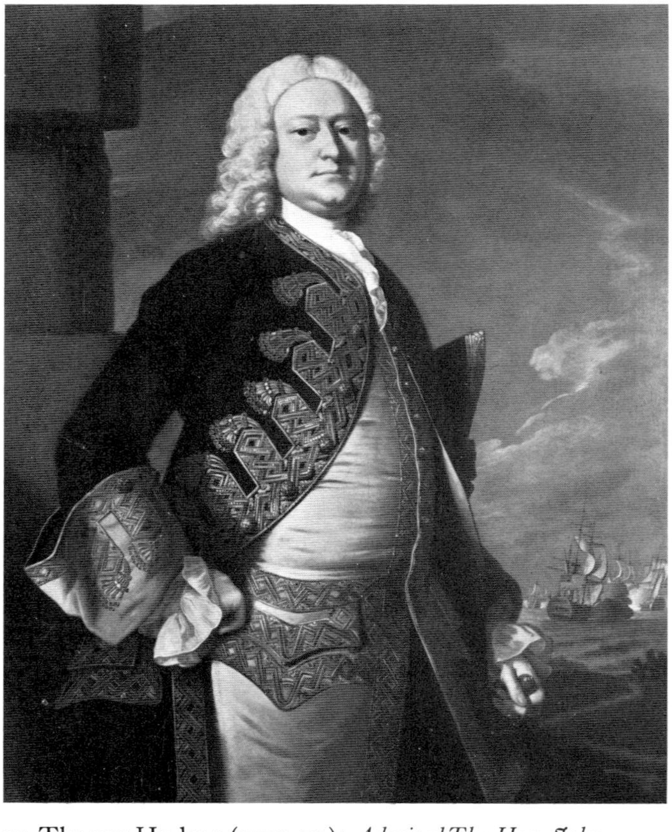

35. Thomas Hudson (1701-79): *Admiral The Hon. John Byng* (1704-57). Canvas, 50×40 in. Signed and dated 1749. London, National Maritime Museum

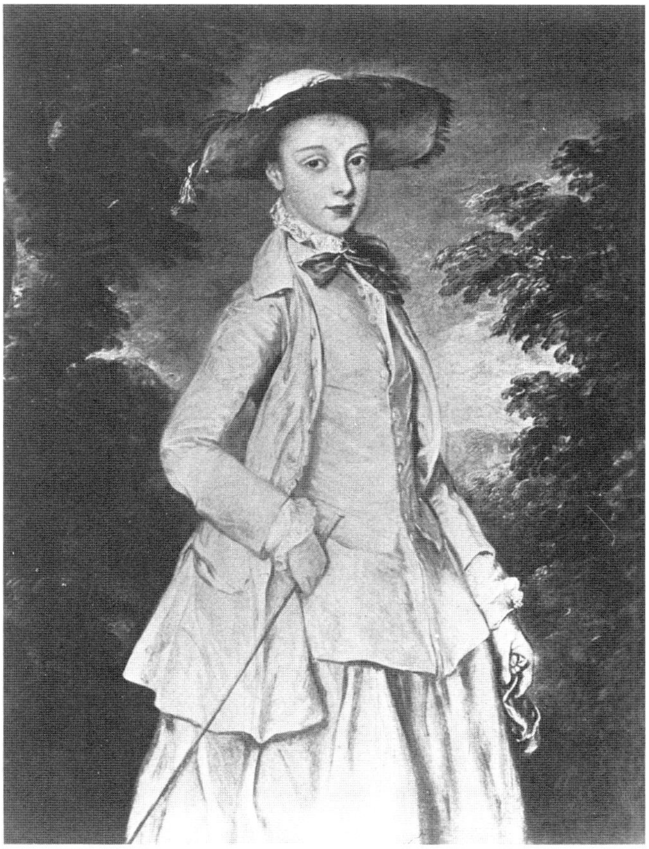

36. *Unkown girl in pink riding habit*. Canvas, 40 × 30 in. About 1759. Last recorded with James Stillman, 1907 (Note 41)

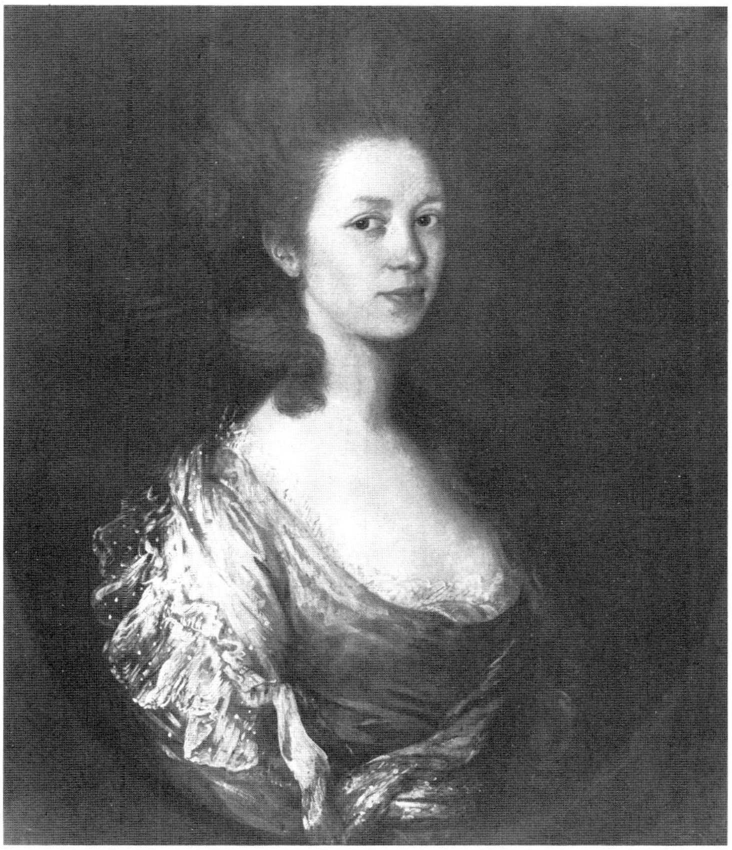

37. *Mrs Samuel Kilderbee, née Mary Wayth* (1723-1811). Canvas, 29½ × 24½ in. About 1757, the costume altered in the 1770s. Ipswich, Christchurch Mansion (Note 33)

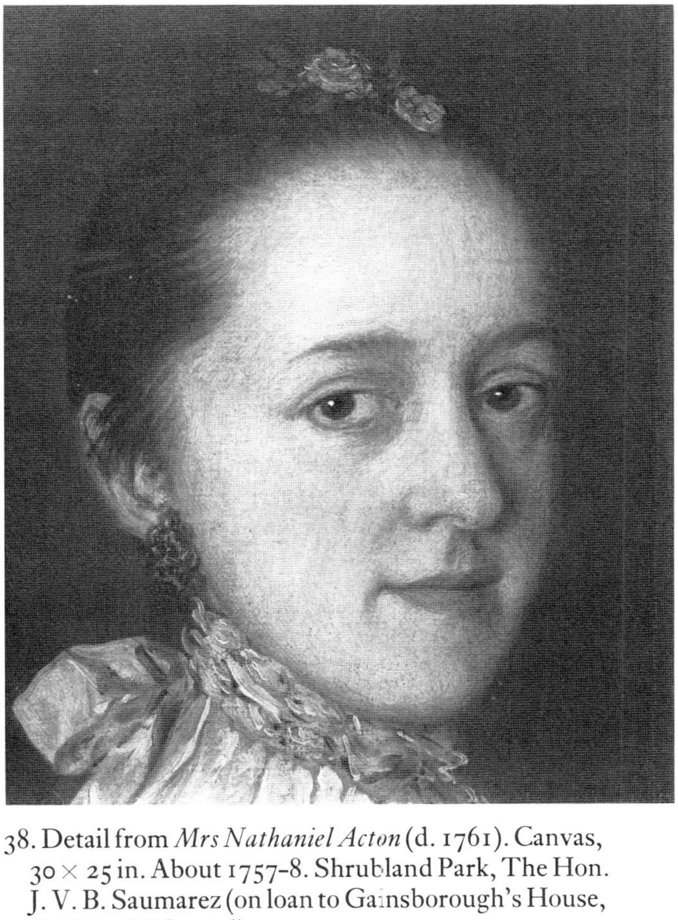

38. Detail from *Mrs Nathaniel Acton* (d. 1761). Canvas, 30 × 25 in. About 1757-8. Shrubland Park, The Hon. J. V. B. Saumarez (on loan to Gainsborough's House, Sudbury) (Note 36)

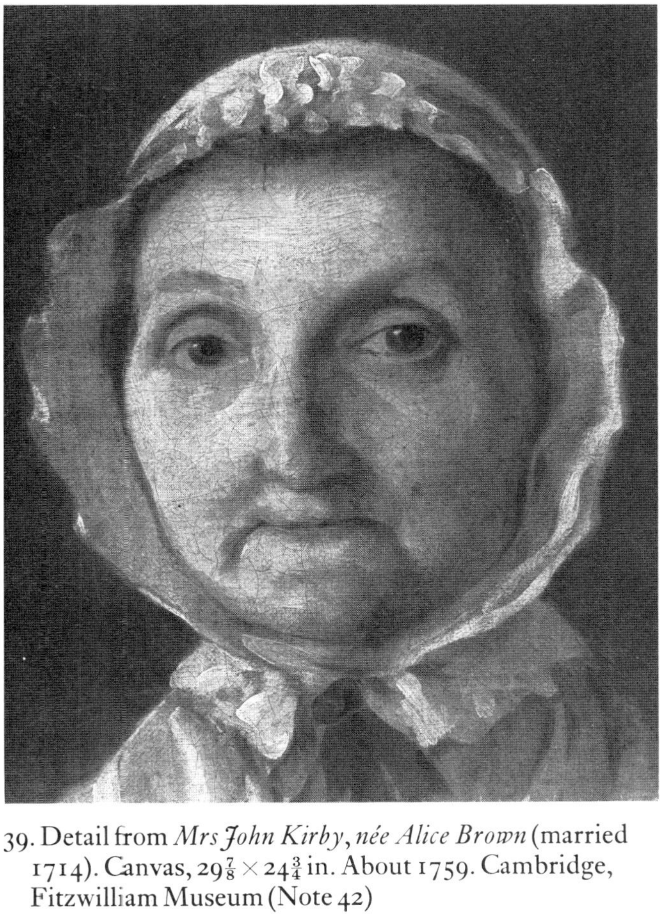

39. Detail from *Mrs John Kirby, née Alice Brown* (married 1714). Canvas, 29⅞ × 24¾ in. About 1759. Cambridge, Fitzwilliam Museum (Note 42)

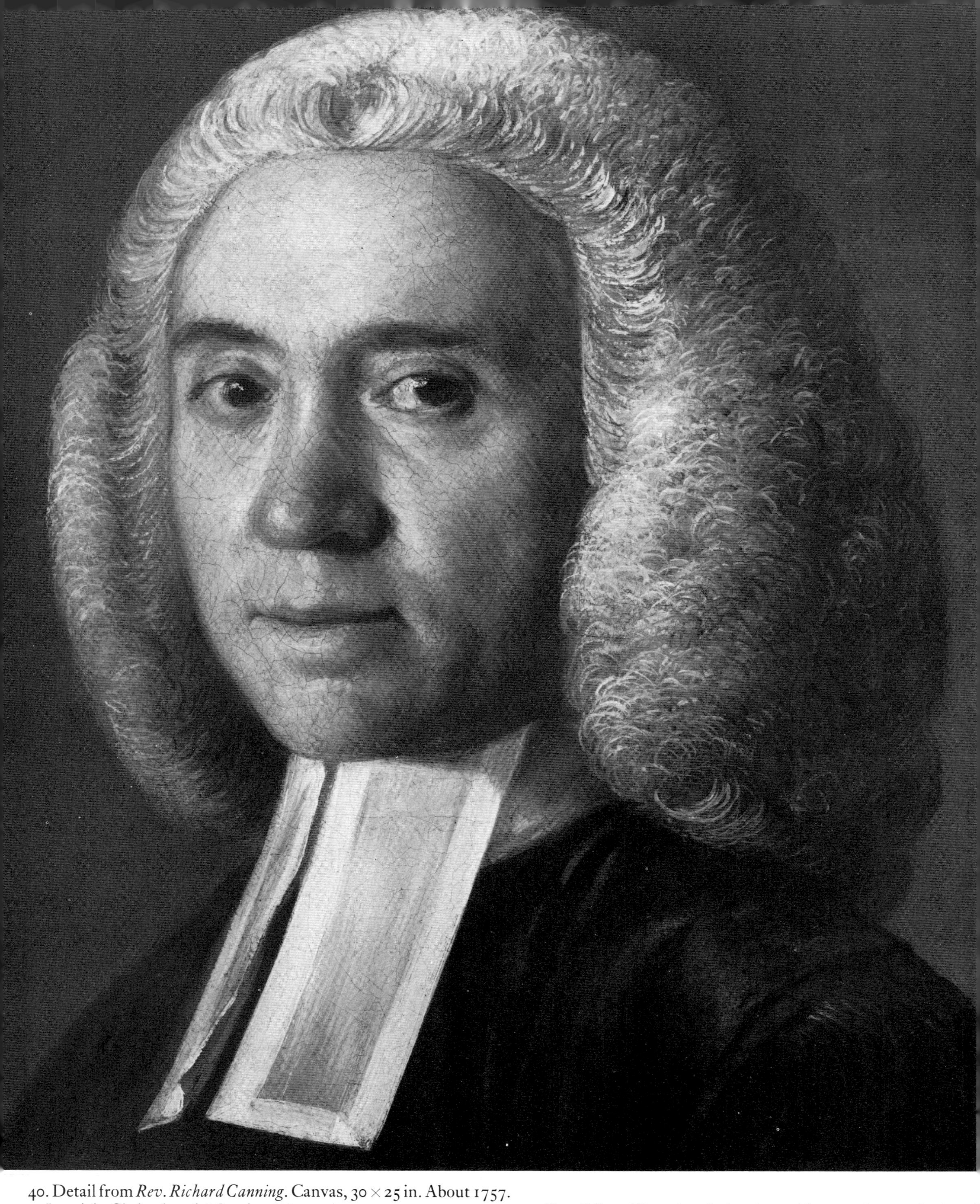

40. Detail from *Rev. Richard Canning*. Canvas, 30 × 25 in. About 1757. Ipswich, Christchurch Mansion (Note 32)

41. Detail from *The painter's daughters, Margaret* (1752–1820) *and Mary* (1748–1826), *holding a cat*. Canvas, $29\frac{3}{4} \times 24\frac{3}{4}$ in. About 1759. London, National Gallery (Note 43)

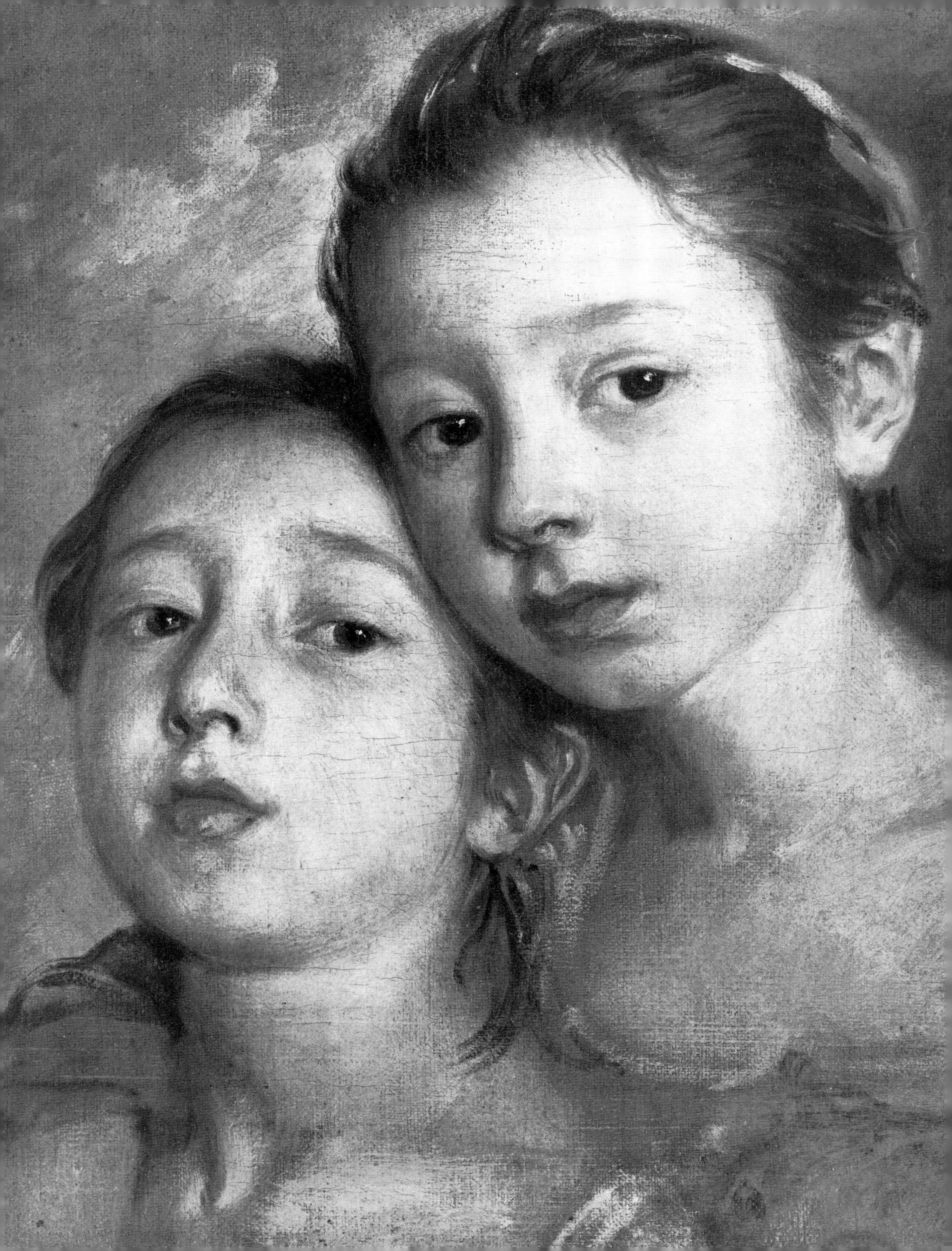

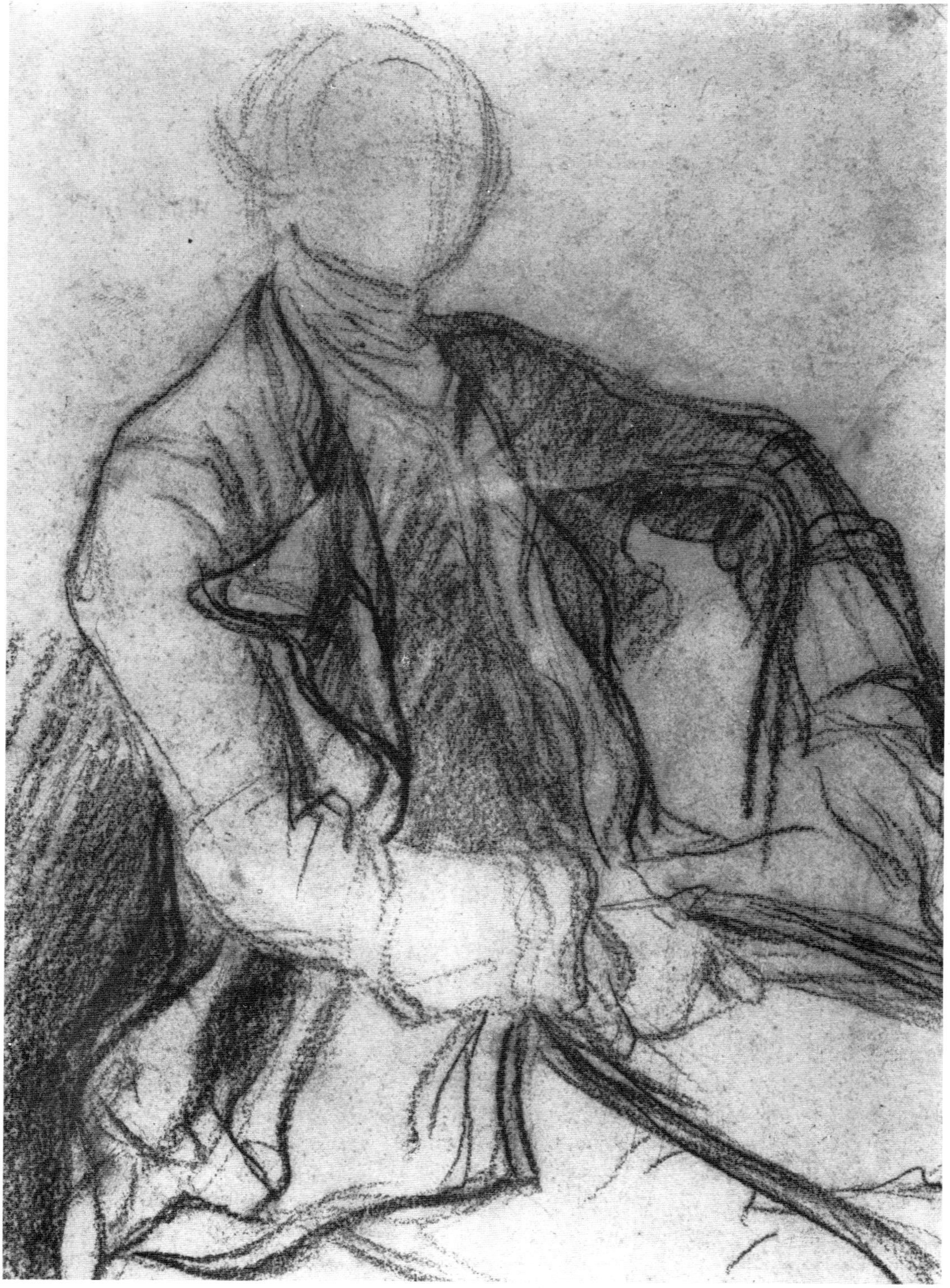

42. Study for *The Hon. Richard Savage Nassau* (1723-80). Black chalk, $11\frac{1}{8} \times 8\frac{3}{16}$ in. About 1757. Berlin, Staatliche Museen (Note 35)

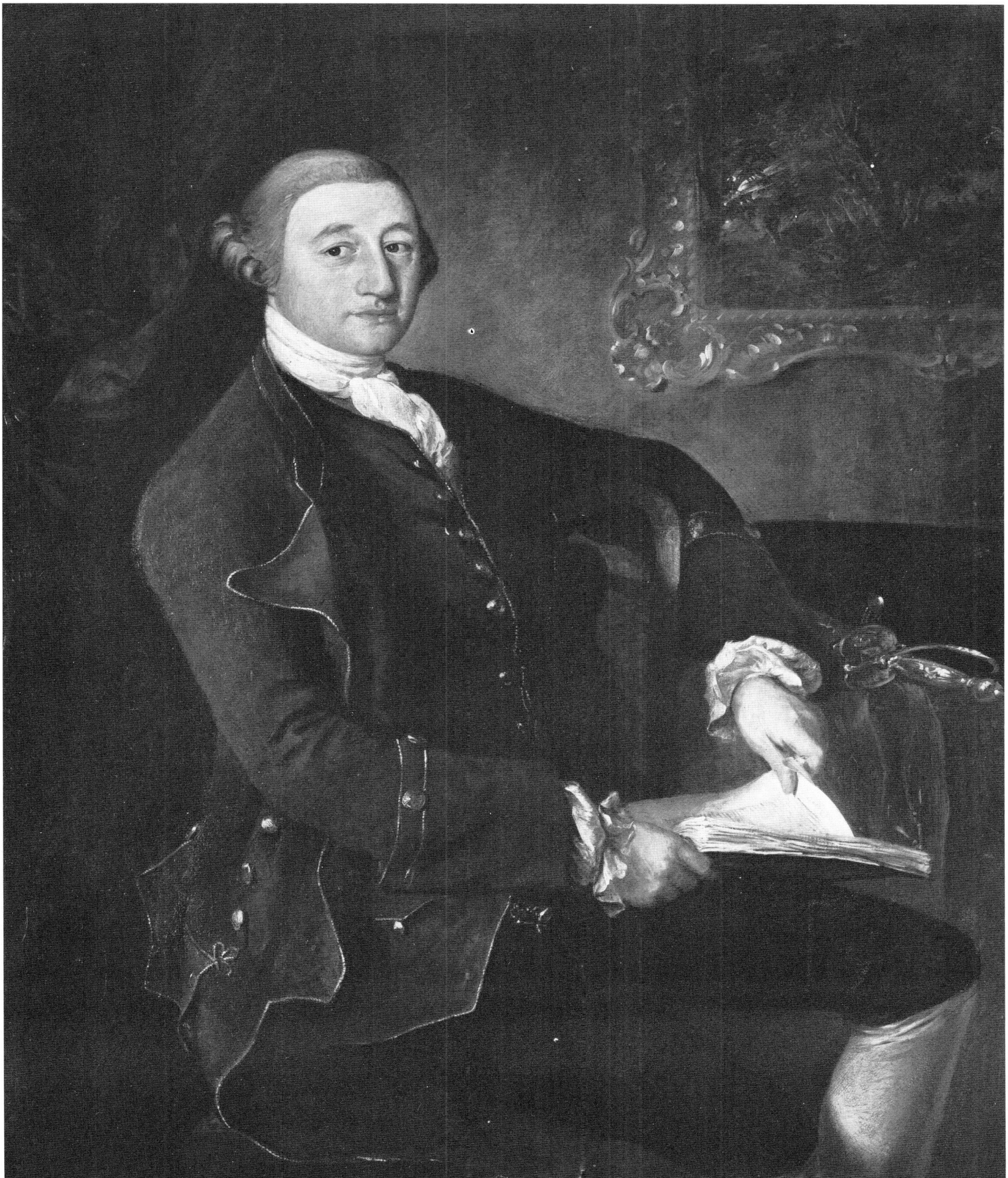

43. *The Hon. Richard Savage Nassau* (1723–80). Canvas, 49 × 38¾ in. About 1757. National Trust for Scotland, Brodick Castle (Note 35)

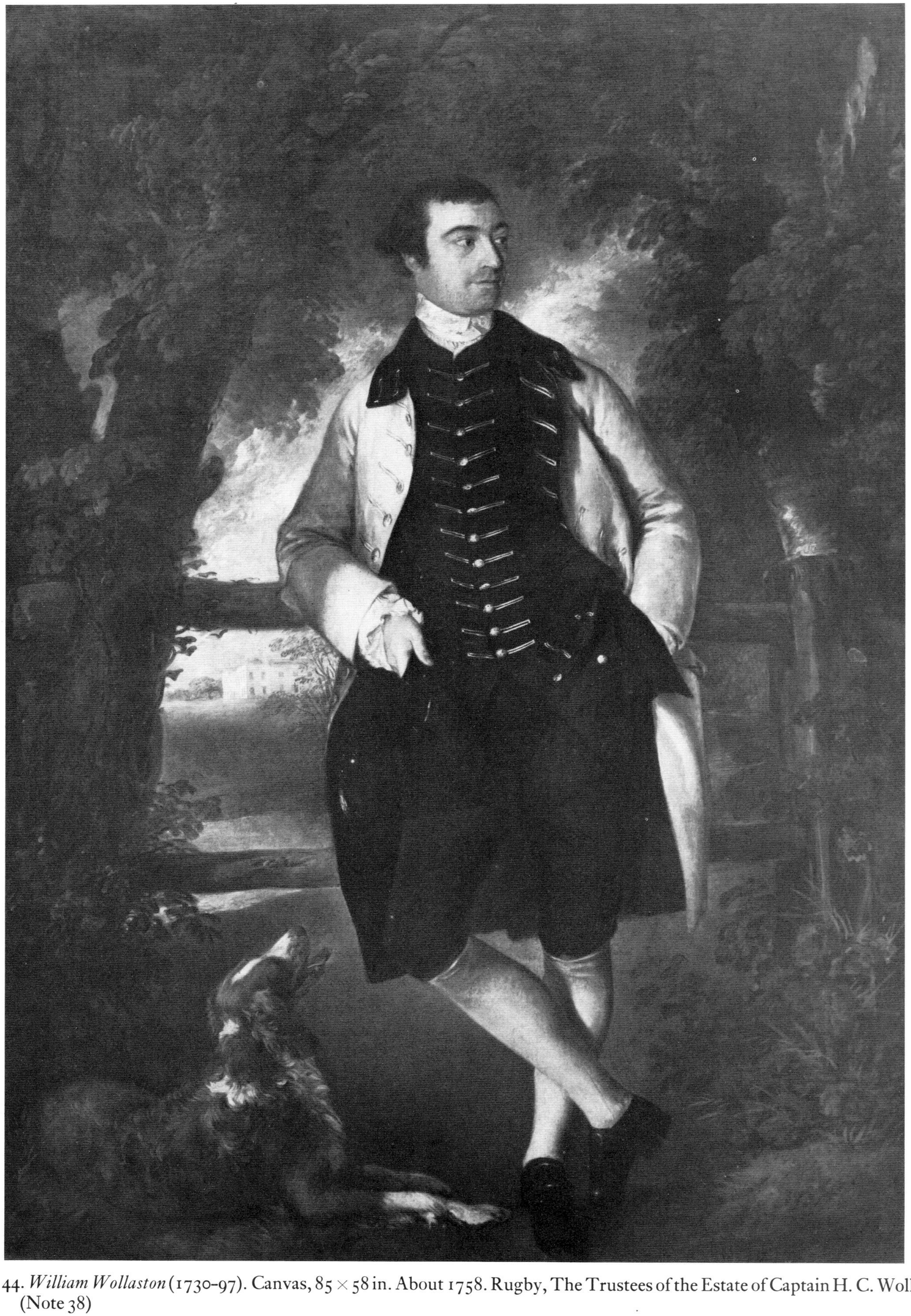

44. *William Wollaston* (1730–97). Canvas, 85 × 58 in. About 1758. Rugby, The Trustees of the Estate of Captain H. C. Wollaston (Note 38)

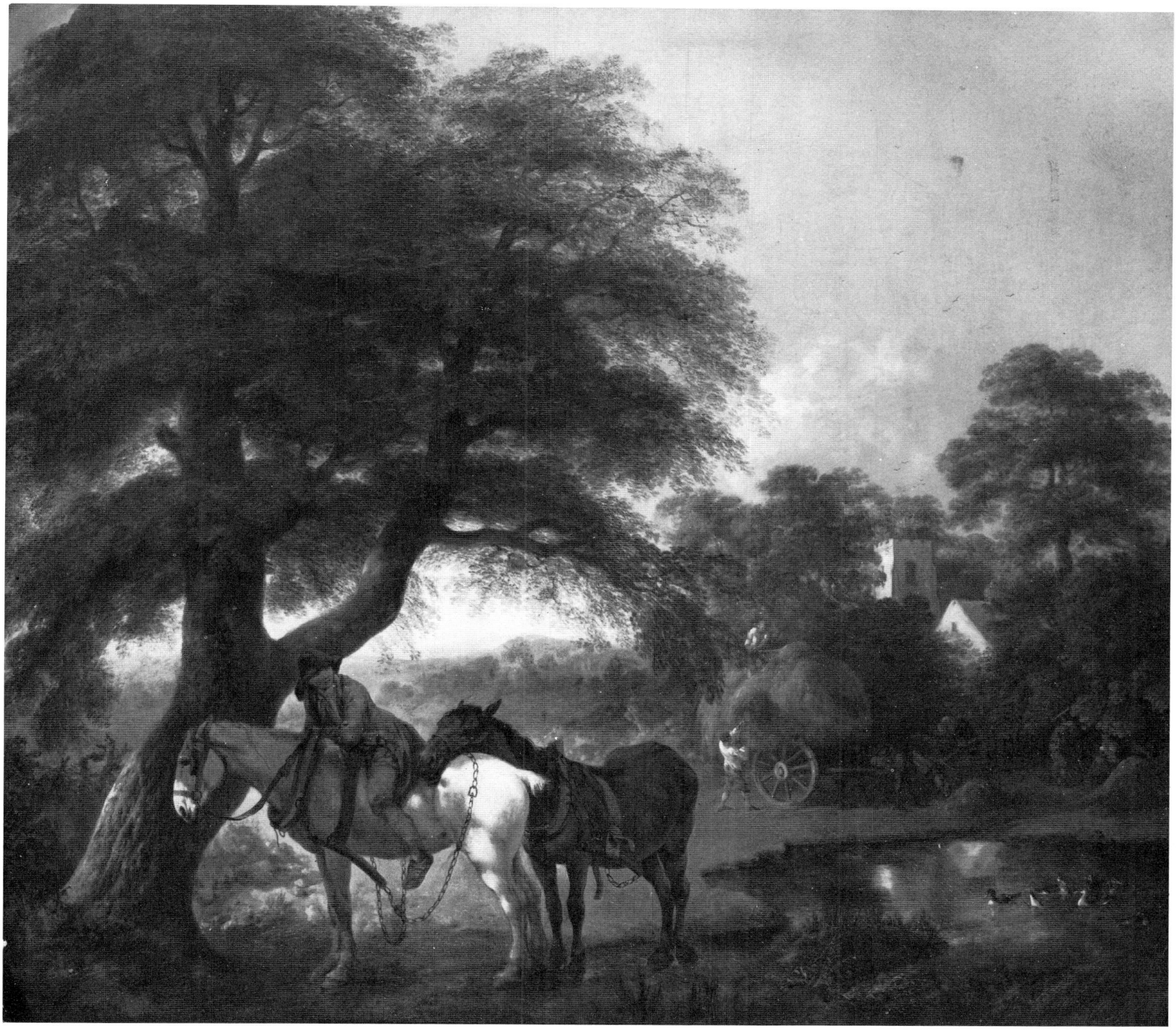

45. *Peasant with two horses : hay cart behind.* Canvas, $37\frac{1}{4} \times 41\frac{1}{4}$ in. Signed. Payment dated July 1755. London, Duke of Bedford (Note 27)

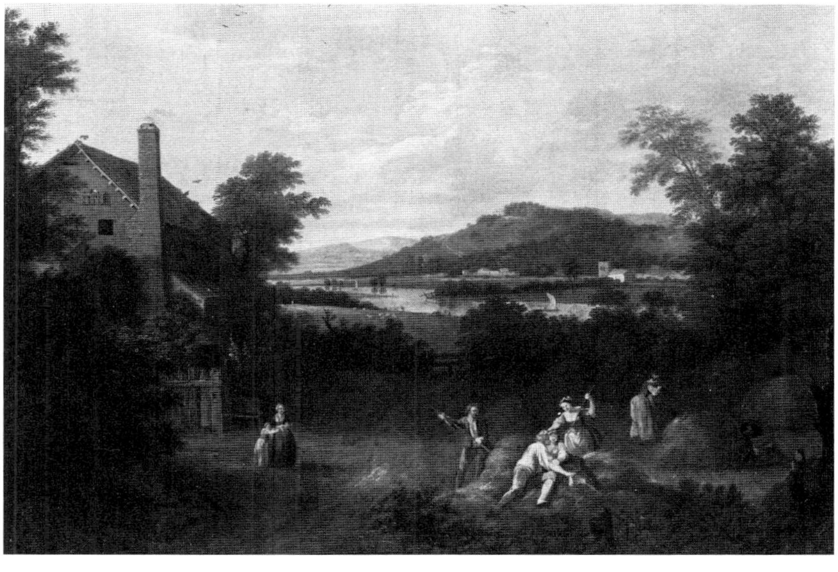

46. George Lambert (1700–65), figures by William Hogarth (1697–1764): detail from *Landscape with farmworkers.* Canvas, $38\frac{1}{2} \times 48\frac{1}{2}$ in. Oak Spring, Virginia, Mr and Mrs Paul Mellon

47. *Wooded landscape with herdsman and cow*. Pencil, $11 \times 15\frac{1}{8}$ in. About 1758-9. Private Collection (Note 46)

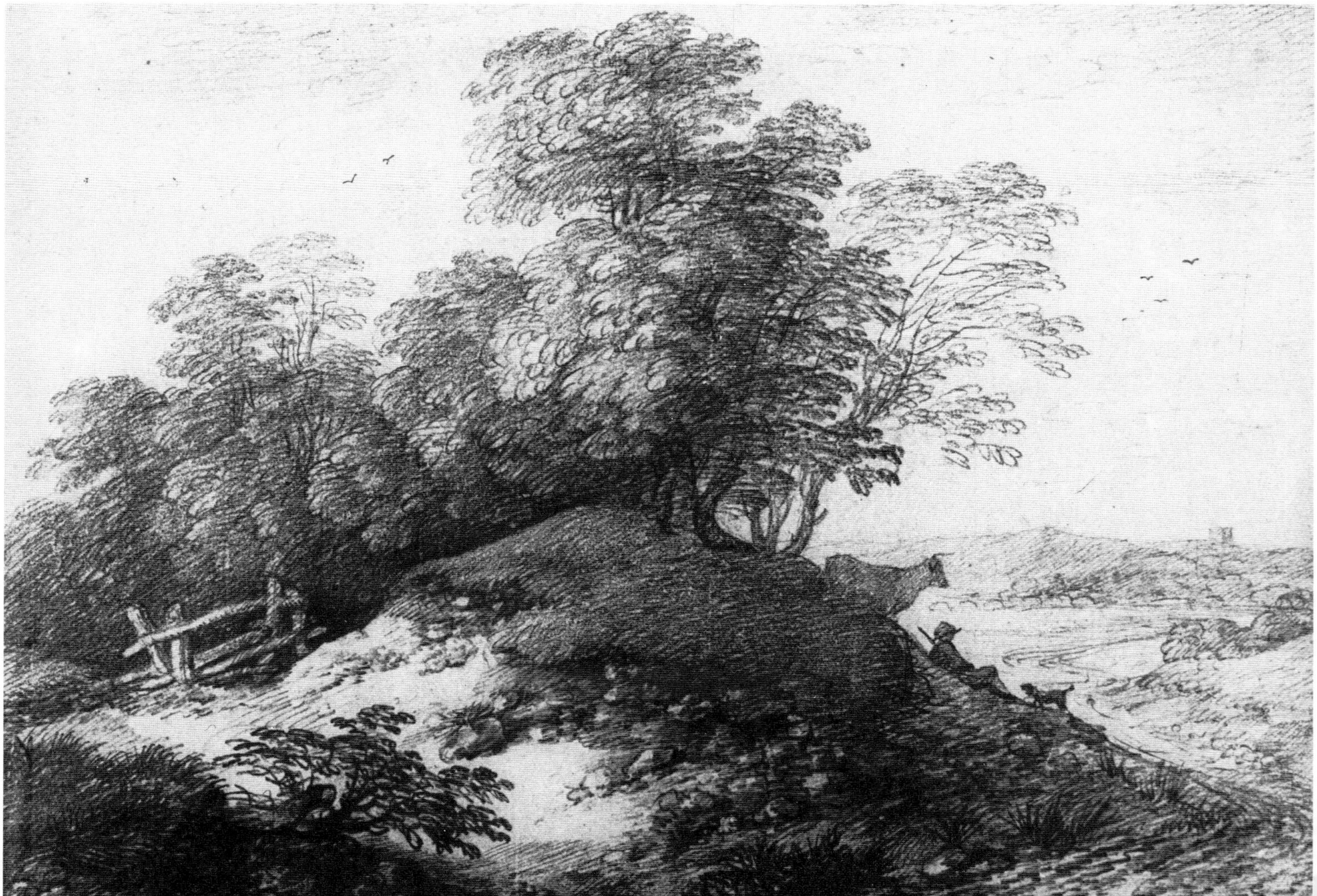

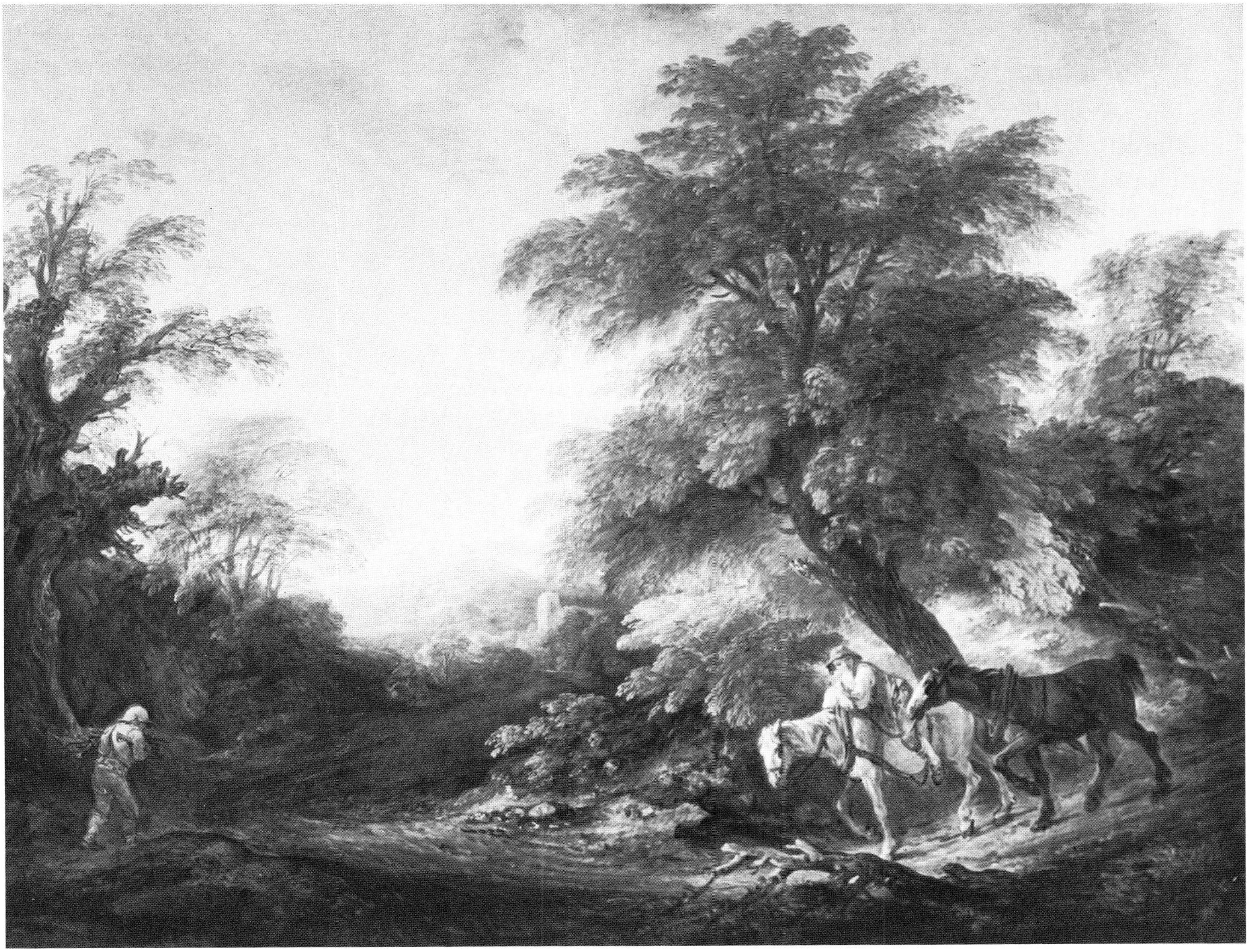

48. *Wooded landscape : boy on horse and woodman returning*. Canvas, 40 × 50¼ in. About 1760. Private Collection (Note 47)

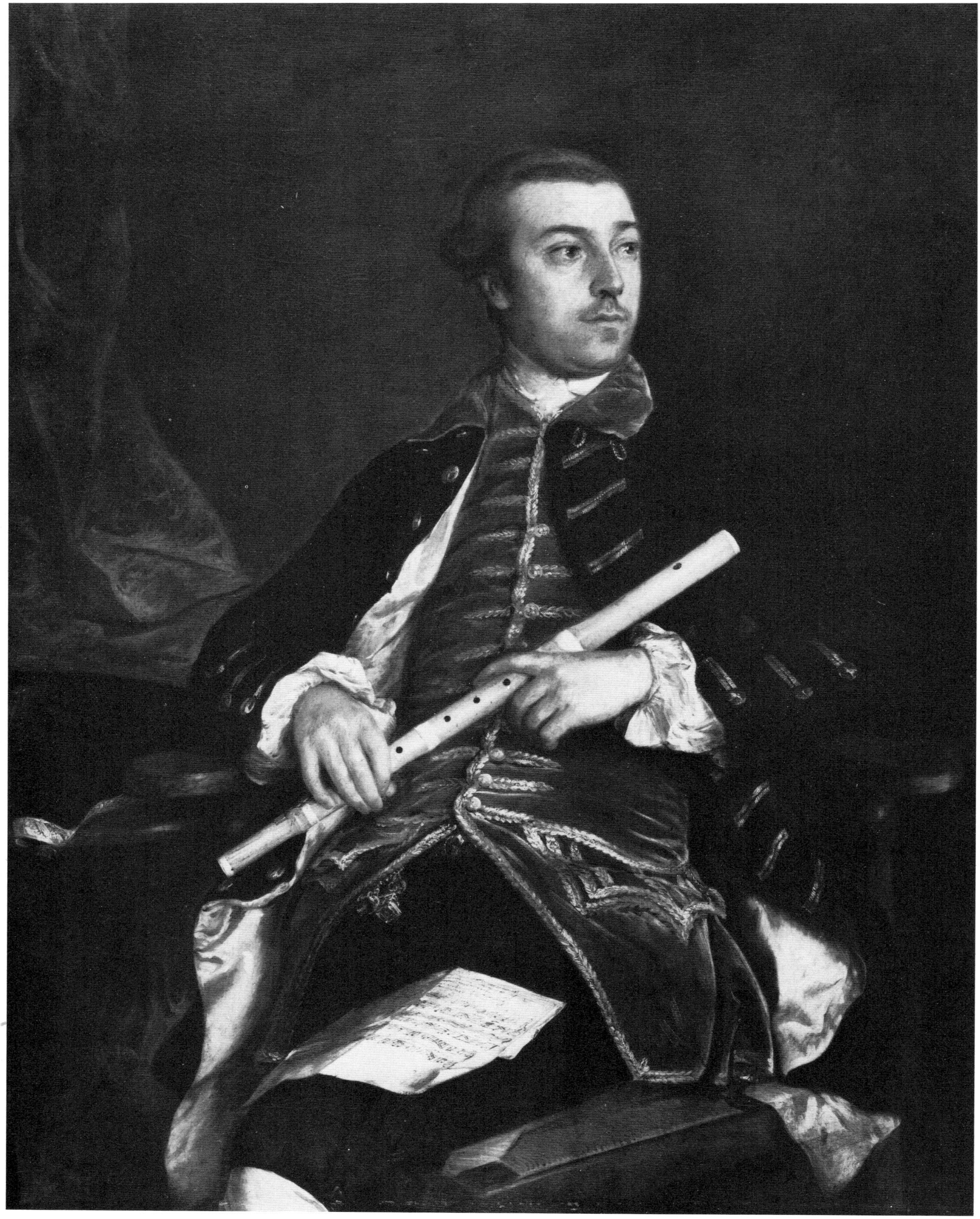

49. *William Wollaston* (1730–97). Canvas, $47\frac{1}{2} \times 38\frac{1}{2}$ in. About 1758–9. Ipswich, Christchurch Mansion (Note 39)

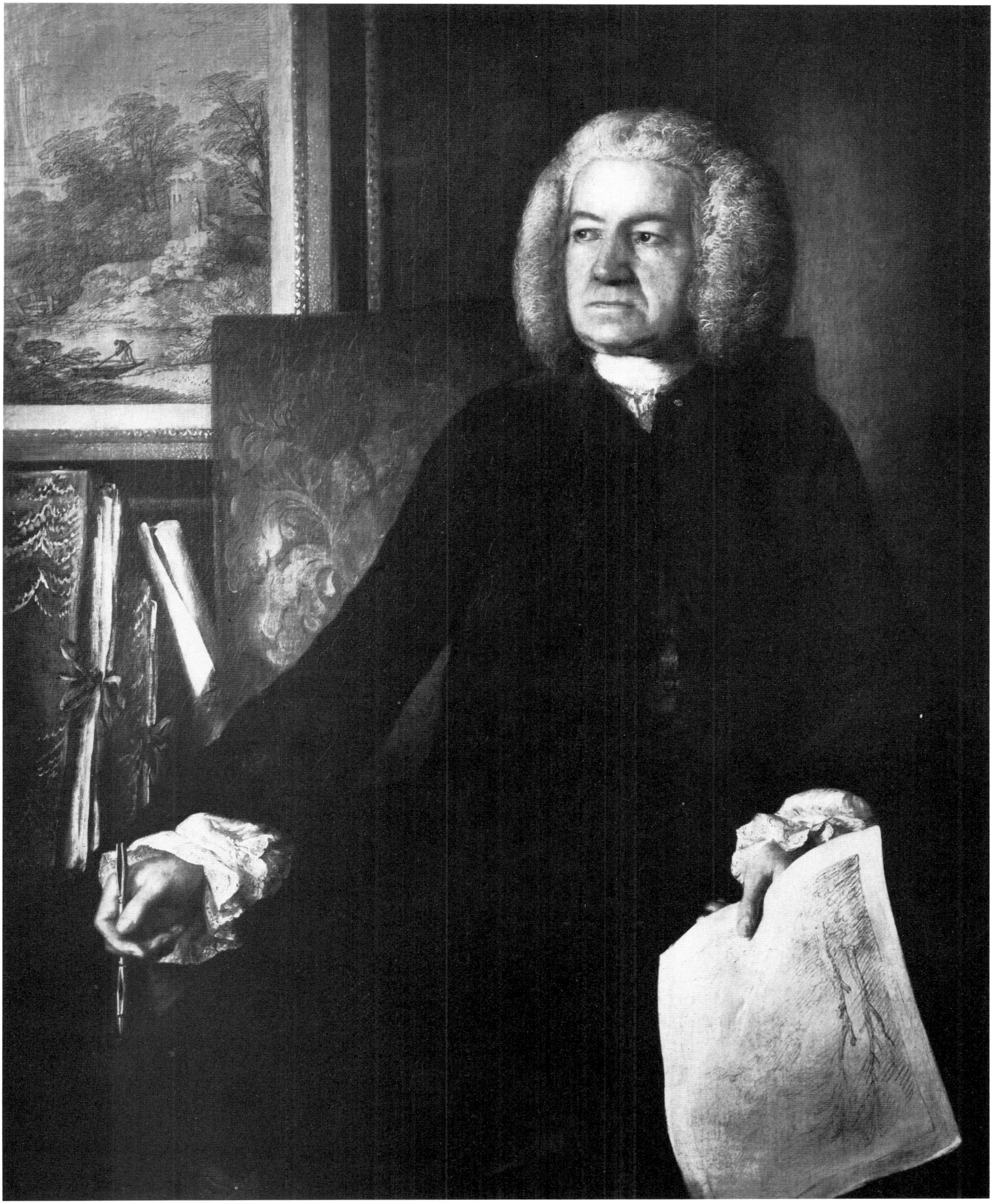

50. *Uvedale Tomkyns Price* (1685-1764). Canvas, 49 × 39 in. About 1760. Munich, Alte Pinakothek (Note 49)

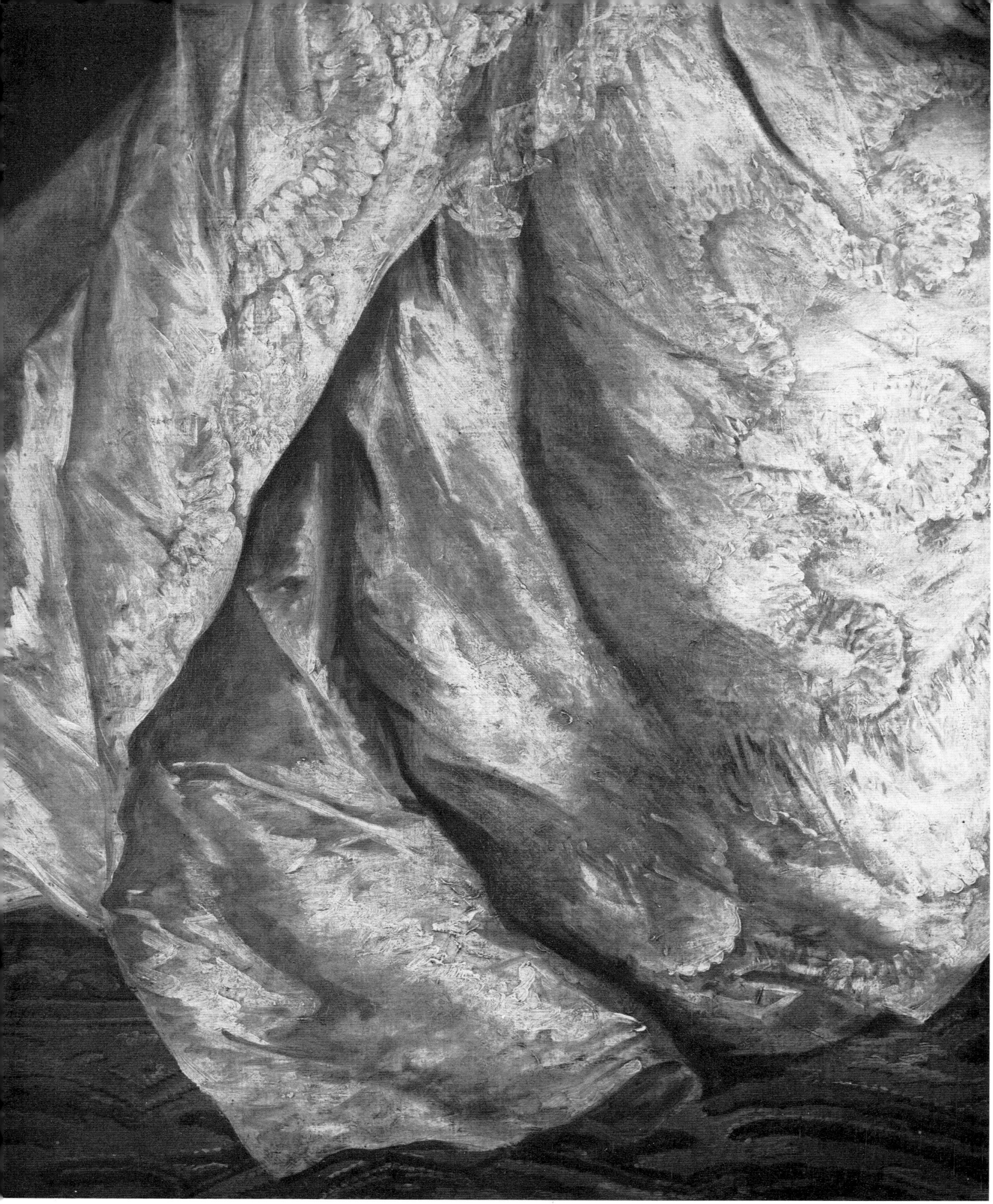

51. Detail from Pl. 54 (Note 48)

52. Detail from *Juliana, Lady Petre* (1759-1833). Canvas, $88\frac{3}{4} \times 57\frac{1}{4}$ in. Painted spring 1788. San Marino, Henry E. Huntington Art Gallery (Note 135)

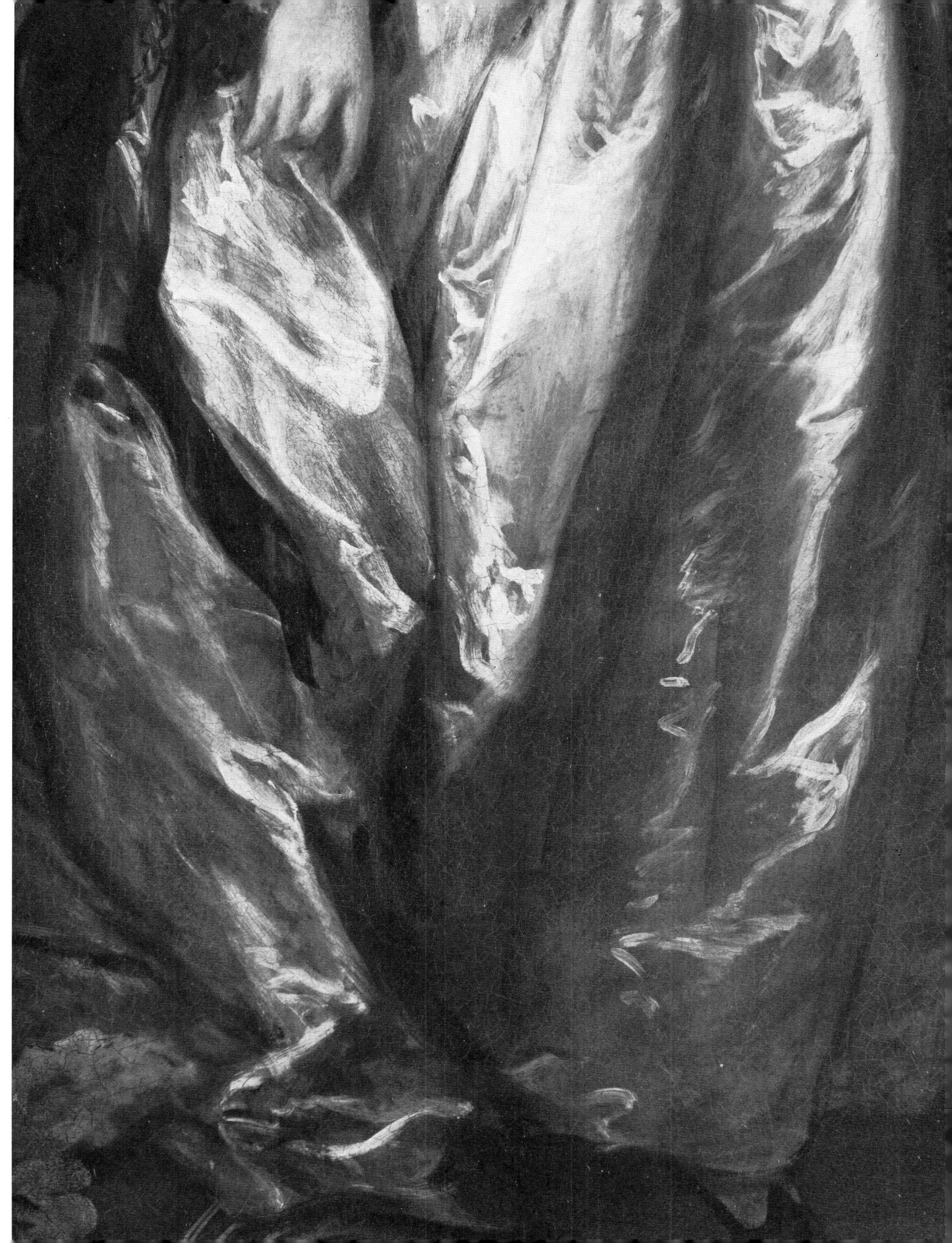

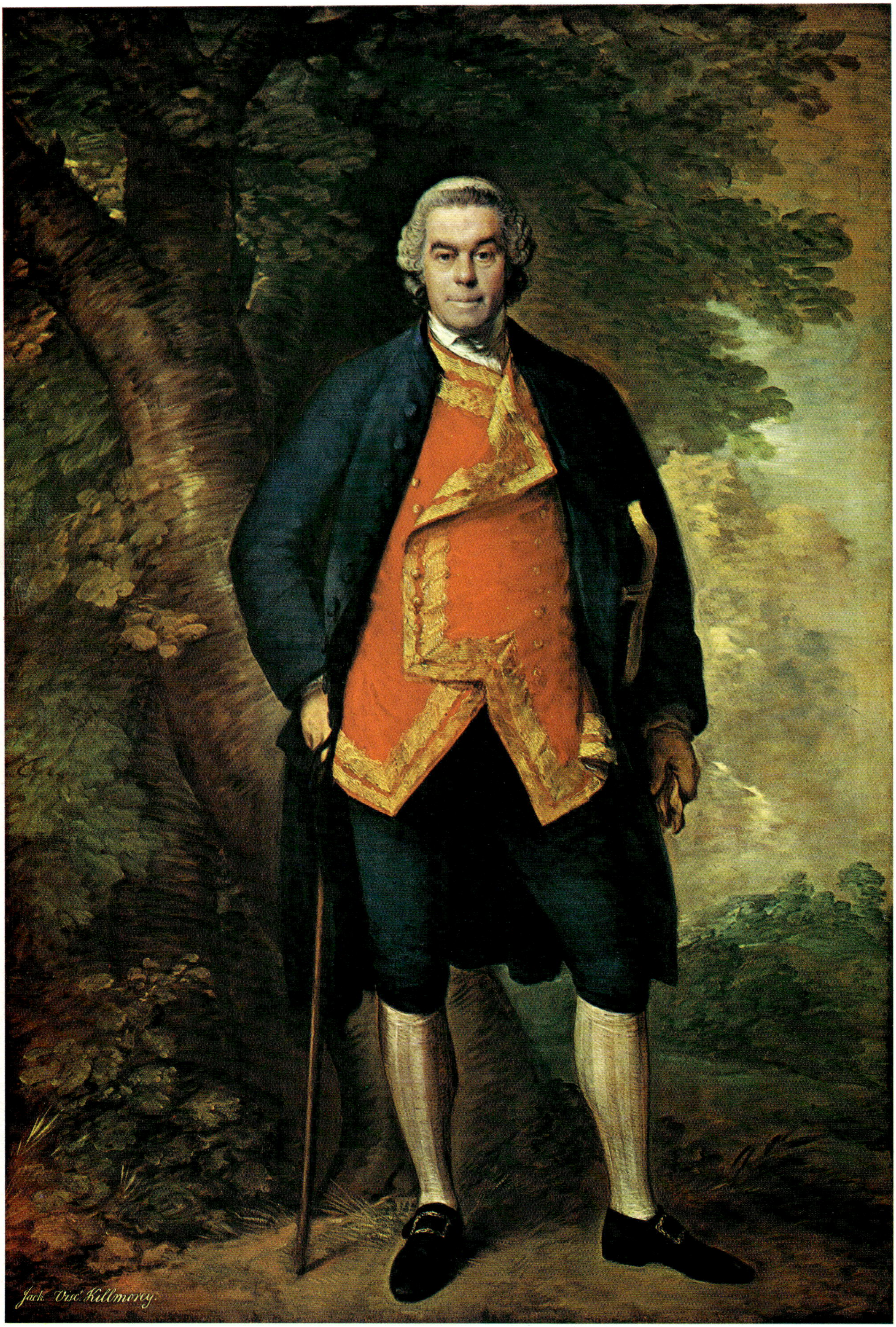
Jack. Visc.t Killmorey.

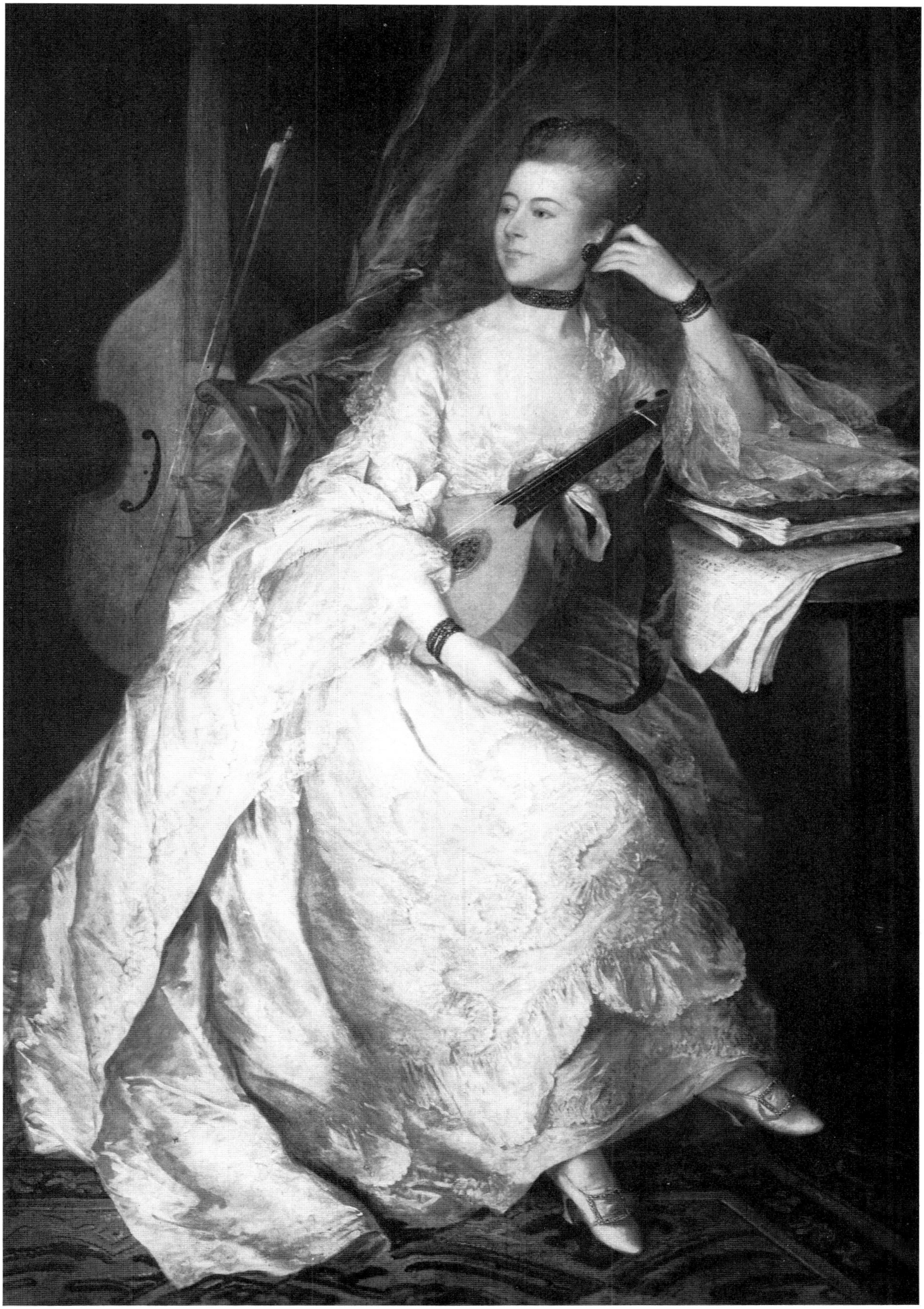

54. *Mrs Philip Thicknesse, née Anne Ford* (1732–1824). Canvas, 77½ × 53 in. Painted 1760. Cincinnati, Art Museum (Note 48)

53. *John, 10th Viscount Kilmorey* (1710–91). Canvas, 92 × 61½ in. About 1768. London, Tate Gallery (Note 66)

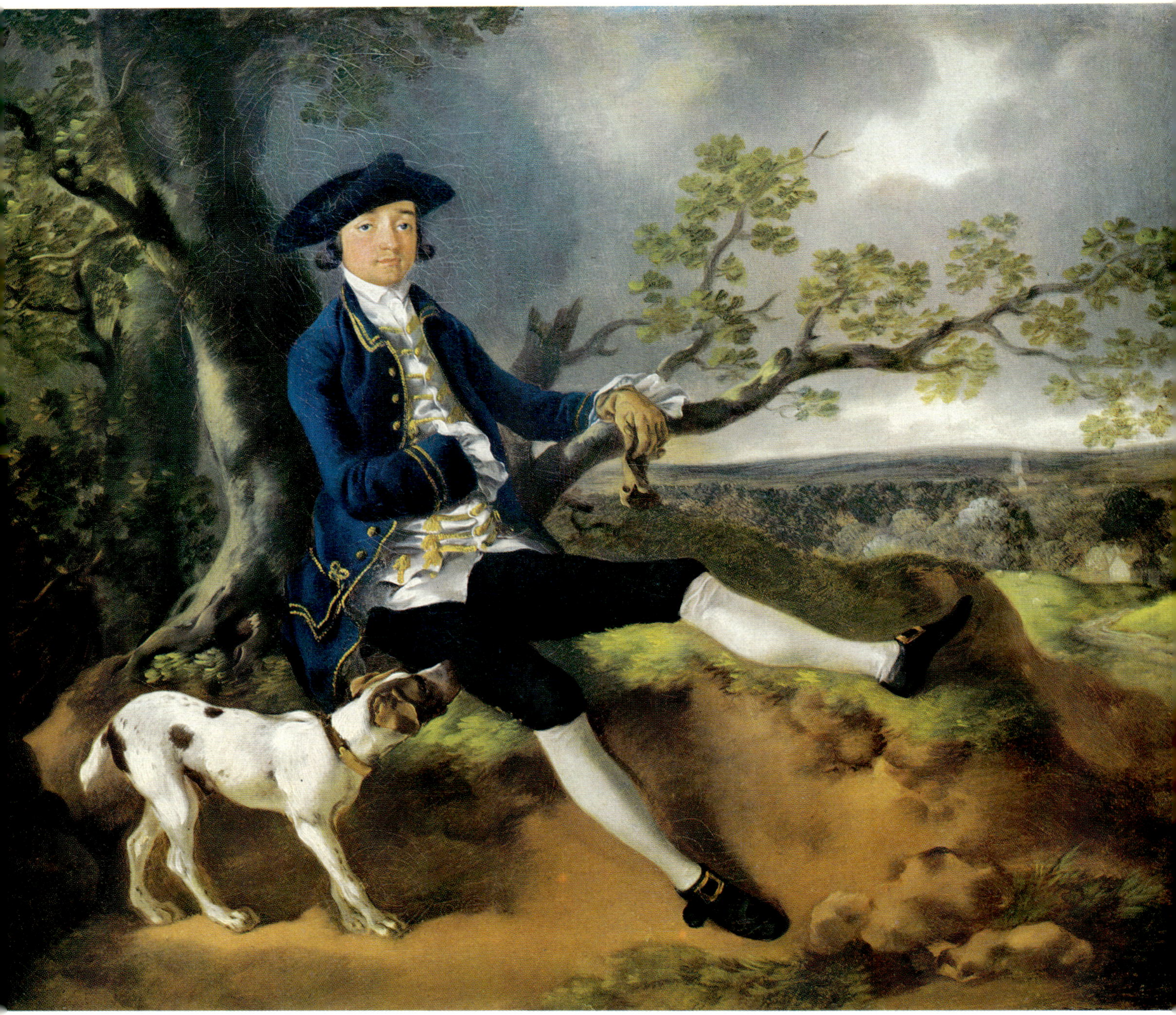

55. *John Plampin* (*c.* 1726–1805). Canvas, $19\frac{3}{4} \times 23\frac{3}{4}$ in. About 1753–4. London, National Gallery (Note 22)

56. *William Poyntz* (1734–1809). Canvas, $92\frac{1}{2} \times 60$ in. Exhibited S. A. 1762 (30). Althorp, Earl Spencer (Note 50)

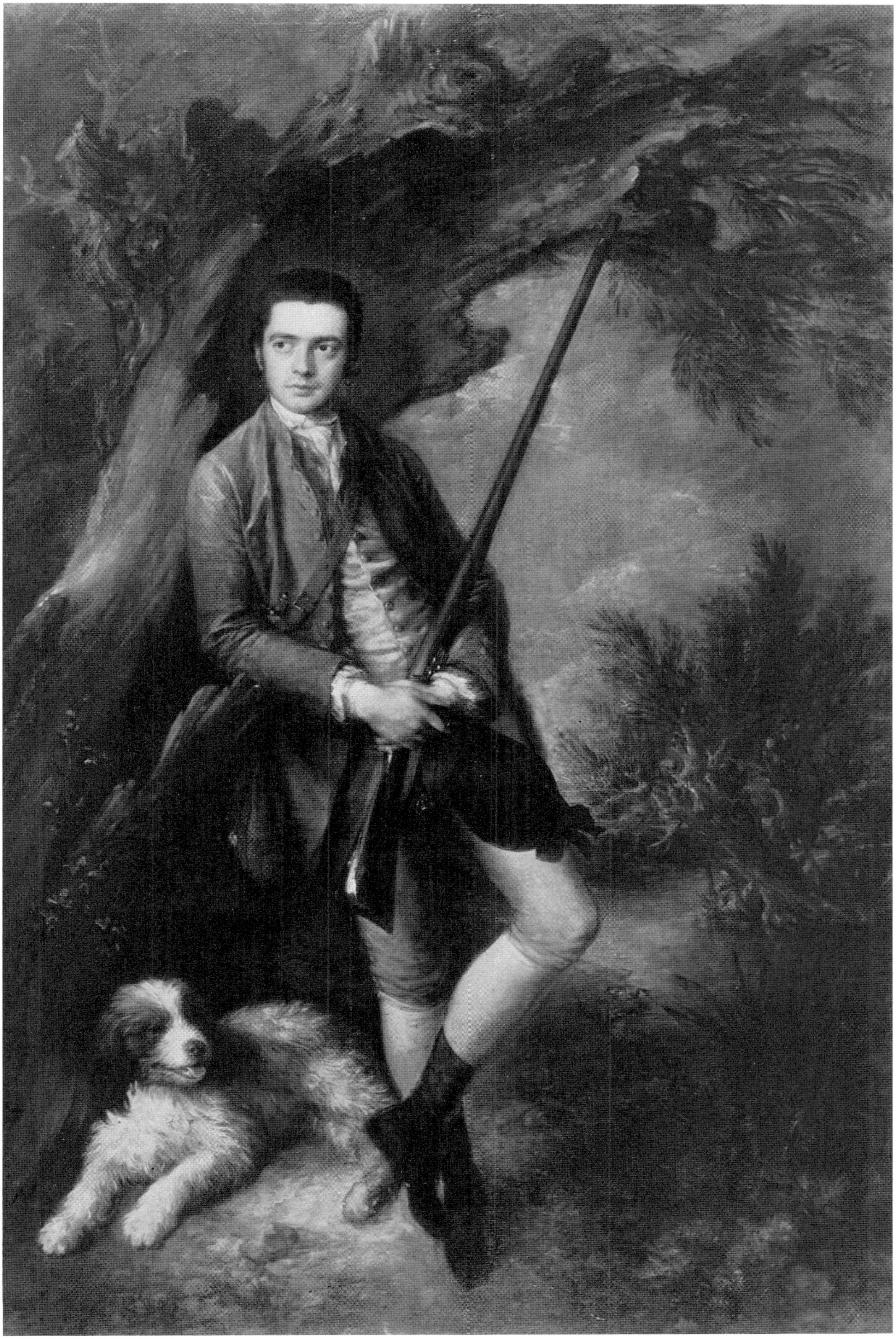

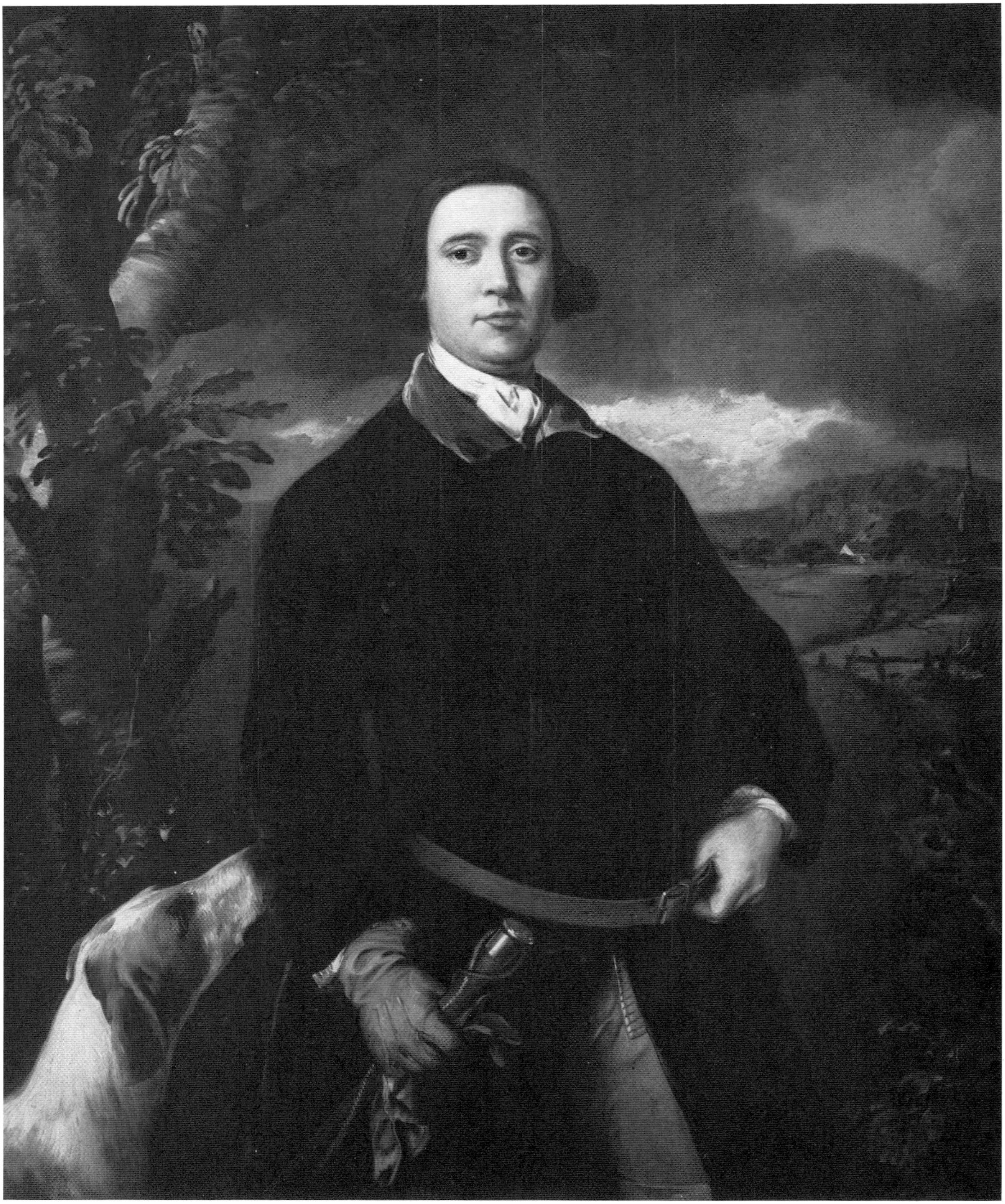

57. *Samuel Kilderbee* (1725–1813). Canvas, $50\frac{1}{2} \times 40\frac{1}{2}$ in. About 1755. San Francisco, M. H. de Young Memorial Museum (Note 30)

58. *The Rev. Sir Henry Bate-Dudley* (1745–1824). Canvas, 88×59 in. Exhibited R. A. 1780 (189) (engraved). Needwood House, Lord Burton (on loan to Marlborough House) (Note 94)

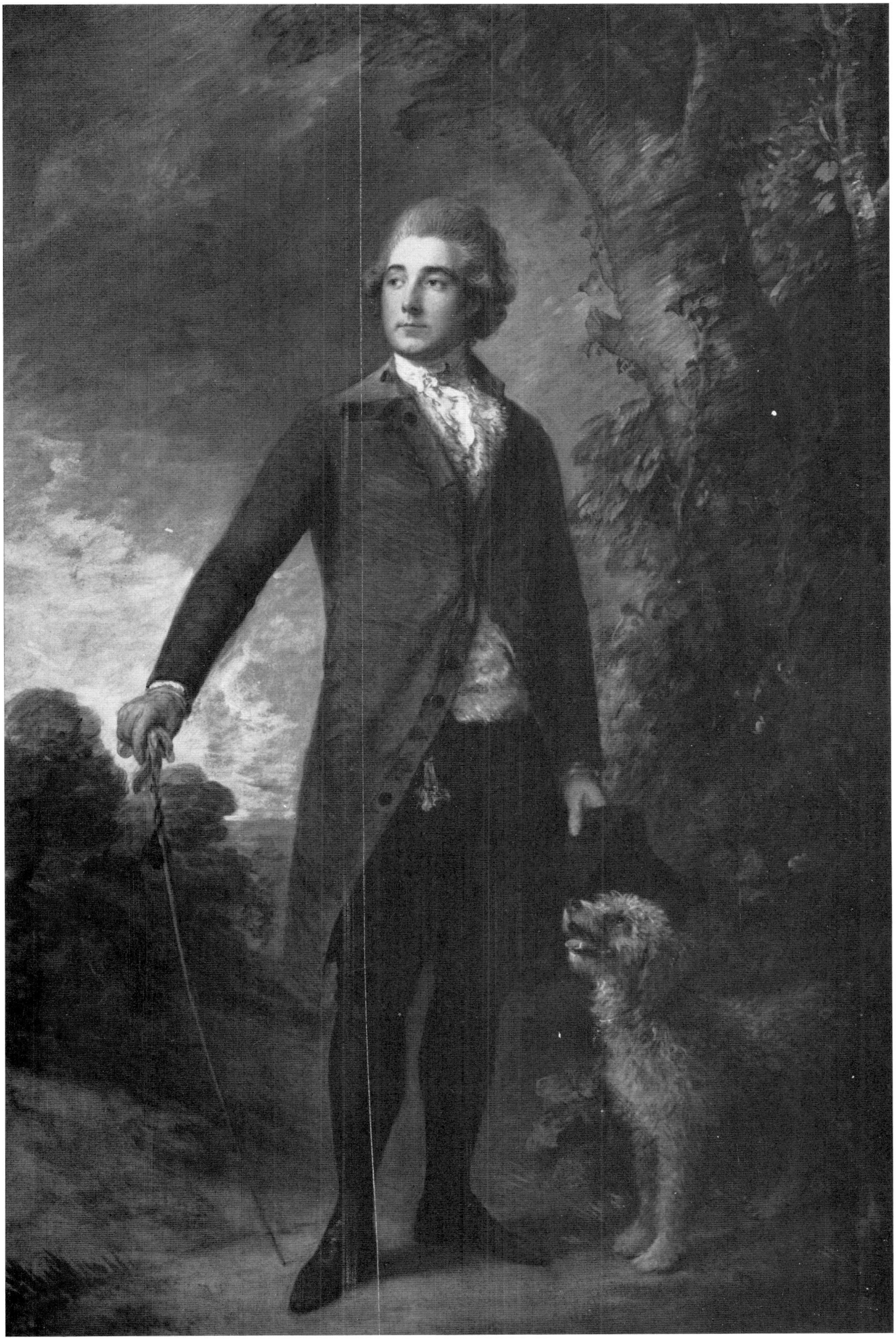

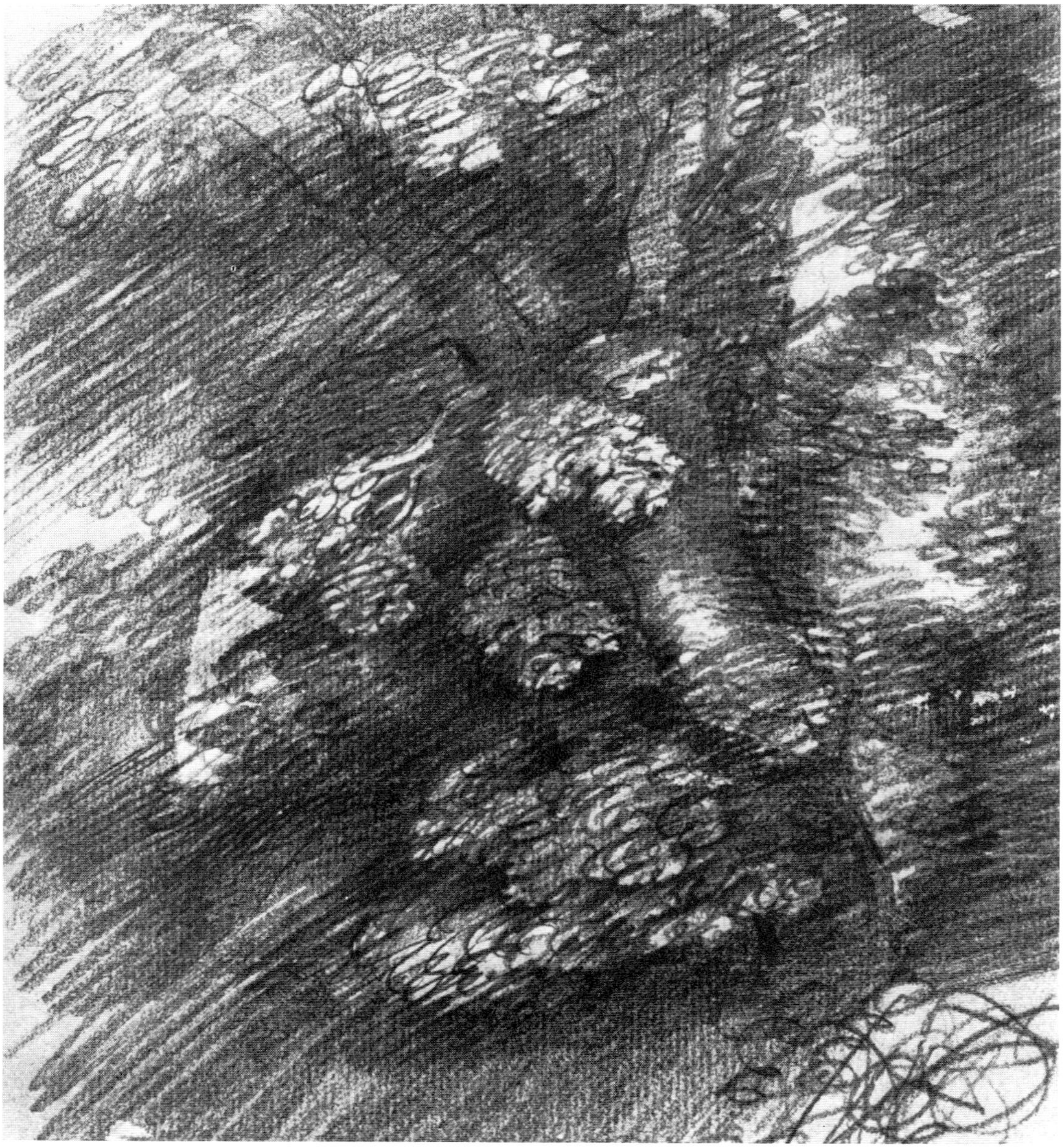

59. *Study of a tree trunk and foliage.* Pencil, $6\frac{3}{16} \times 5\frac{3}{4}$ in. Later 1750s. London, British Museum (Note 45)

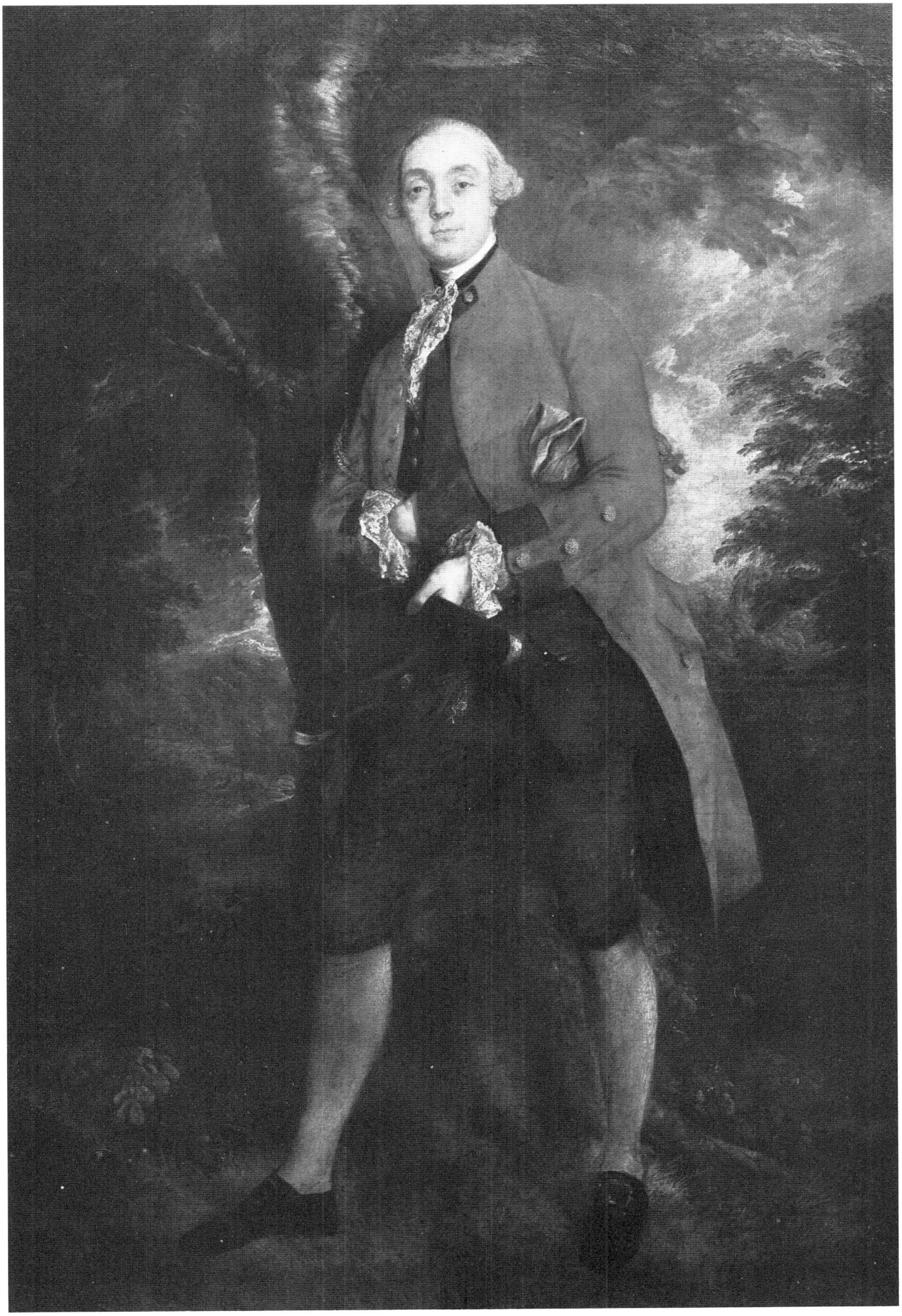

60. *General James Johnston* (1721–97). Canvas, $89\frac{3}{8} \times 57\frac{1}{2}$ in. About 1763–4. Dublin, National Gallery of Ireland (Note 56)

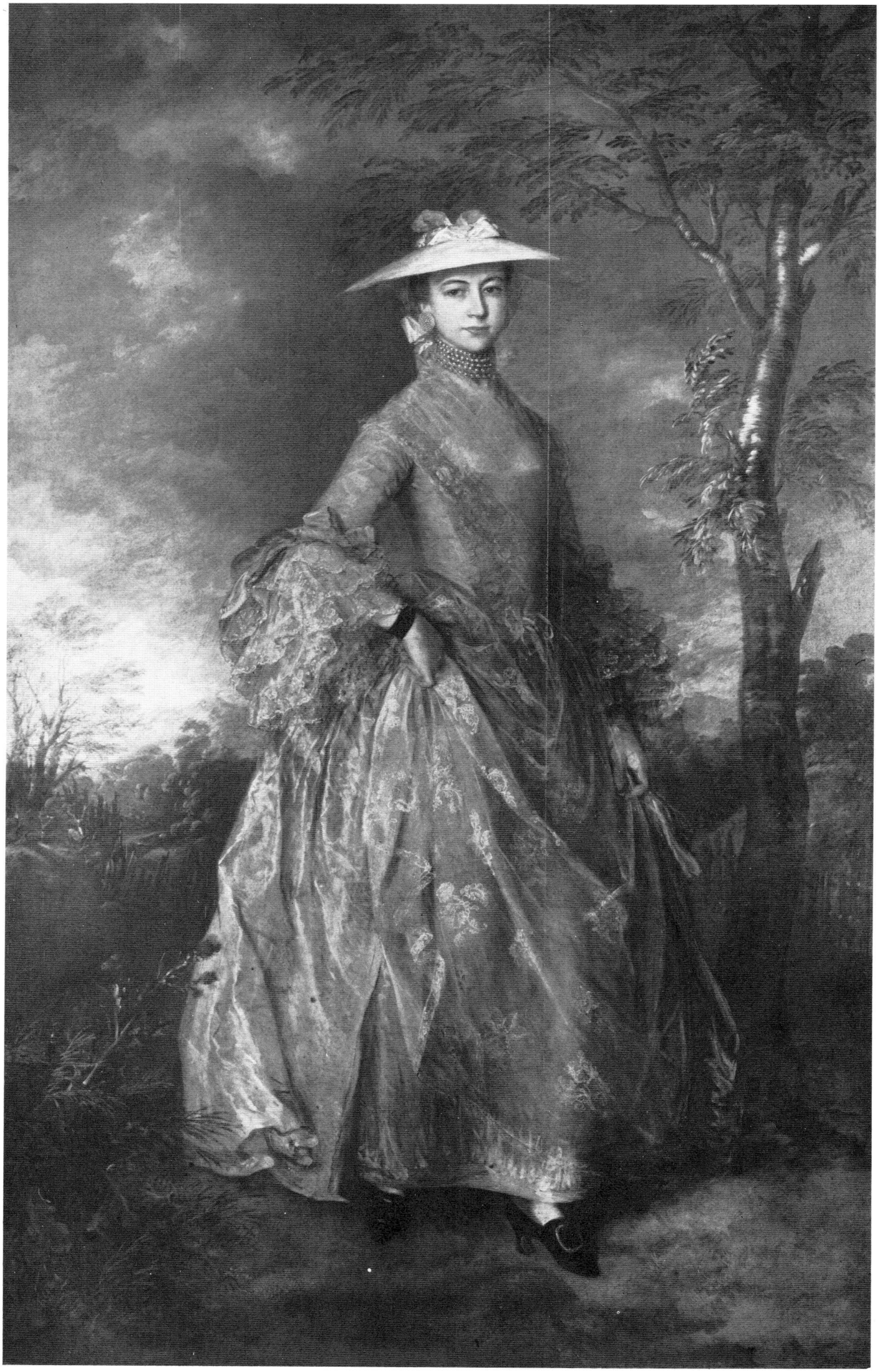

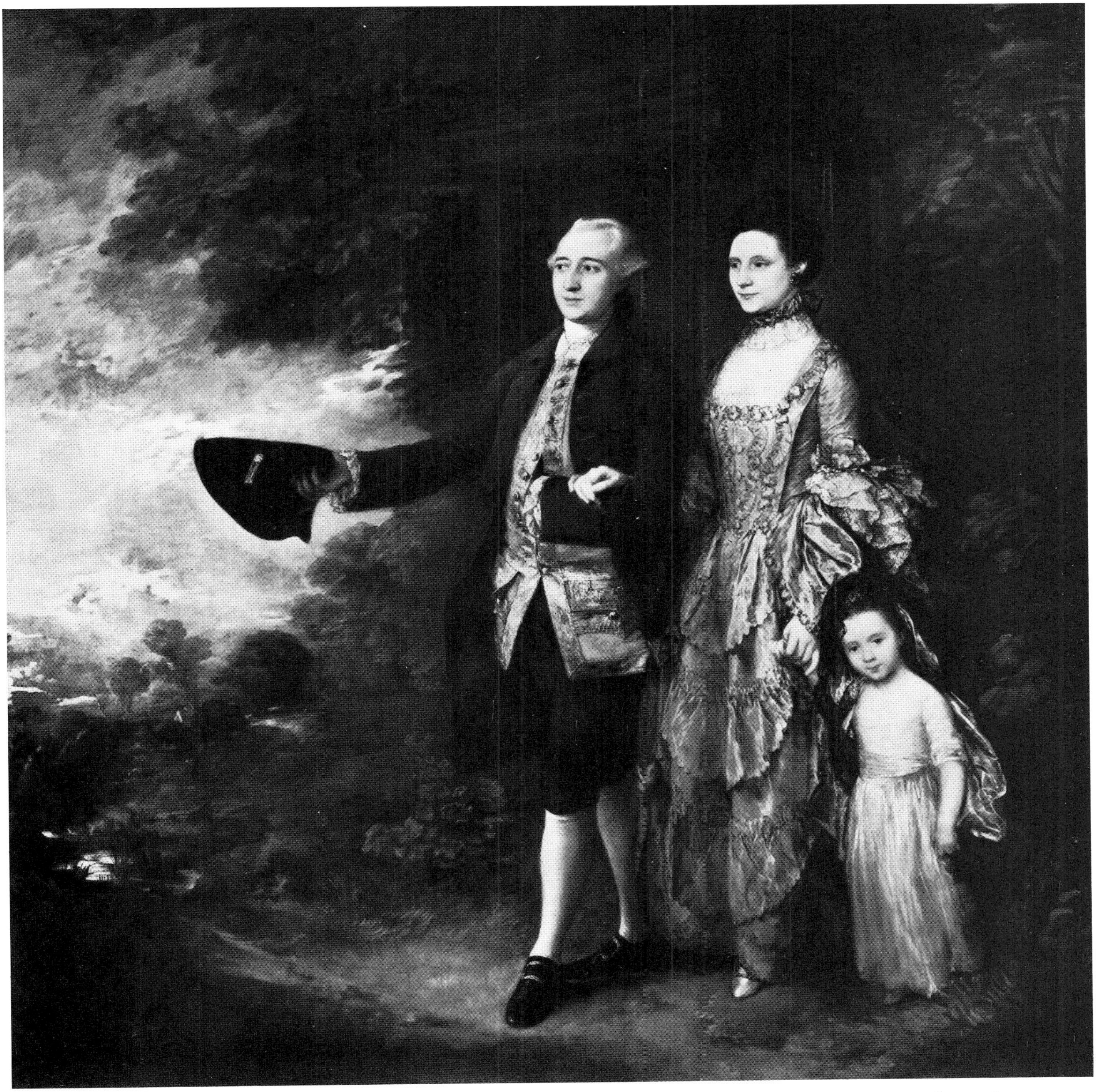

62. *George and Louisa Byam, with their daughter Sarah* (b. 1760). Canvas, 98 × 94 in. About 1764. Marlborough, Marlborough College (Note 57)

61. *Mary, Countess Howe* (1732–1800). Canvas, 96 × 60 in. About 1763–4. London, Iveagh Bequest, Kenwood (Note 55)

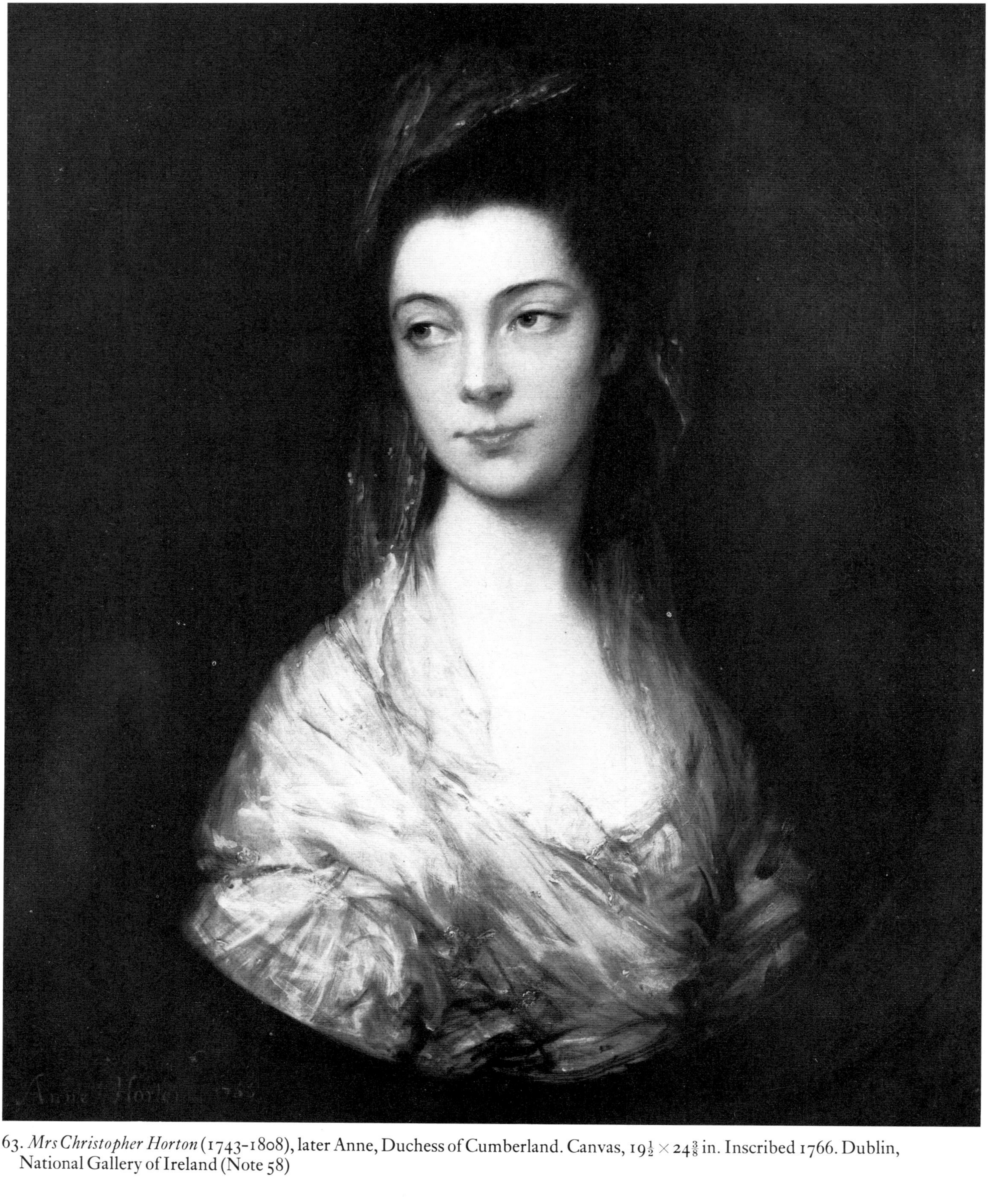

63. *Mrs Christopher Horton* (1743–1808), later Anne, Duchess of Cumberland. Canvas, $19\frac{1}{2} \times 24\frac{3}{8}$ in. Inscribed 1766. Dublin, National Gallery of Ireland (Note 58)

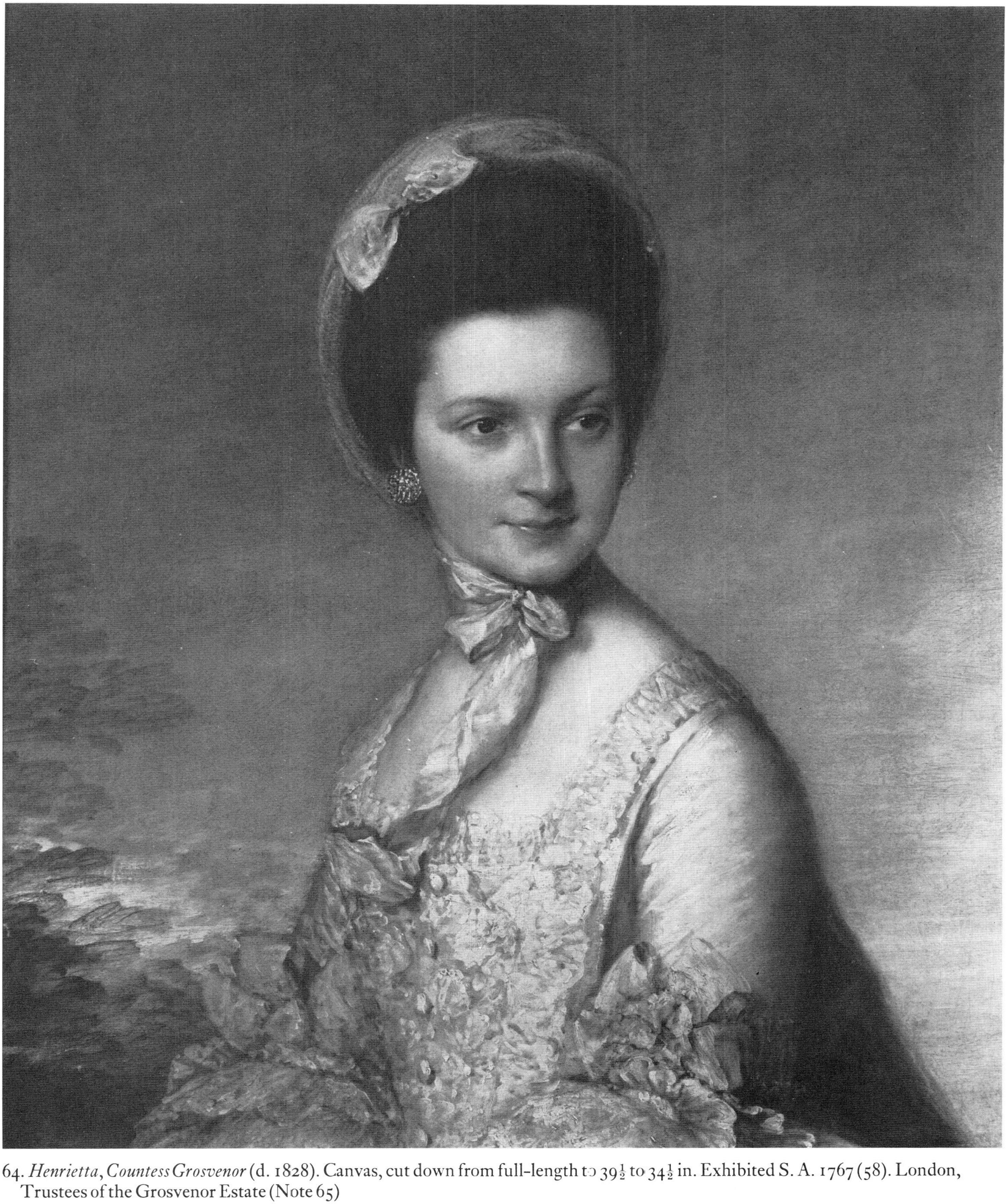

64. *Henrietta, Countess Grosvenor* (d. 1828). Canvas, cut down from full-length to $39\frac{1}{2}$ to $34\frac{1}{2}$ in. Exhibited S. A. 1767 (58). London, Trustees of the Grosvenor Estate (Note 65)

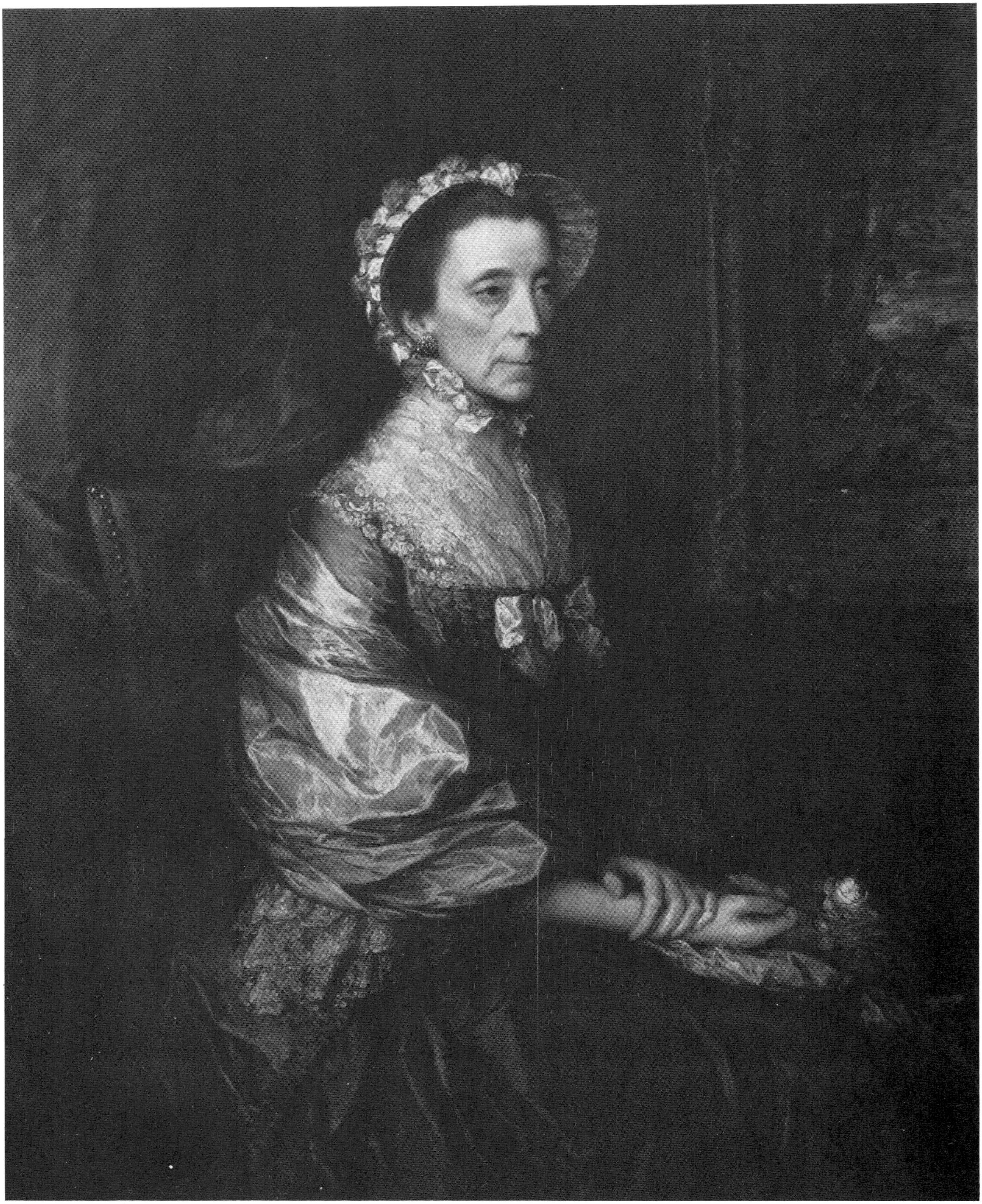

65. *Mary, Duchess of Montagu* (1711–75). Canvas, $49\frac{1}{2} \times 39\frac{1}{2}$ in. About 1768. Bowhill, Duke of Buccleuch and Queensberry (Note 67)

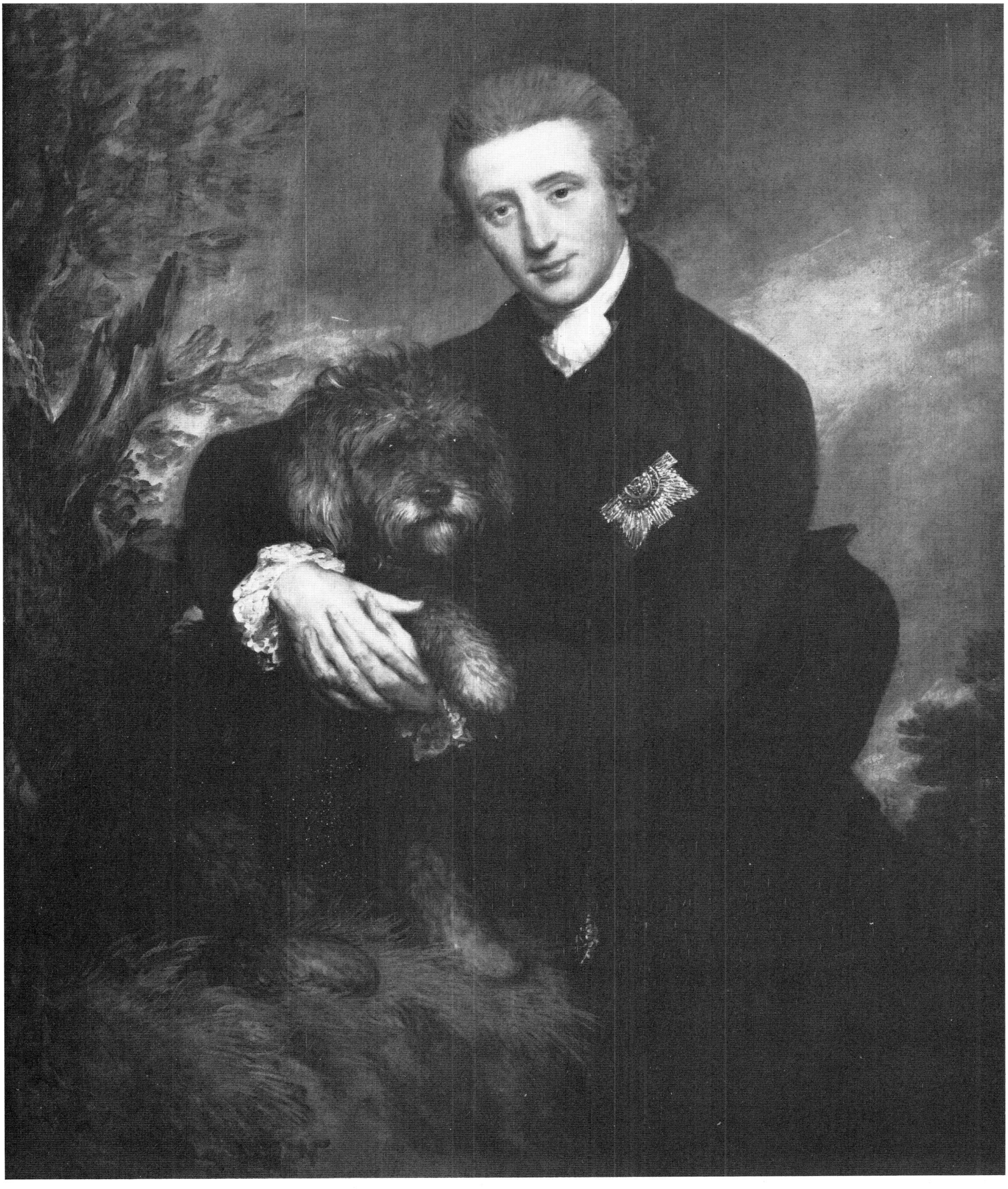

66. *Henry, 3rd Duke of Buccleuch* (1746–1812). Canvas, 48½ × 38 in. Receipt for payment dated November 1770. Engraved 1771. Bowhill, Duke of Buccleuch and Queensberry (Note 74)

Overleaf:

67. Detail from Pl. 66 (Note 74)

68. Detail from Pl. 62 (Note 57)

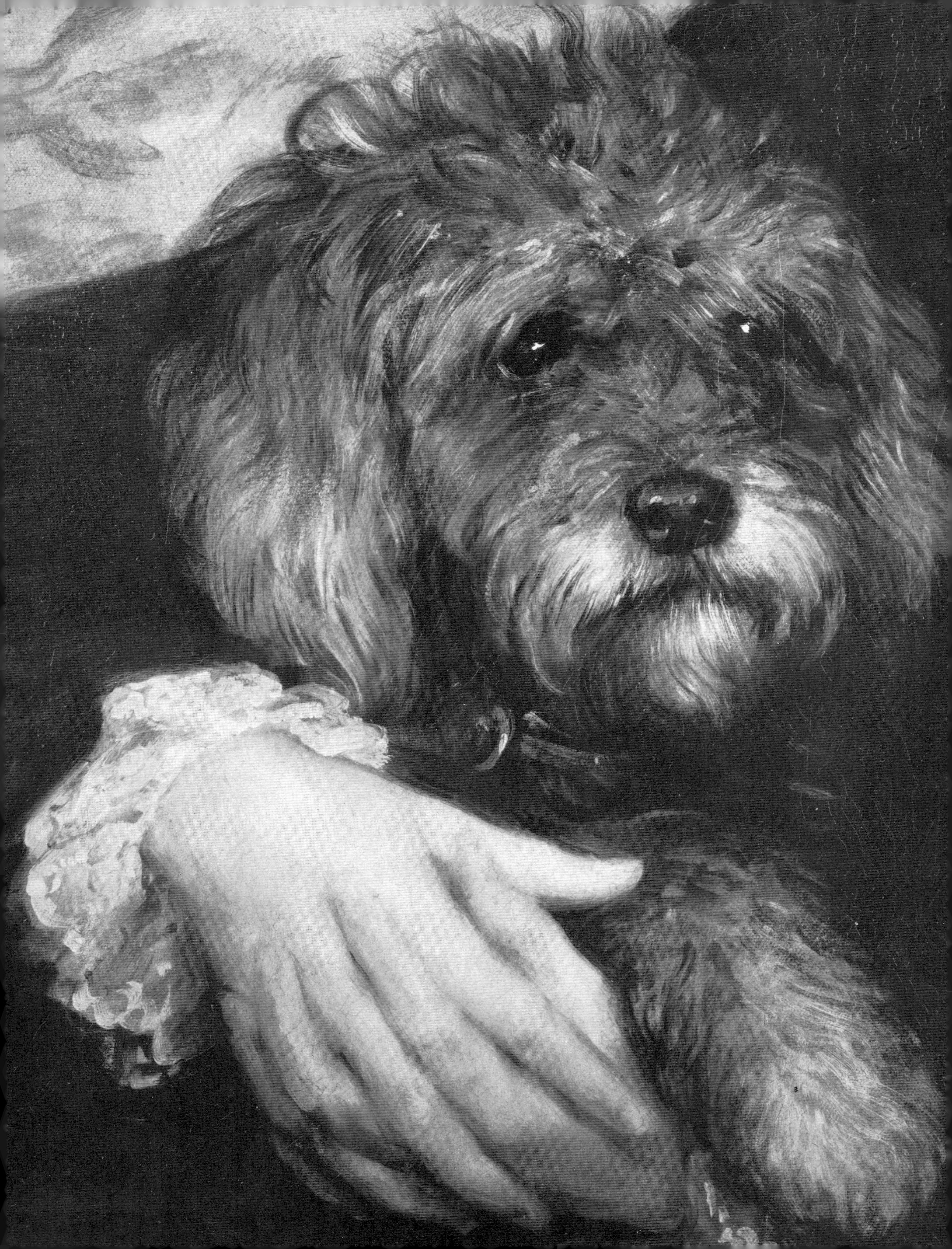

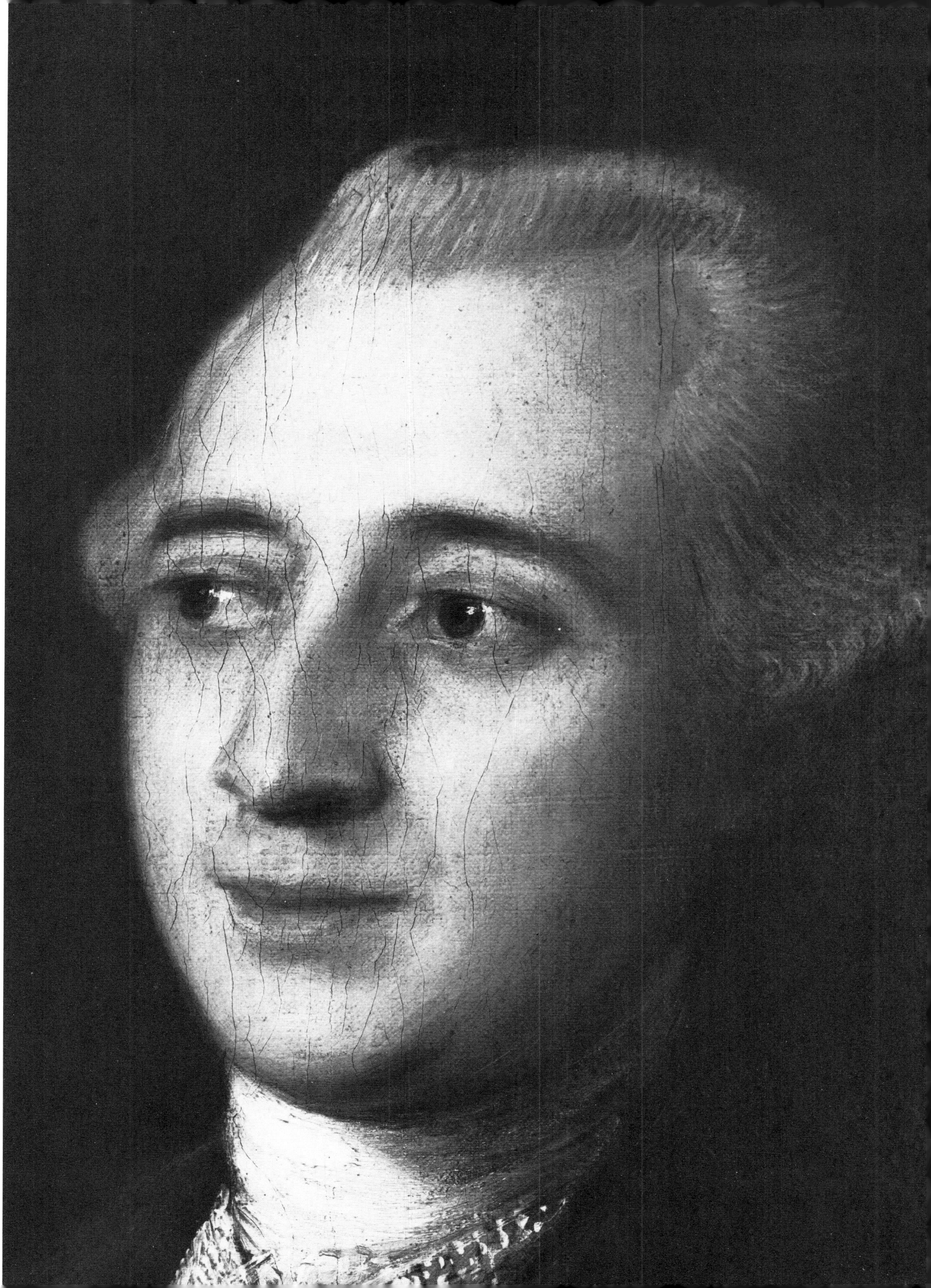

69. *Wooded landscape with herdsman and cattle.* Black chalk and watercolour, heightened with white, 9 $\frac{5}{16}$ × 12 $\frac{1}{2}$ in. Stamped in monogram. Mid 1760s. Driffield, Major Michael Ingram (Note 54)

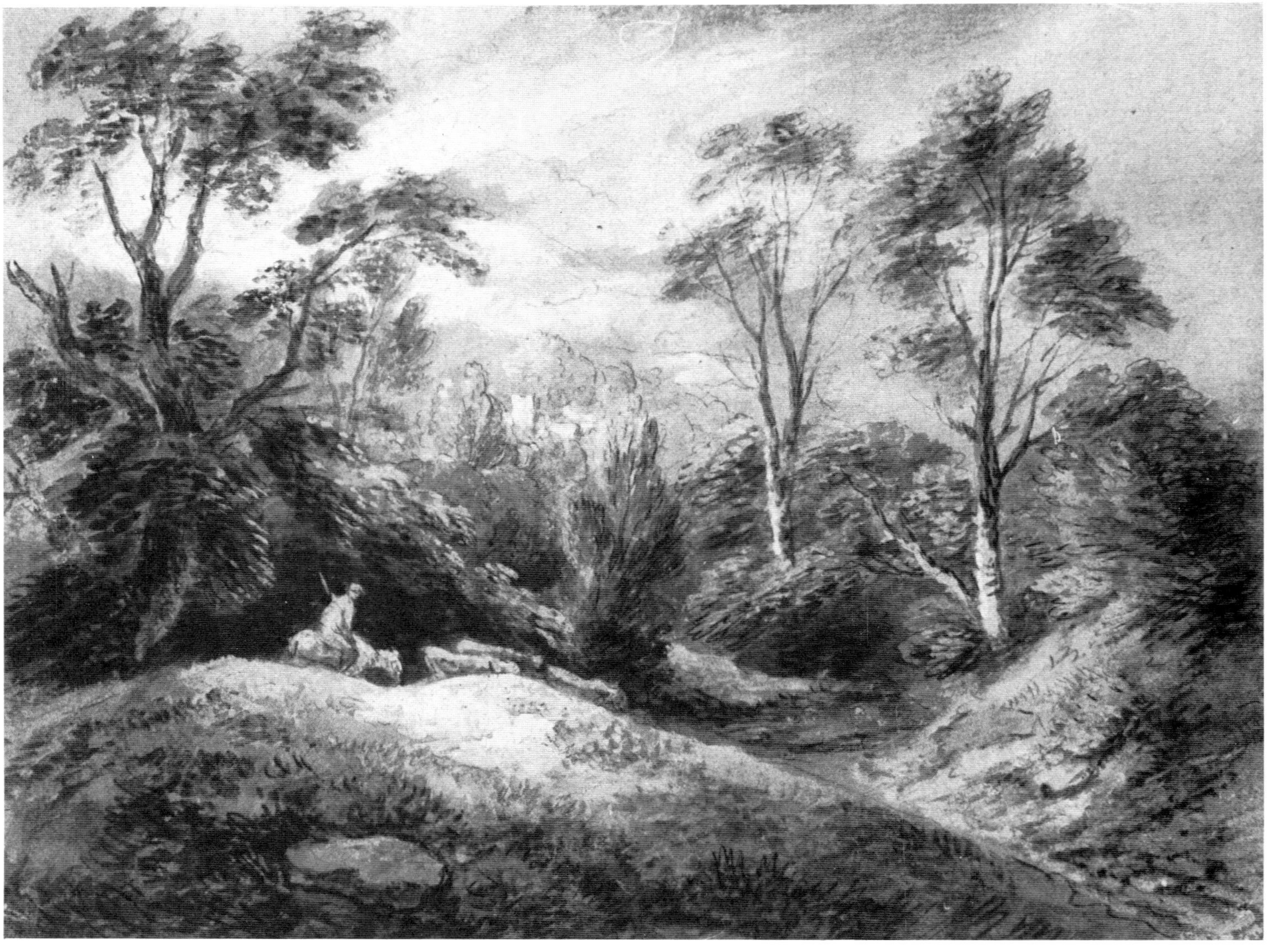

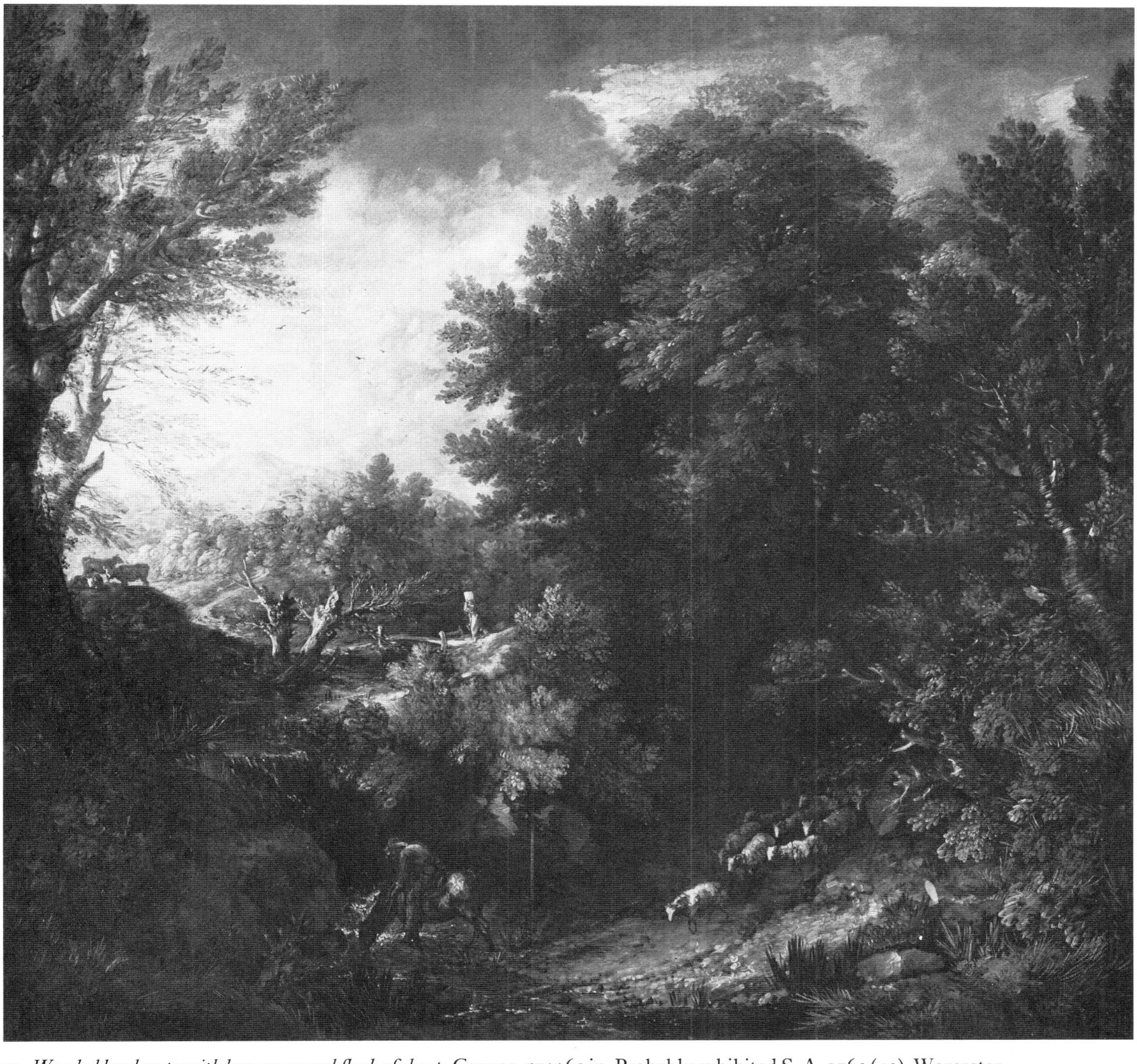

70. *Wooded landscape with horseman and flock of sheep*. Canvas, 57 × 62 in. Probably exhibited S. A. 1763 (43). Worcester, Massachusetts, Art Museum (Note 51)

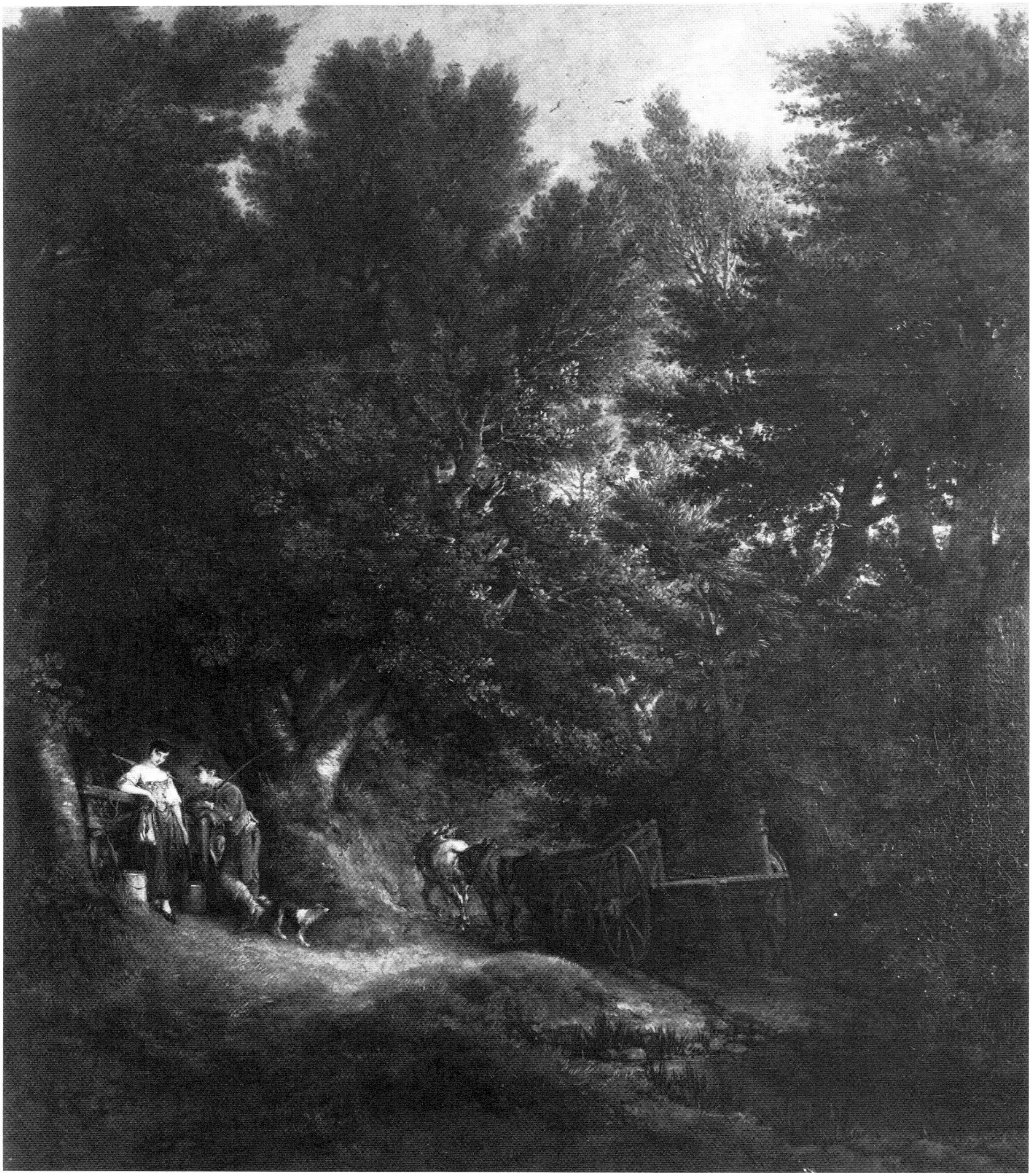

71. *Wooded landscape with milkmaid and drover*. Canvas, 57 × 47 in. Exhibited S. A. 1766 (53). Scampston Hall, Sir Thomas Legard Bt (Note 60)

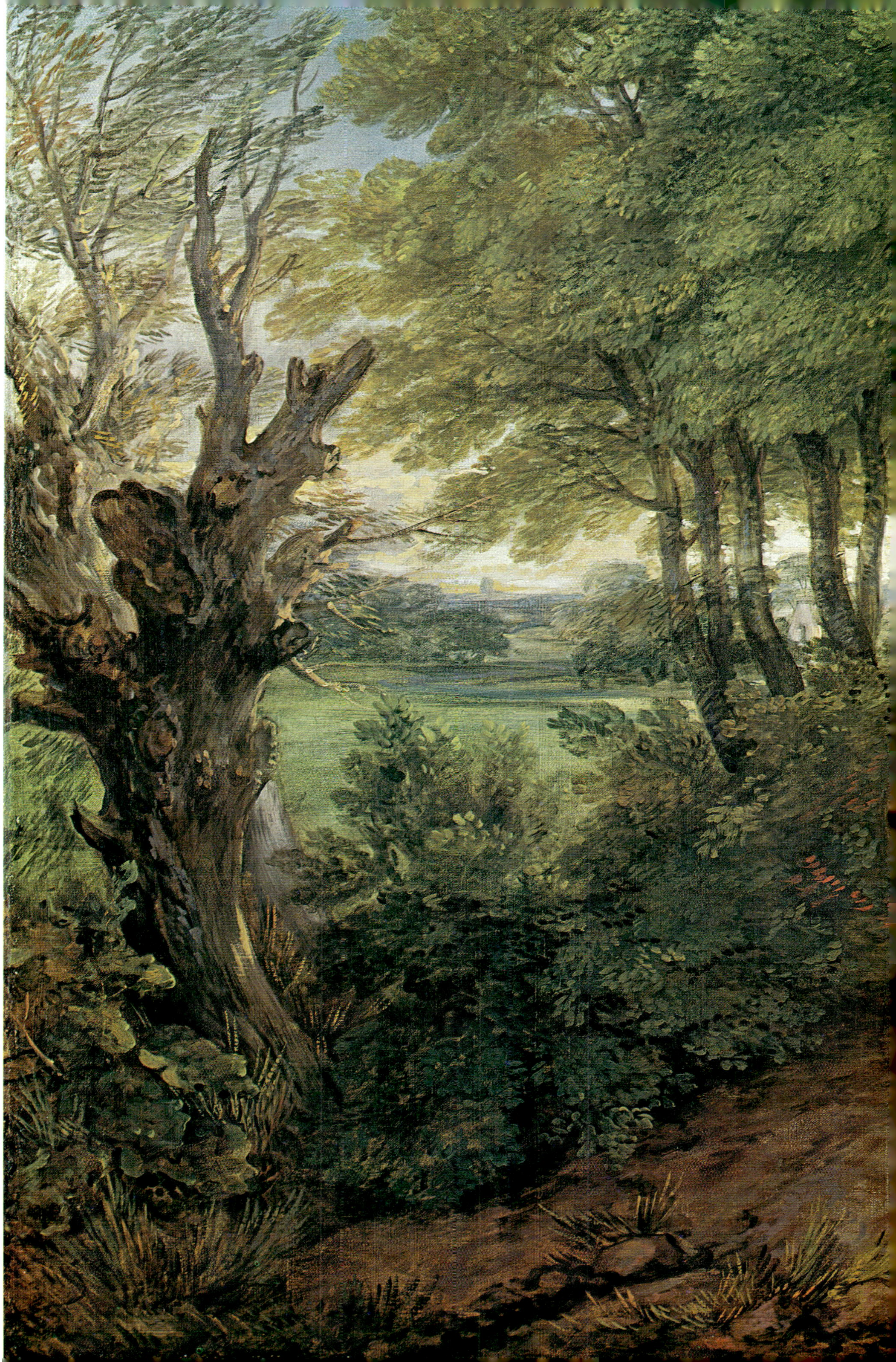

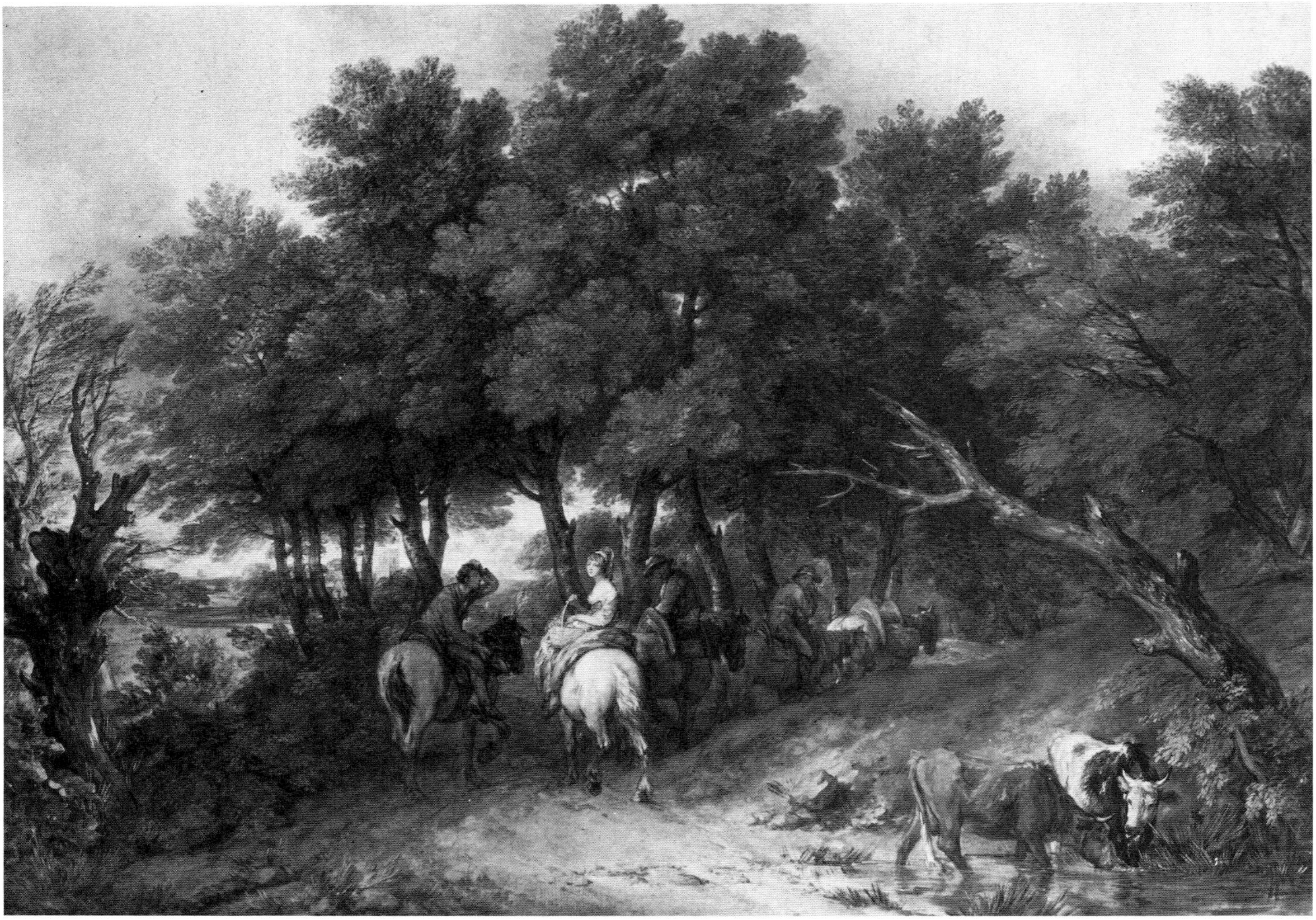

73. *Peasants returning from market through a wood*. Canvas, $47\frac{1}{2} \times 67$ in. About 1767–8. Toledo, Ohio, Museum of Art (Note 62)

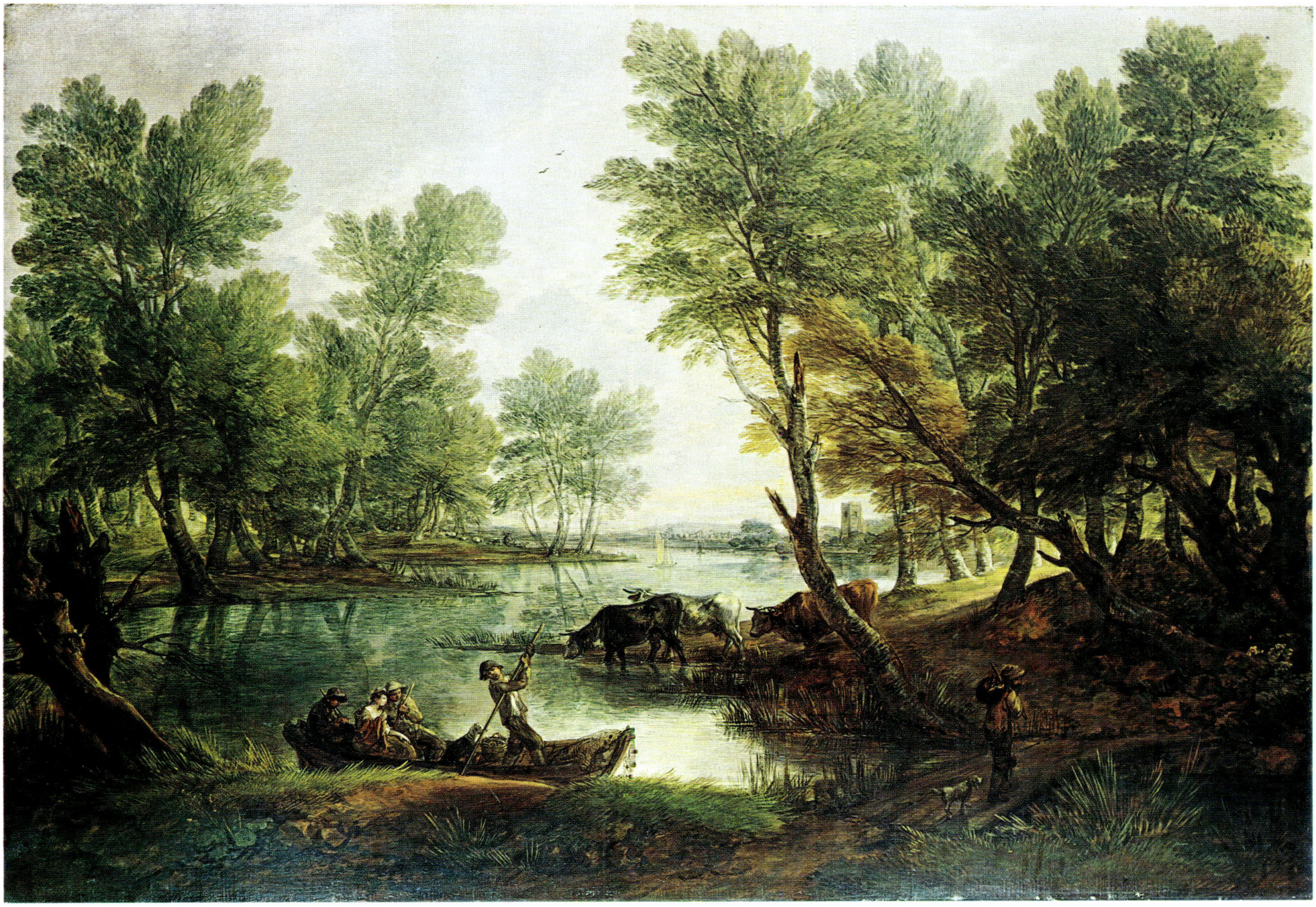

74. *River landscape with figures in a boat*. Canvas, 47 × 66¼ in. About 1768-70. Philadelphia, Museum of Art (Note 63)

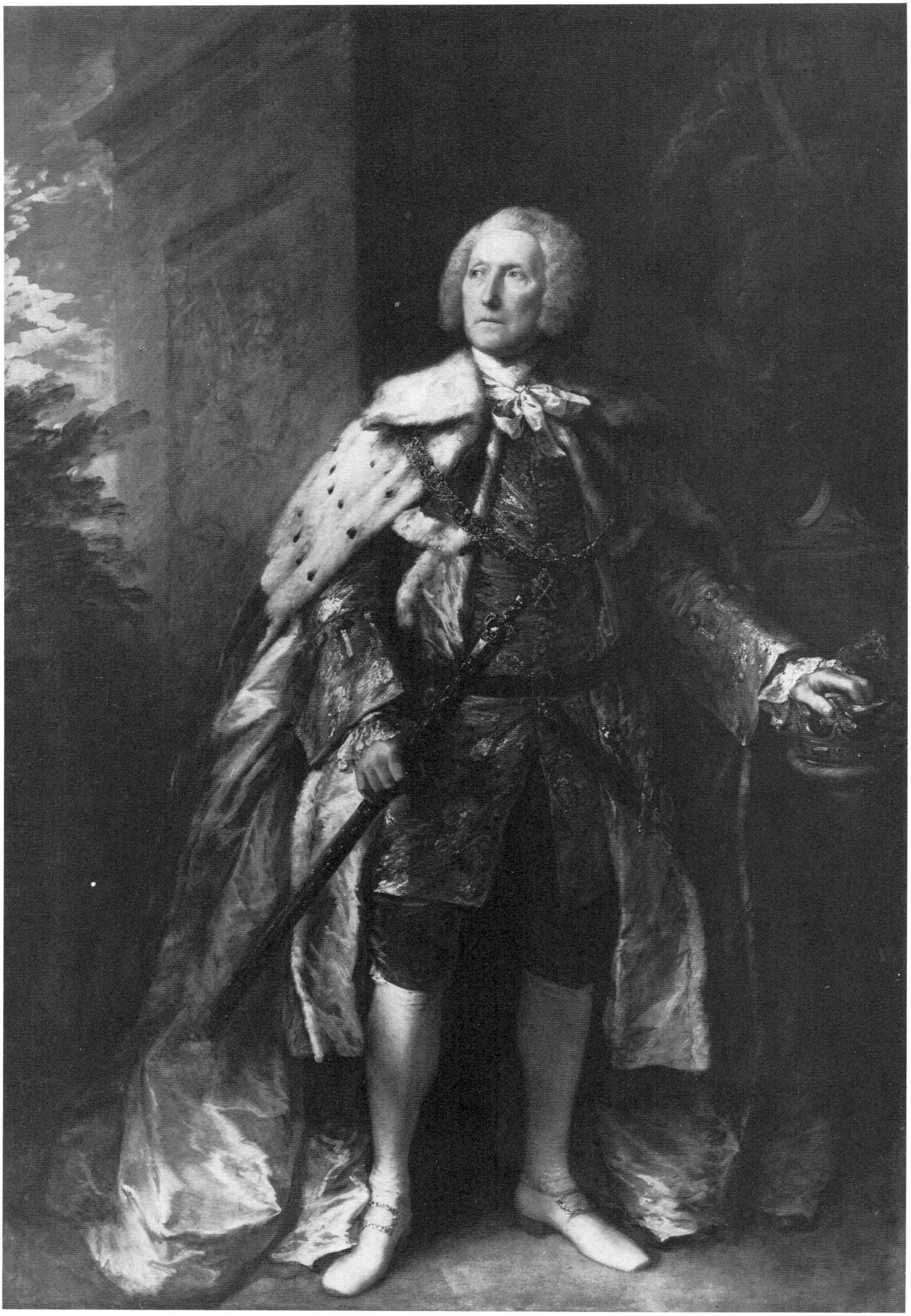

75. *John, 4th Duke of Argyll* (1694–1770). Canvas, 91 × 60½ in. Exhibited S. A. 1767 (59). Edinburgh, Scottish National Portrait Gallery (Note 64)

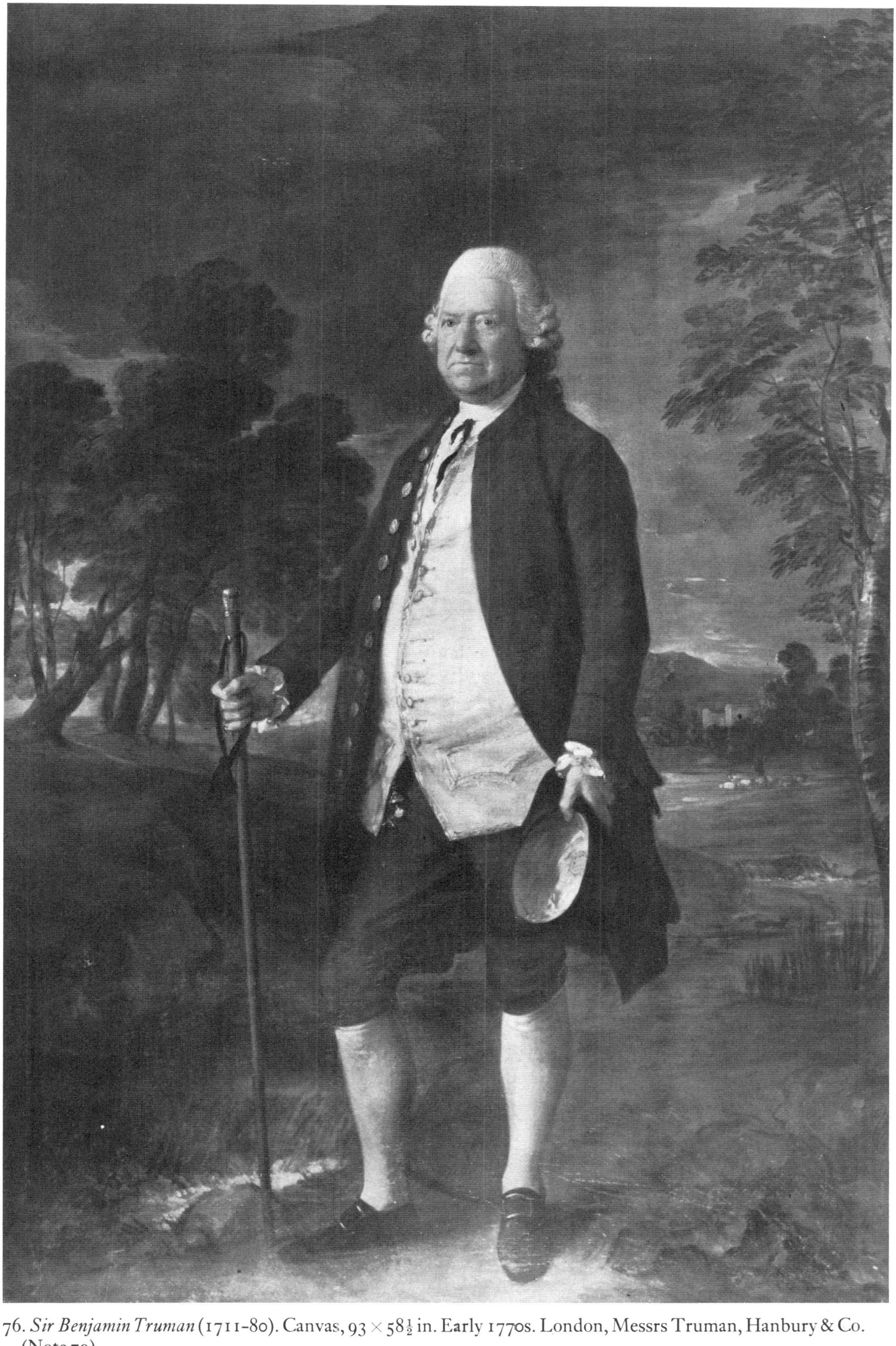

76. *Sir Benjamin Truman* (1711-80). Canvas, 93 × 58½ in. Early 1770s. London, Messrs Truman, Hanbury & Co. (Note 79)

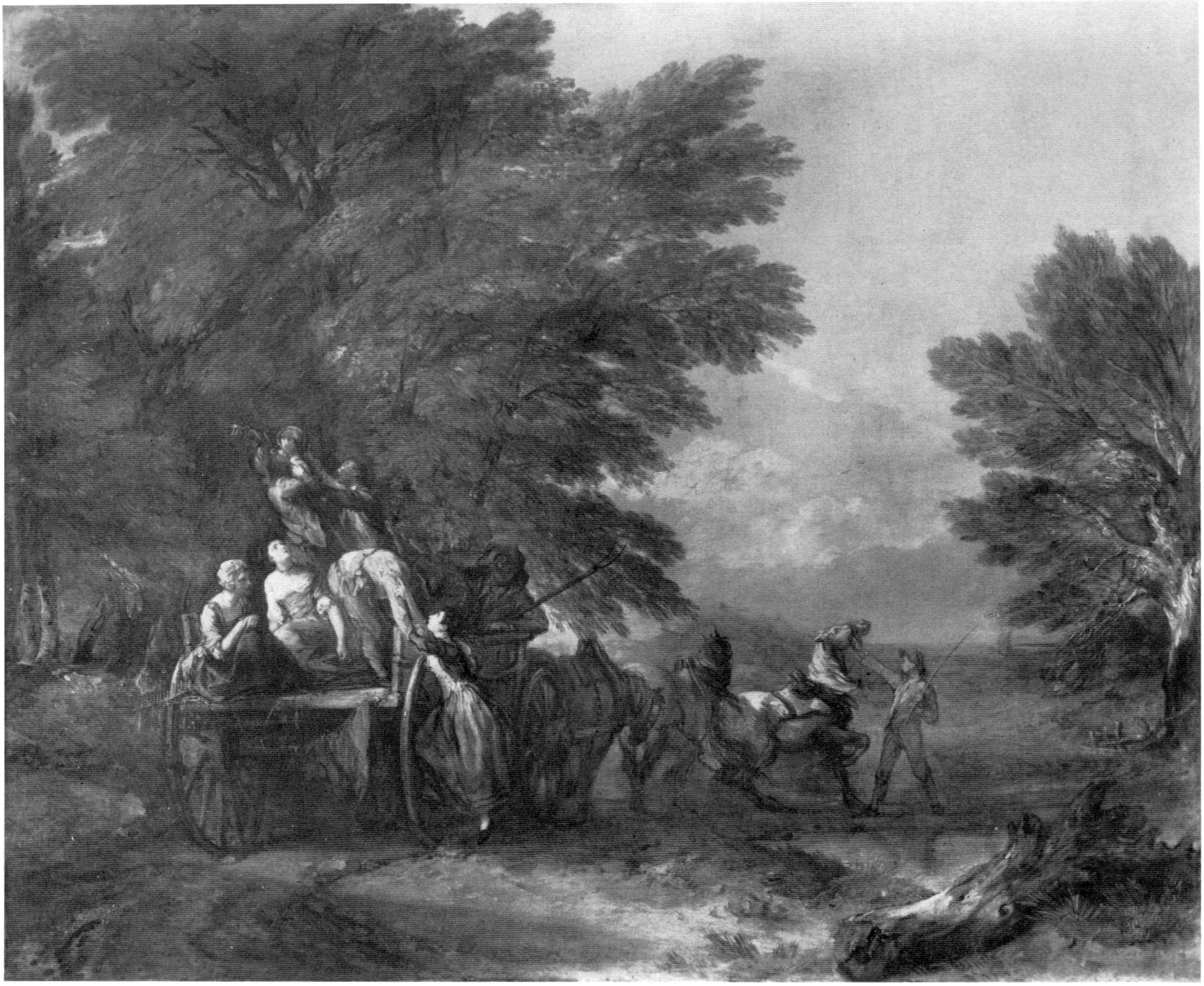

77. *The Harvest Waggon*. Canvas, $47\frac{1}{2} \times 57$ in. Exhibited S. A. 1767 (71). Birmingham, Barber Institute of Fine Arts (Note 61)

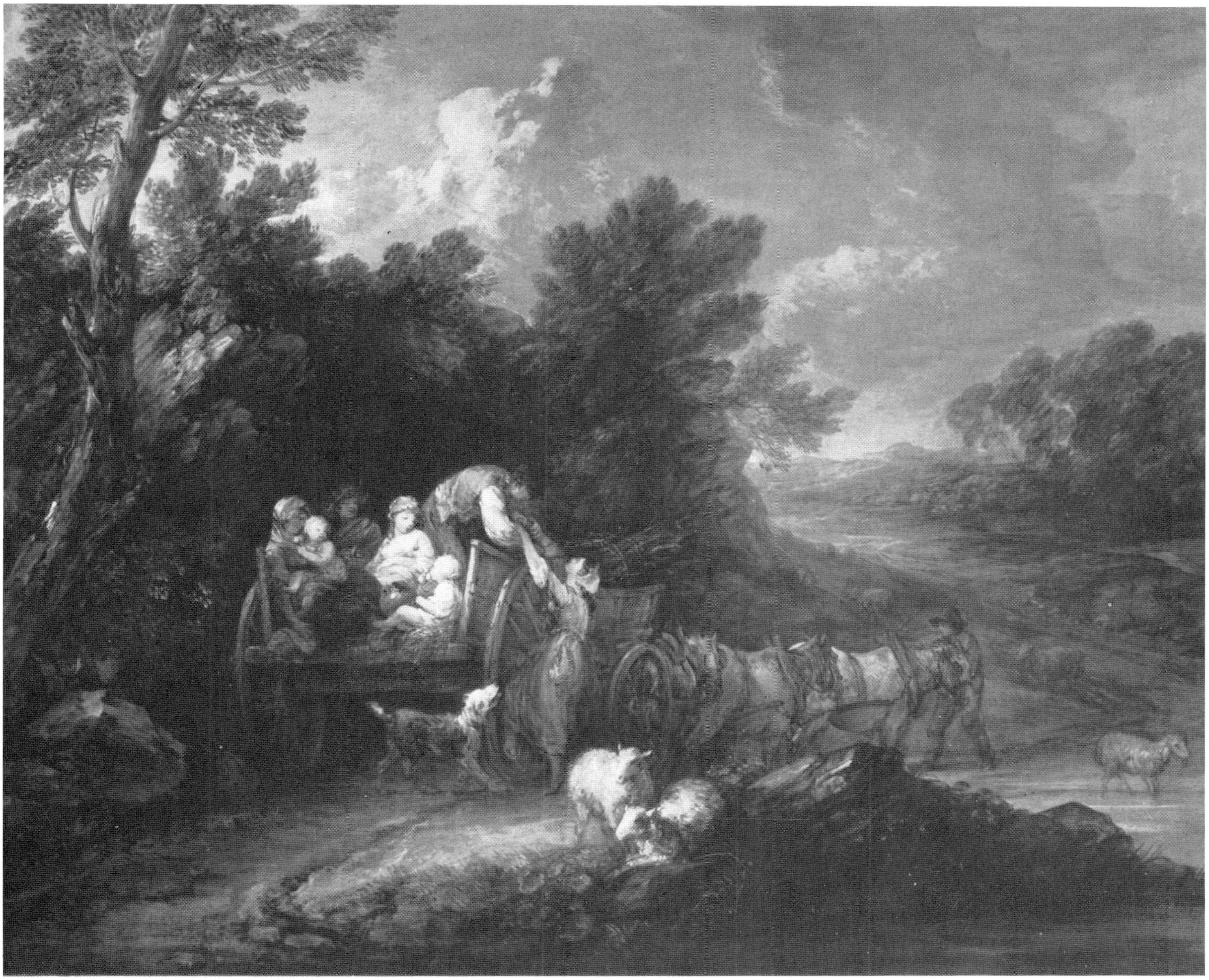

78. *The Harvest Waggon*. Canvas, 48 × 59 in. Signed. Painted winter 1784–5. Toronto, Art Gallery (Note 114)

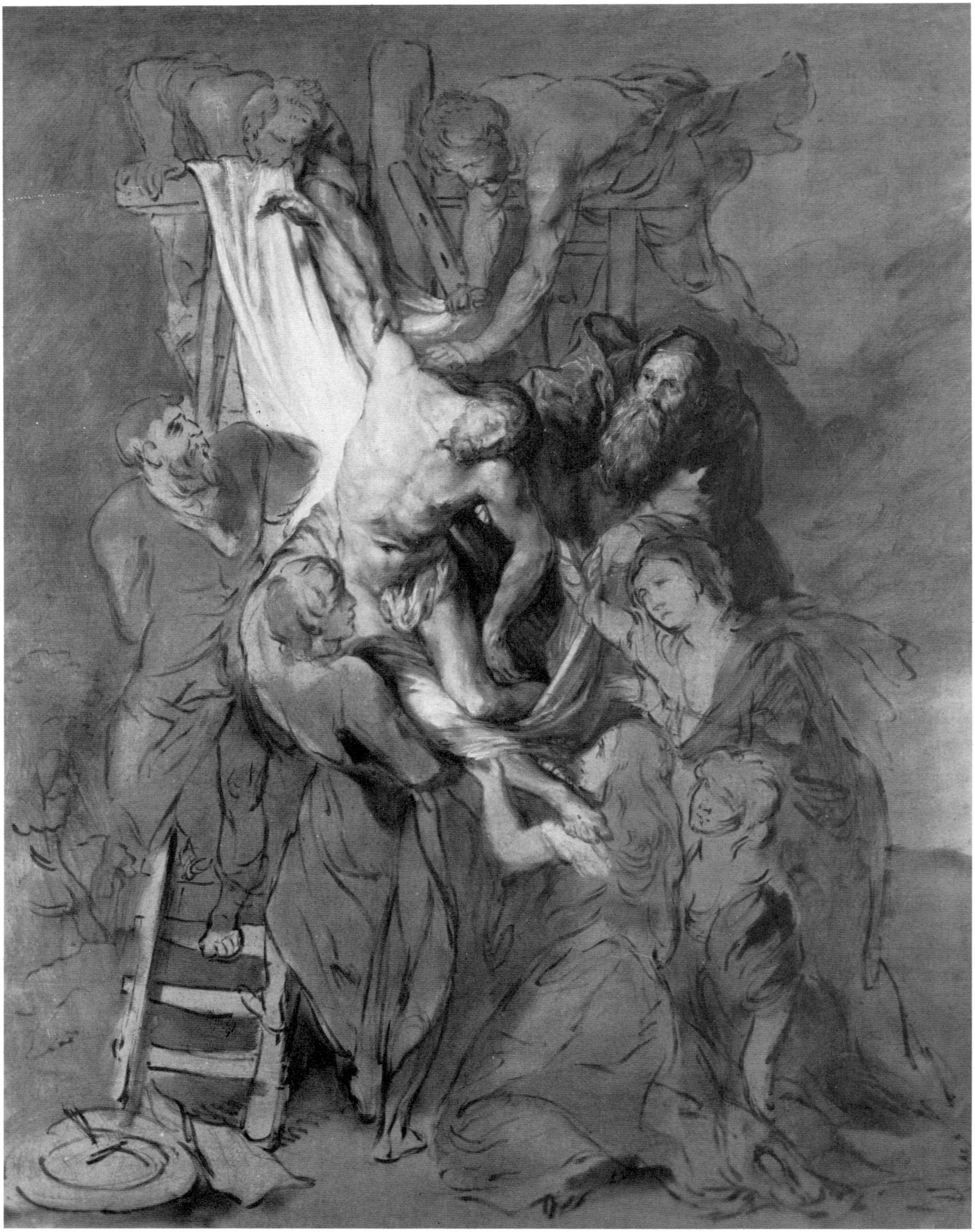

79. *The Descent from the Cross* (after Rubens). Canvas, 48 × 38½ in. Early to mid 1760s. Private Collection (Note 52)

80. Detail from Pl. 77 (Note 61)

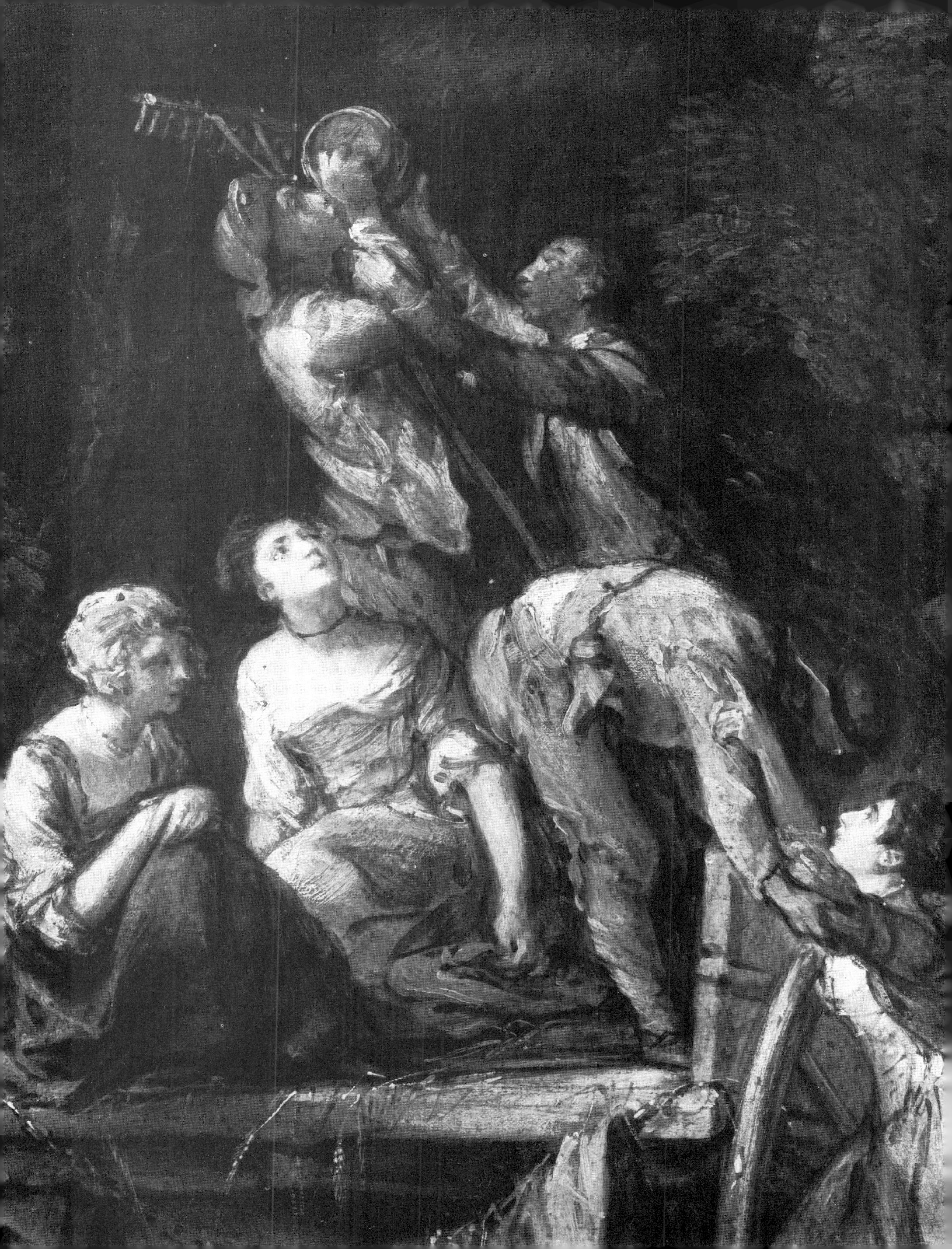

81. *Wooded landscape with boy reclining in a cart*. Pen and brown ink with grey and brown washes, $6\frac{15}{16} \times 8\frac{11}{16}$ in. Later 1760s. London, British Museum (Note 69)

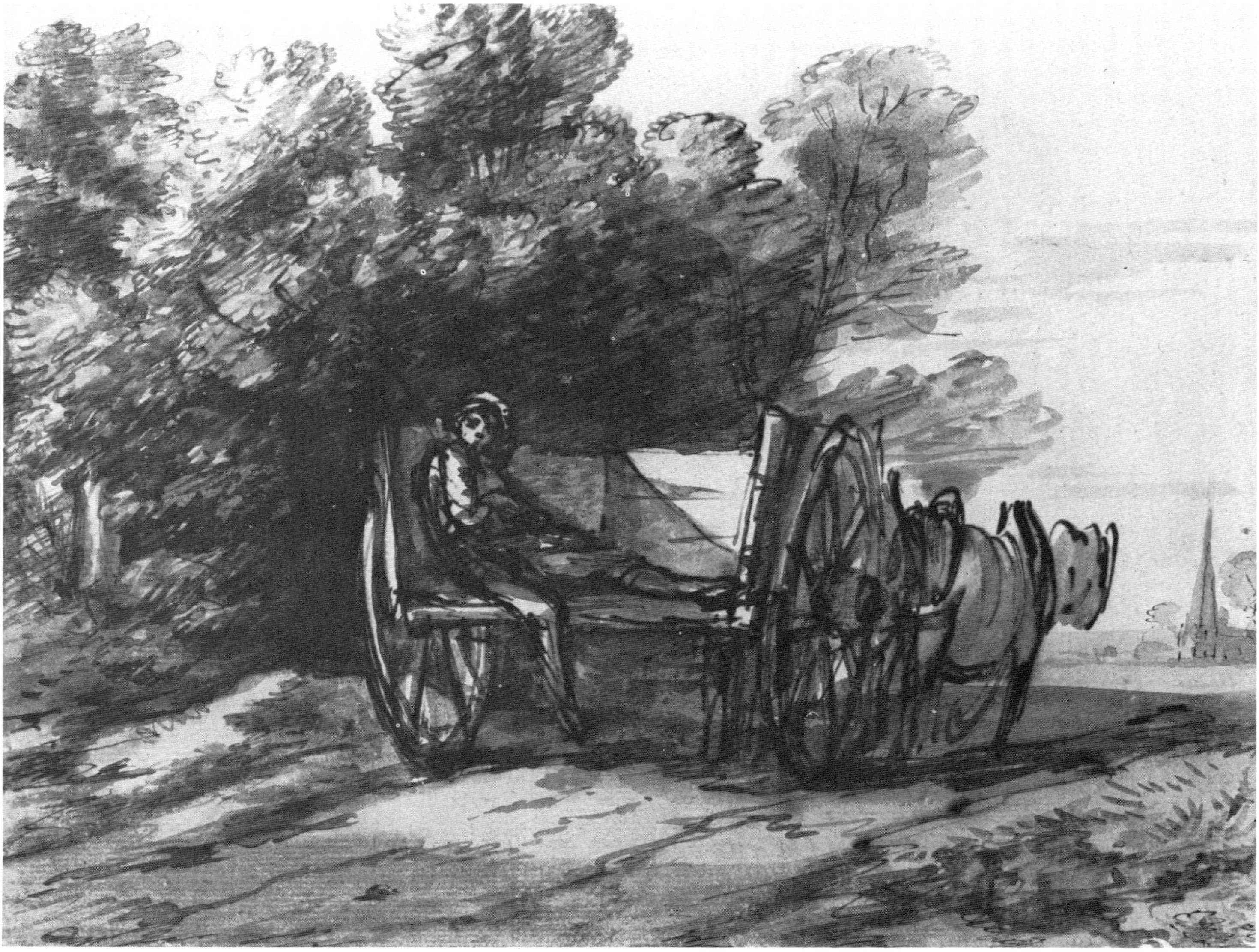

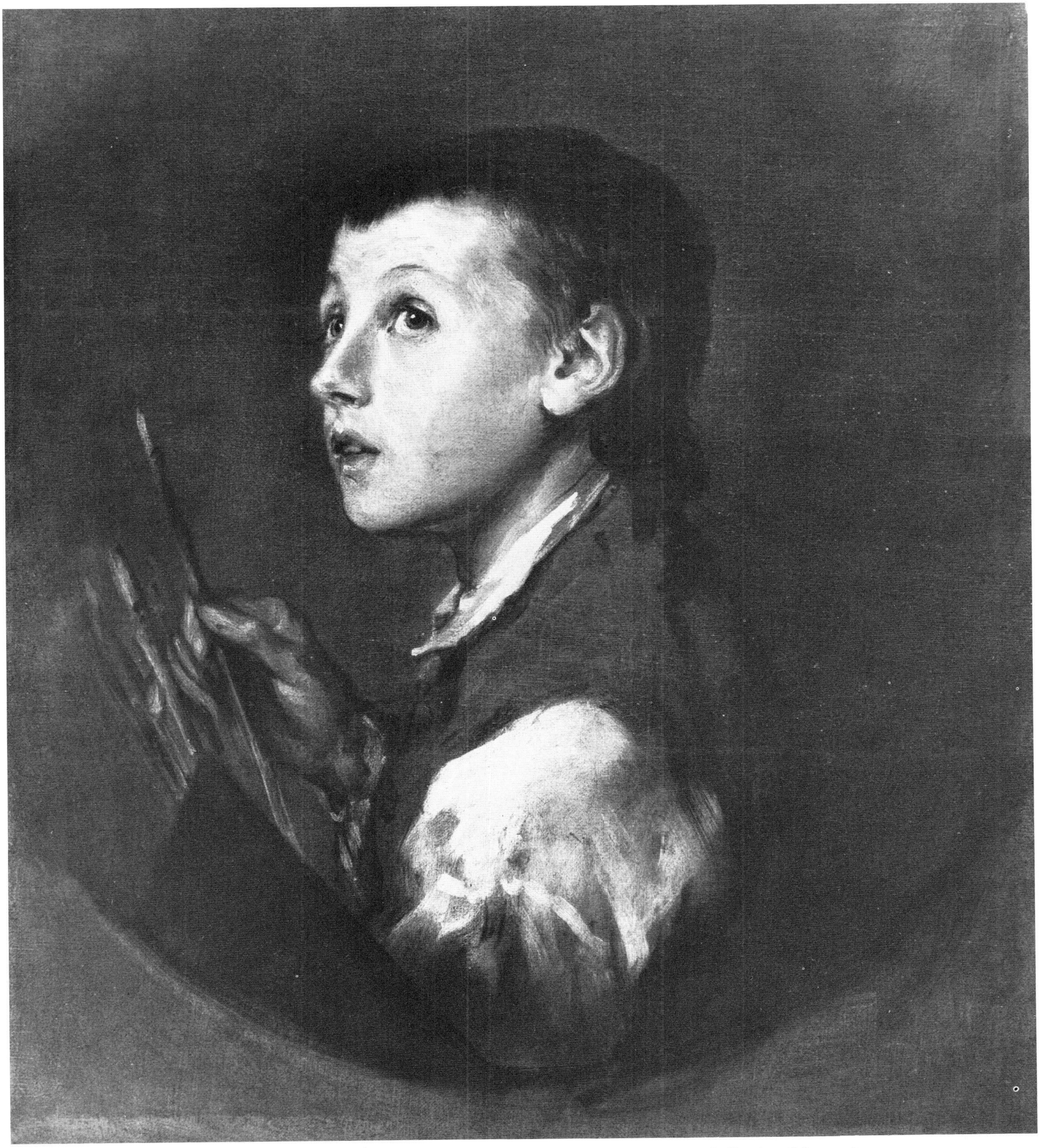

82. Unknown youth, known as '*The Pitminster Boy*'. Canvas, 23 × 20 in. Later 1760s. Private Collection (Note 70)

83. *Studies of a cat*. Black chalk and stump and white chalk on buff paper, 13 $\frac{1}{16}$ × 18 $\frac{1}{16}$ in. Signed. Mid to later 1760s. Amsterdam, Rijksmuseum (Note 68)

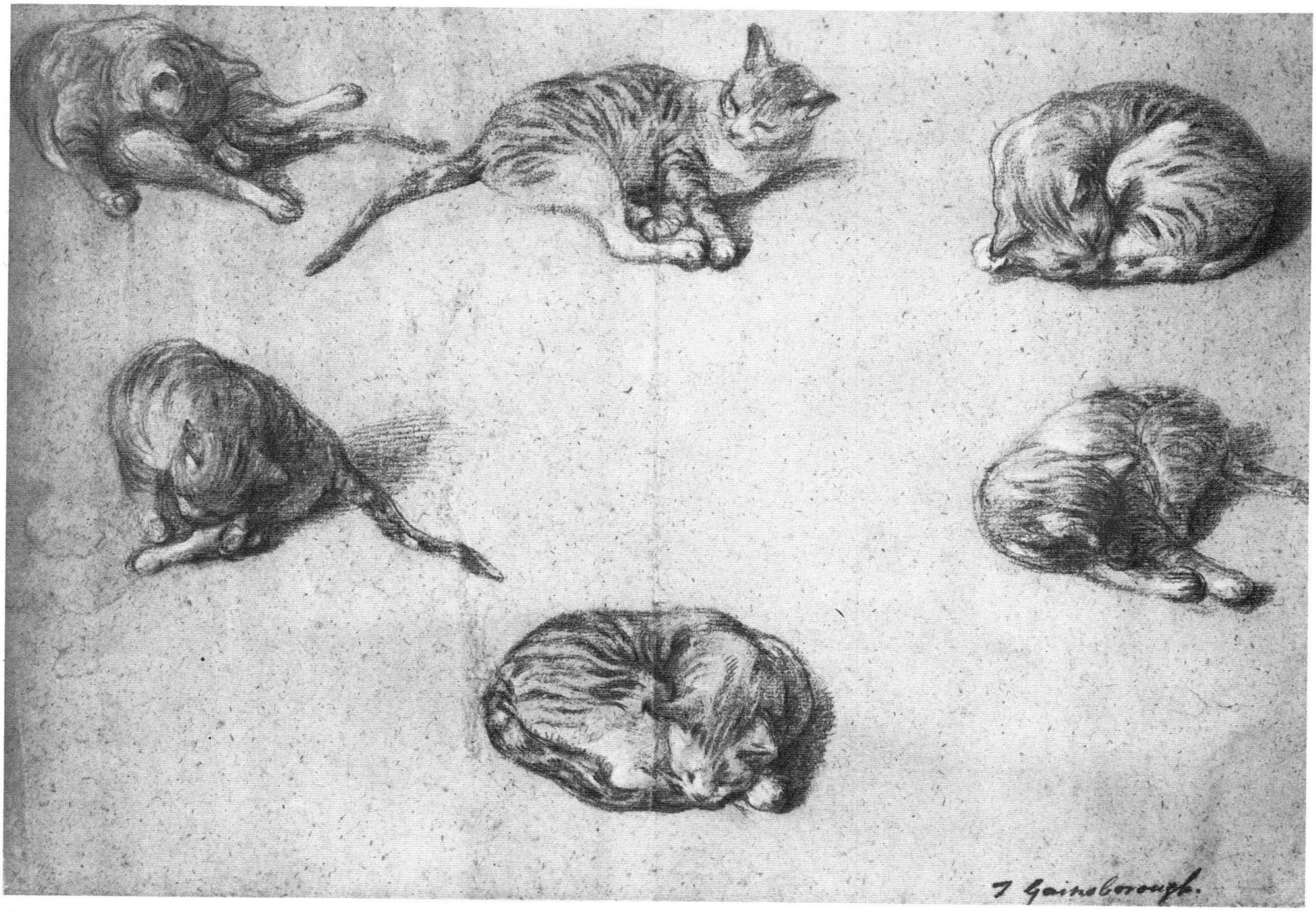

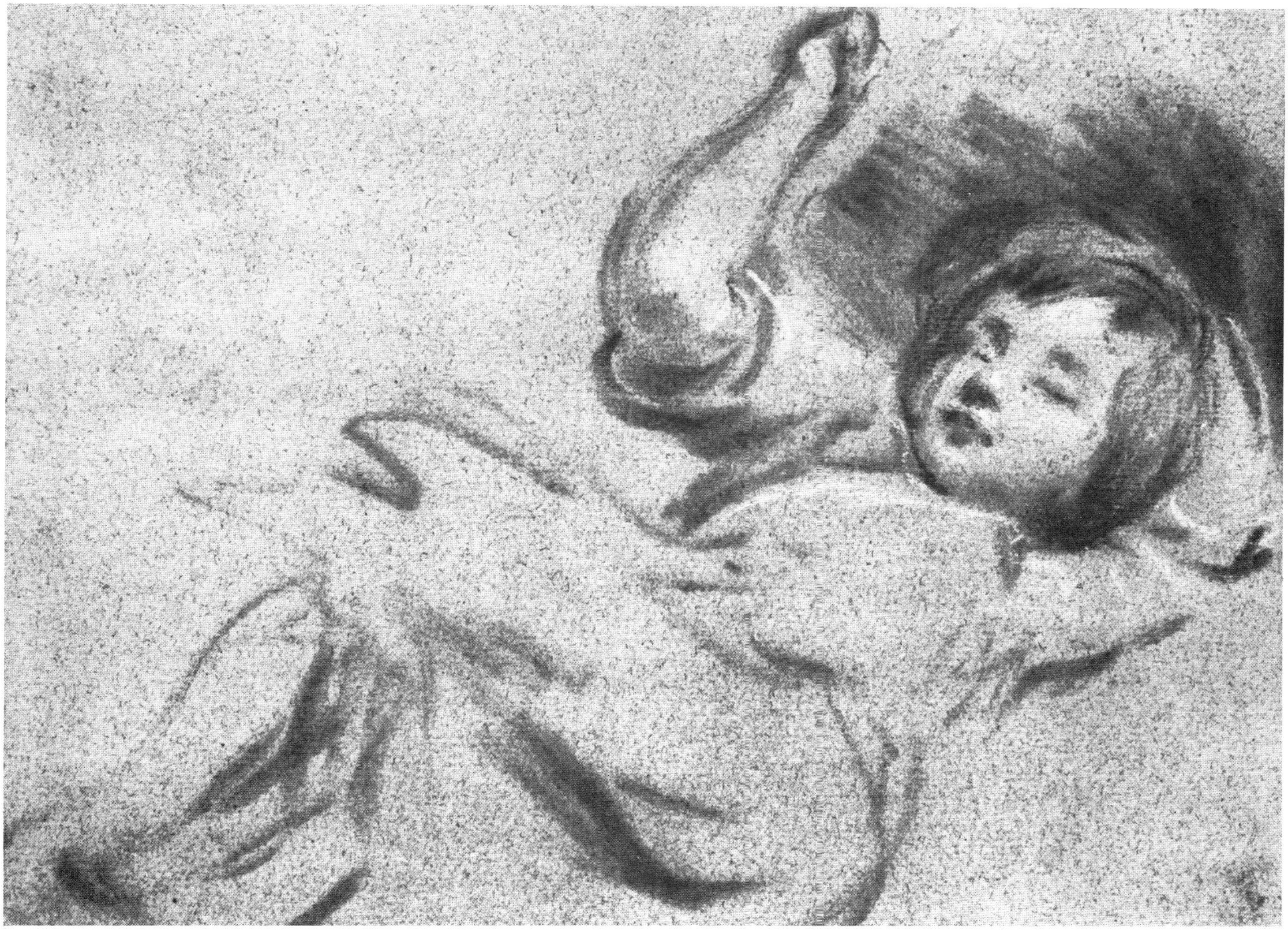

84. *Study of a child asleep*. Black chalk and stump and white chalk on blue paper, $5\frac{3}{4} \times 7\frac{9}{16}$ in. Early 1780s. Private Collection (Note 106)

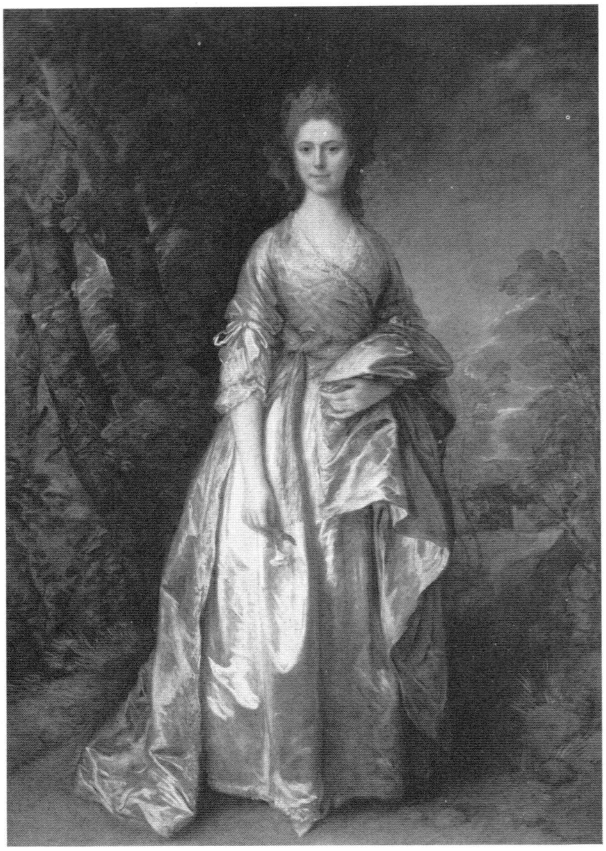

85. *Maria Marow, Lady Eardley* (1743–94). Canvas, $58\frac{1}{2} \times 85$ in. About 1766. Formerly Havana, The Hon. Oscar B. Cintas (Note 59)

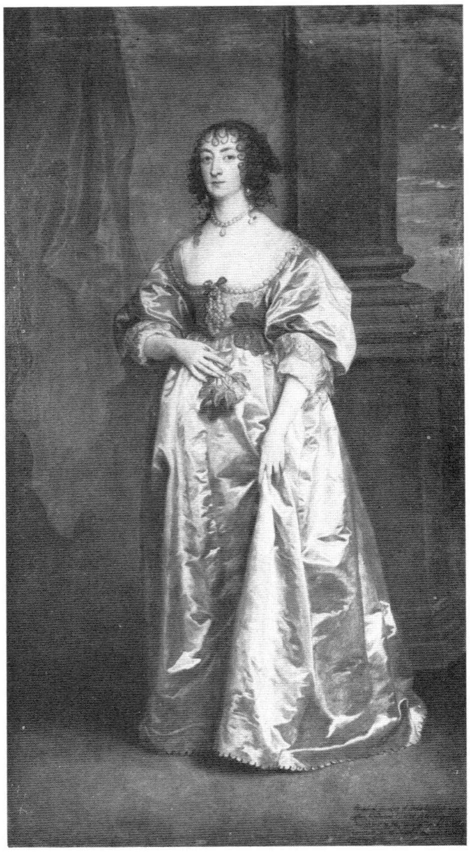

86. Sir Anthony Van Dyck (1599–1641): *Elizabeth Howard, Countess of Peterborough* (1603–71). Canvas, $91 \times 49\frac{1}{4}$ in. Drayton, Lionel Stopford Sackville

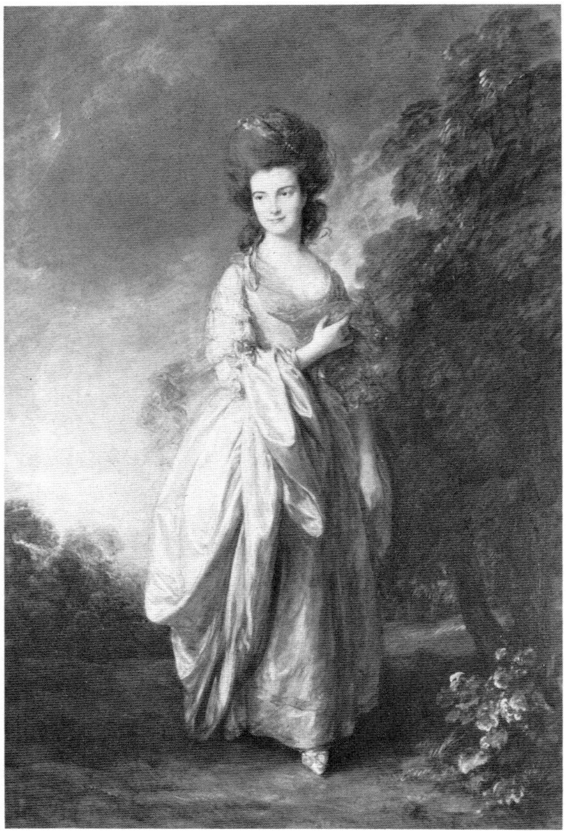

87. *Mrs Henry Beaufoy* (*c.* 1754–1826). Canvas, $90 \times 58\frac{3}{4}$ in. Exhibited R. A. 1780 (84). San Marino, Henry E. Huntington Art Gallery (Note 96)

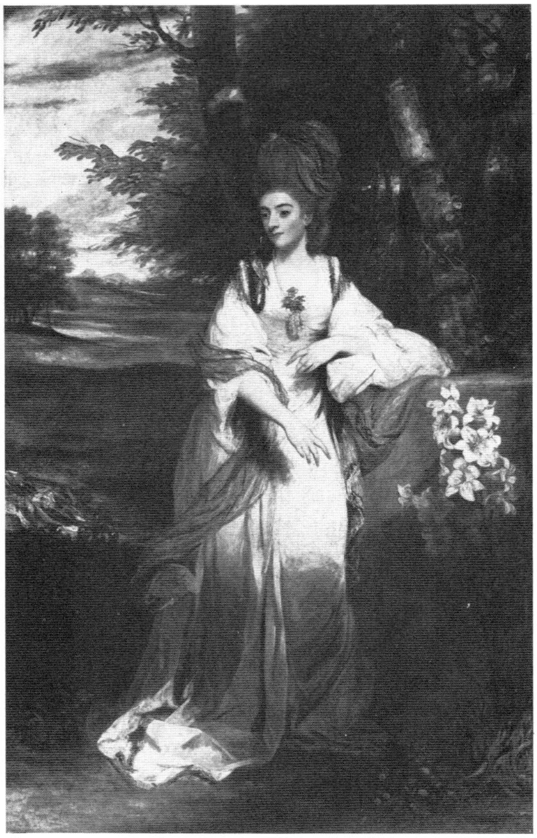

88. Sir Joshua Reynolds (1723–92): *Catherine, Lady Bamfylde* (*c.* 1754–1832). Canvas, $93\frac{3}{4} \times 58\frac{1}{4}$ in. Exhibited R. A. 1777 (283). London, Tate Gallery

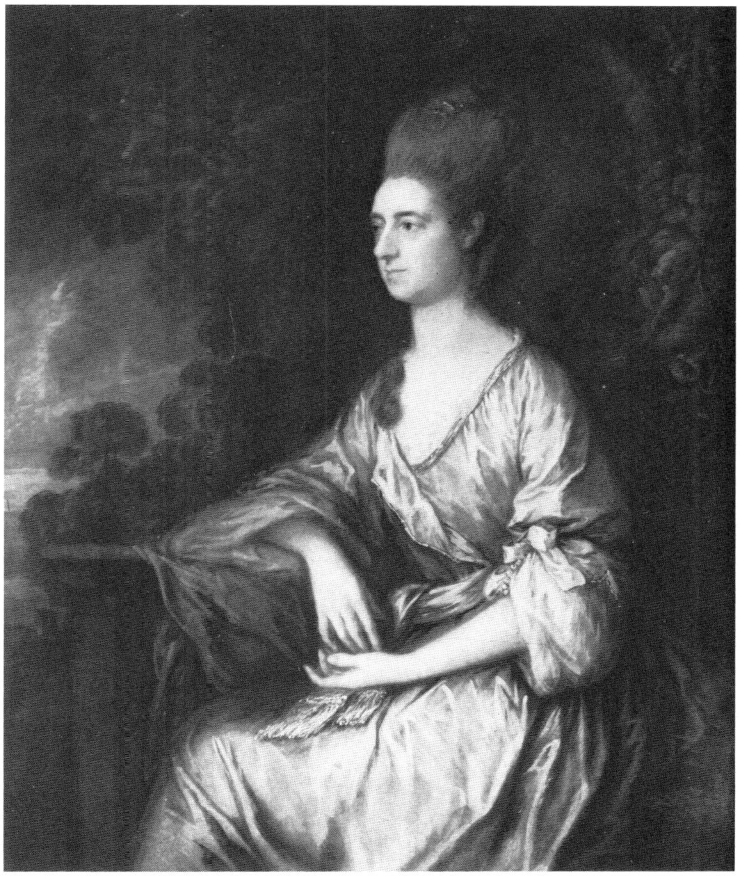

89. *Frances Catherine, Countess of Dartmouth* (*c.* 1733–1805). Canvas, 49 × 39 in. Receipt for payment dated May 1769. Patshull, Earl of Dartmouth (Note 71)

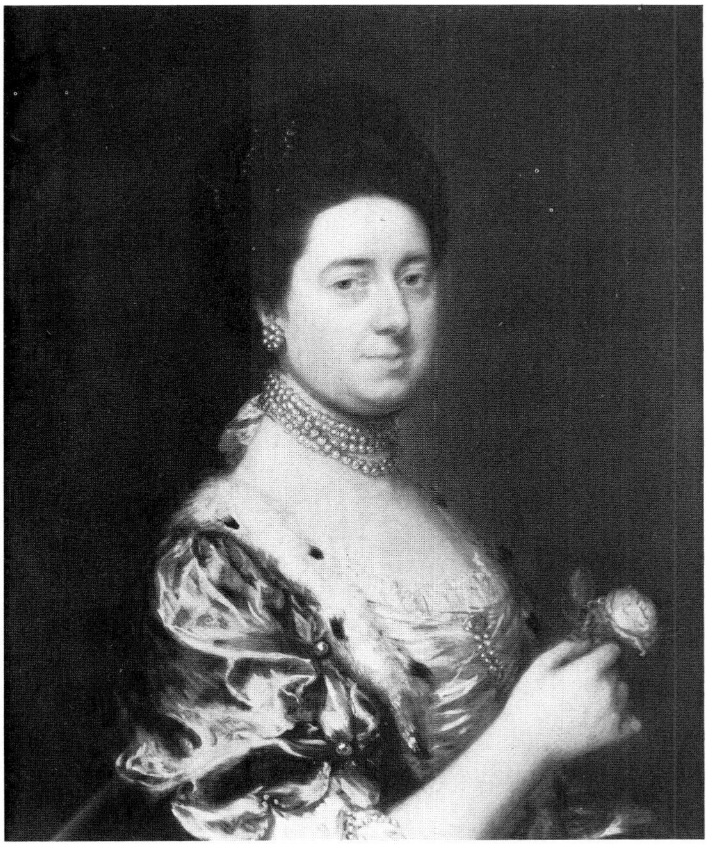

90. *Frances Catherine, Countess of Dartmouth* (*c.* 1733–1805). Canvas, 30 × 25 in. About 1771. Patshull, Earl of Dartmouth (Note 71)

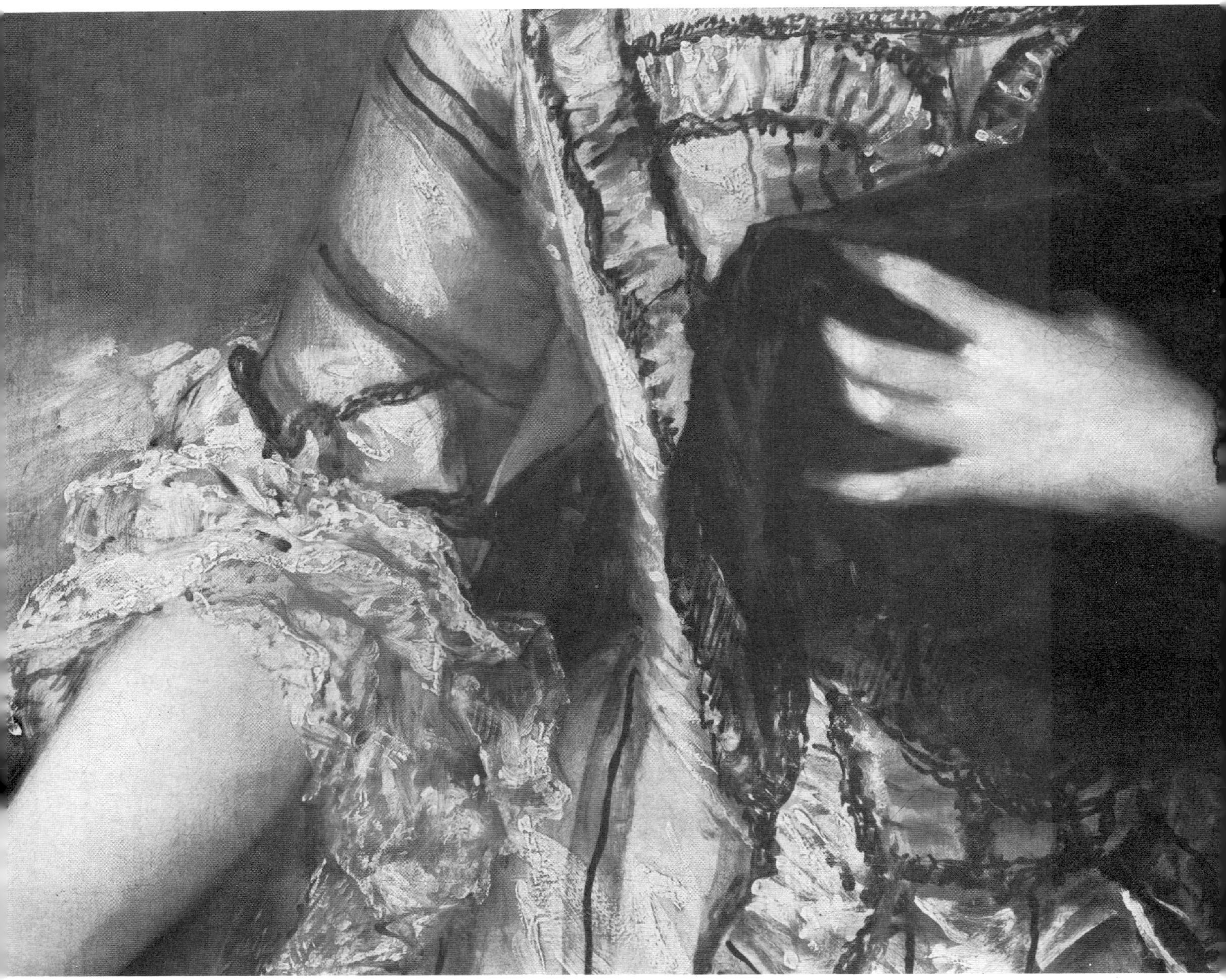

91. Detail from Pl. 92 (Note 72)

92. *Isabella, Viscountess Molyneux, later Countess of Sefton* (1748–1819). Canvas, 92 × 60 in. Exhibited R. A. 1769 (35). Liverpool, Walker Art Gallery (Note 72)

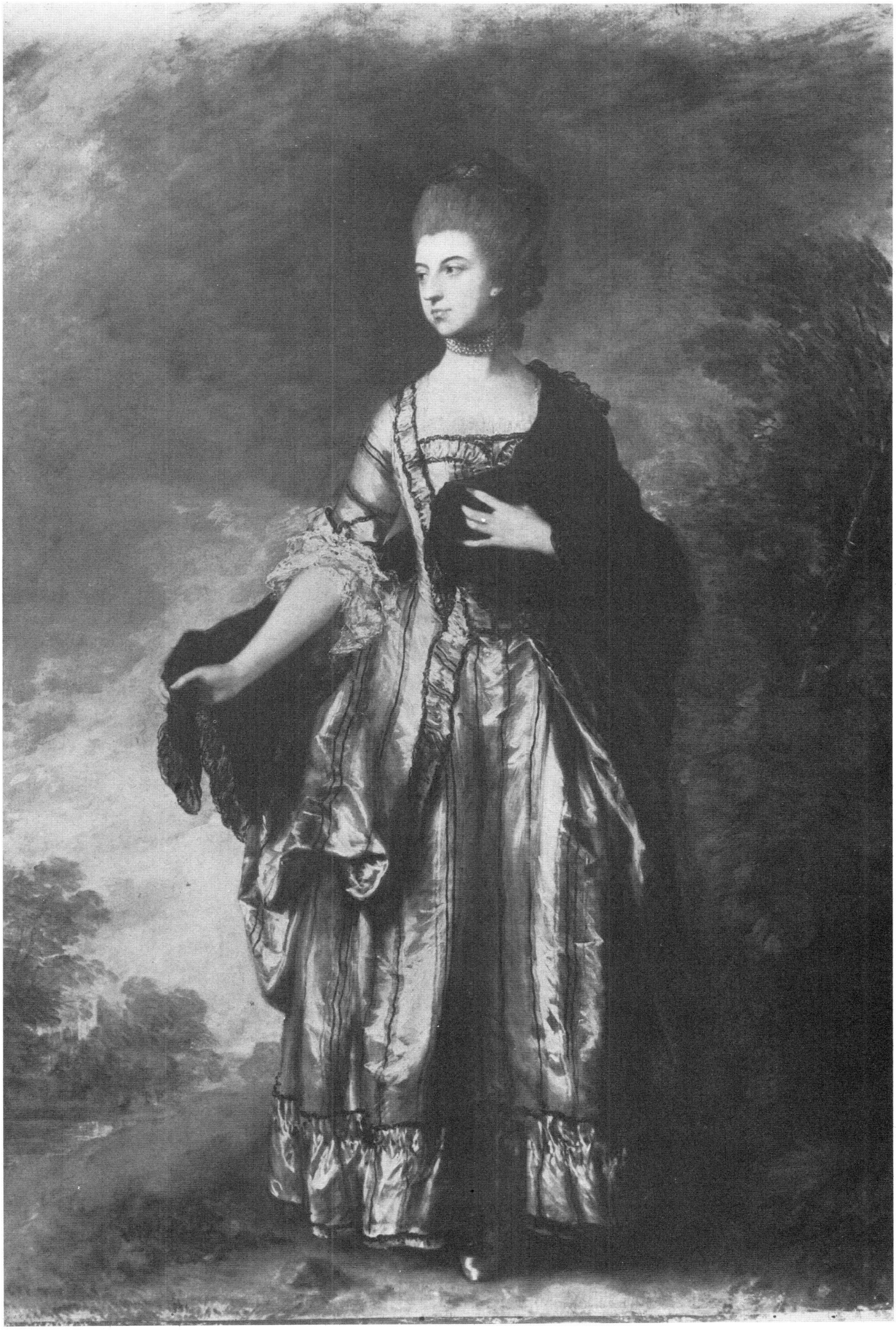

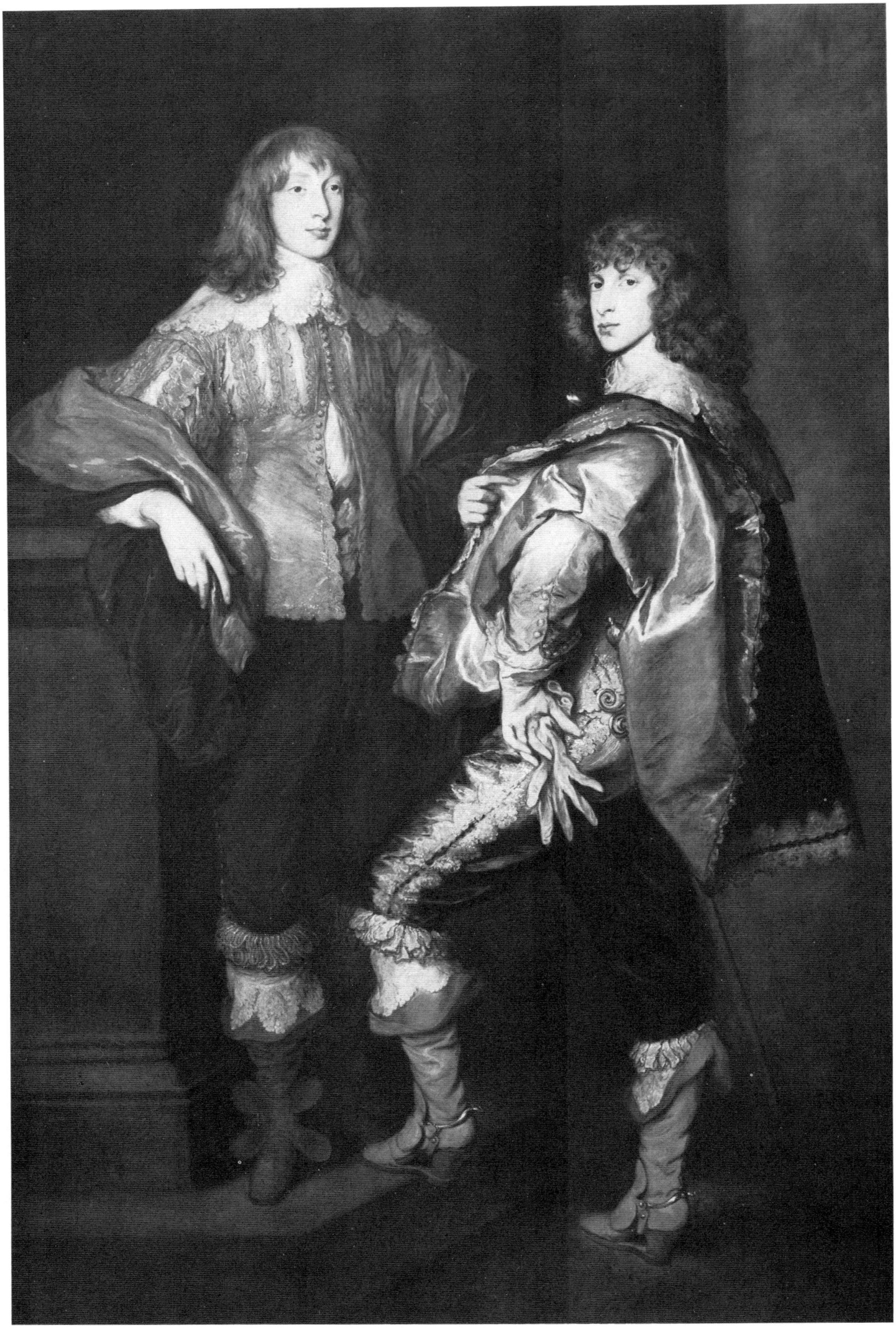

93. *Lords John and Bernard Stuart* (after Van Dyck). Canvas, $92\frac{1}{2} \times 57\frac{1}{2}$ in. Early to mid 1760s. St Louis, Missouri, Art Museum (Note 53)

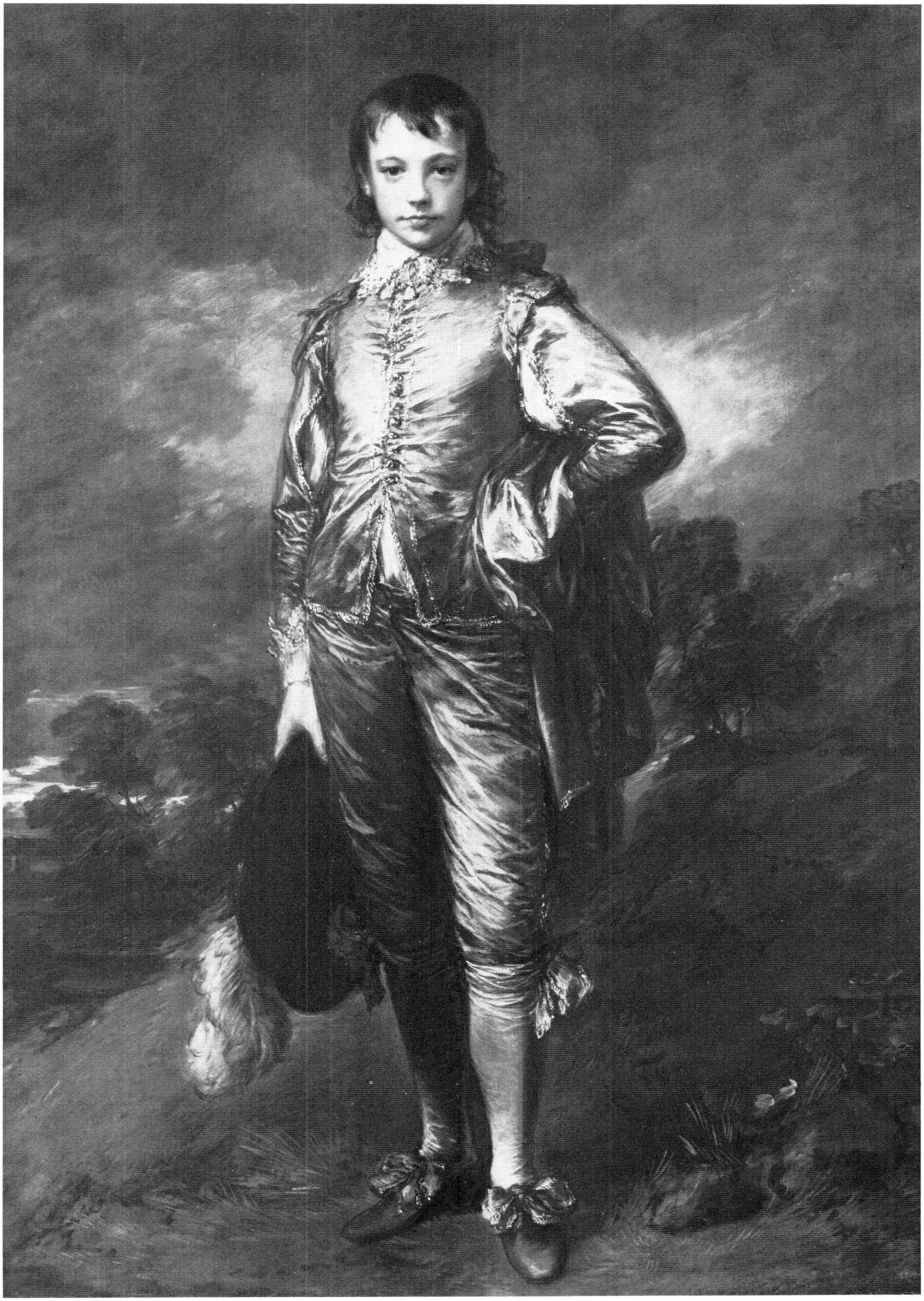

94. Jonathan Buttall (d. 1805), known as '*The Blue Boy*'. Canvas, 70 × 48 in. Exhibited R. A. 1770 (85). San Marino, Henry E. Huntington Art Gallery (Note 73)

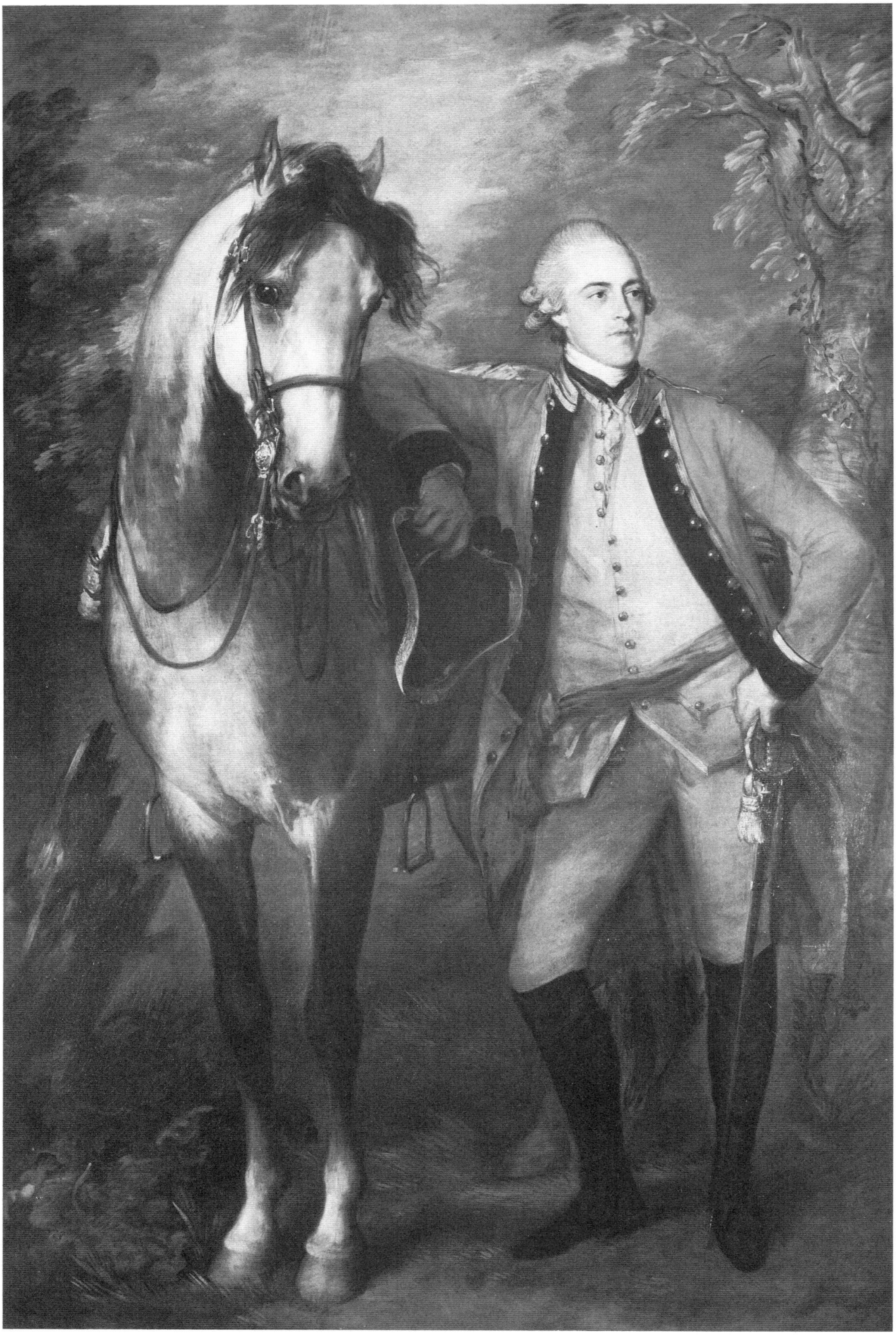

95. *Edward, 2nd Viscount Ligonier* (1740–82). Canvas, $92\frac{1}{2} \times 61\frac{1}{2}$ in. Painted 1770. Exhibited R. A. 1771 (76). San Marino, Henry E. Huntington Art Gallery (Note 75)

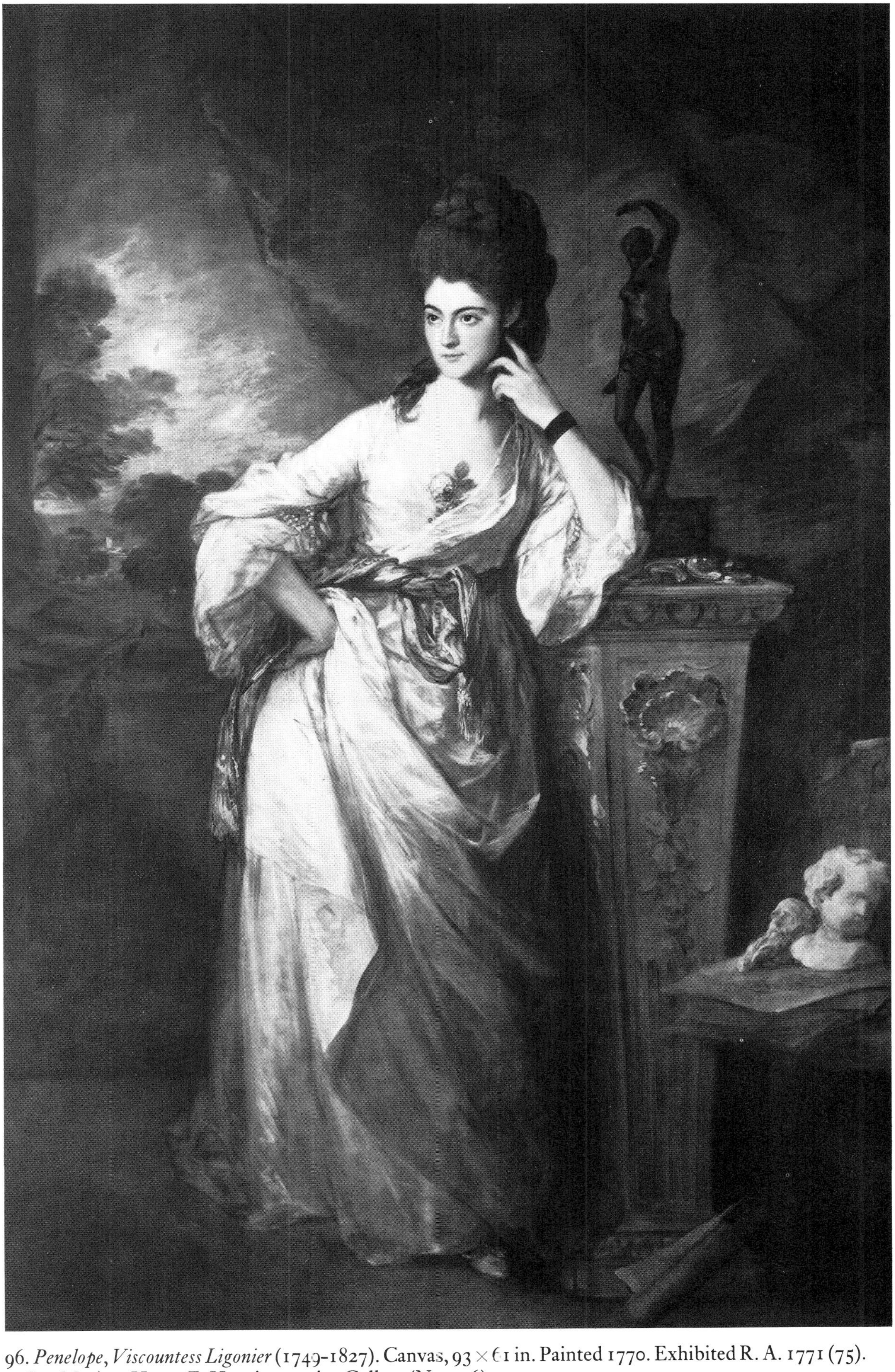

96. *Penelope, Viscountess Ligonier* (1749–1827). Canvas, 93 × 61 in. Painted 1770. Exhibited R. A. 1771 (75). San Marino, Henry E. Huntington Art Gallery (Note 76)

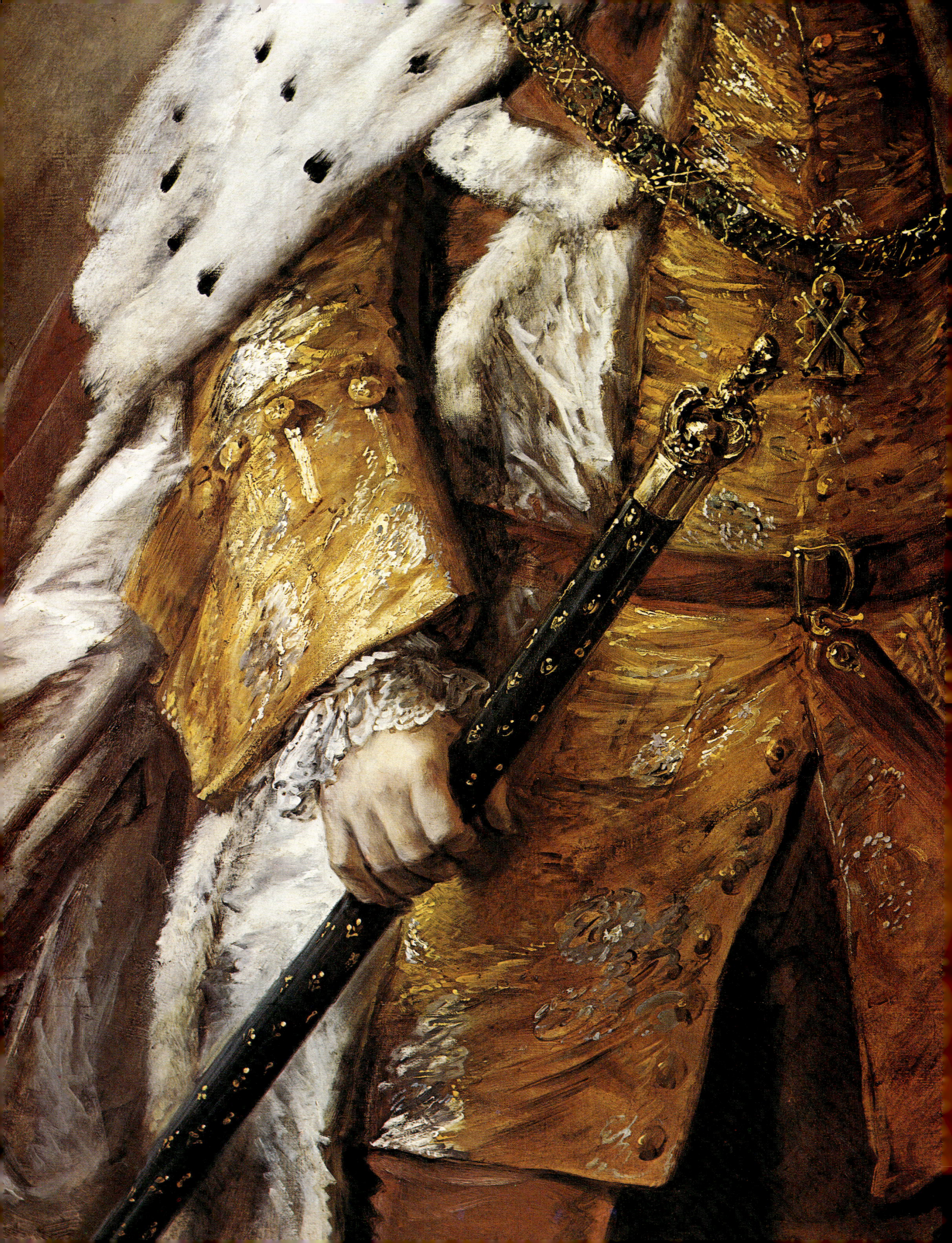

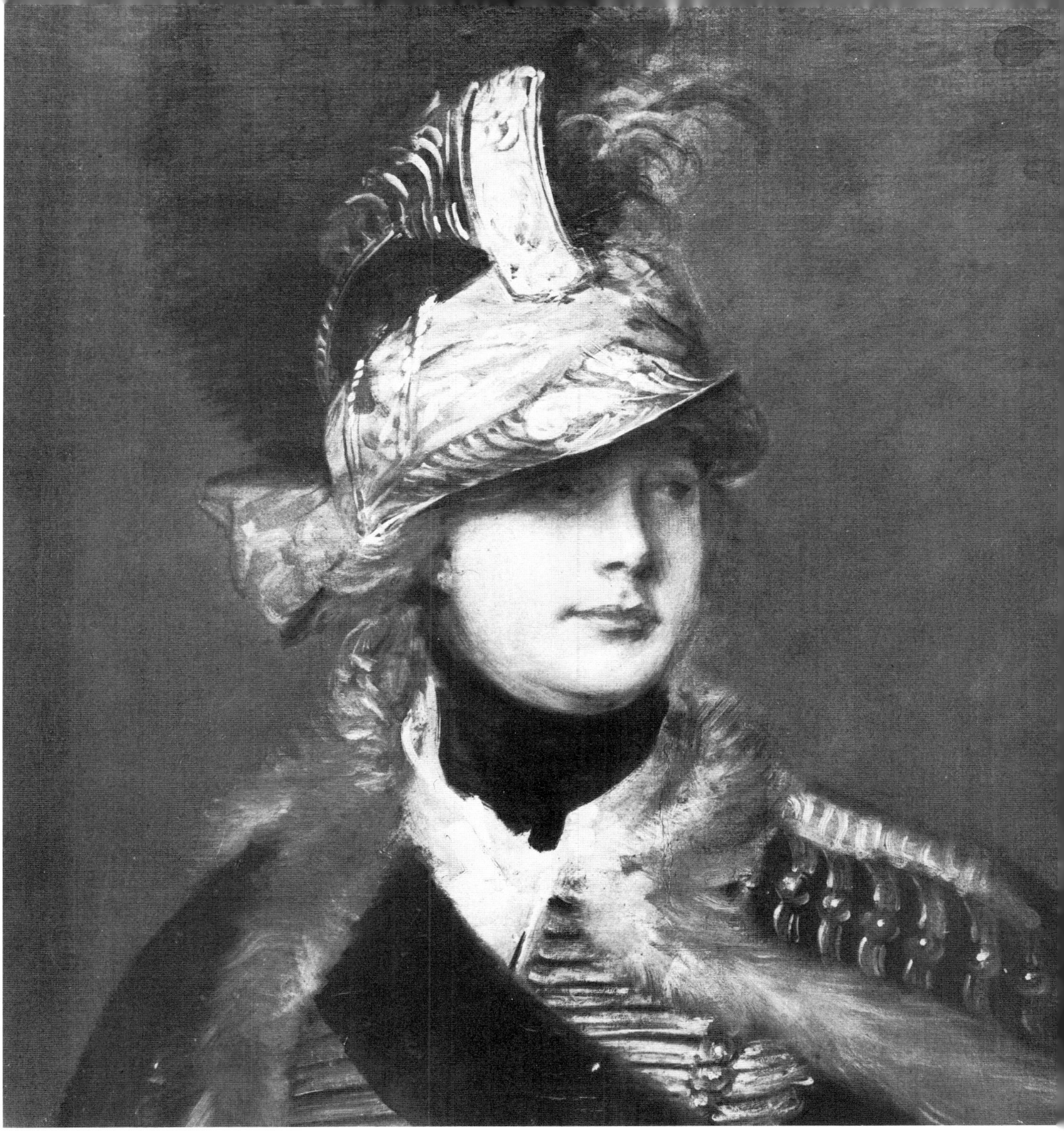

98. Detail from *George, Prince of Wales, later George IV* (1762-1830). Canvas, $88\frac{3}{4} \times 60\frac{1}{2}$ in. Painted winter 1784. Finished by an early nineteenth-century artist, possibly Jacques-Laurent Agasse. Private Collection (Note 112)

97. Detail from Pl. 75 (Note 64)

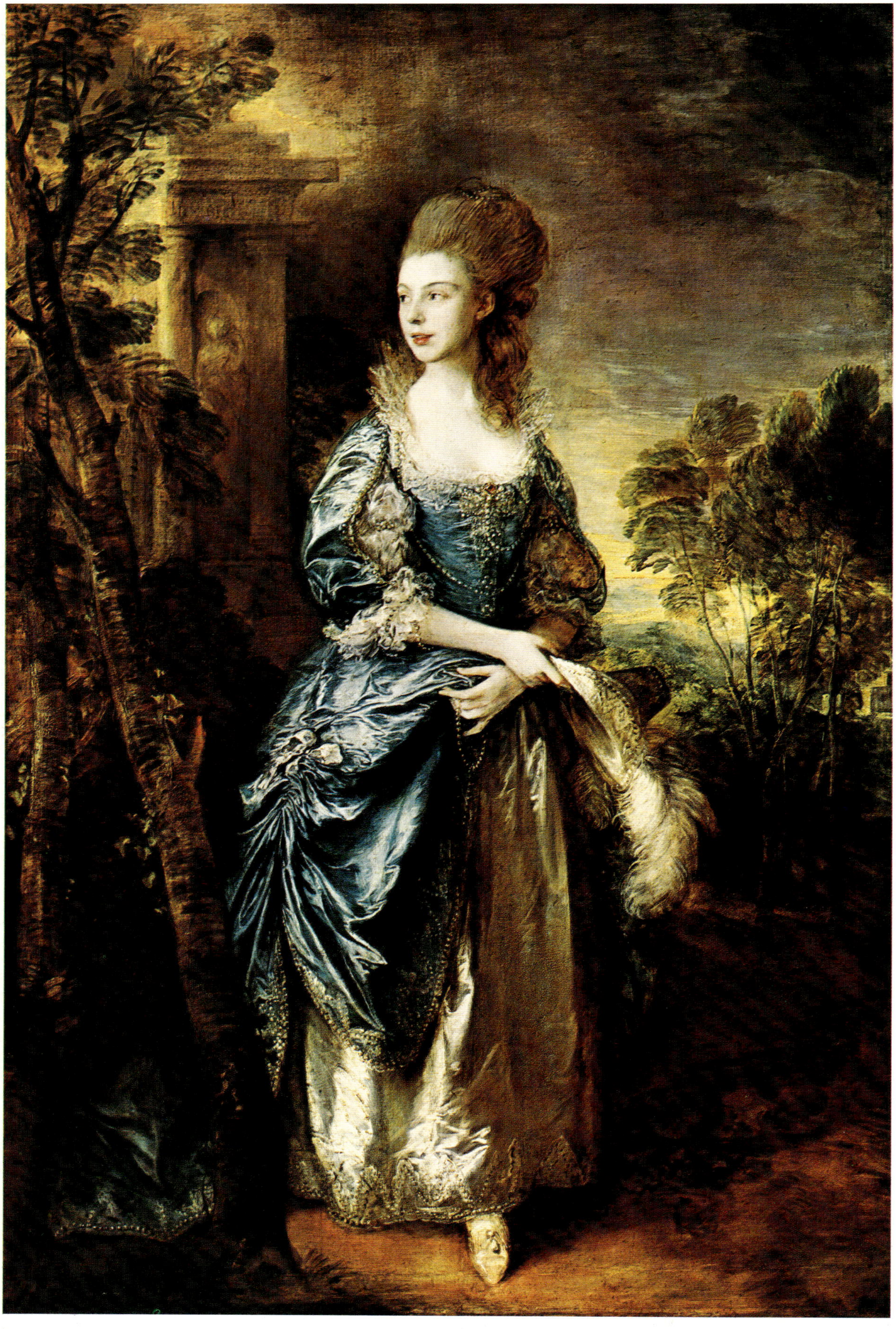

99. *The Hon. Frances Duncombe* (1757–1827). Canvas, $92\frac{1}{4} \times 62\frac{1}{8}$ in. About 1778. New York, Frick Collection (Note 92)

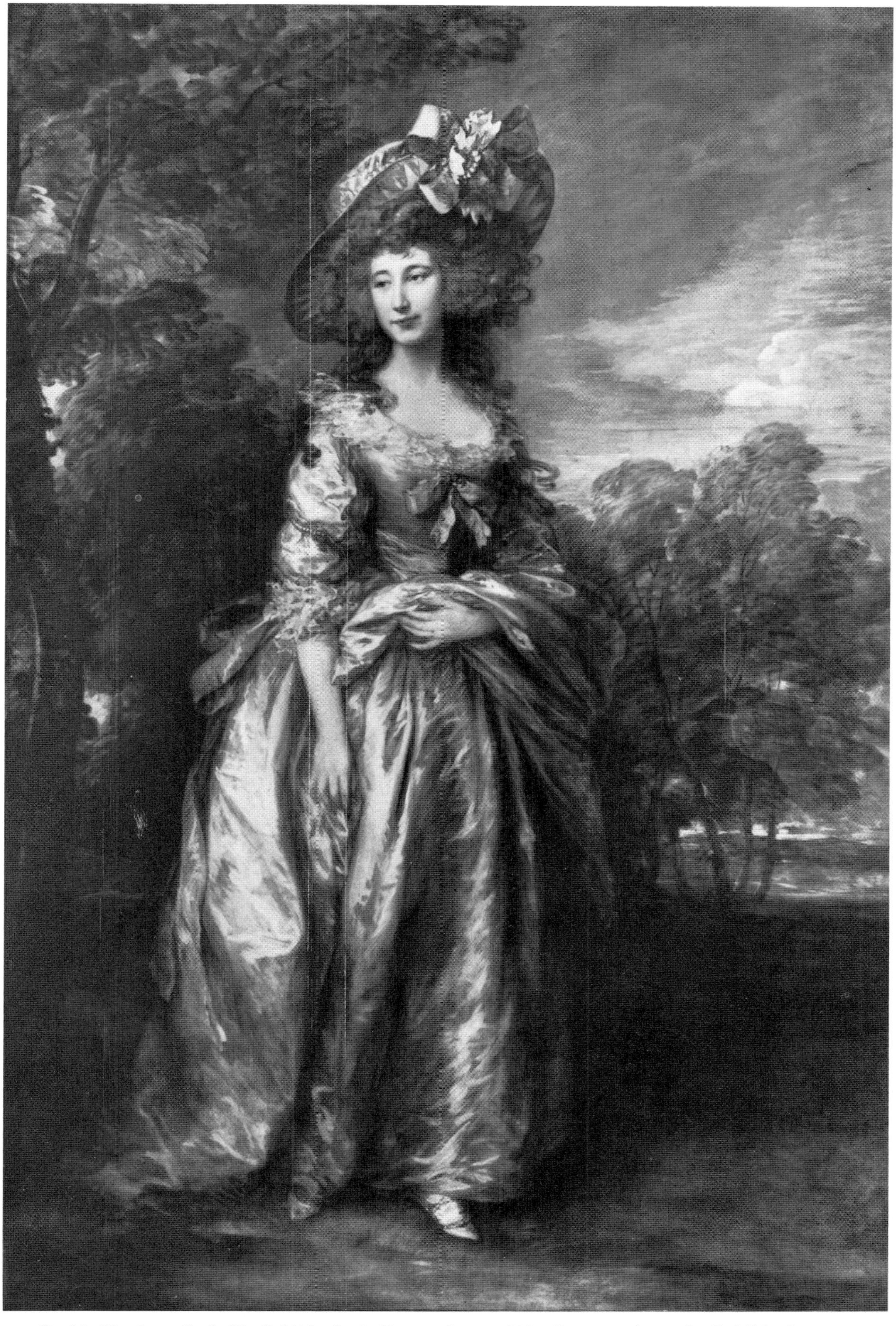

100. *Sophia Charlotte, Lady Sheffield* (d. 1815). Canvas, $89\frac{1}{2} \times 58\frac{3}{4}$ in. Begun spring 1785. Exhibited Schomberg House, April 1786. National Trust, Waddesdon Manor (Note 121)

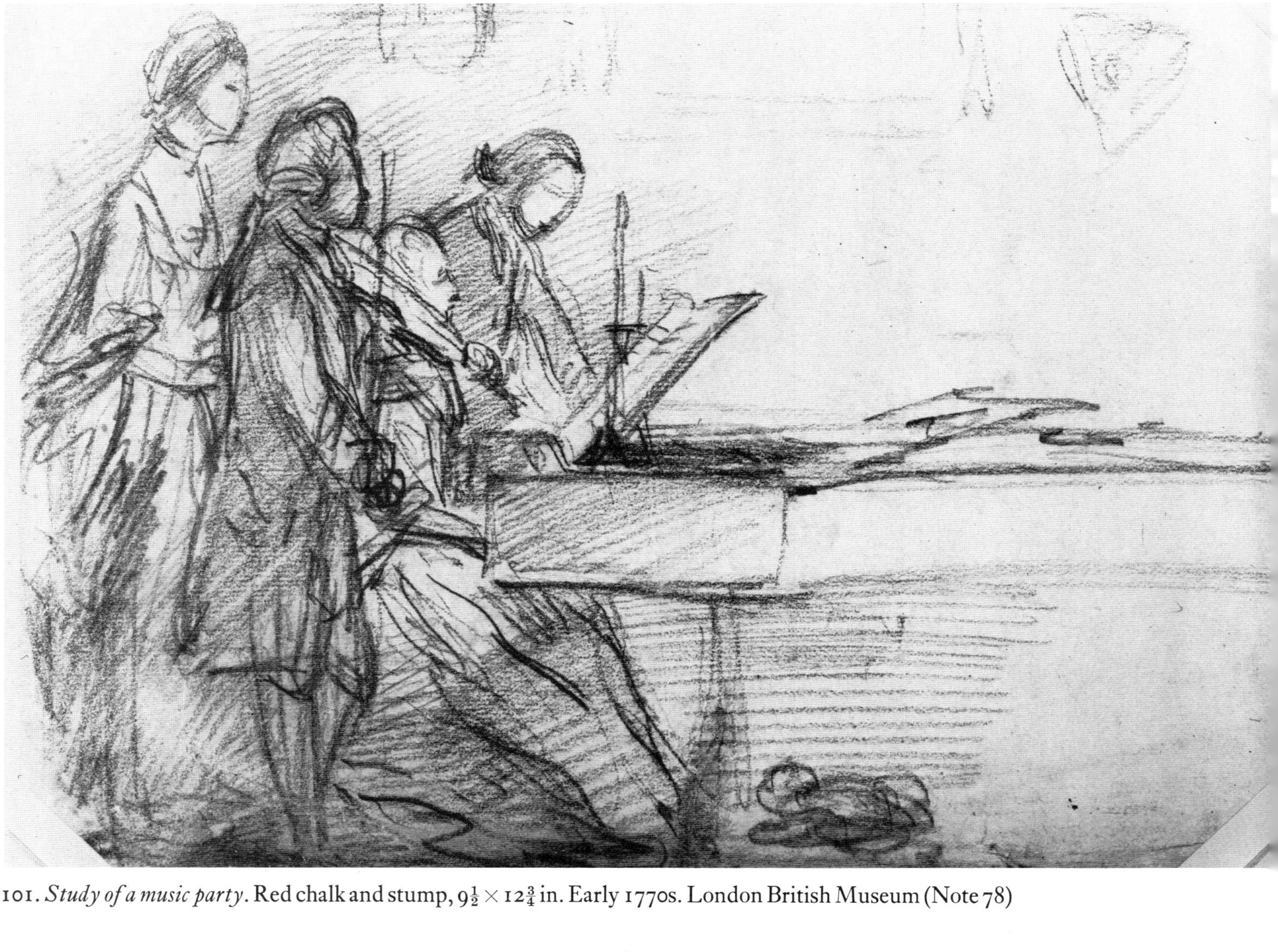

101. *Study of a music party*. Red chalk and stump, $9\frac{1}{2} \times 12\frac{3}{4}$ in. Early 1770s. London British Museum (Note 78)

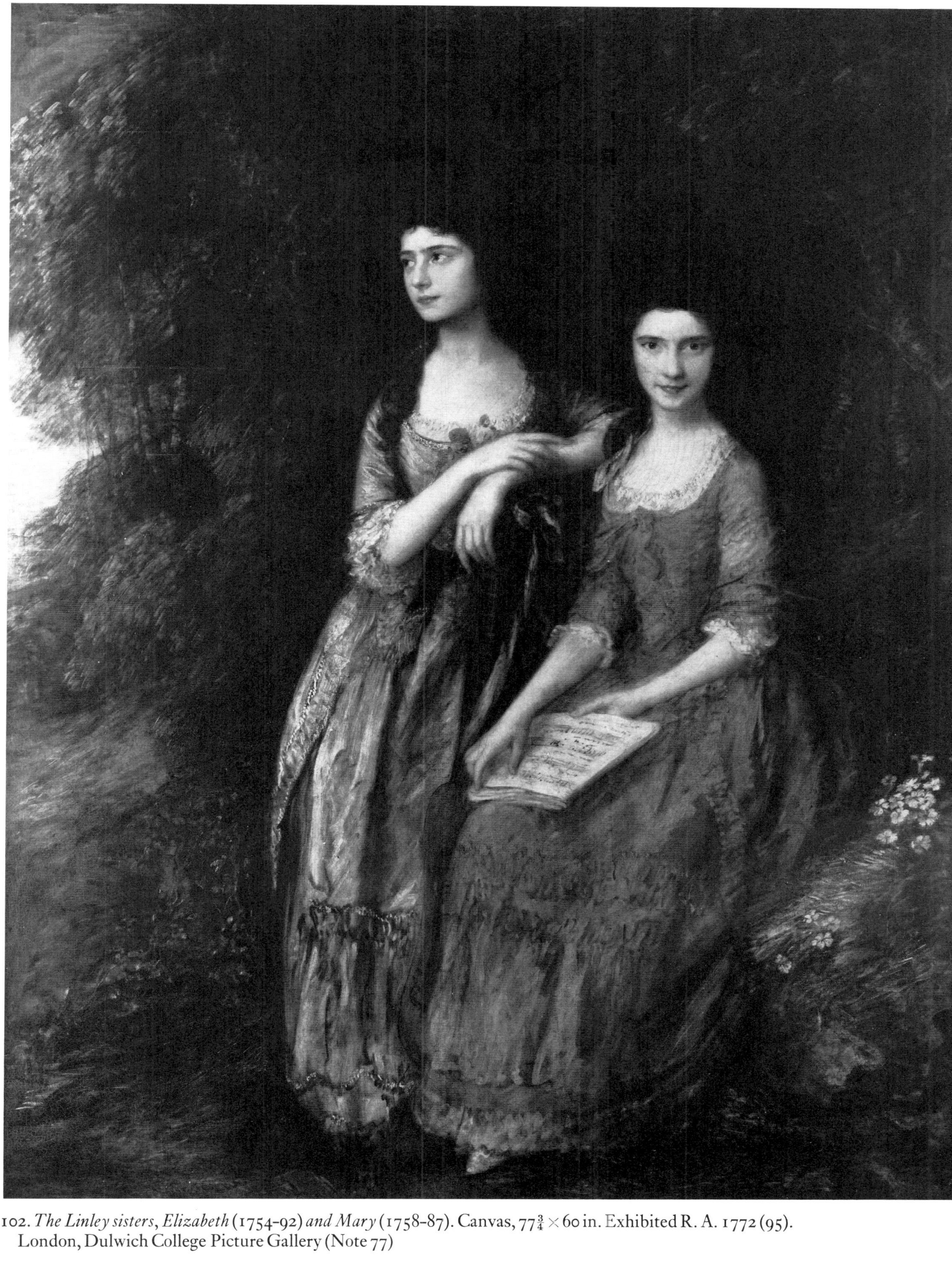

102. *The Linley sisters*, *Elizabeth* (1754-92) *and Mary* (1758-87). Canvas, $77\frac{3}{4} \times 60$ in. Exhibited R. A. 1772 (95). London, Dulwich College Picture Gallery (Note 77)

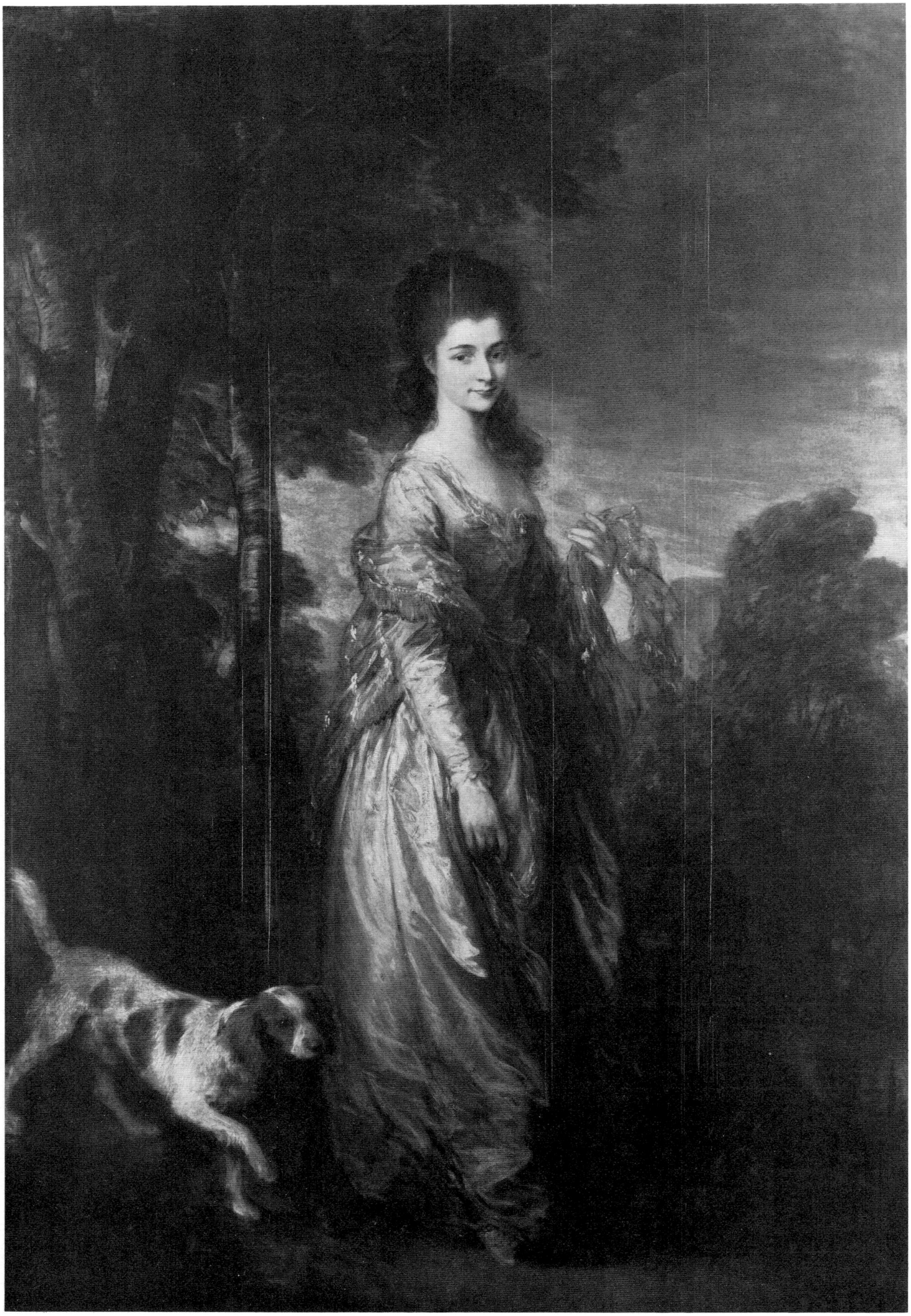

103. *Mrs William Lowndes-Stone* (?1758–1837). Canvas, $91\frac{3}{4} \times 60\frac{1}{2}$ in. About 1775. Lisbon, Gulbenkian Foundation (Note 84)

104. Detail from Pl. 103 (Note 84)

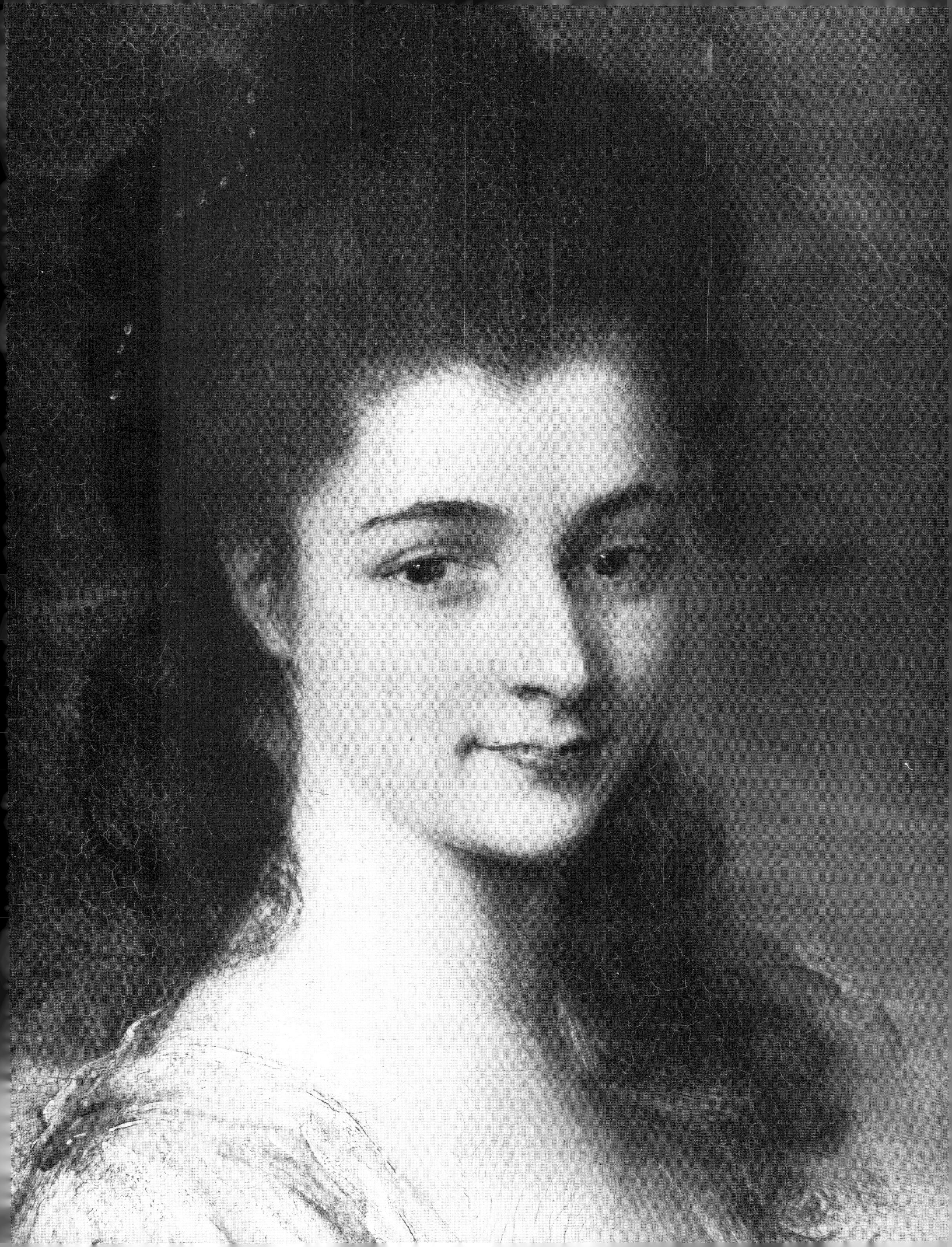

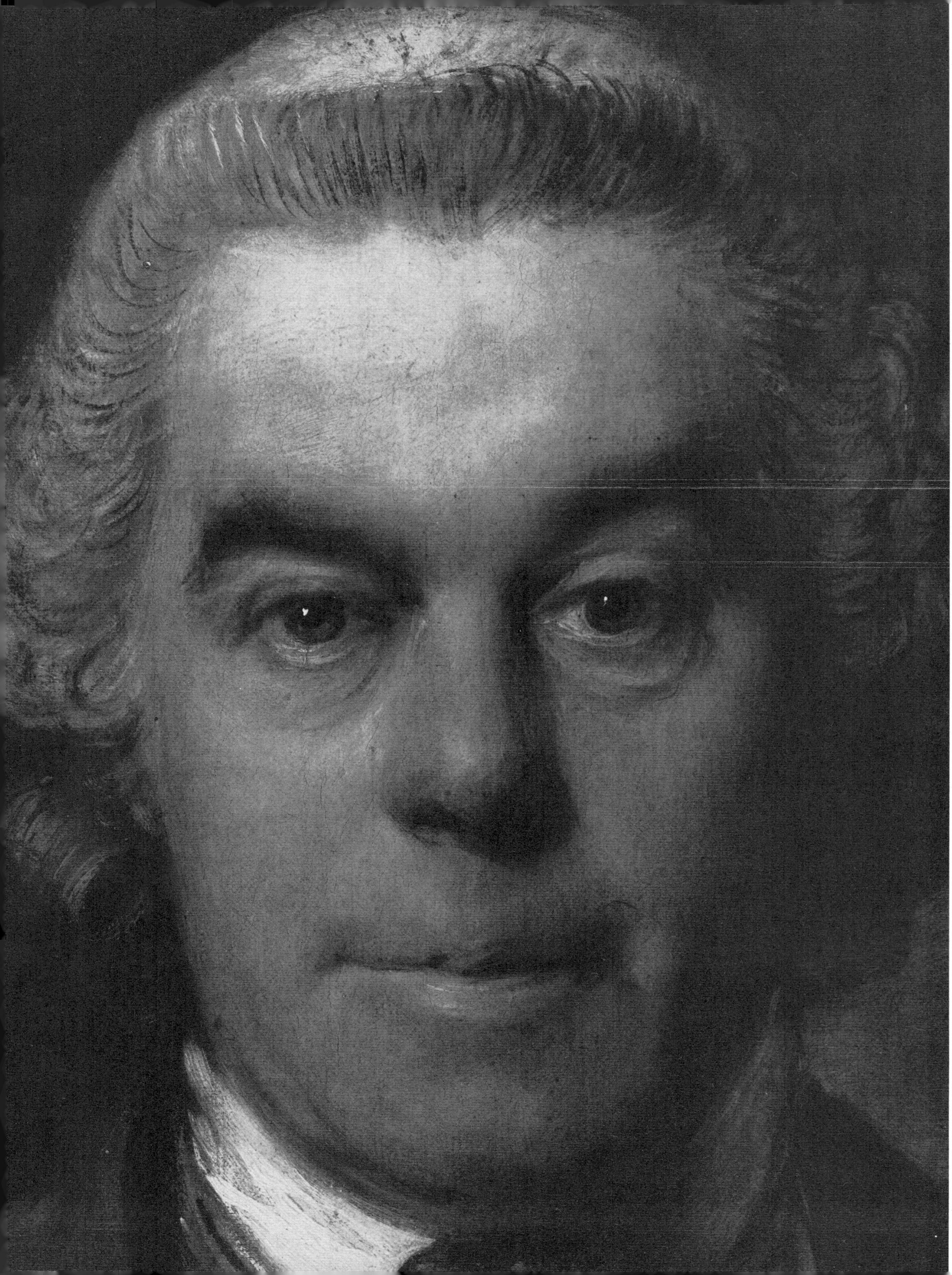

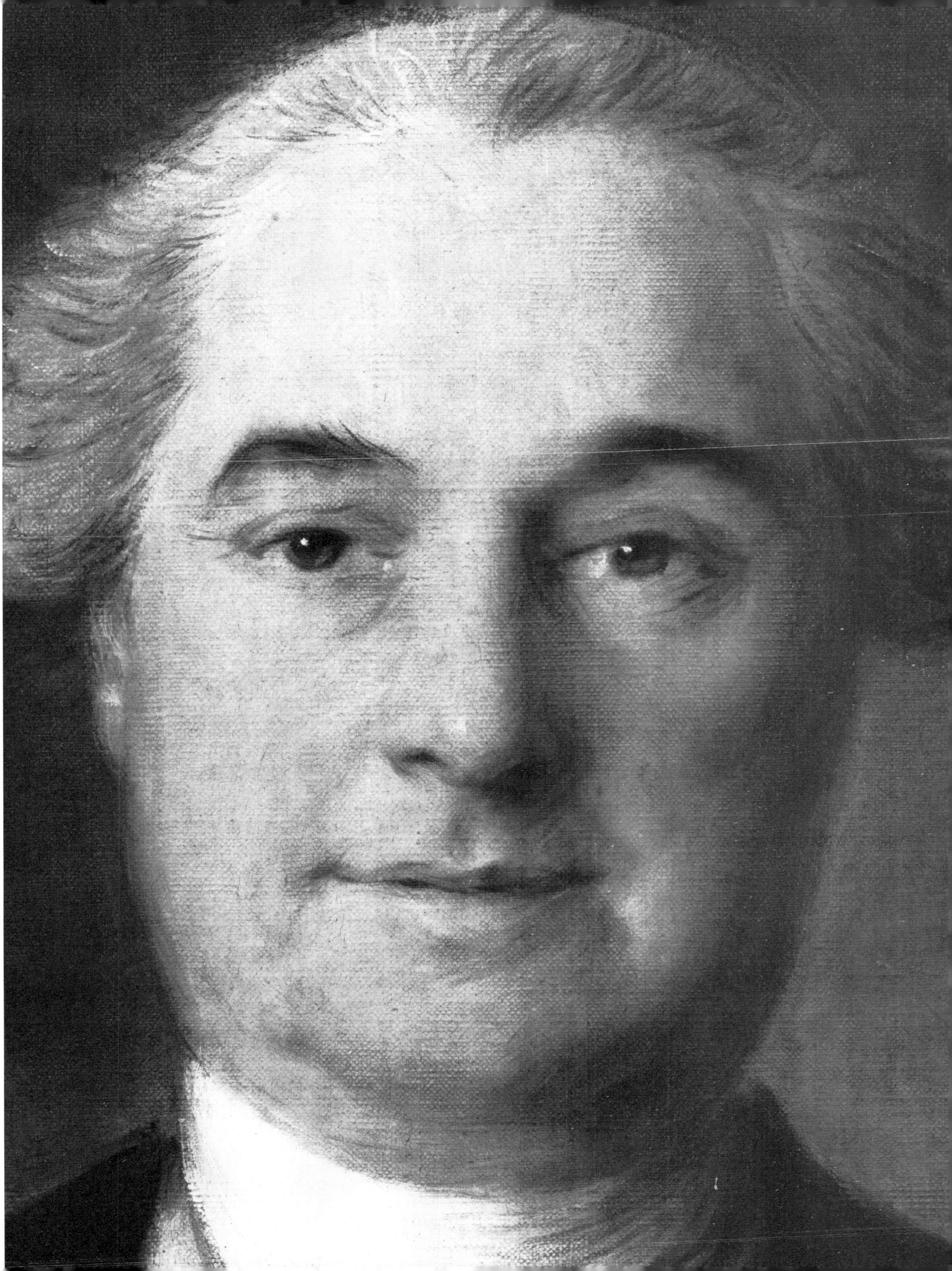

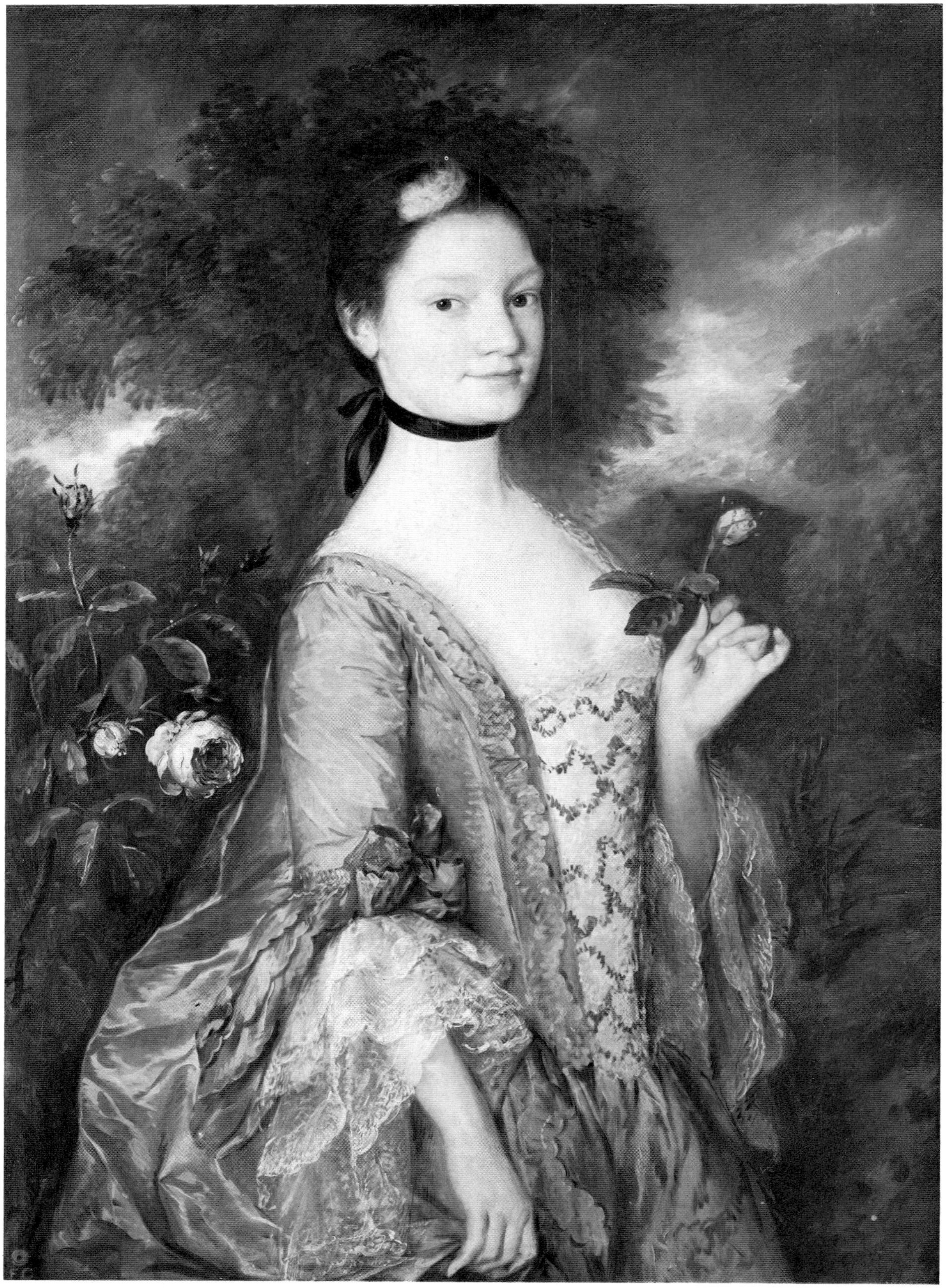

107. *Sarah, Lady Innes* (d. 1770). Canvas, 40 × 28⅝ in. About 1757. New York, Frick Collection (Note 34)

On the preceding pages:

105. Detail from Pl. 53 (Note 66)

106. Detail from *William, 2nd Viscount Gage* (1718-91). Canvas, 91½ × 59 in. Exhibited R. A. 1777 (134). Firle Place, Viscount Gage (Note 90)

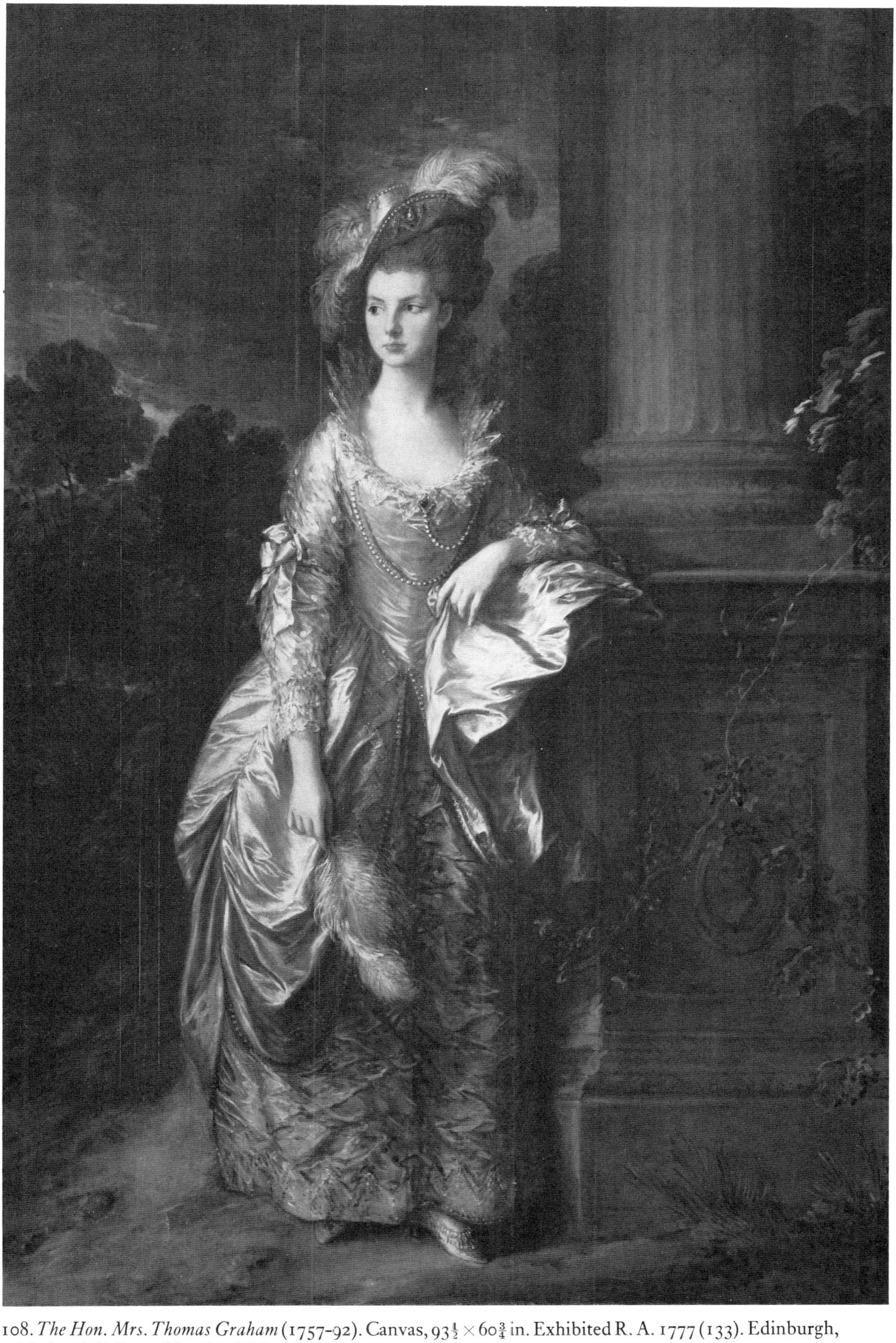

108. *The Hon. Mrs. Thomas Graham* (1757–92). Canvas, $93\frac{1}{2} \times 60\frac{3}{4}$ in. Exhibited R. A. 1777 (133). Edinburgh, National Gallery of Scotland (Note 88)

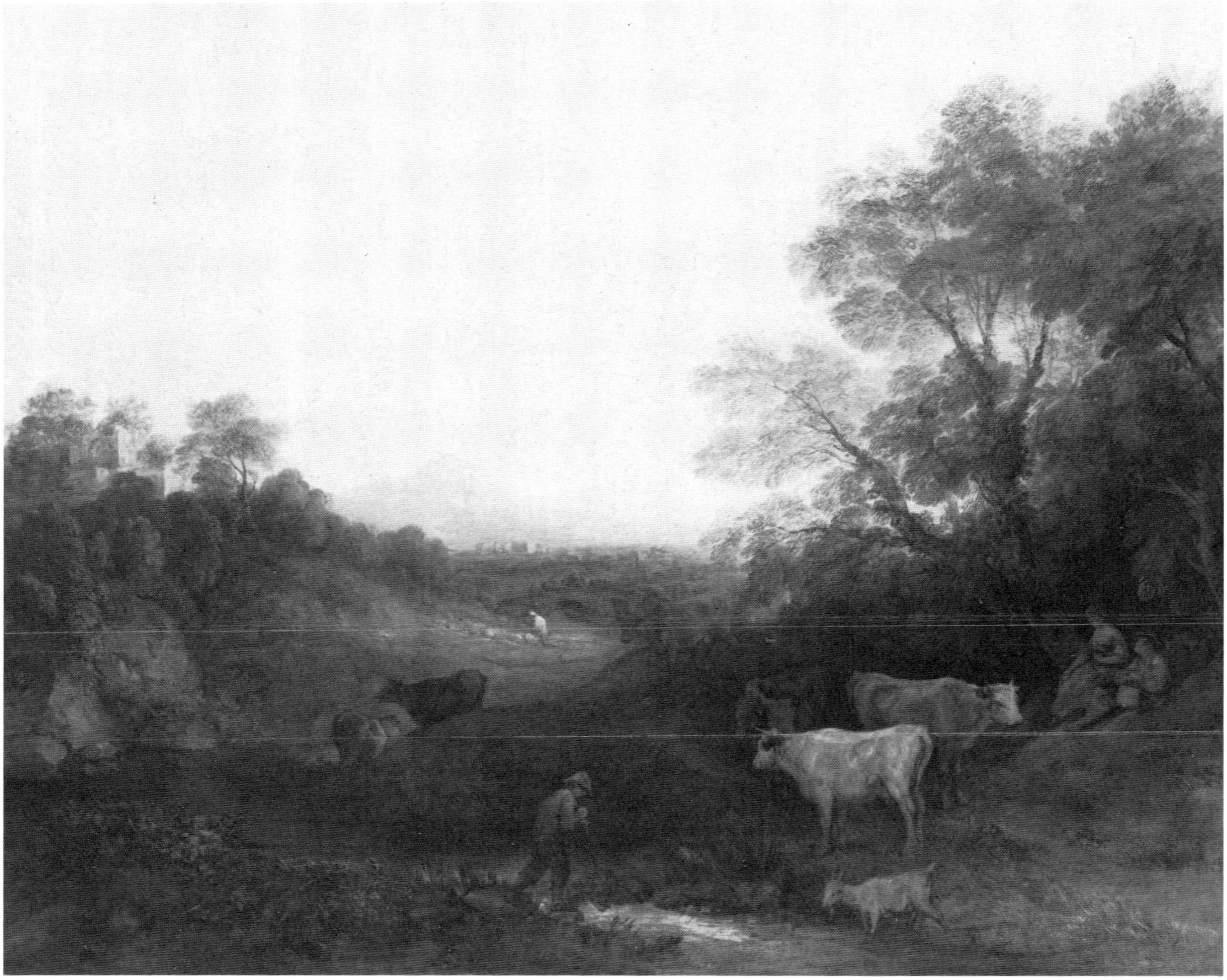

109. *Wooded stream with pastoral figures and distant bridge*. Canvas, 47¼ × 57¼ in. Early 1770s. Oak Spring, Virginia, Mr and Mrs Paul Mellon (Note 83)

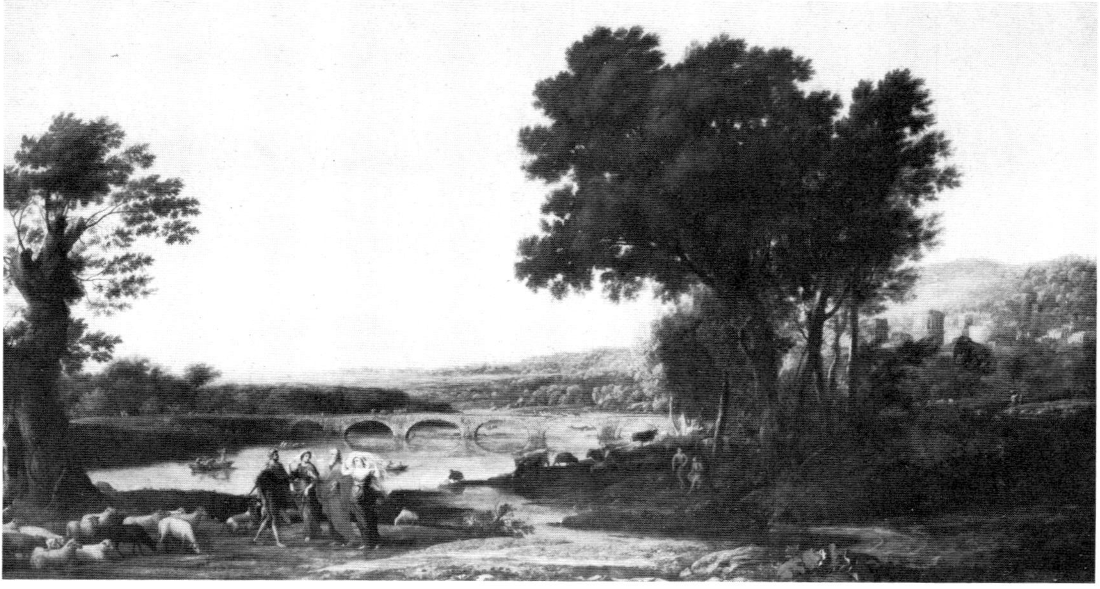

110. Claude Lorraine (1600–82): *Jacob and Laban*. Canvas, 56 × 99 in. National Trust, Petworth House

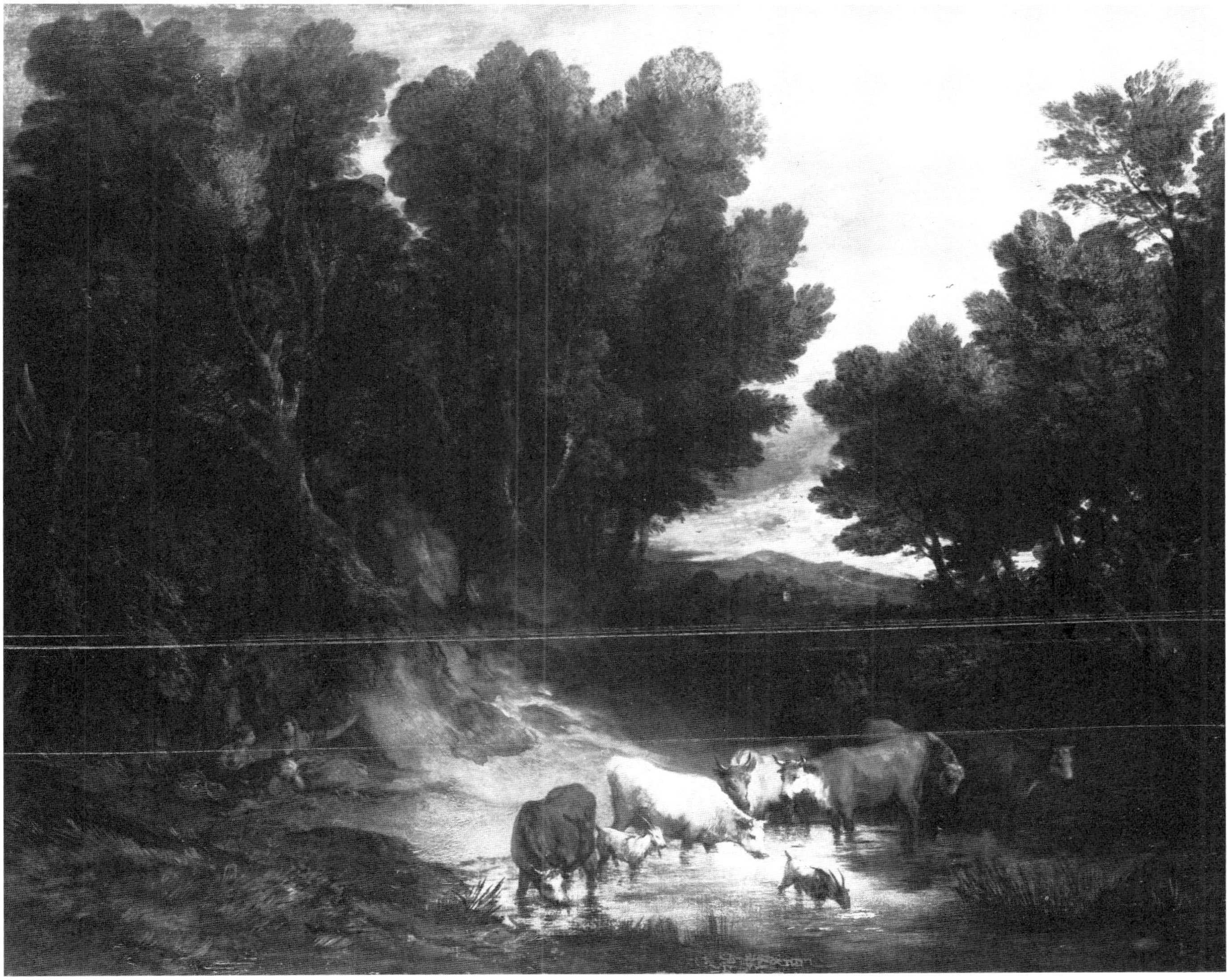

111. *The Watering Place*. Canvas, 58 × 71 in. Exhibited R. A. 1777 (136). London, National Gallery (Note 87)

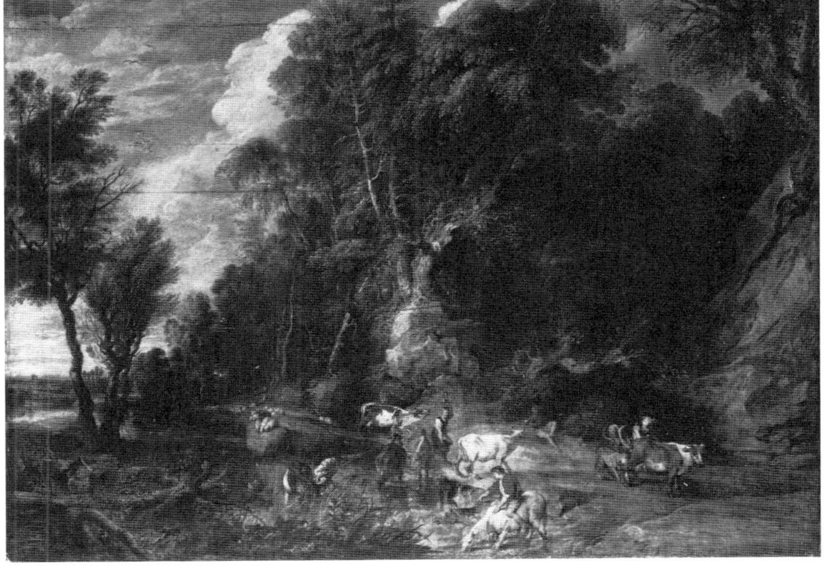

112. Sir Peter Paul Rubens (1577–1640): *The Watering Place*. Panel, $38\frac{5}{8} \times 52\frac{3}{4}$ in. London, National Gallery

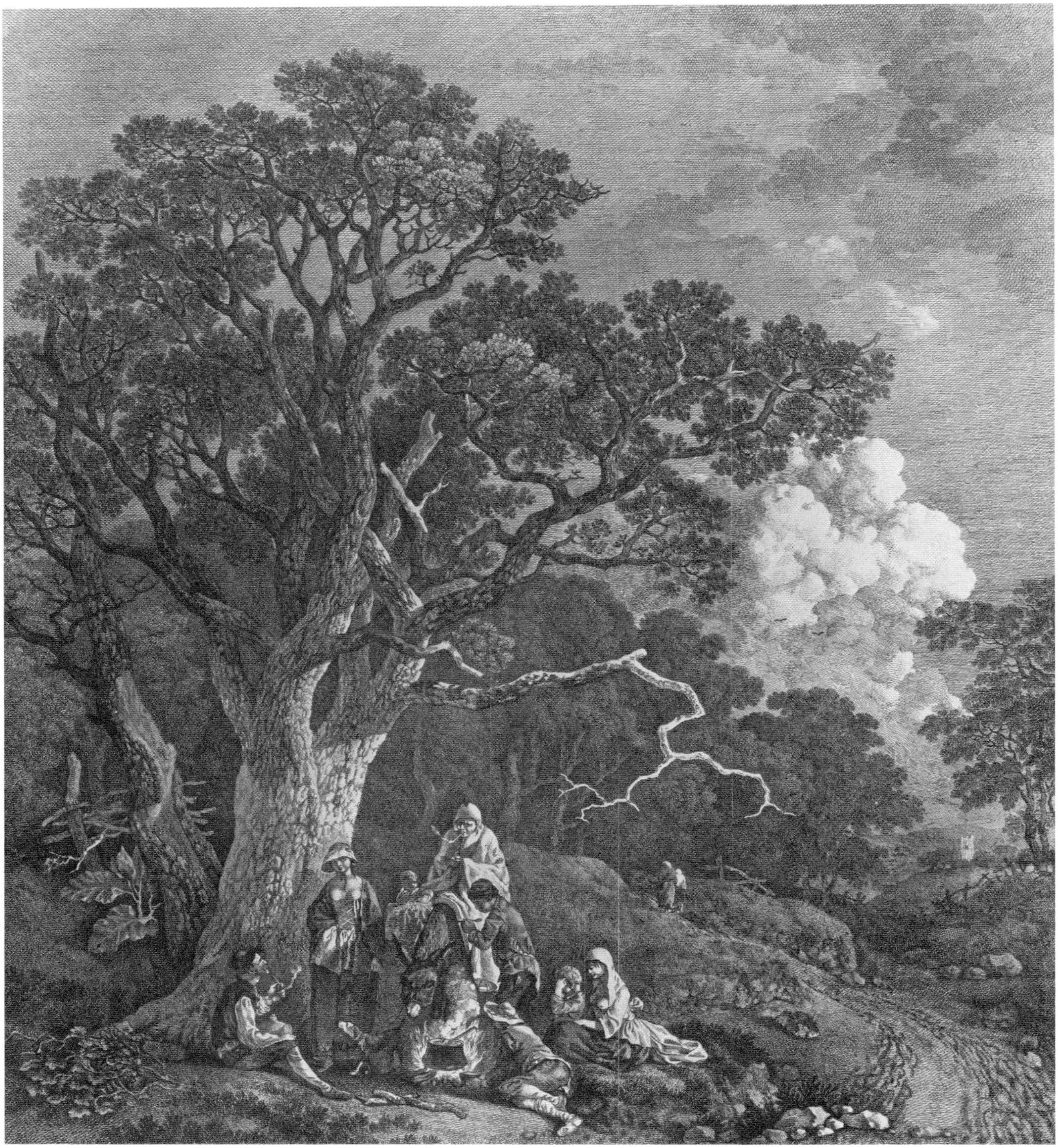

113. *Wooded landscape with gipsies round a camp fire*. Engraving by J. Wood, $18\frac{5}{8} \times 16\frac{9}{16}$ in., after Gainsborough's original etching, about 1753–4. London, British Museum (Note 24)

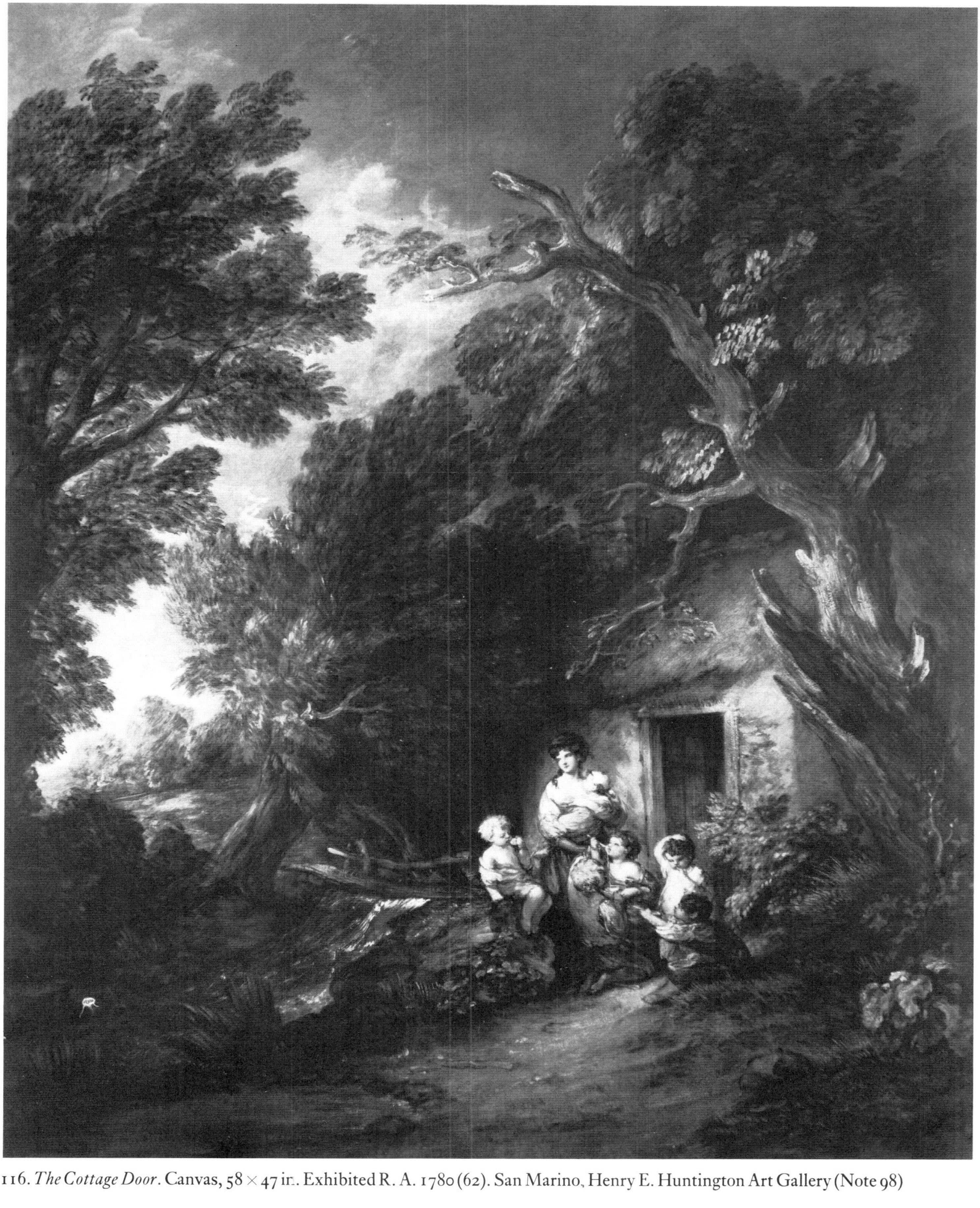

116. *The Cottage Door*. Canvas, 58 × 47 in. Exhibited R. A. 1780 (62). San Marino, Henry E. Huntington Art Gallery (Note 98)

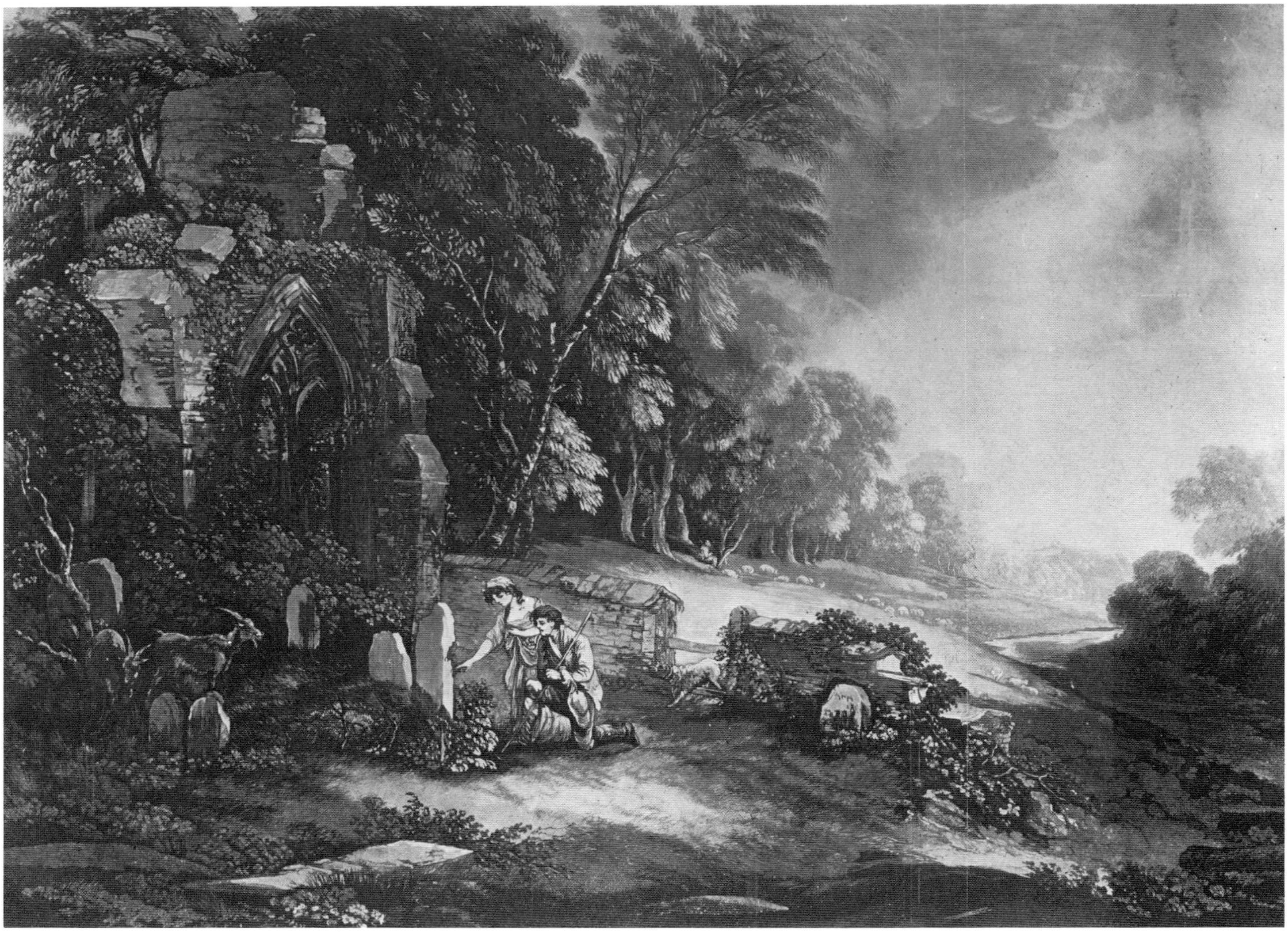

117. *Wooded landscape with peasants reading tombstone and ruined church.* Aquatint by M. C. Prestal after the painting by Gainsborough known as '*The Country Churchyard*' exhibited R. A. 1780 (319), published by R. Pollard, 12 May 1790. London, British Museum (Note 99)

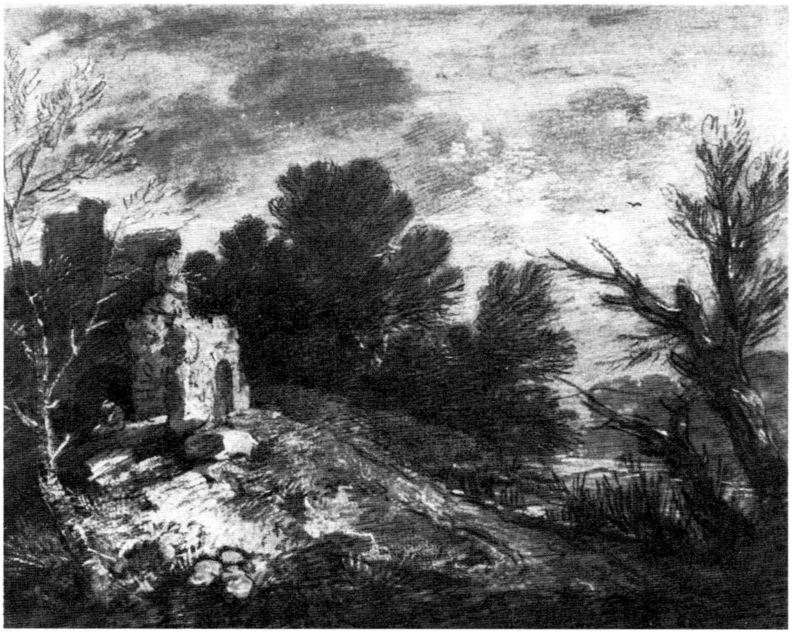

118. *Wooded landscape with figure and ruined castle.* Black chalk and stump and white chalk on grey-blue paper, $9\frac{11}{16} \times 12\frac{1}{8}$ in. Early 1770s. Private Collection (Note 82)

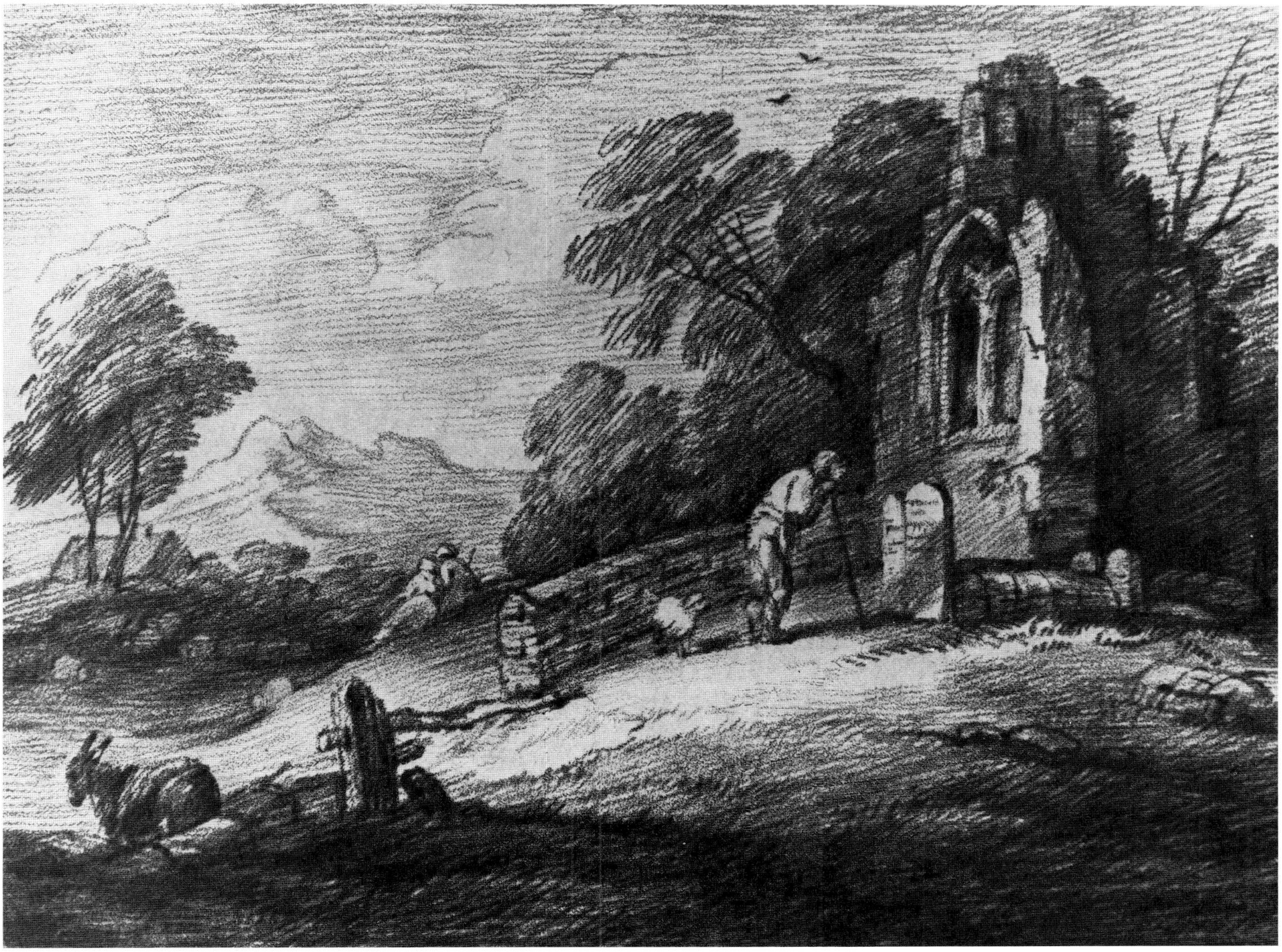

119. *Wooded landscape with peasant reading tombstone, rustic lovers and ruined church.* Soft-ground etching, $11\frac{11}{16} \times 15\frac{1}{2}$ in. Second state. 1779–80. San Marino, Henry E. Huntington Art Gallery (Note 99)

120. *Cattle ferry*. Oil on brown prepared paper, varnished, 8 $\frac{9}{16}$ × 11 $\frac{7}{8}$ in. Mid to later 1780s. Birmingham, City Museum and Art Gallery (Note 117)

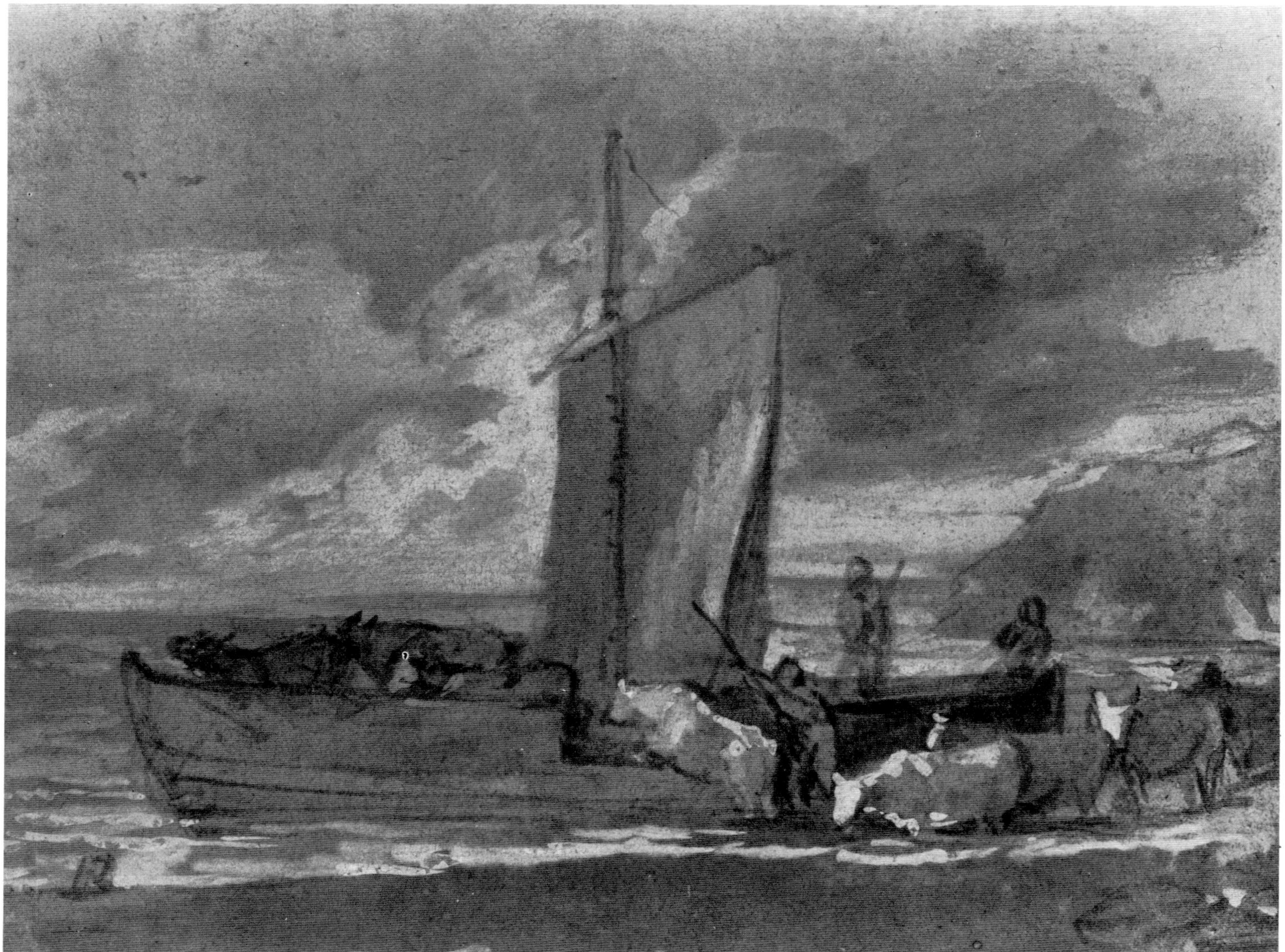

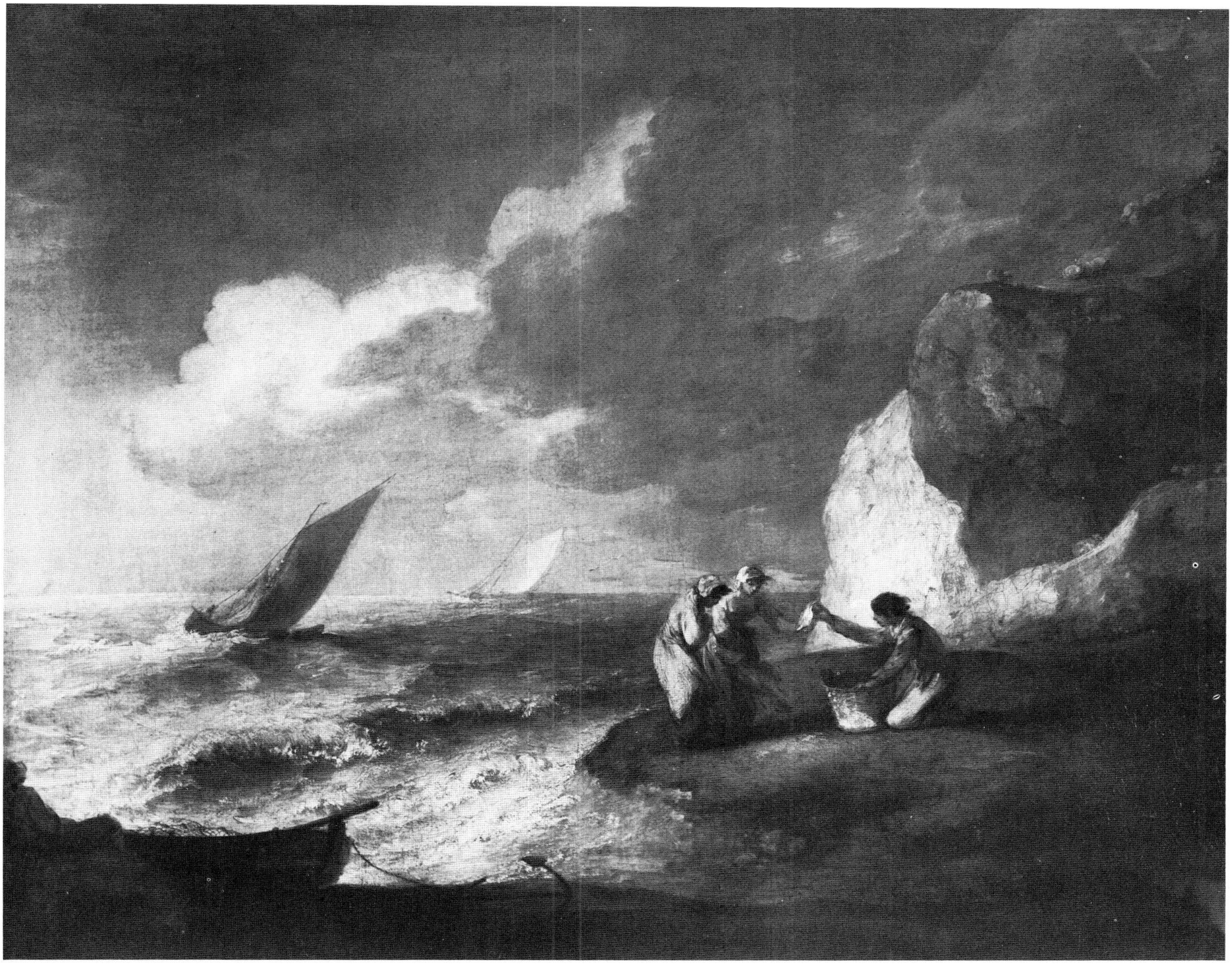

121. *Coast scene : selling fish*. Canvas, $39\frac{1}{2} \times 50$ in. Exhibited R. A. 1781 (94). London, Trustees of the Grosvenor Estate (Note 100)

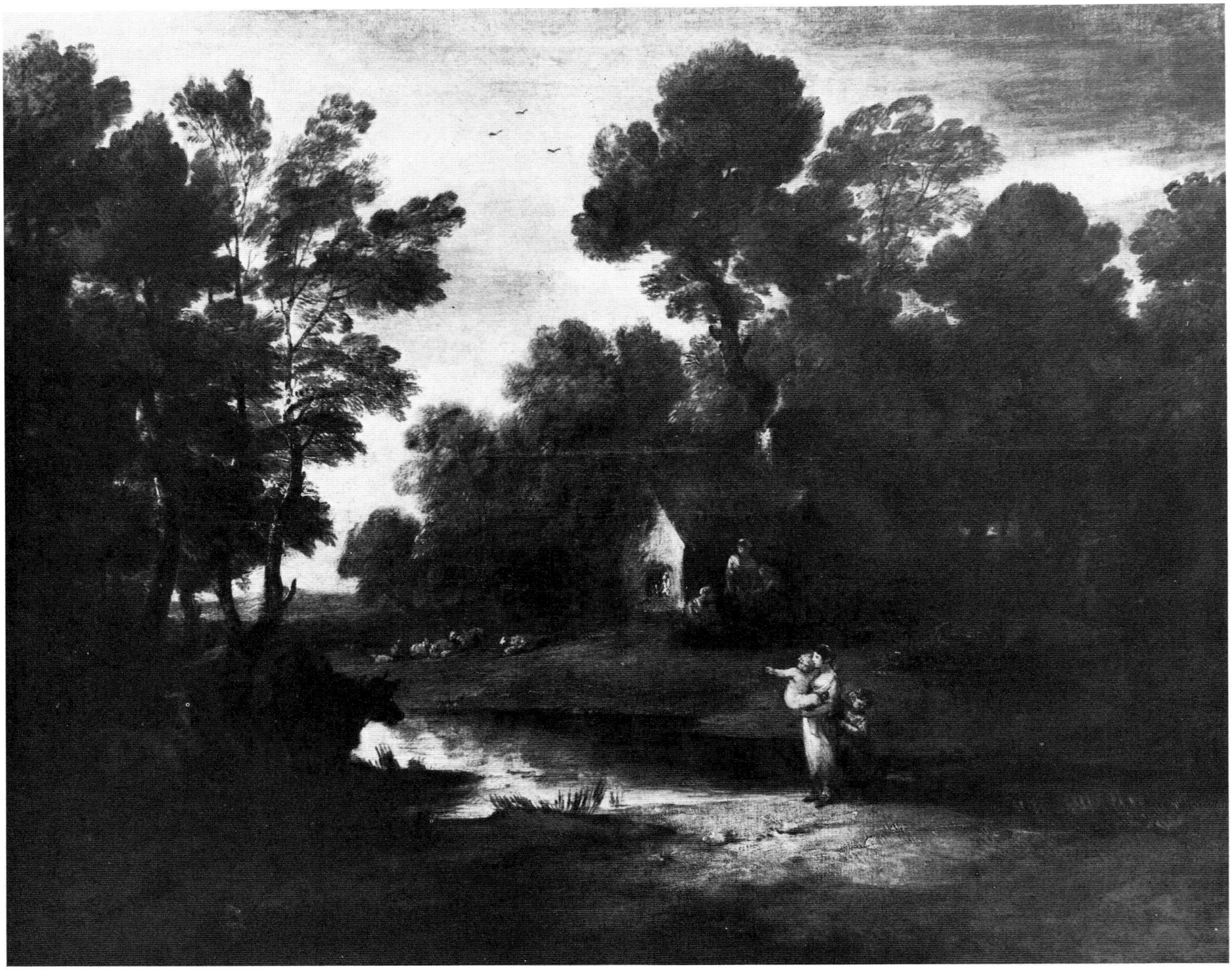

122. *Pool in the woods with cottage, figures and cattle.* Canvas, 47 × 57 in. Exhibited R. A. 1782 (166). Private Collection (Note 104)

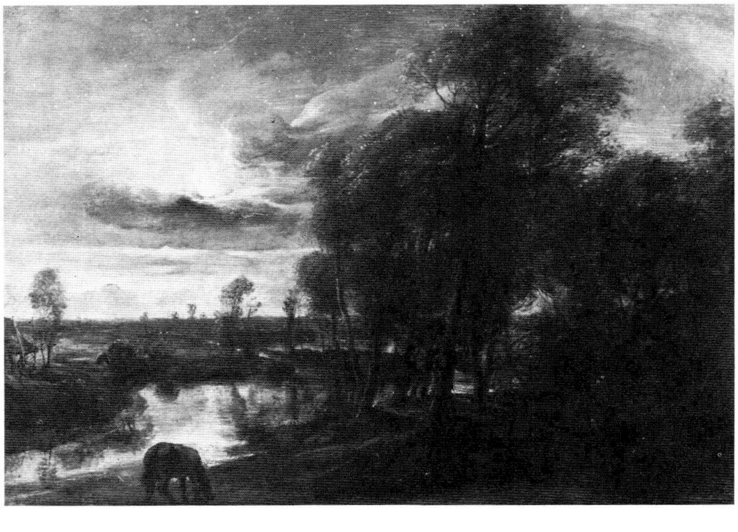

123. Sir Peter Paul Rubens (1577–1640): *A moonlight landscape.* Panel, $24\frac{3}{4}$ × 35 in. London, Count Antoine Seilern

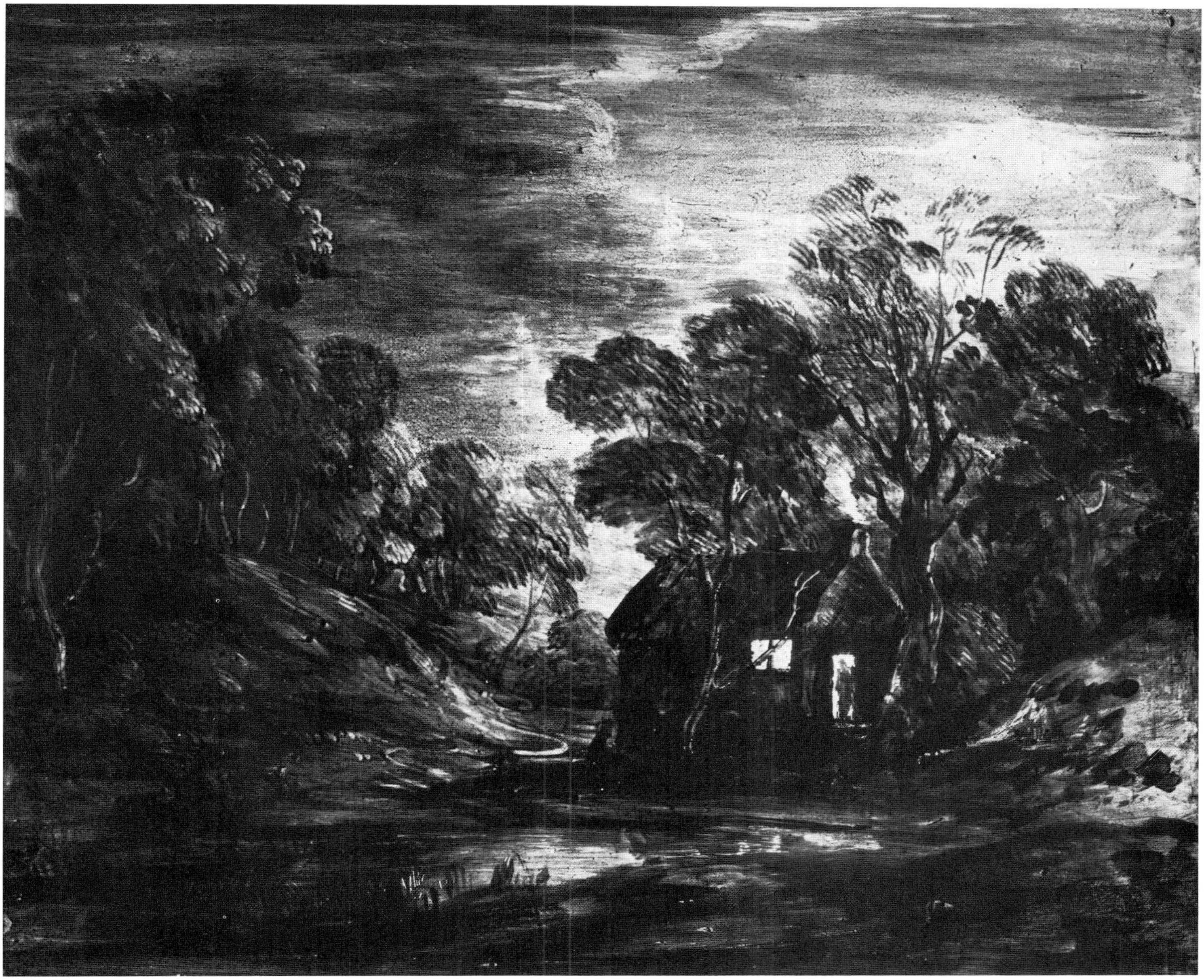

124. *Cottage with figure beside a woodland pool.* Transparency on glass, 11 × 13¼ in. About 1782. London, Victoria and Albert Museum (Note 105)

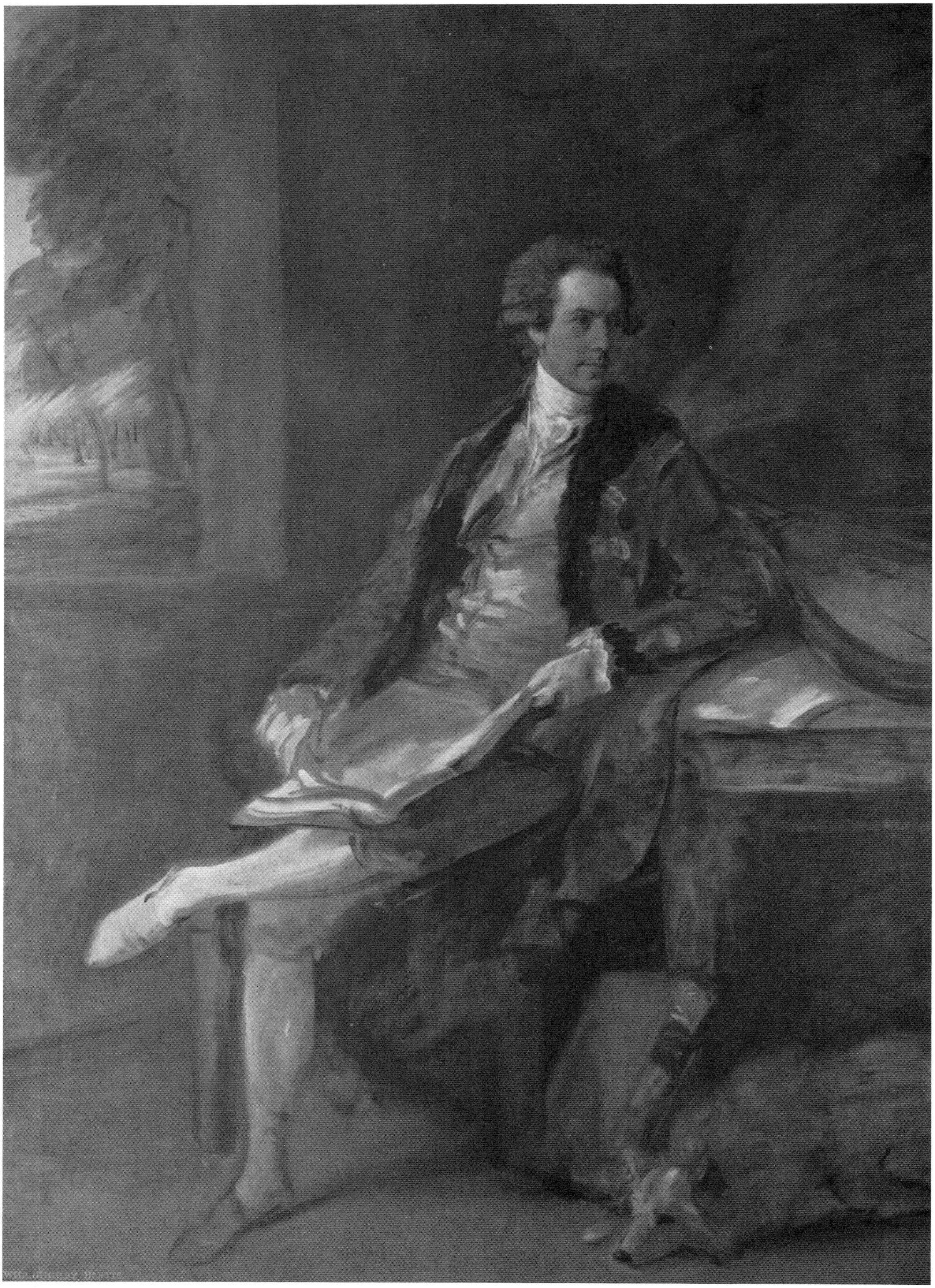

125. *Willoughby, 4th Earl of Abingdon* (1740–99). Canvas, 82 × 57 in. (unfinished). Mid 1770s. London, Private Collection (Note 86)

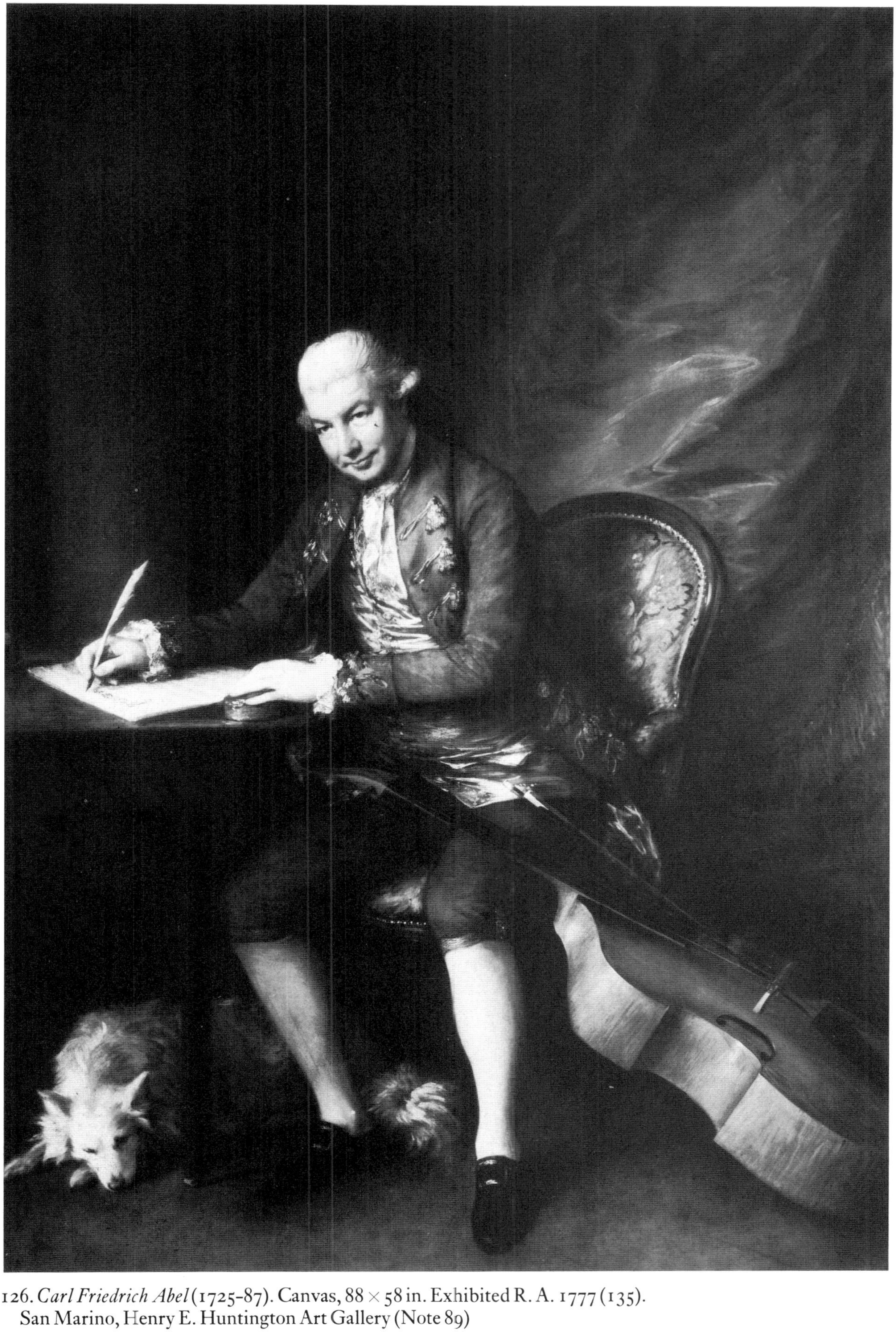

126. *Carl Friedrich Abel* (1725-87). Canvas, 88 × 58 in. Exhibited R. A. 1777 (135).
San Marino, Henry E. Huntington Art Gallery (Note 89)

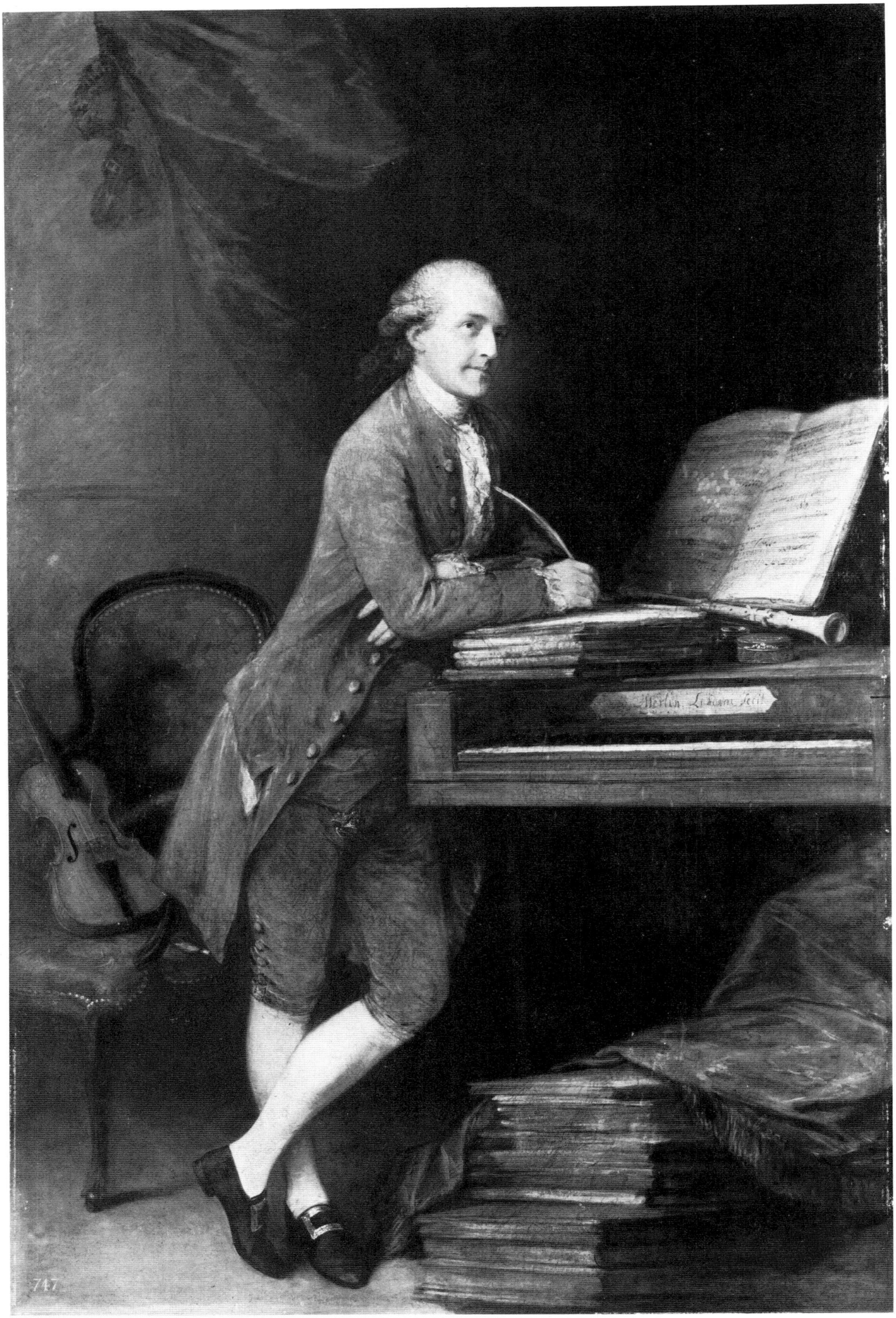

127. *Johann Christian Fischer* (1733–1800). Canvas, 90 × 59¼ in. Exhibited R. A. 1780 (222). London, Buckingham Palace (Note 95) (reproduced by gracious permission of Her Majesty The Queen)

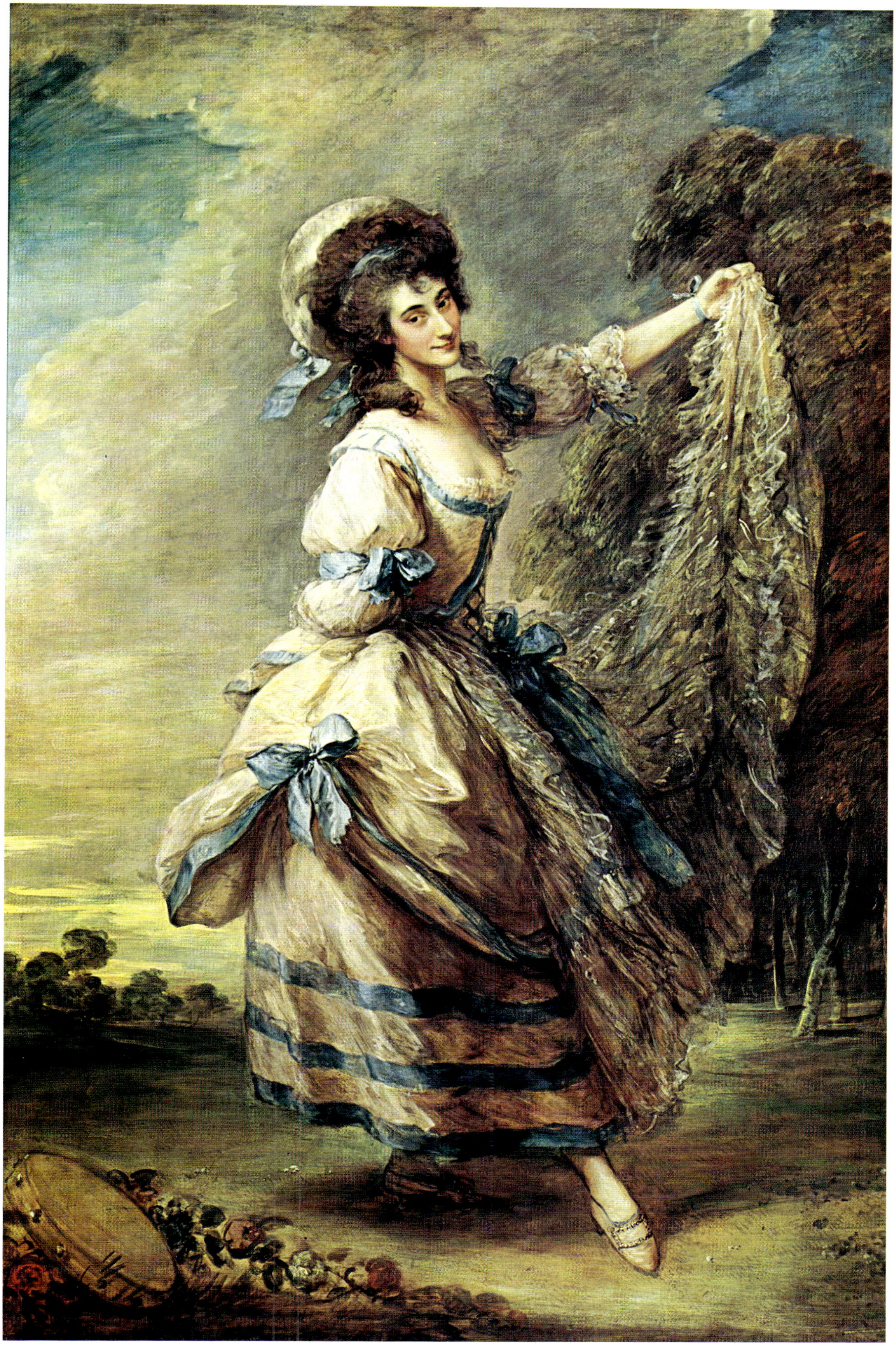

128. *Giovanna Baccelli* (d. 1801). Canvas, $88\frac{1}{2} \times 57$ in. Exhibited R. A. 1782 (230) (engraved 1784). Swinton Park, Earl of Swinton (Note 102)

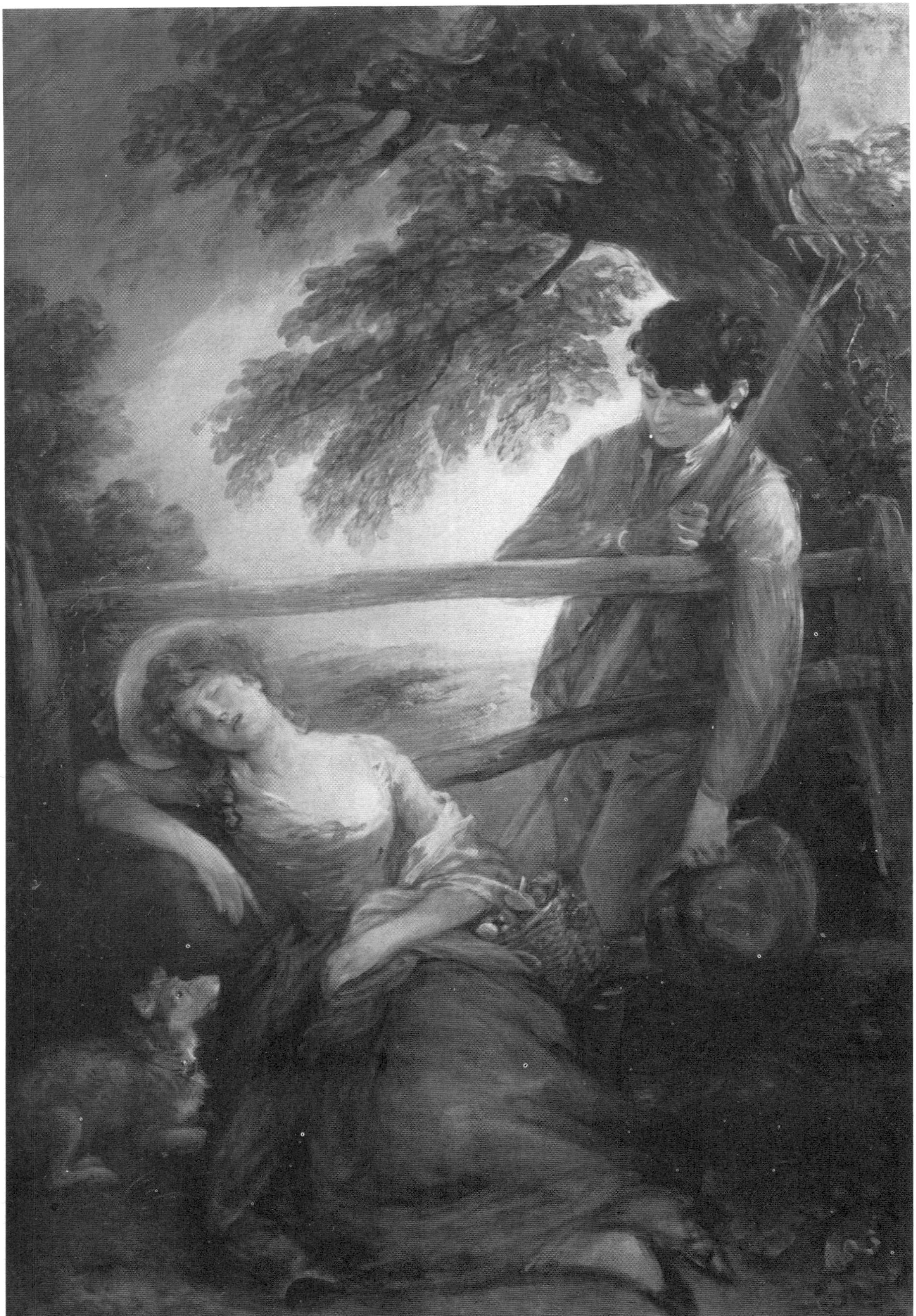

129. *Haymaker and sleeping girl.* Canvas, 89 × 58½ in. About 1785. Boston, Museum of Fine Arts (Note 125)

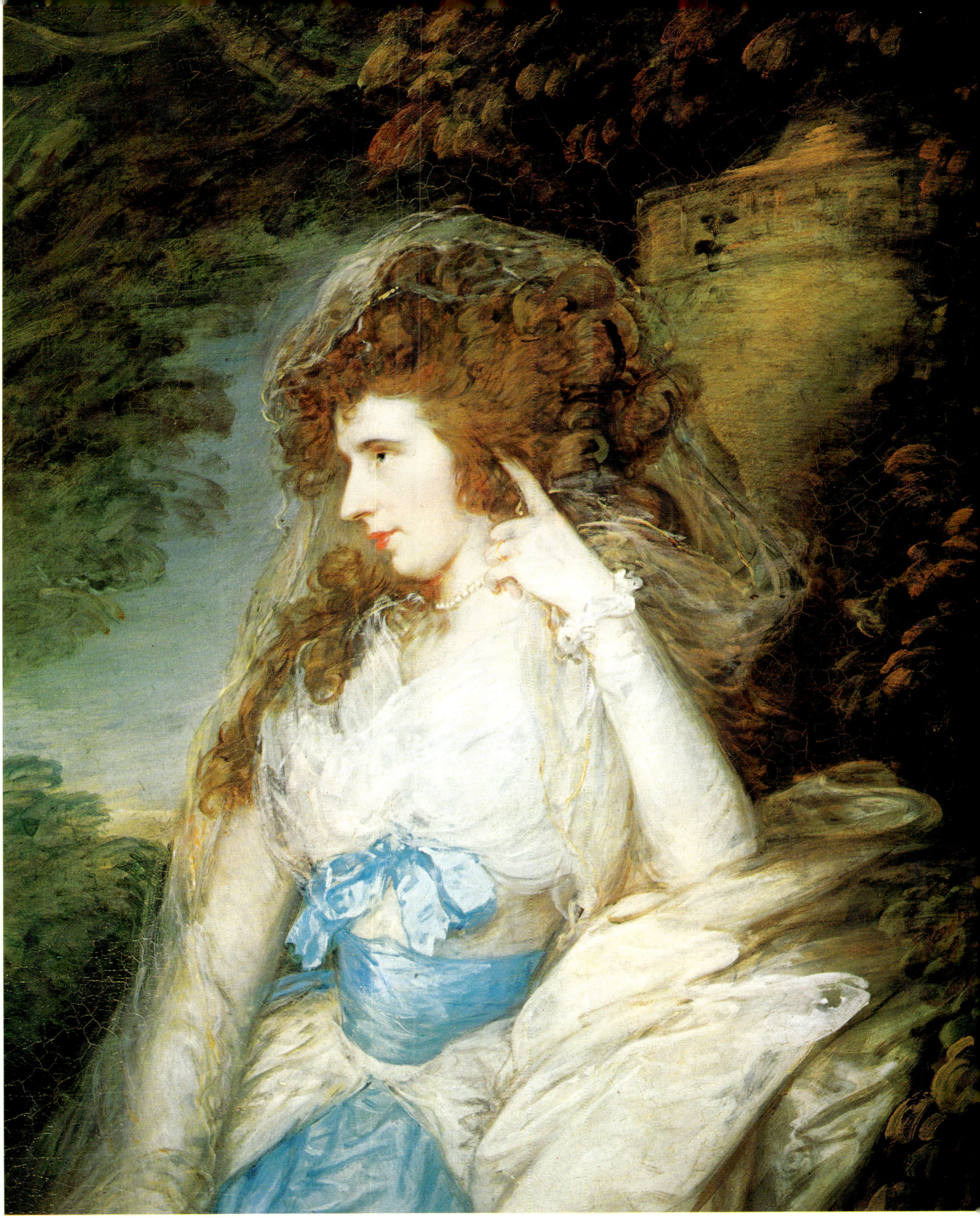

130. Detail from *Mary, Lady Bate-Dudley*. Canvas, 87 × 57 in. Painted summer 1787. Needwood House, Lord Burton (on loan to Marlborough House) (Note 134)

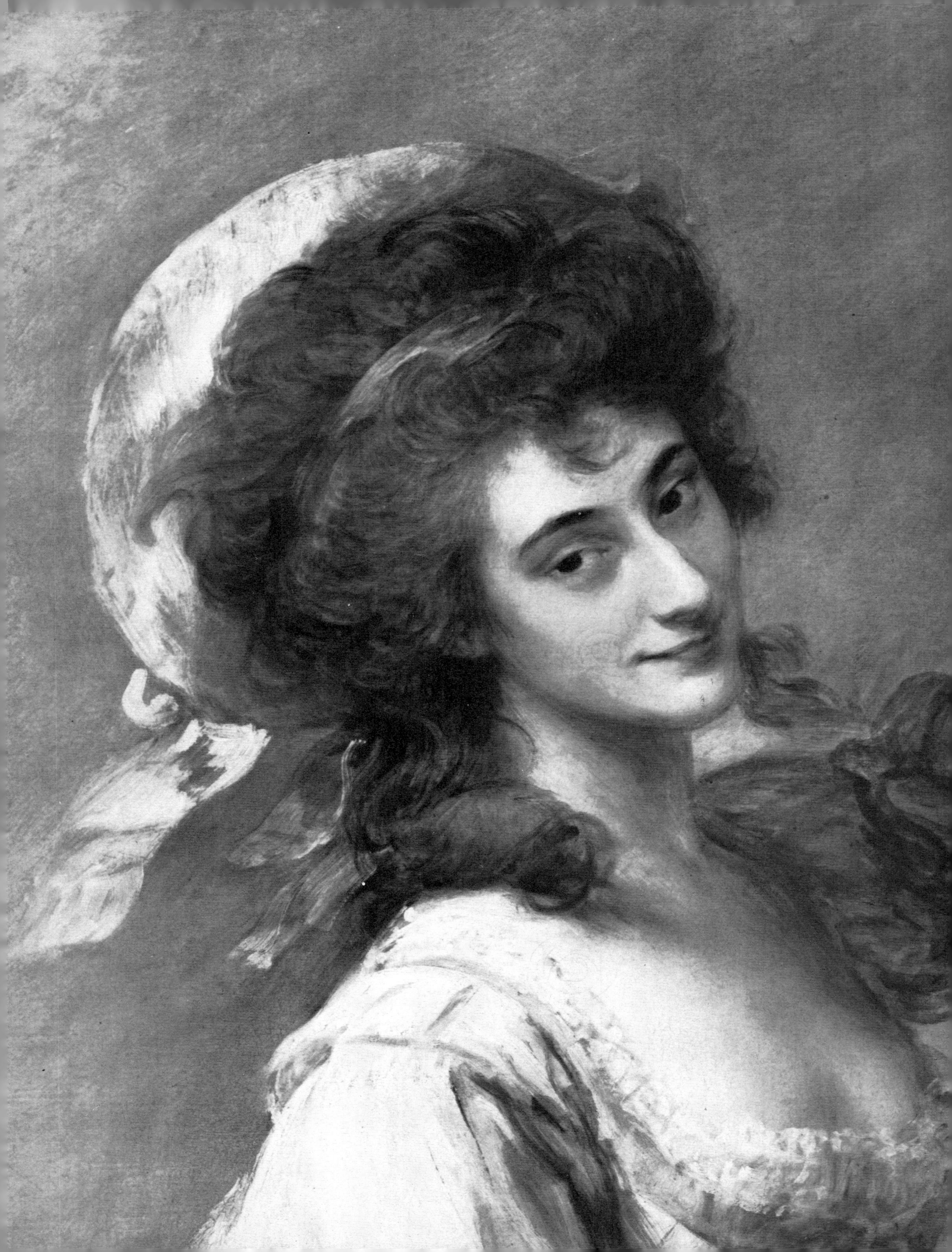

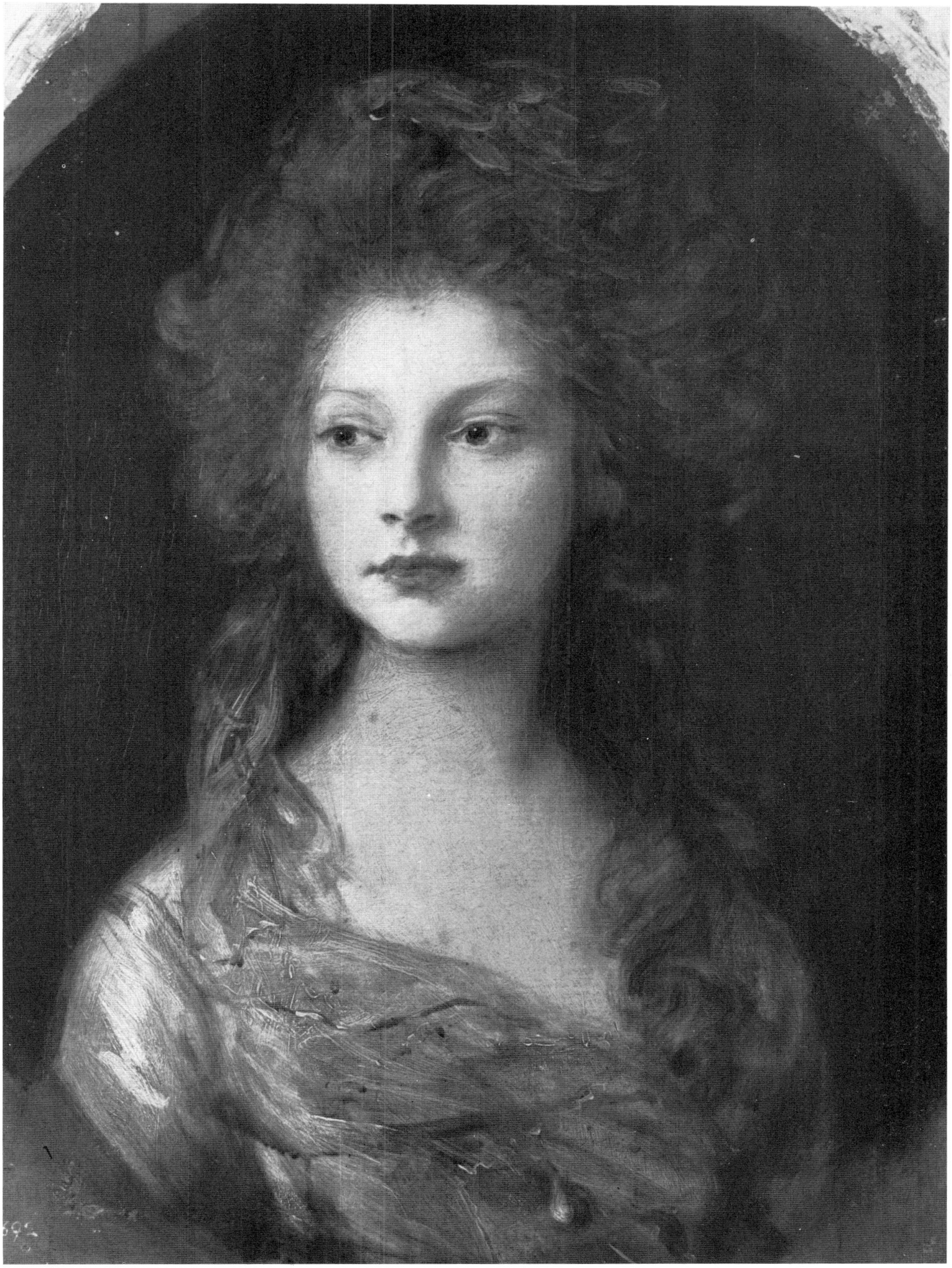

132. *Princess Elizabeth* (1770–1840). Canvas, $22\frac{3}{8} \times 17\frac{3}{8}$ in. (oval). Originally inscribed on the back with the date September 1782. Exhibited R. A. 1783 (134). Windsor Castle (Note 107) (reproduced by gracious permission of Her Majesty The Queen)

131. Detail from Pl. 128 (Note 102)

133. *Wooded landscape with herdsman and cows*. Aquatint. About 1787. Published by J & J Boydell, 1 August 1797. San Marino, Henry E. Huntington Art Gallery (Note 133)

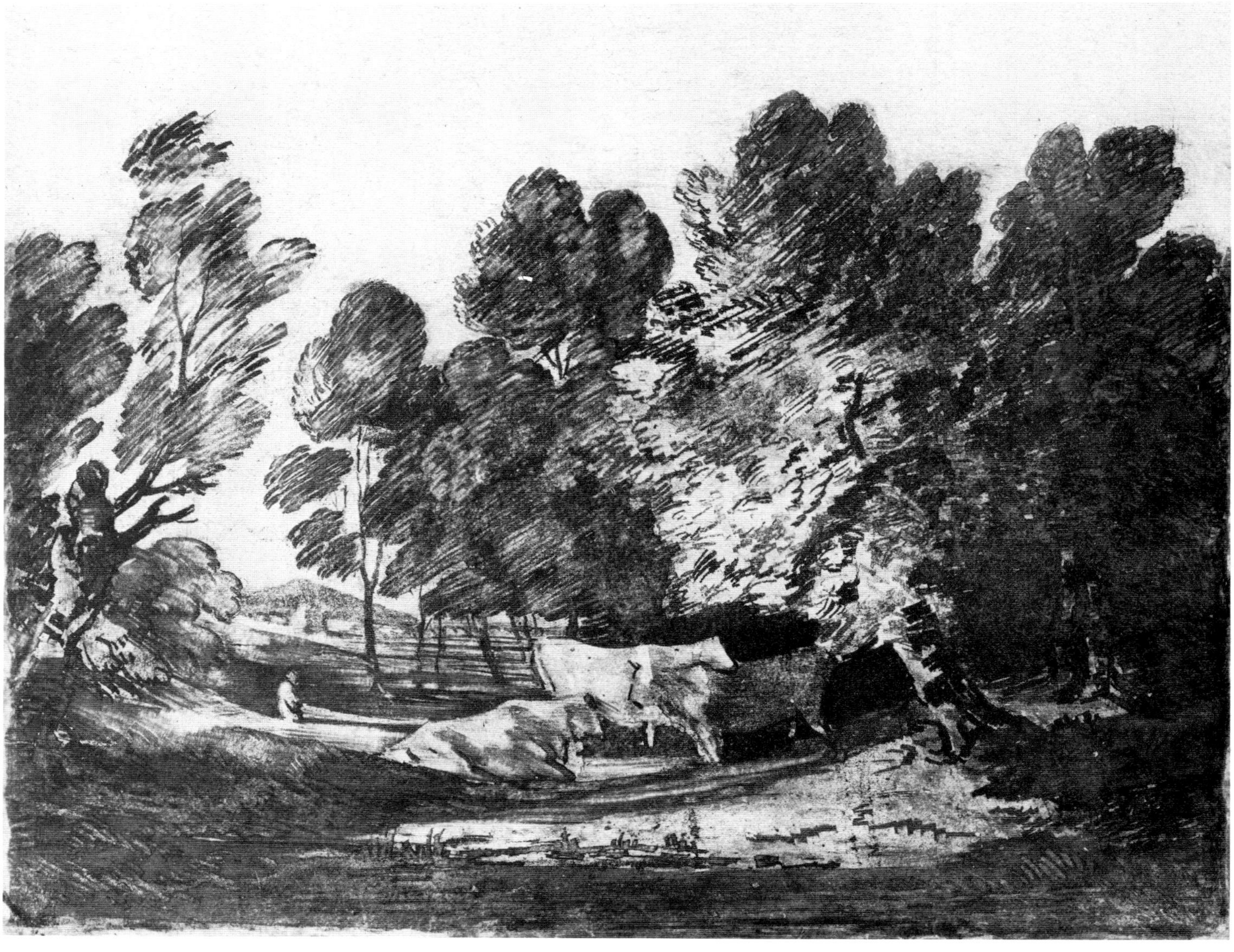

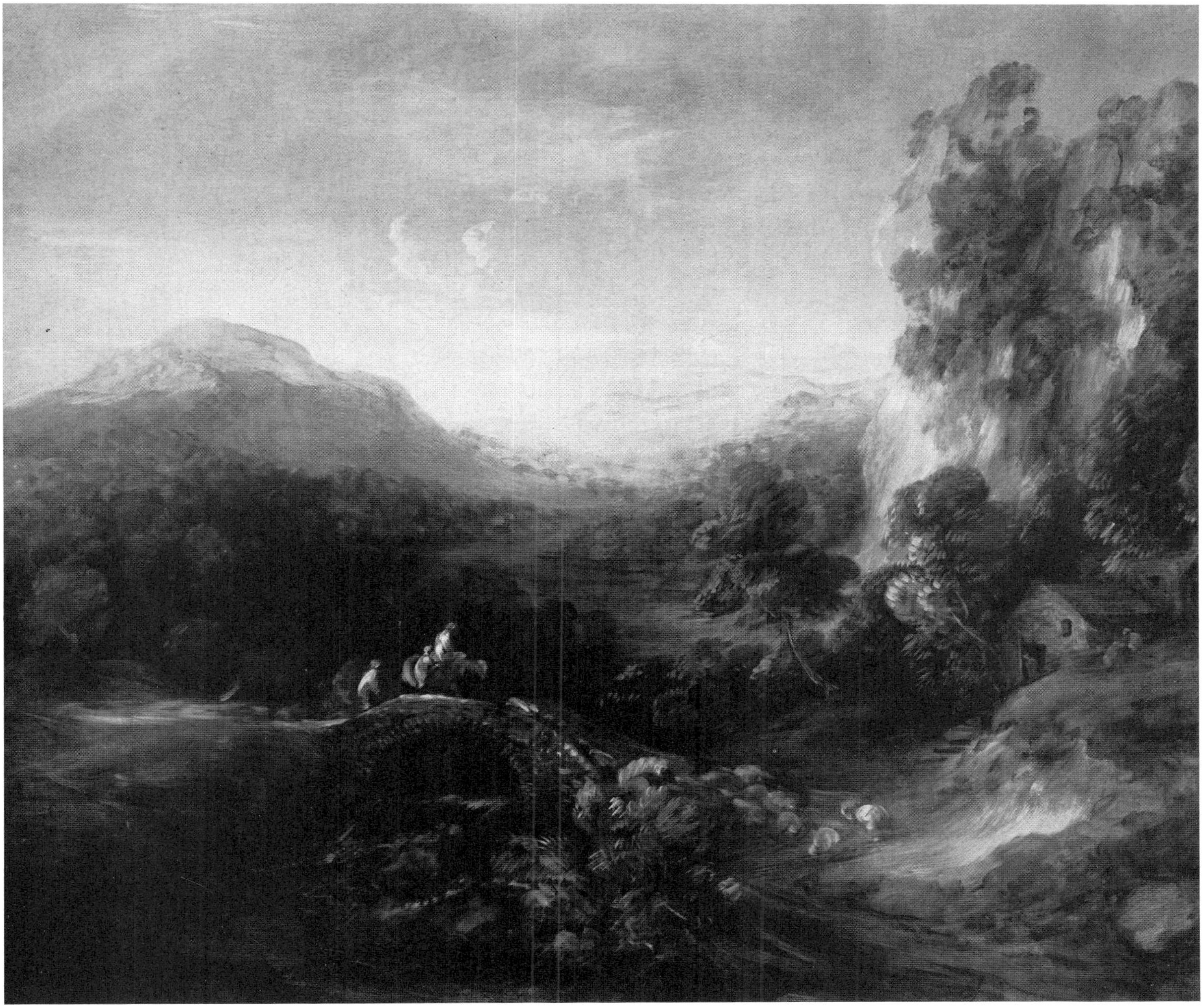

134. *Mountain landscape with peasants crossing a bridge*. Canvas, $44\frac{1}{2} \times 52\frac{1}{2}$ in. (unfinished). About 1784. Washington, National Gallery of Art (Note 113)

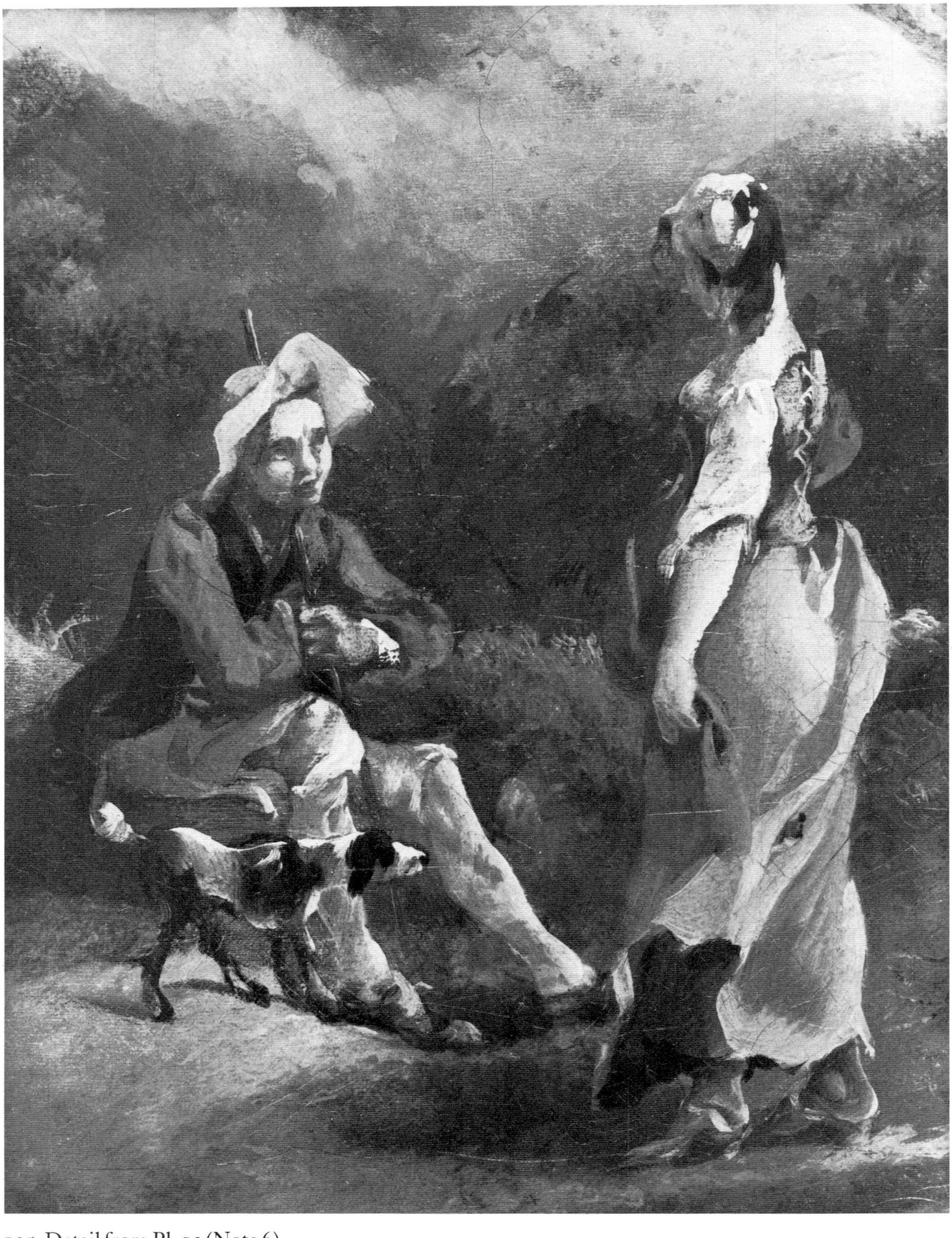

135. Detail from Pl. 13 (Note 6)

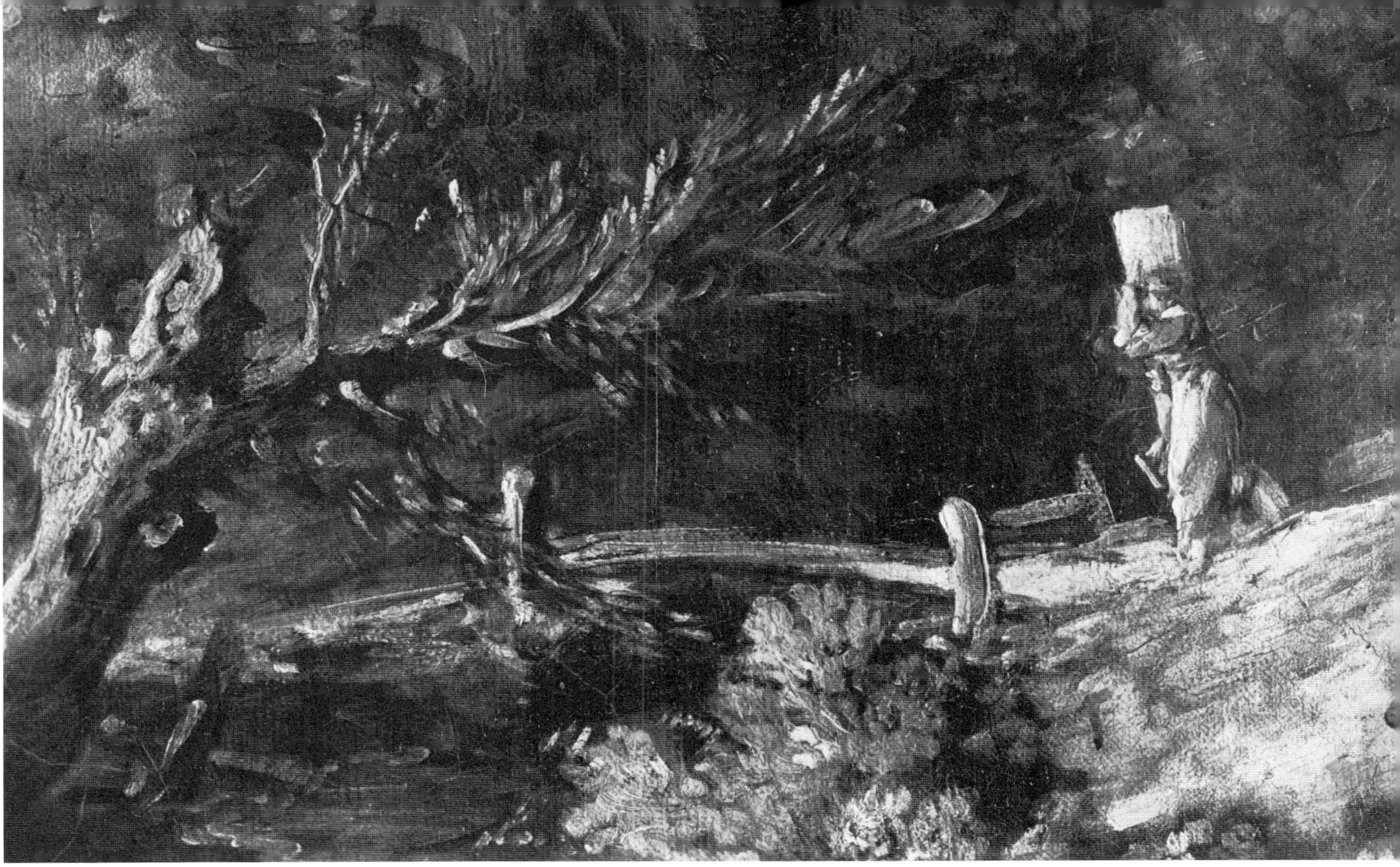

136. Detail from Pl. 70 (Note 51)

137. Detail from Pl. 134 (Note 113)

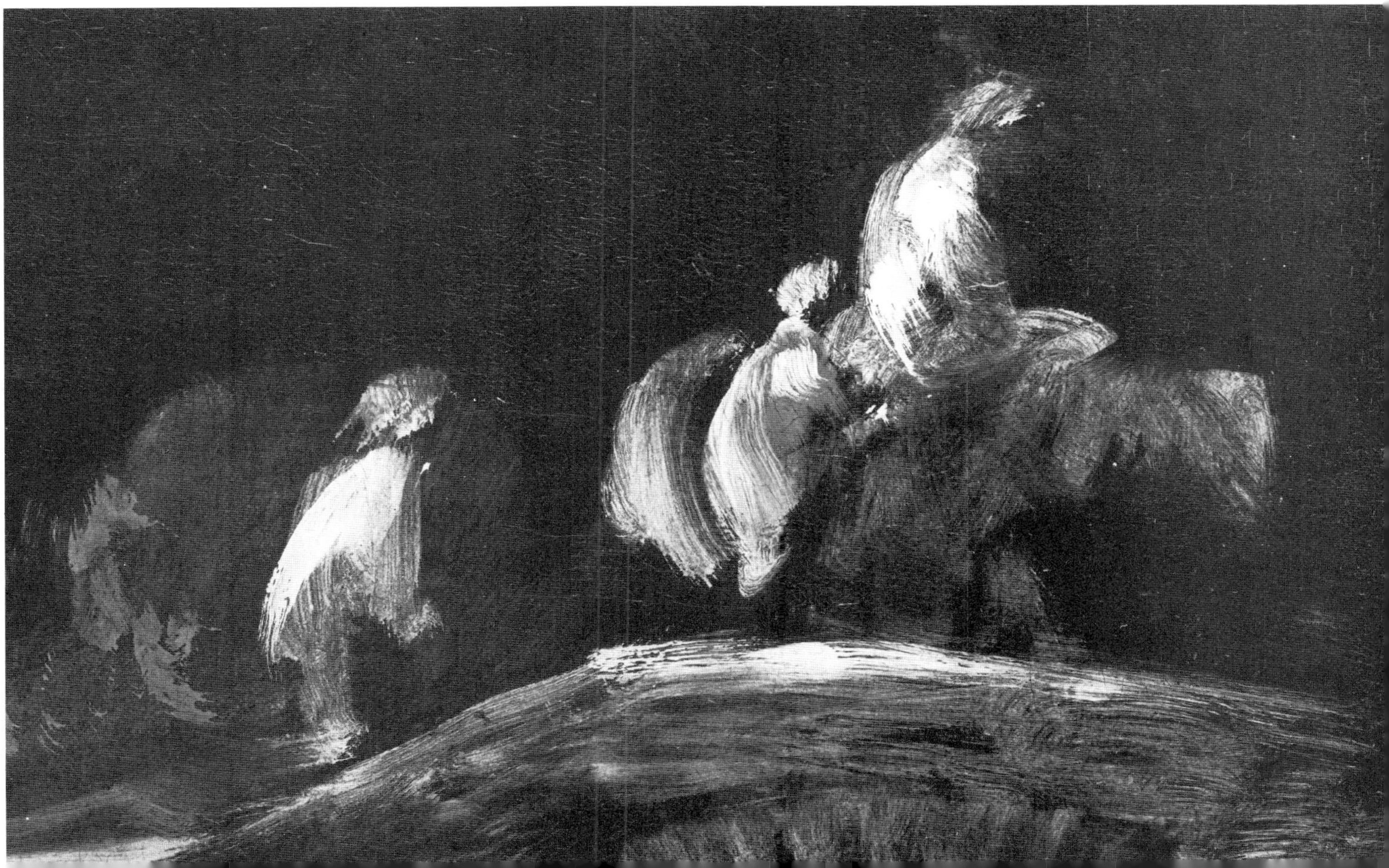

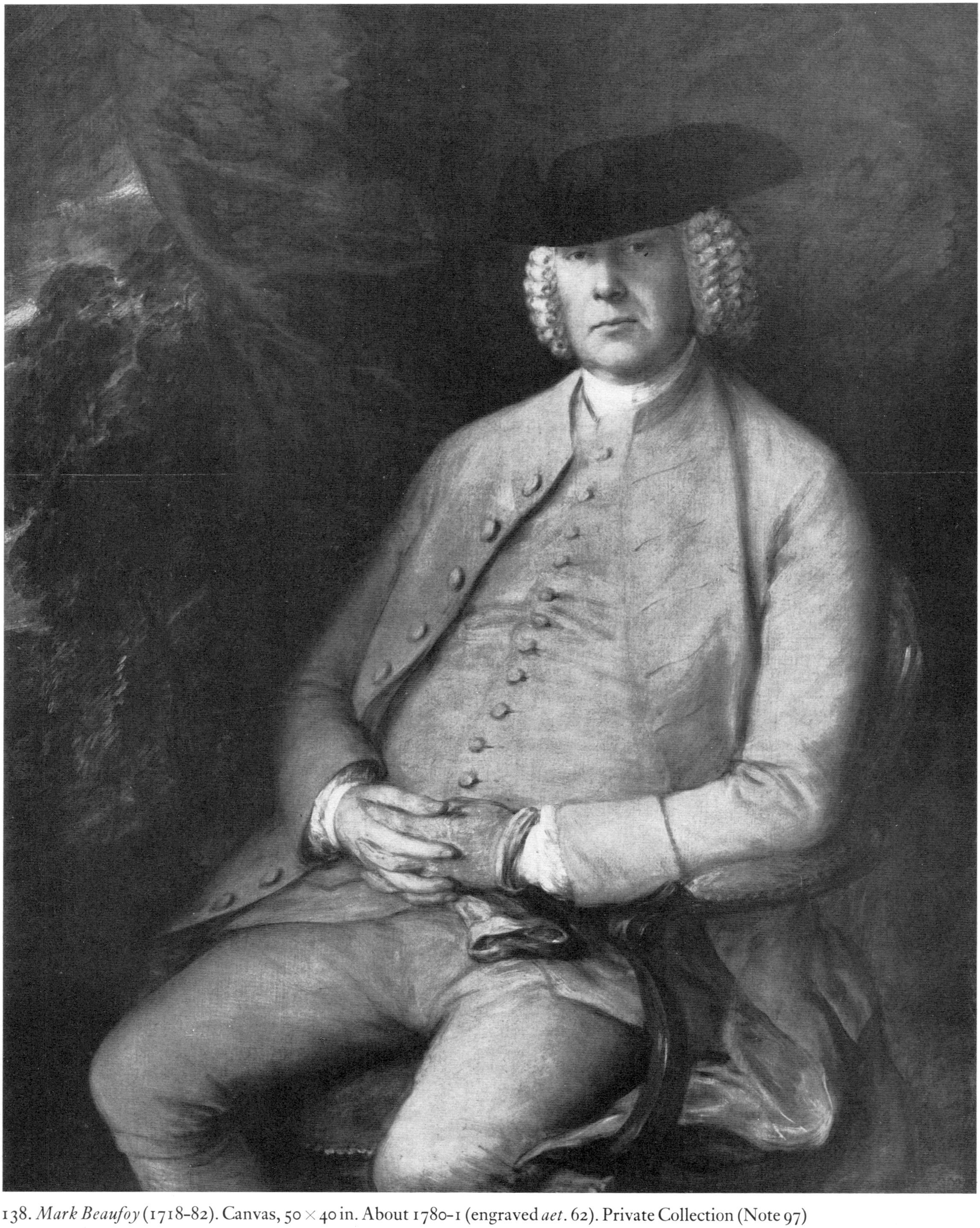

138. *Mark Beaufoy* (1718–82). Canvas, 50 × 40 in. About 1780–1 (engraved *aet*. 62). Private Collection (Note 97)

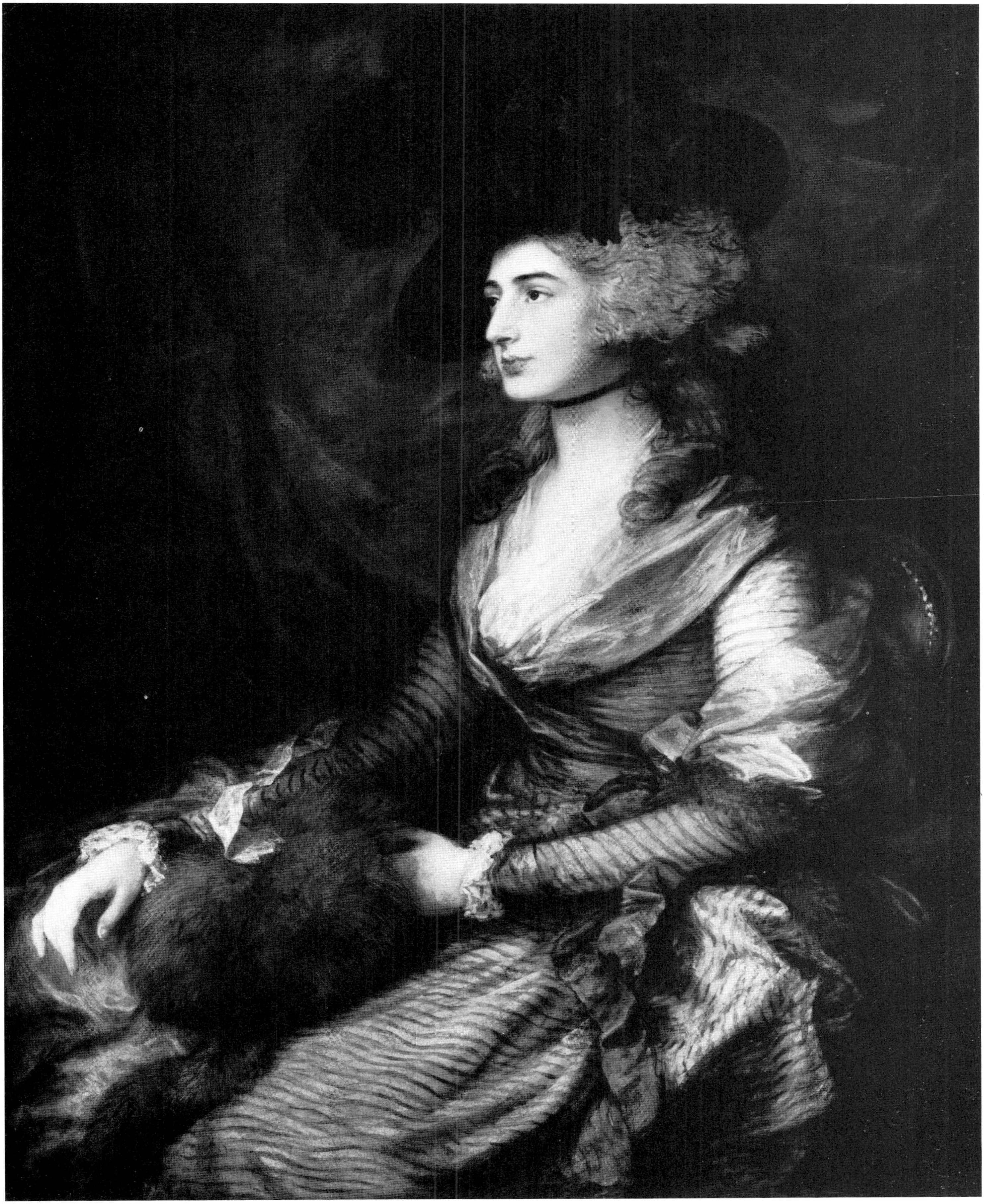

139. *Mrs Sarah Siddons* (1755–1831). Canvas, $49\frac{3}{4} \times 39\frac{1}{4}$ in. Painted March 1785. London, National Gallery (Note 120)

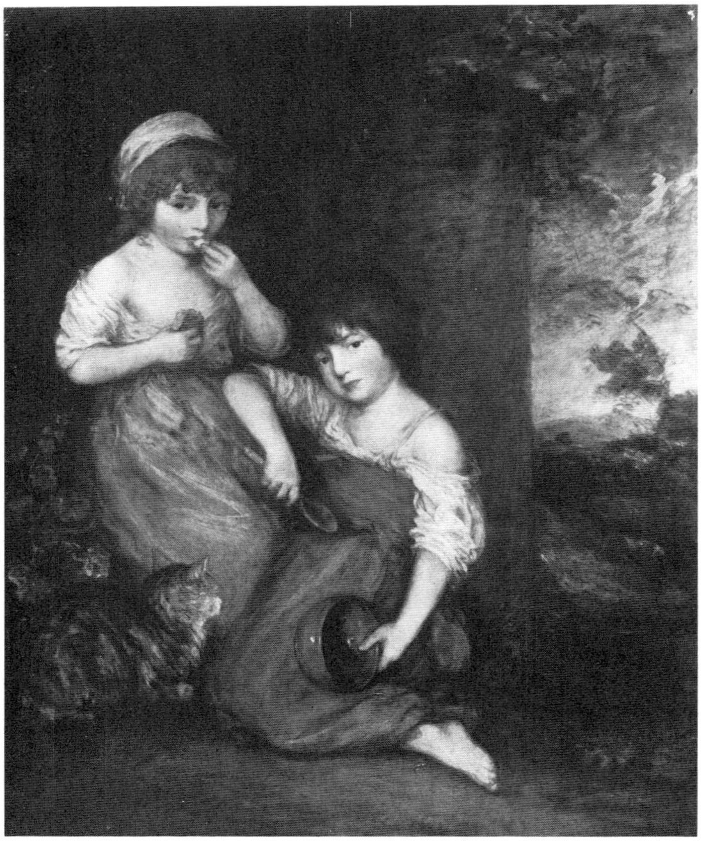

140. *Young Hobbinol and Ganderetta*. Canvas, $49\frac{1}{2} \times 39\frac{1}{2}$ in. Exhibited Macklin's 'Poets' Gallery', April 1788 (engraved 1790). Los Angeles, Mrs Mildred Browning Greene (Note 137)

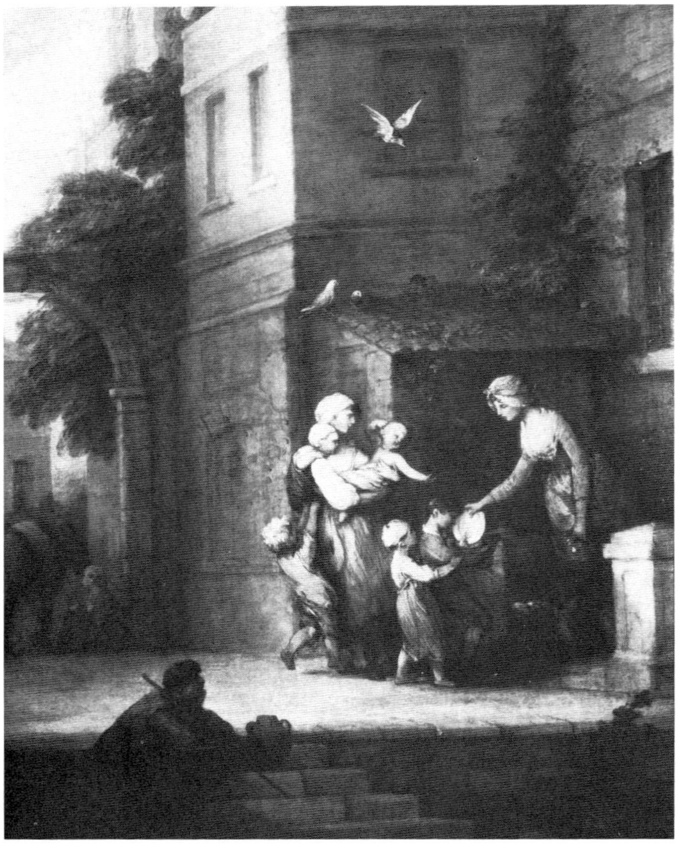

141. *Peasant family receiving charity*. Canvas, cut down to 39×30 in. Exhibited Schomberg House July 1784: retouched and improved autumn 1787. Private Collection (Note 111)

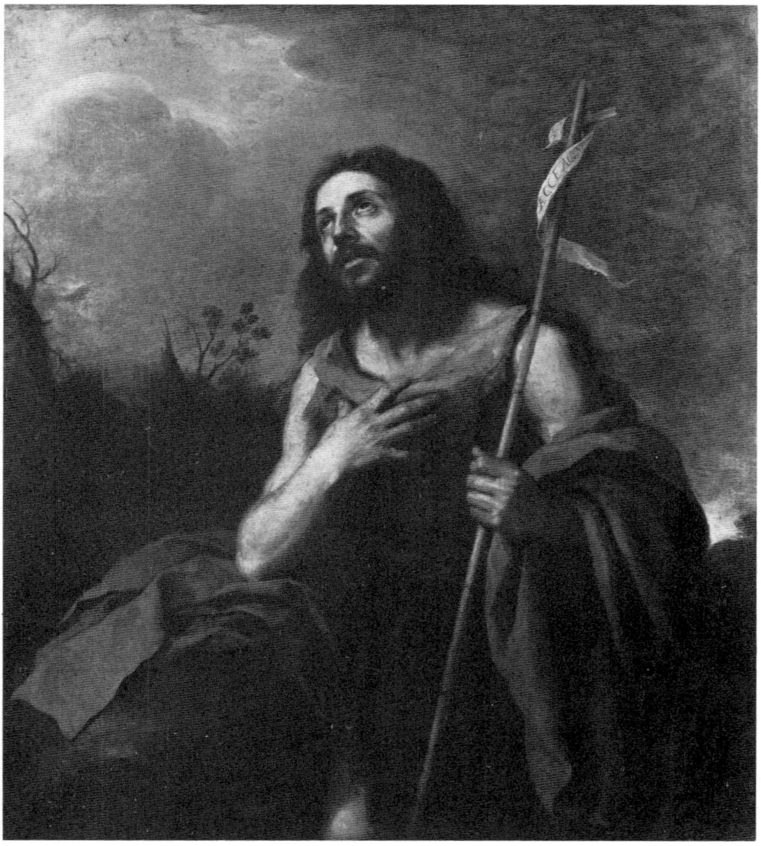

142. Follower of Bartolomé Esteban Murillo (1617–82): *St John the Baptist*. Canvas, $47\frac{1}{4} \times 41\frac{1}{2}$ in. London, National Gallery

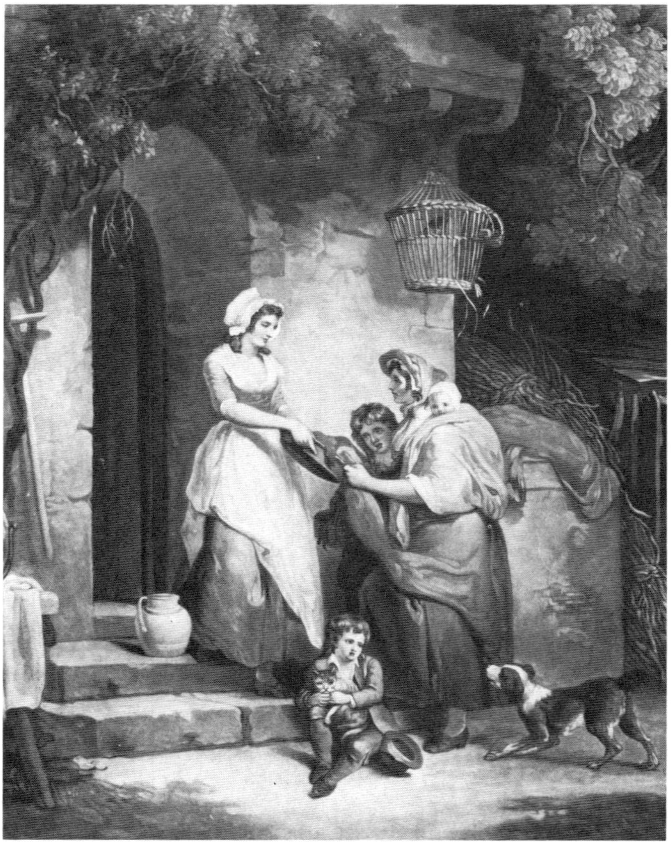

143. Francis Wheatley (1747–1801): *Rustic Benevolence*. Detail from the mezzotint by G. Keating, published 1 August 1797. London, British Museum

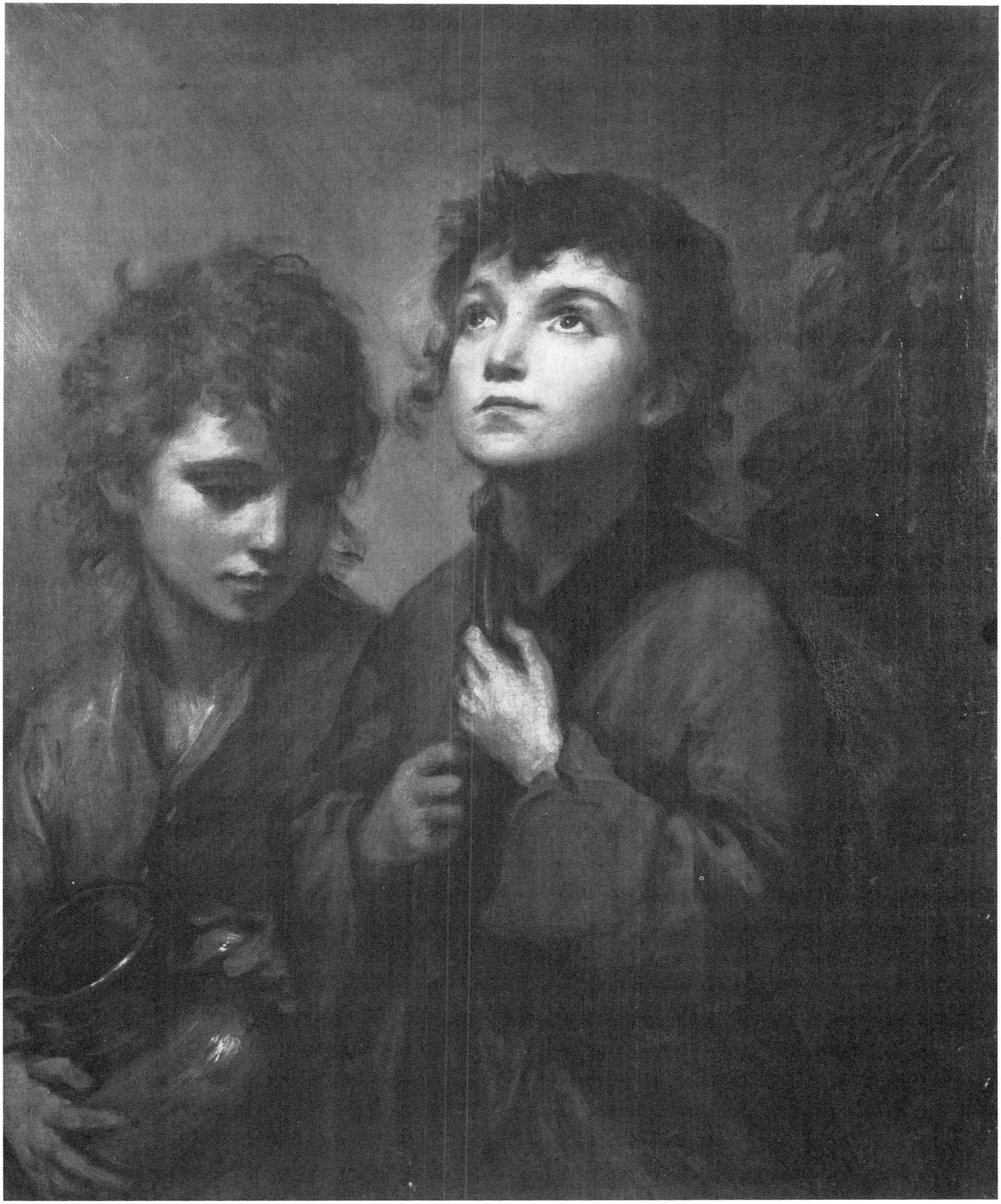

144. *Beggar Boys*. Canvas, 29 × 25 in. Painted spring 1785. Private Collection (Note 123)

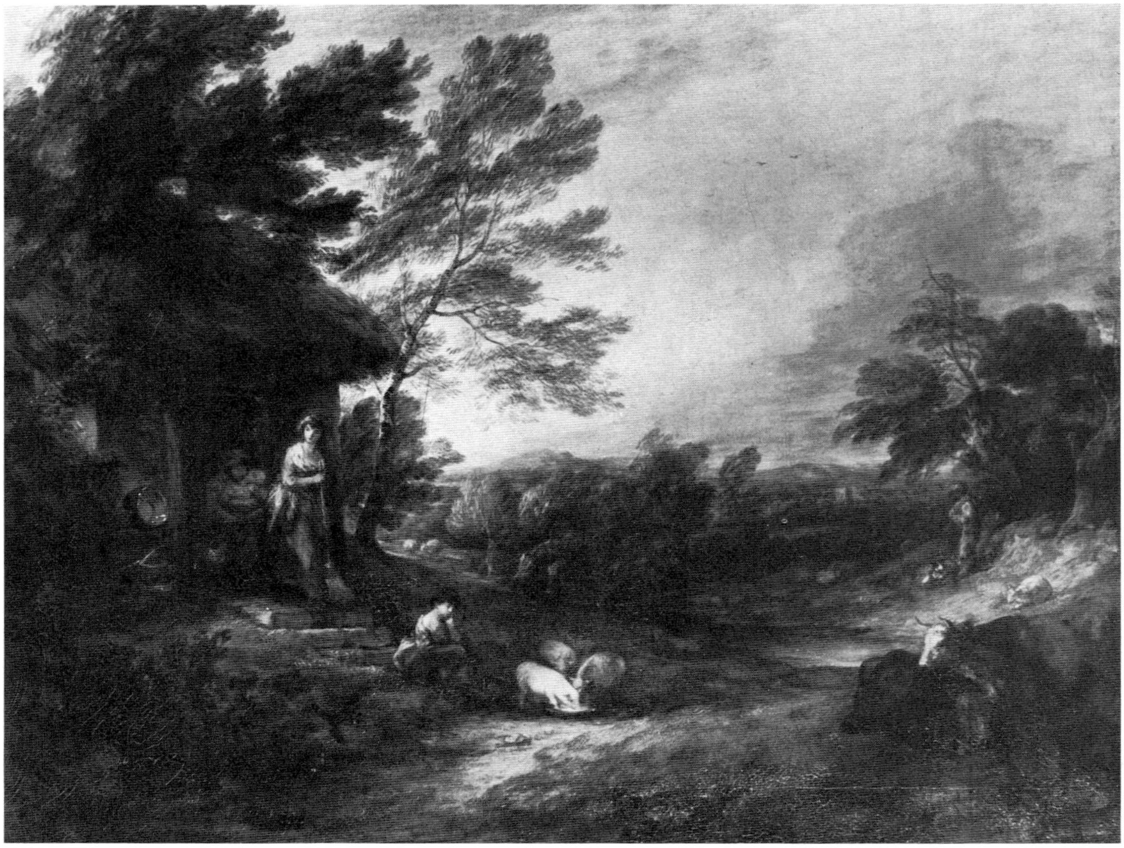

145. *The cottage door with girl with pigs*. Canvas, $38\frac{3}{4} \times 48\frac{3}{4}$ in. Painted summer 1786. London, Mrs H. Scudamore (on permanent loan to the Victoria and Albert Museum) (Note 128)

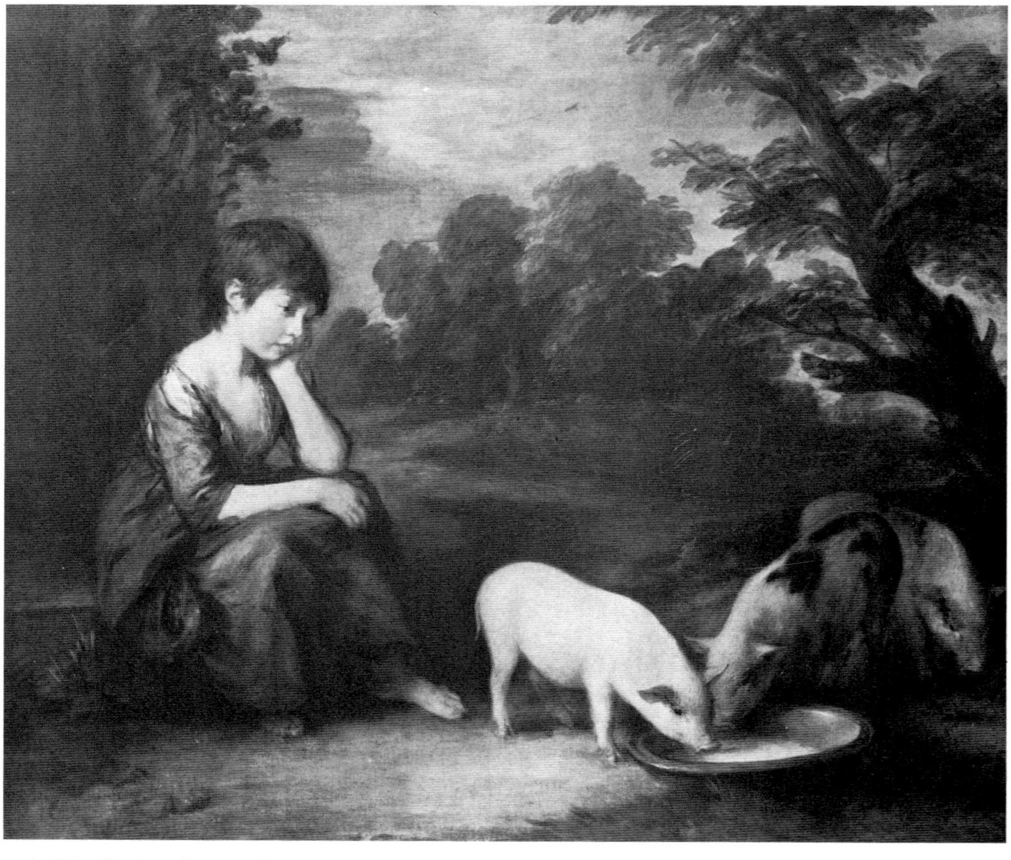

146. *The Girl with Pigs*. Canvas, $49\frac{1}{2} \times 58\frac{1}{2}$ in. Exhibited R. A. 1782 (127) (engraved 1783). Castle Howard, George Howard (Note 101)

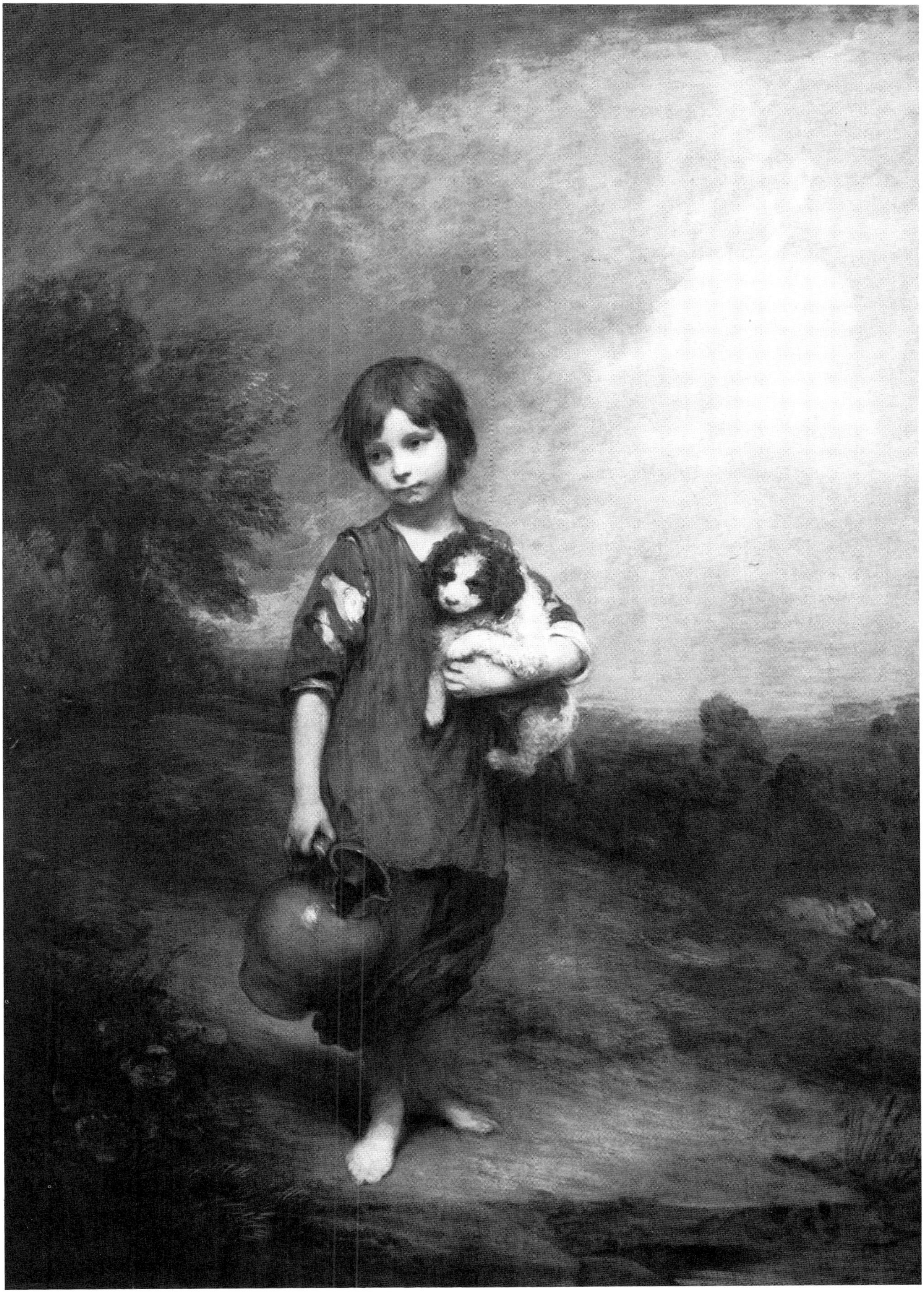

147. *The Cottage Girl with Dog and Pitcher*. Canvas; $68\frac{1}{2} \times 49$ in. Painted spring 1785 (engraved 1806). Russborough, Sir Alfred Beit, Bt (Note 124)

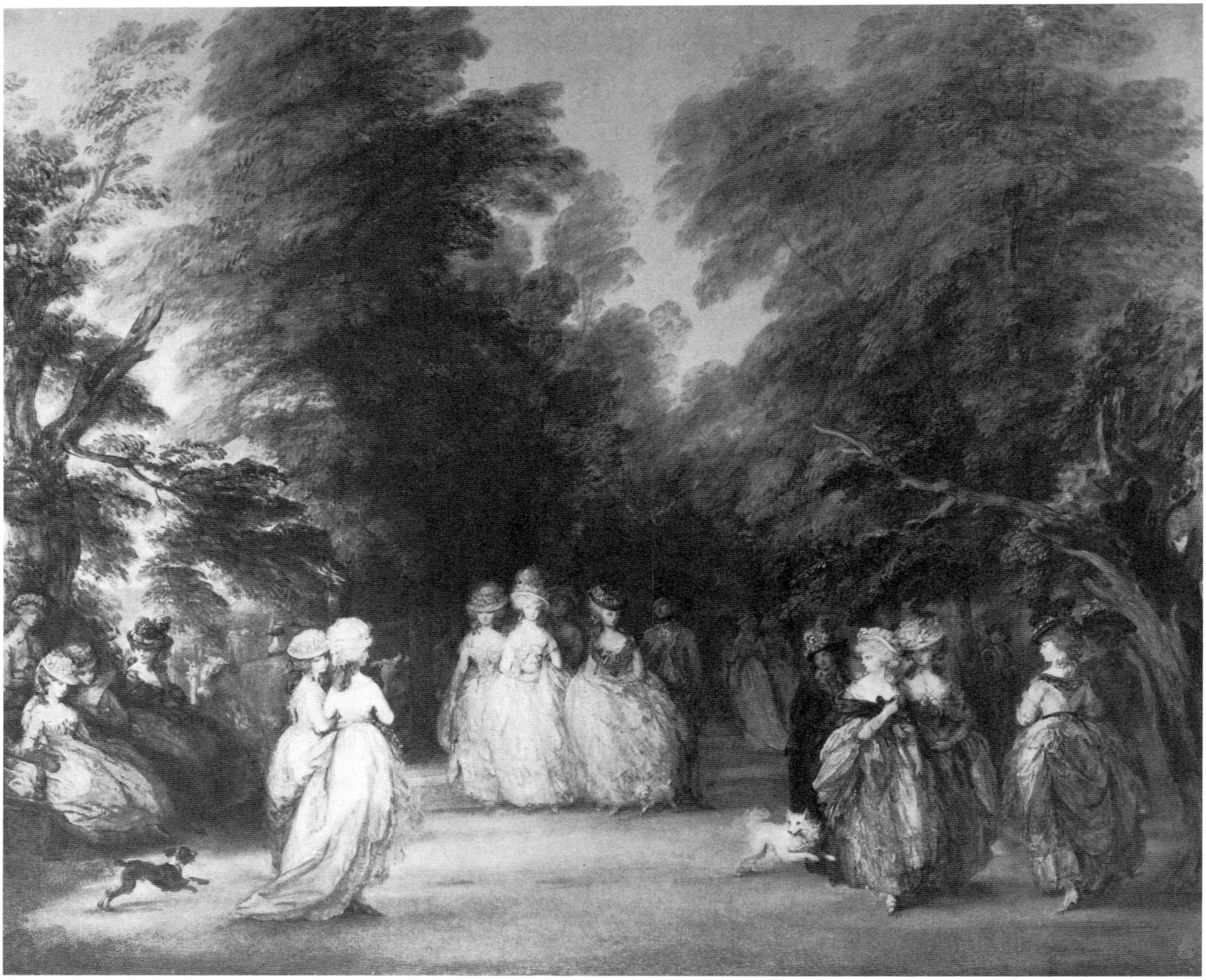

148. *The Mall*. Canvas, $47\frac{1}{2} \times 57\frac{7}{8}$ in. Painted winter 1783. Exhibited Schomberg House, July 1784. New York, Frick Collection (Note 109)

149. Detail from *Grace Dalrymple, Mrs John Elliott* (1758?–1823). Canvas, $30\frac{1}{8} \times 25$ in. Probably R. A. 1782 (184). New York, Frick Collection (Note 103)

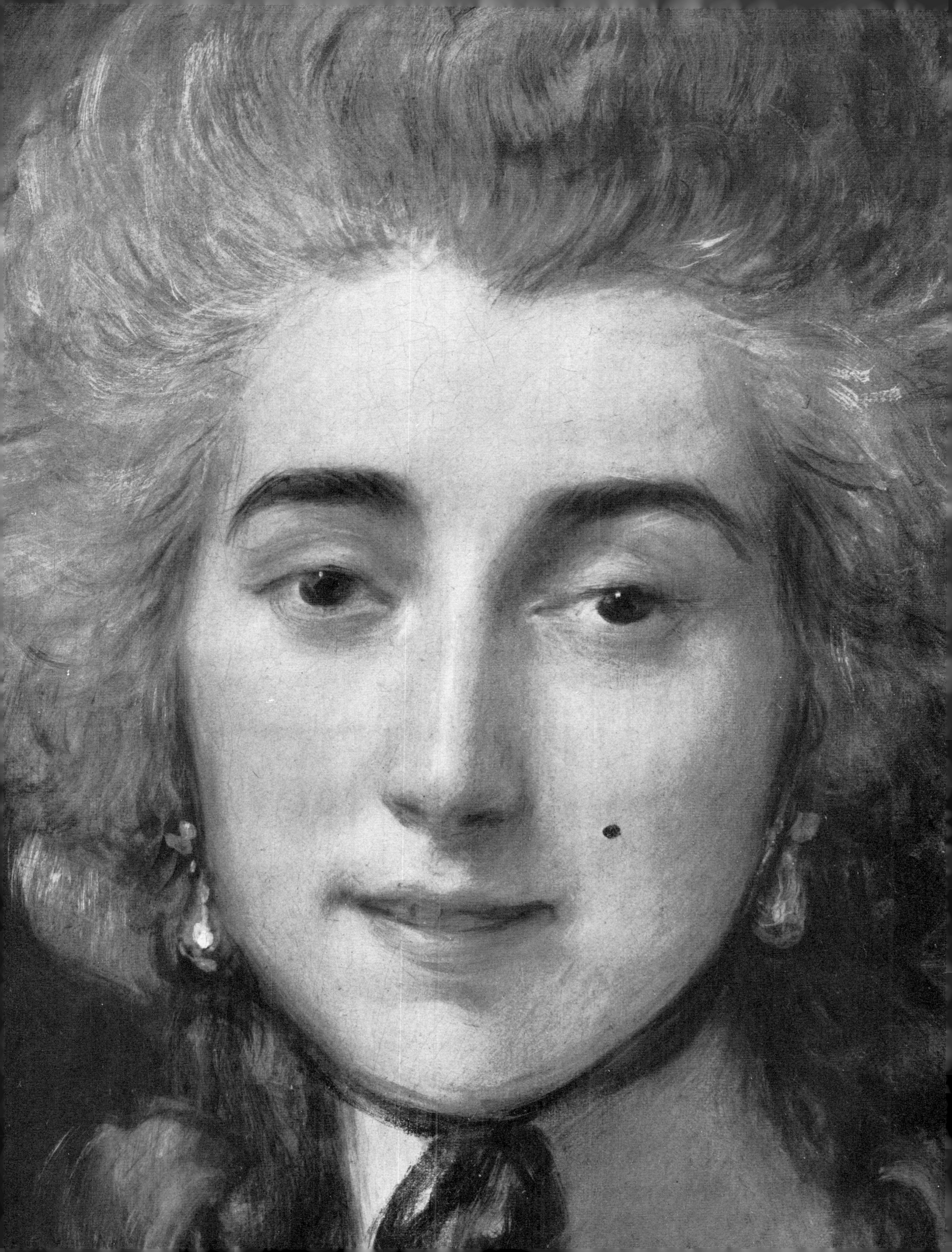

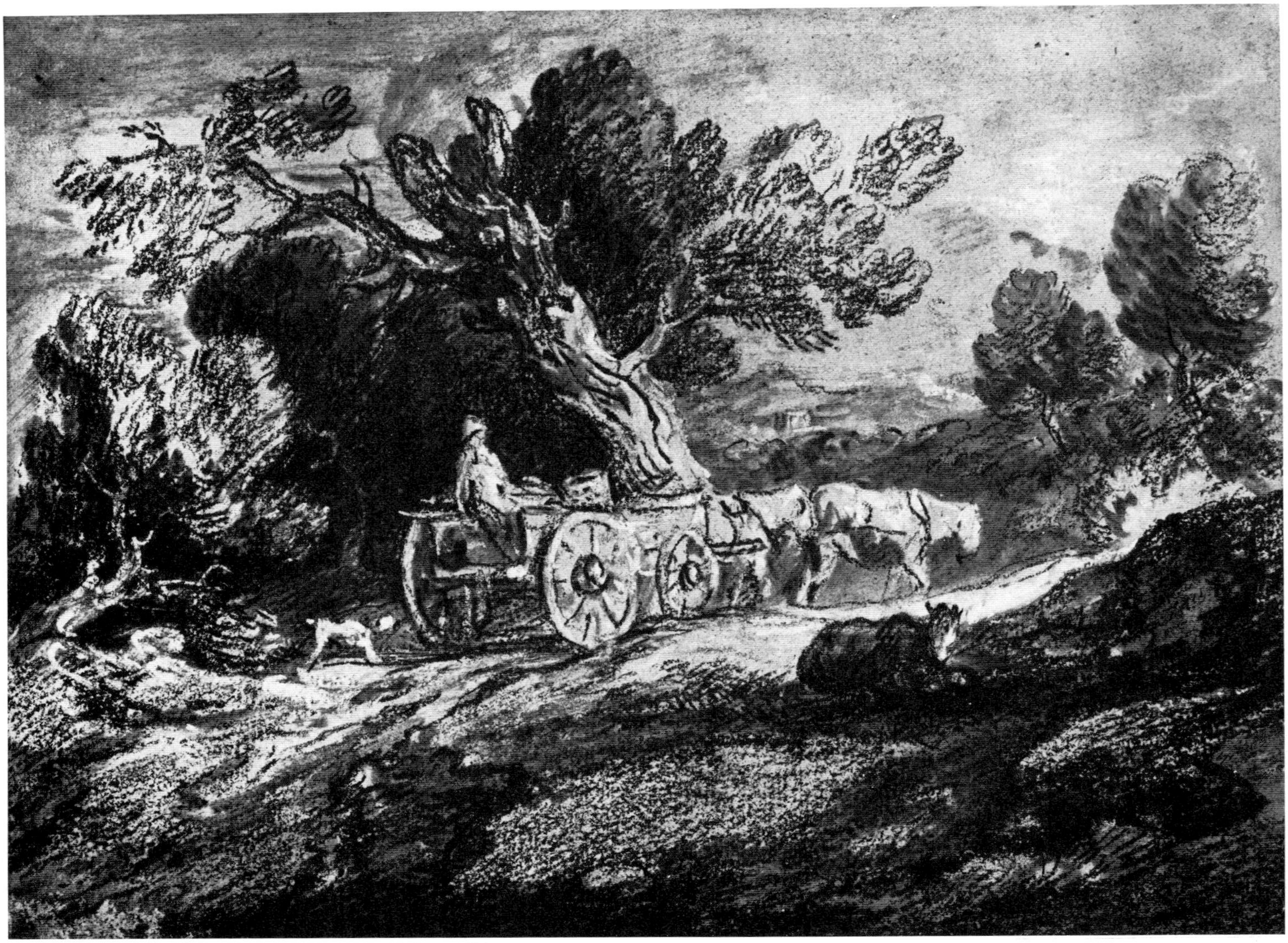

150. *Wooded landscape with country cart*. Black chalk and stump and white chalk on buff paper, $11\frac{1}{8} \times 14\frac{15}{16}$ in. Mid 1780s. London, Victoria and Albert Museum (Note 116)

151. Study of a lady for '*The Richmond Water-walk*'. Black chalk and stump on buff paper, heightened with white, $19\frac{5}{16} \times 12\frac{1}{4}$ in. About 1785. London, British Museum (Note 122)

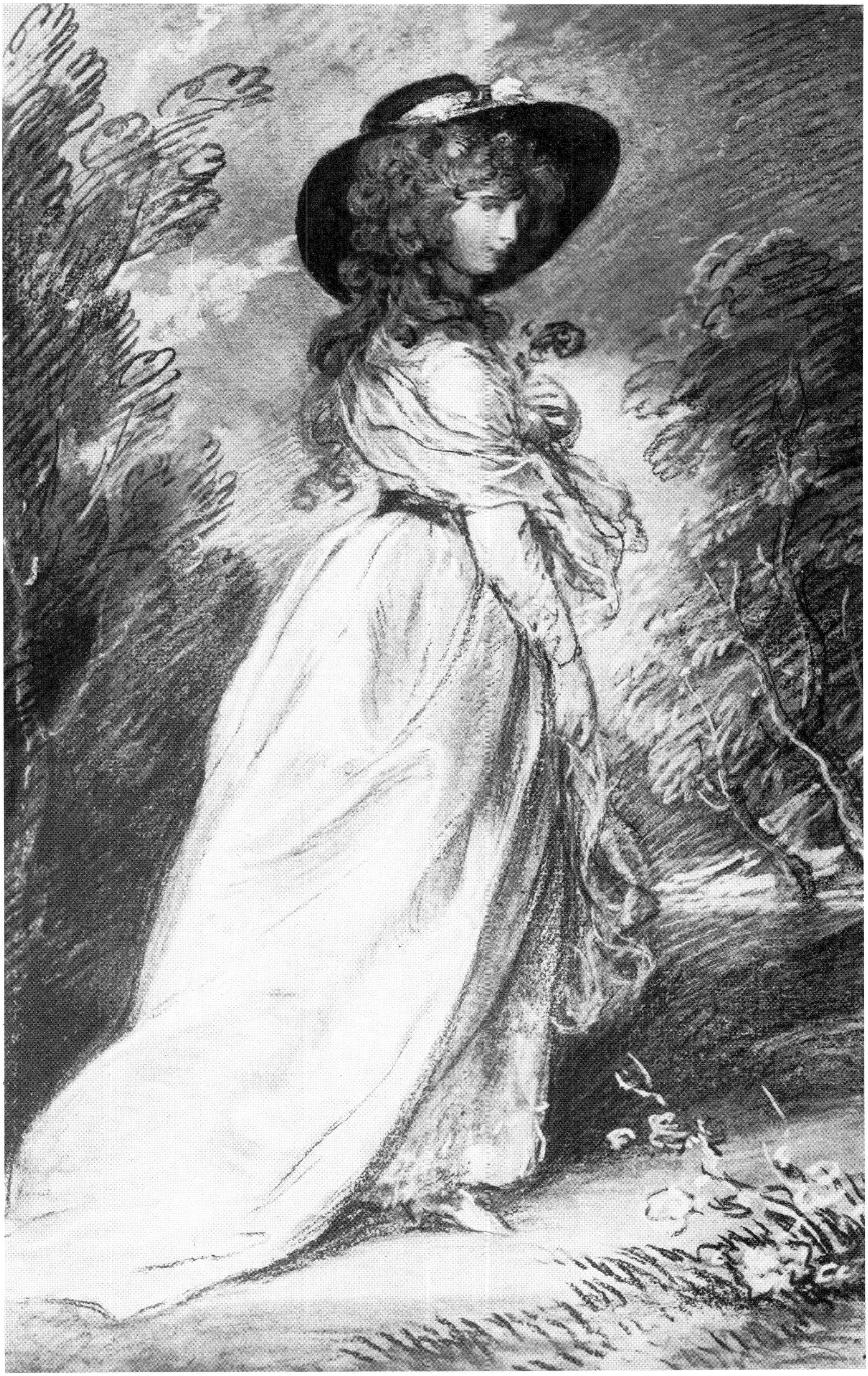

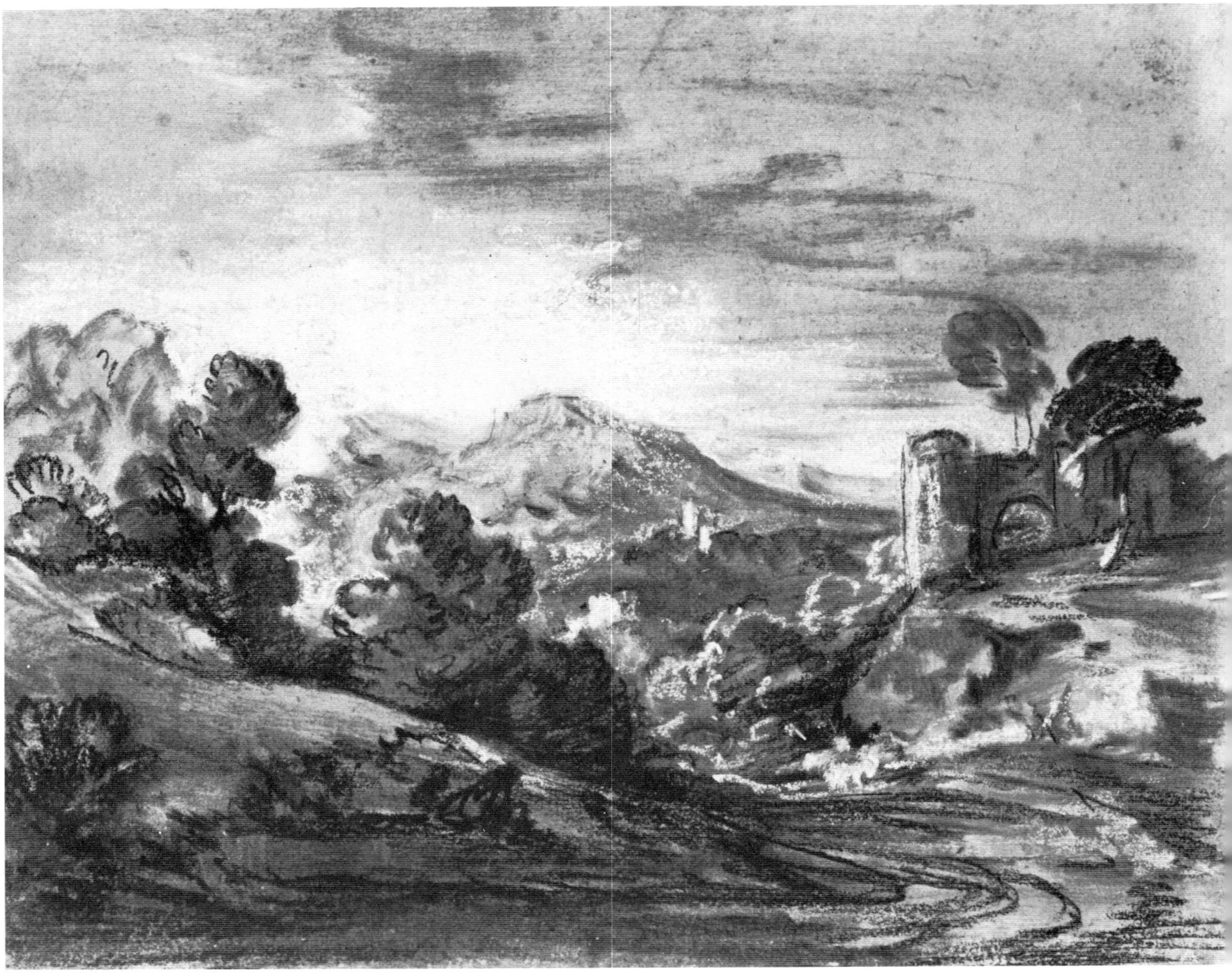

152. *Wooded landscape with castle*. Black chalk and stump and white chalk on grey paper, $10\frac{5}{16} \times 12\frac{7}{8}$ in. About 1787–8. Oak Spring, Virginia, Mr and Mrs Paul Mellon (Note 139)

153. *Mrs Richard Brinsley Sheridan, née Elizabeth Linley* (1754–92). Canvas, $86\frac{1}{2} \times 60\frac{1}{2}$ in. Painted spring 1785, slightly altered winter 1786 Washington, National Gallery of Art (Note 119)

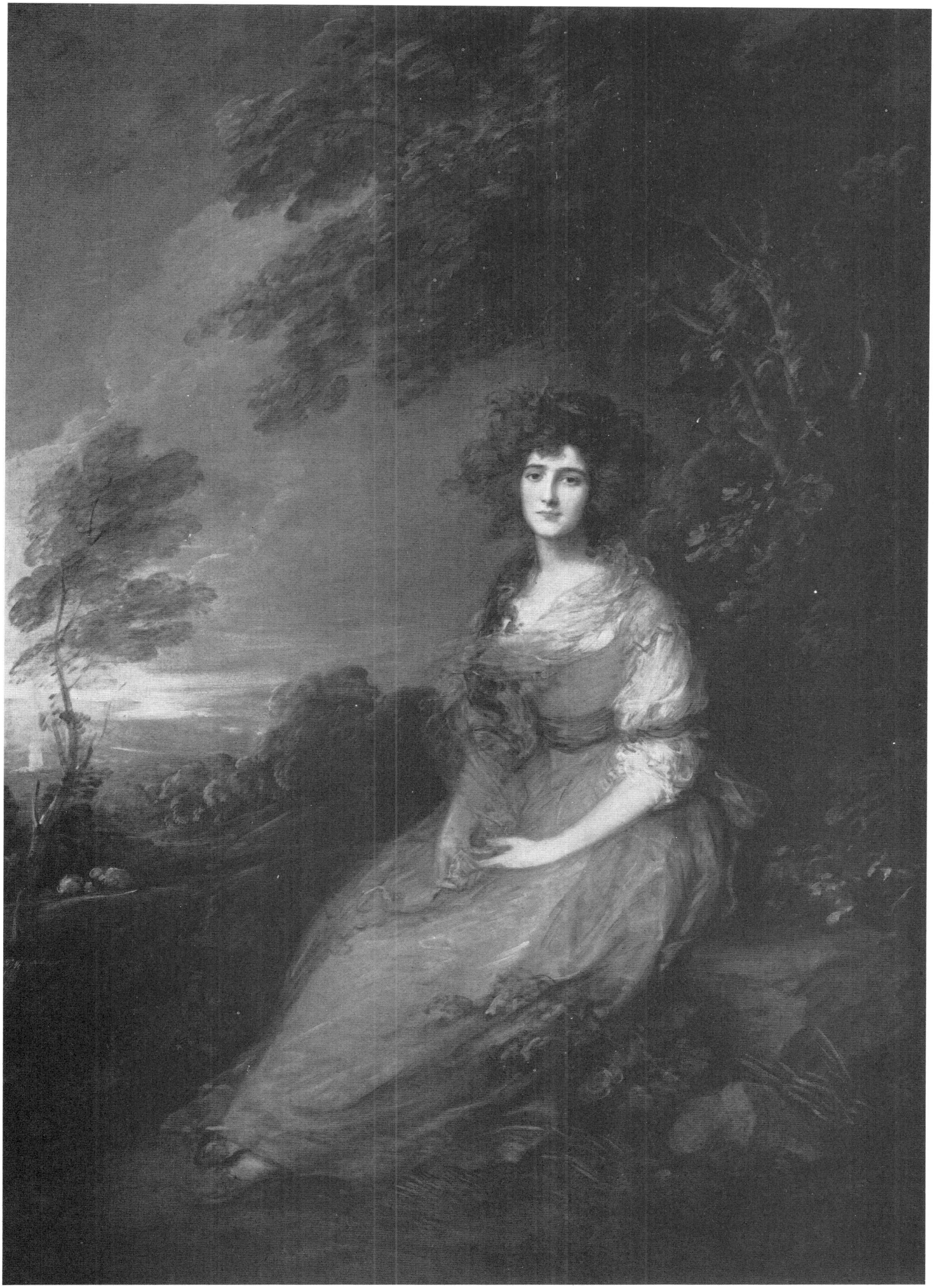

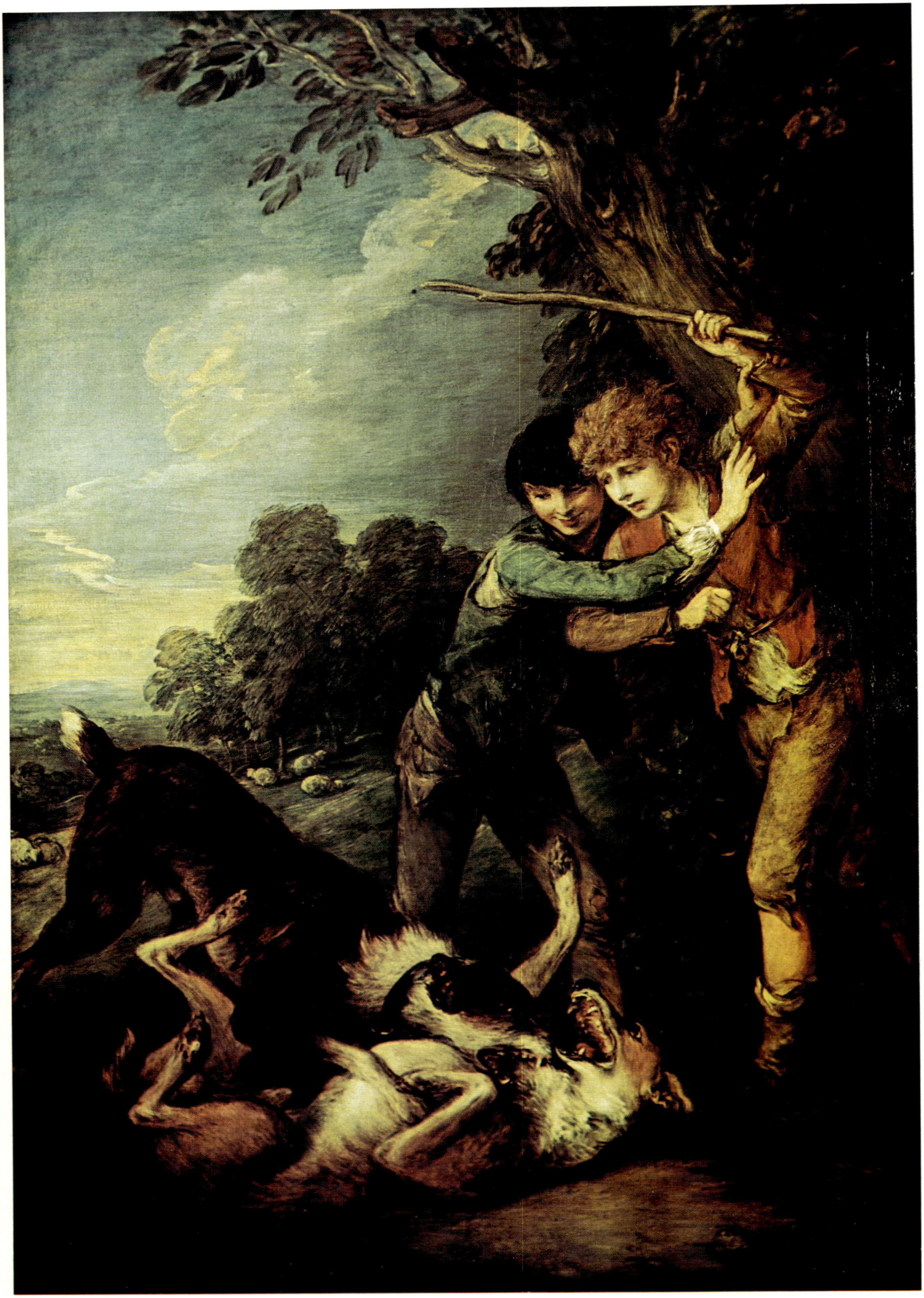

154. *Two shepherd boys with dogs fighting*. Canvas, 88 × 62 in. Exhibited R. A. 1783 (35) (engraved 1791). London, Iveagh Bequest, Kenwood (Note 108)

155. *Greyhounds coursing a fox*. Canvas, 70 × 93 in. About 1784-5. Mentmore, Earl of Rosebery (Note 115)

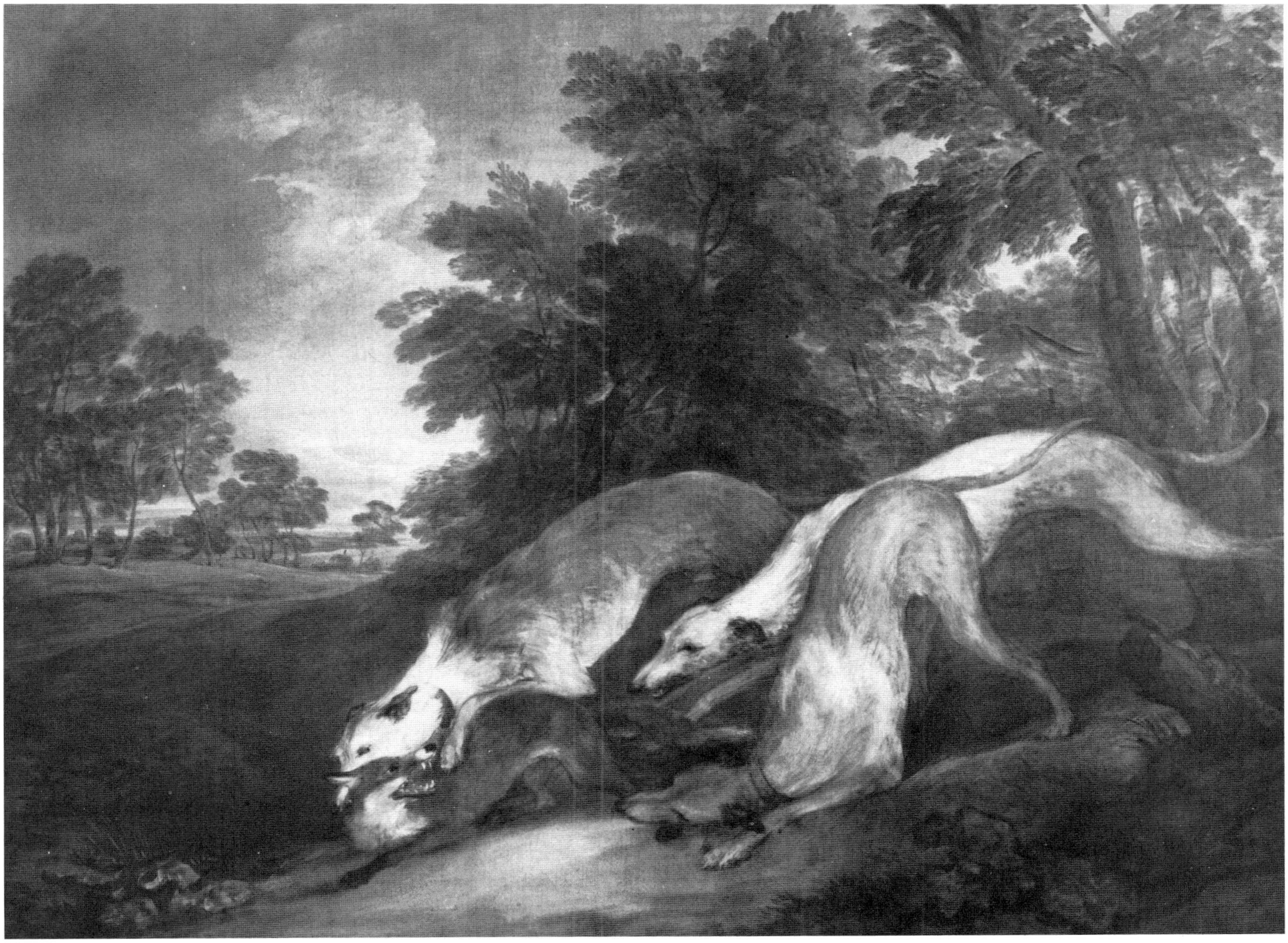

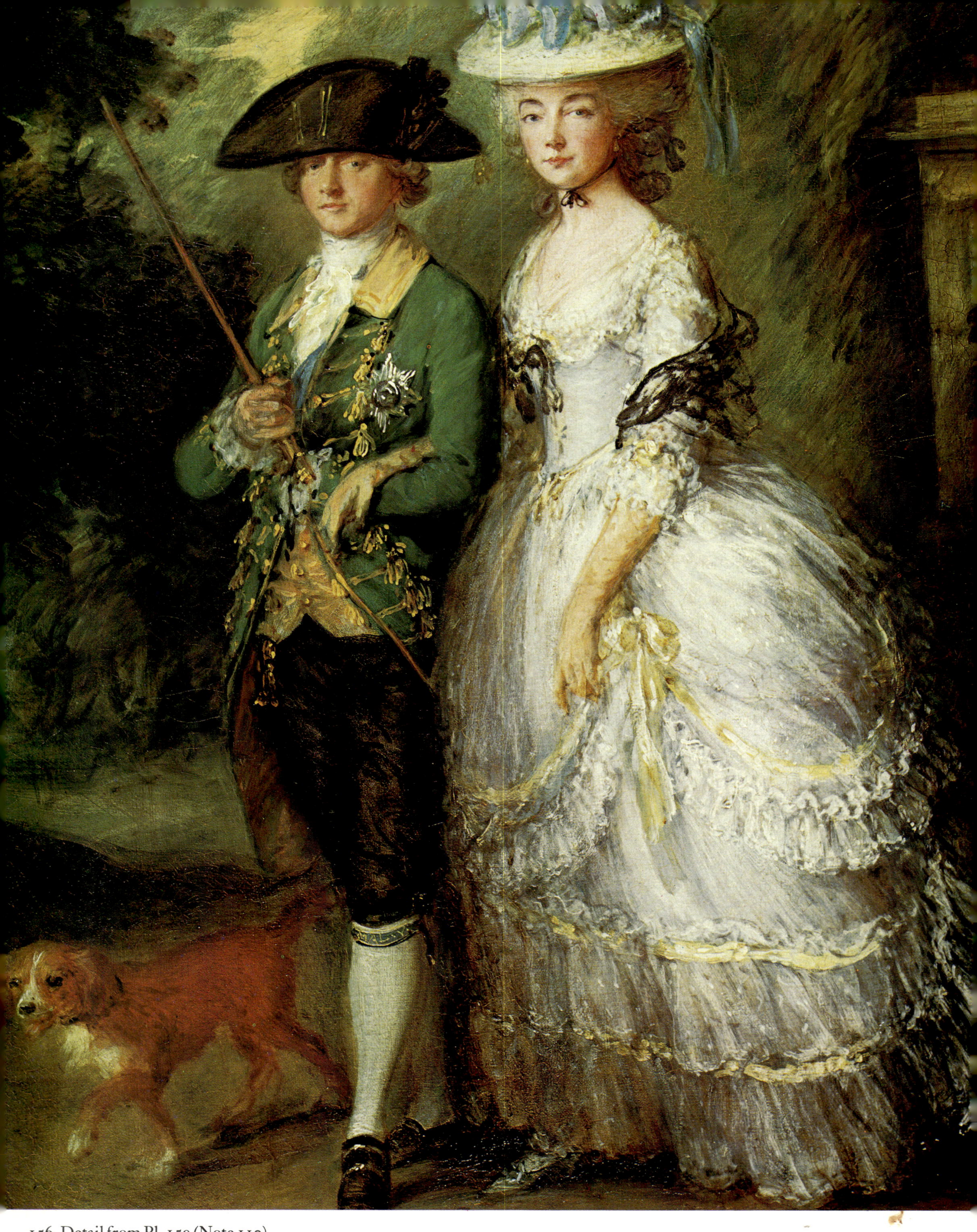

156. Detail from Pl. 159 (Note 110)

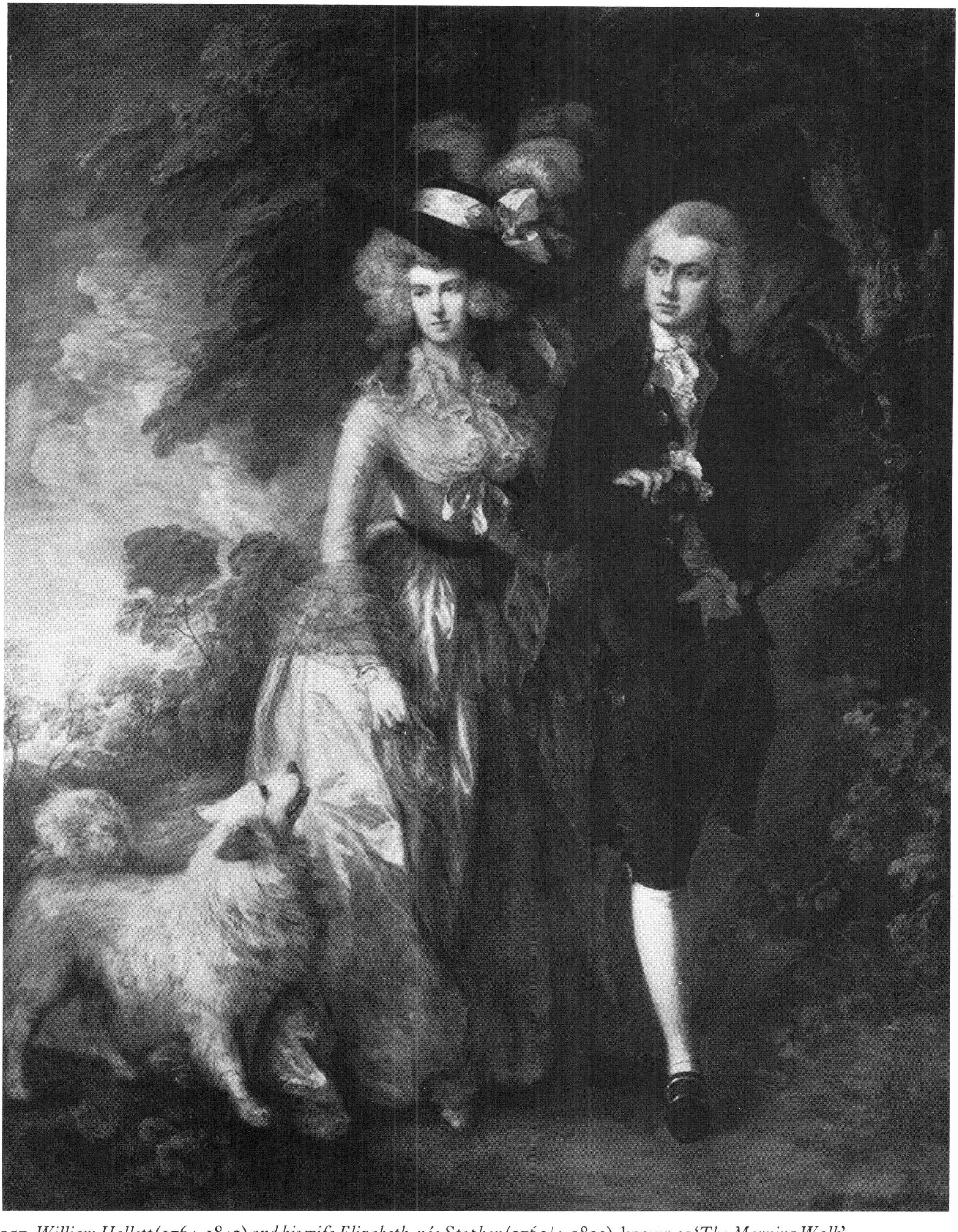

157. *William Hallett* (1764–1842) *and his wife Elizabeth, née Stephen* (1763/4–1833), known as '*The Morning Walk*'. Canvas, 93 × 70½ in. Painted autumn 1785. London, National Gallery (Note 127)

156. Detail from Pl. 159 (Note 110)

160. Detail from Pl. 157 (Note 127)

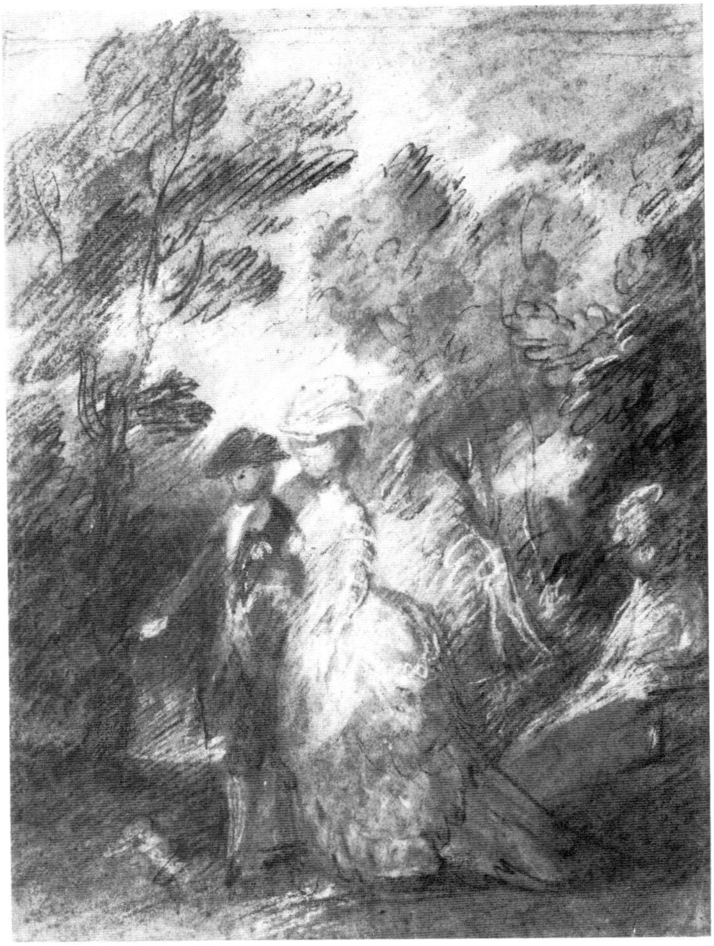

158. Second study for *The Duke and Duchess of Cumberland*. Black chalk and stump and white chalk on buff paper, $16\frac{7}{8} \times 12\frac{7}{16}$ in. About 1783–5. London, British Museum (Note 110)

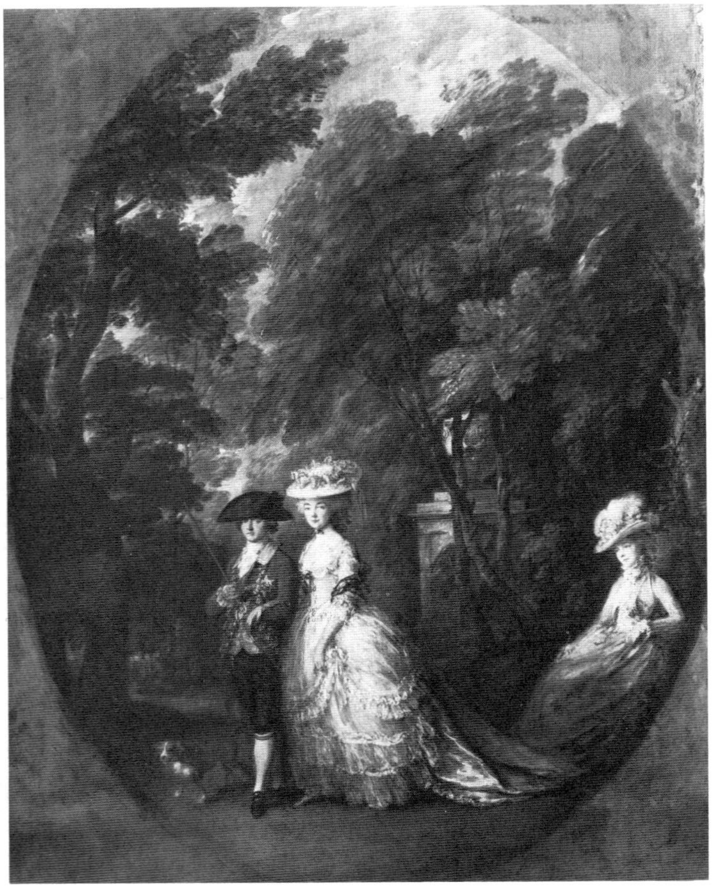

159. *Henry Frederick, Duke of Cumberland* (1745–90) *with his wife Anne, formerly Mrs Horton* (1743–1808), *attended by Lady Elizabeth Luttrell* (d.1799). Canvas, $64\frac{1}{2} \times 49$ in. (oval). About 1783–5. Windsor Castle (Note 110) (reproduced by gracious permission of Her Majesty The Queen)

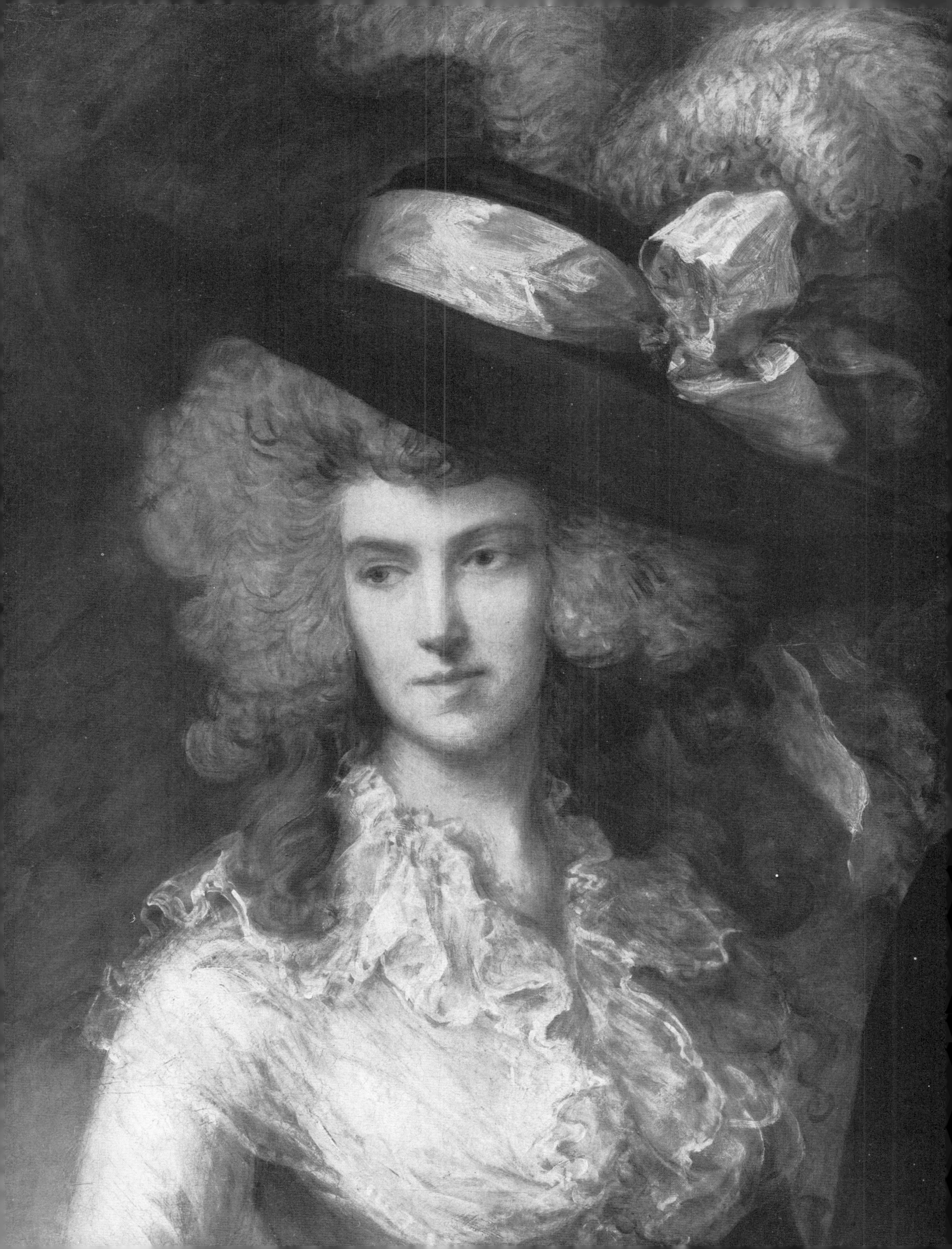

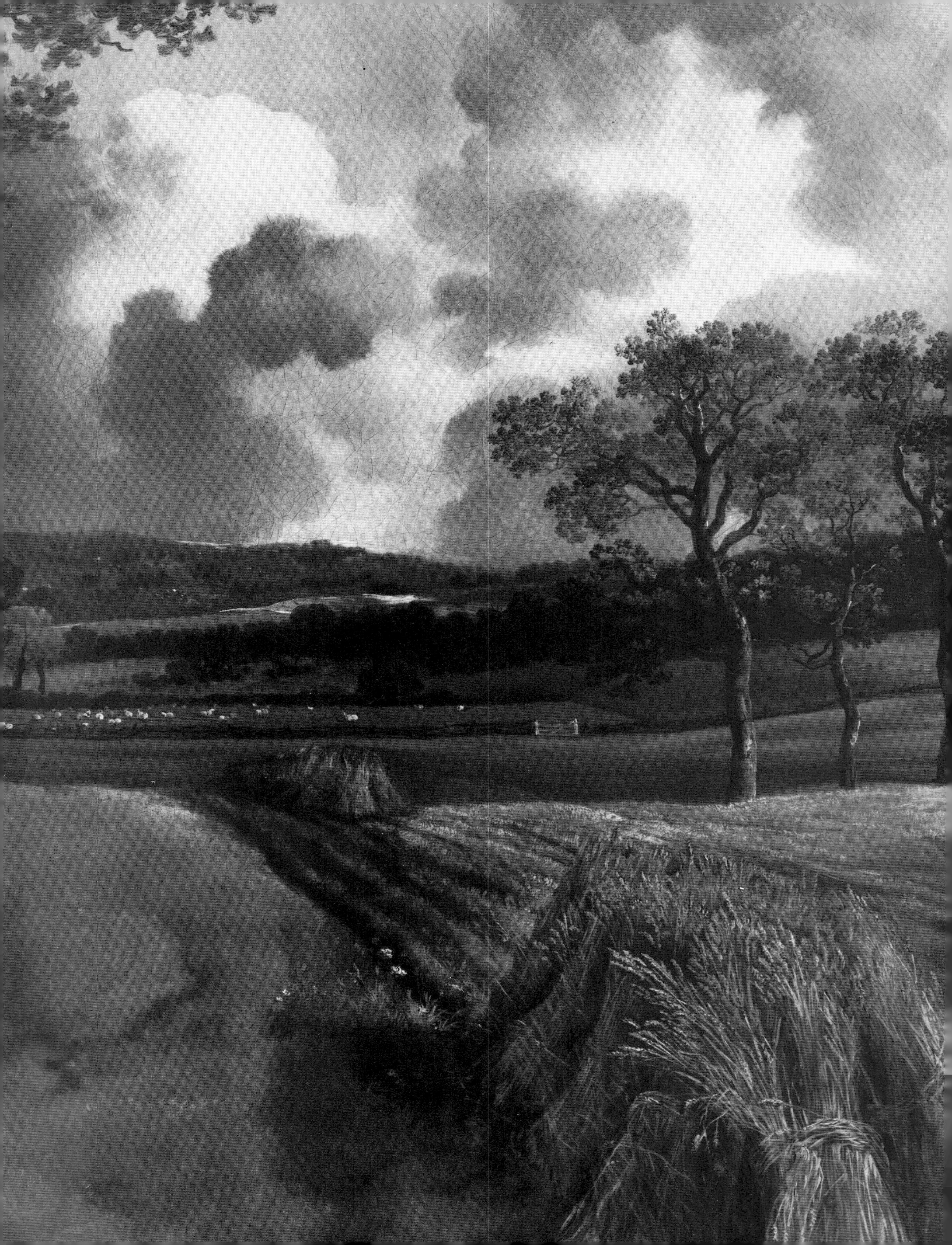

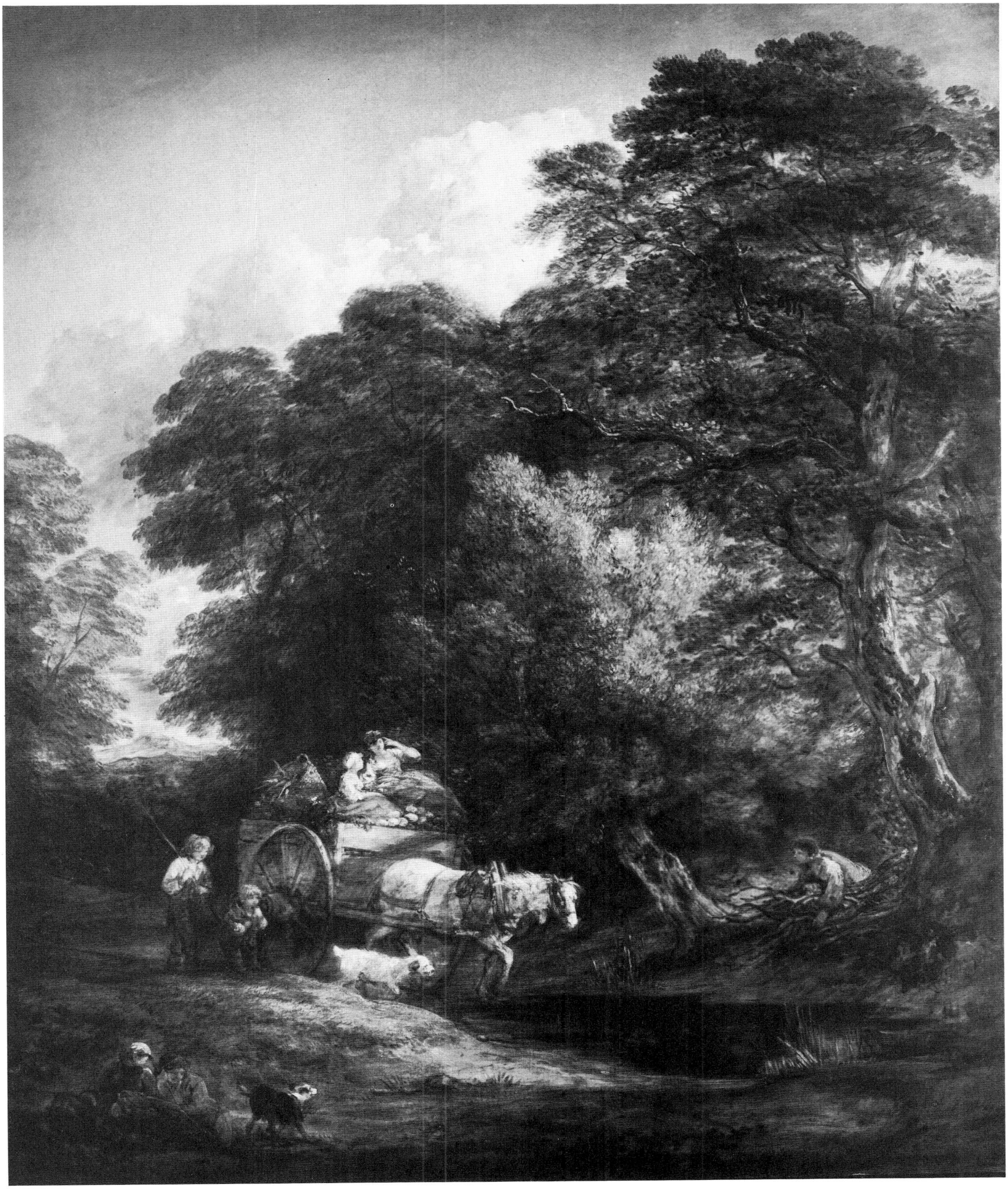

162. *The Market Cart*. Canvas, $72\frac{1}{2} \times 60\frac{1}{4}$ in. Painted winter 1786. London, Tate Gallery (Note 129)

161. Detail from Pl. 21 (Note 12)

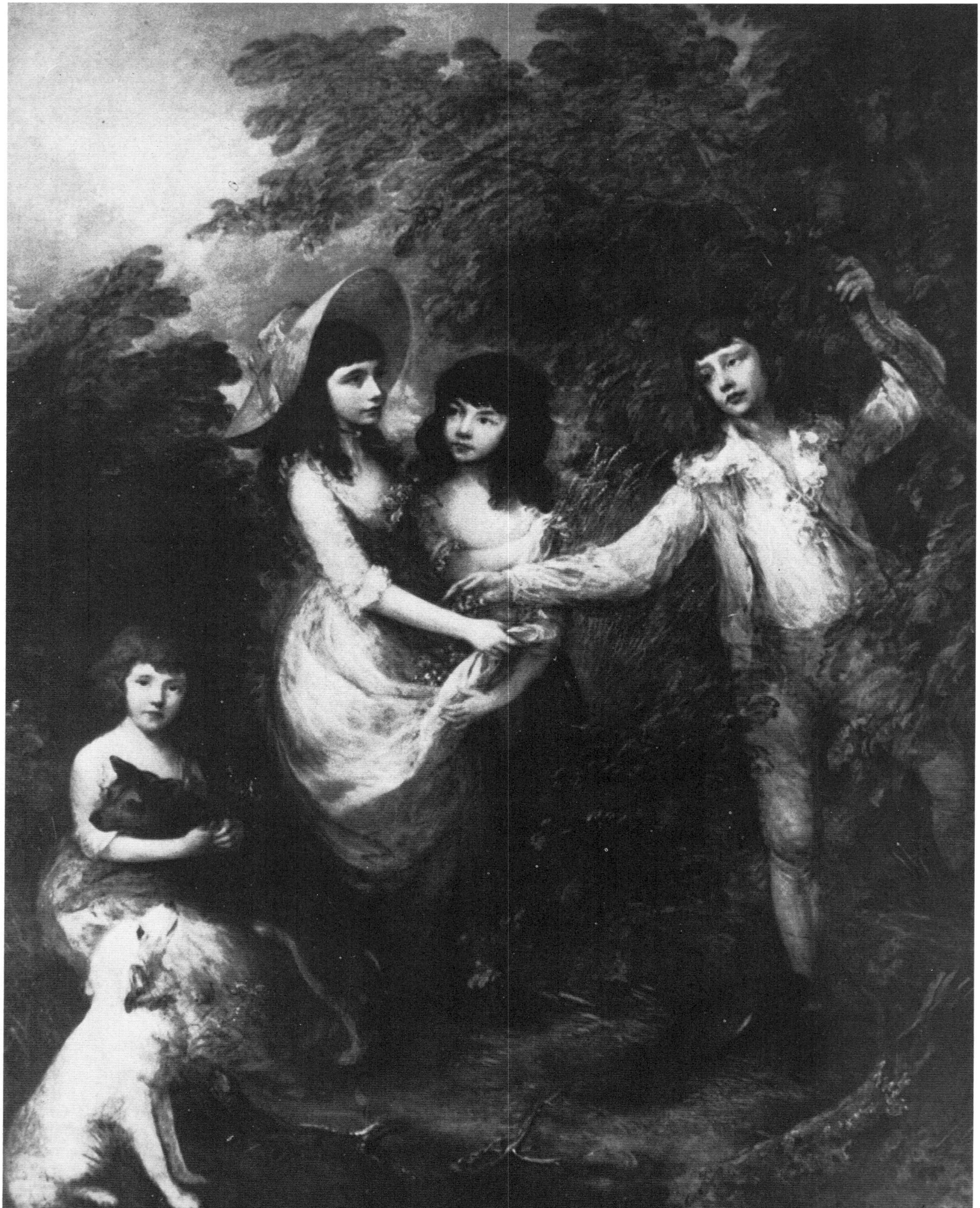

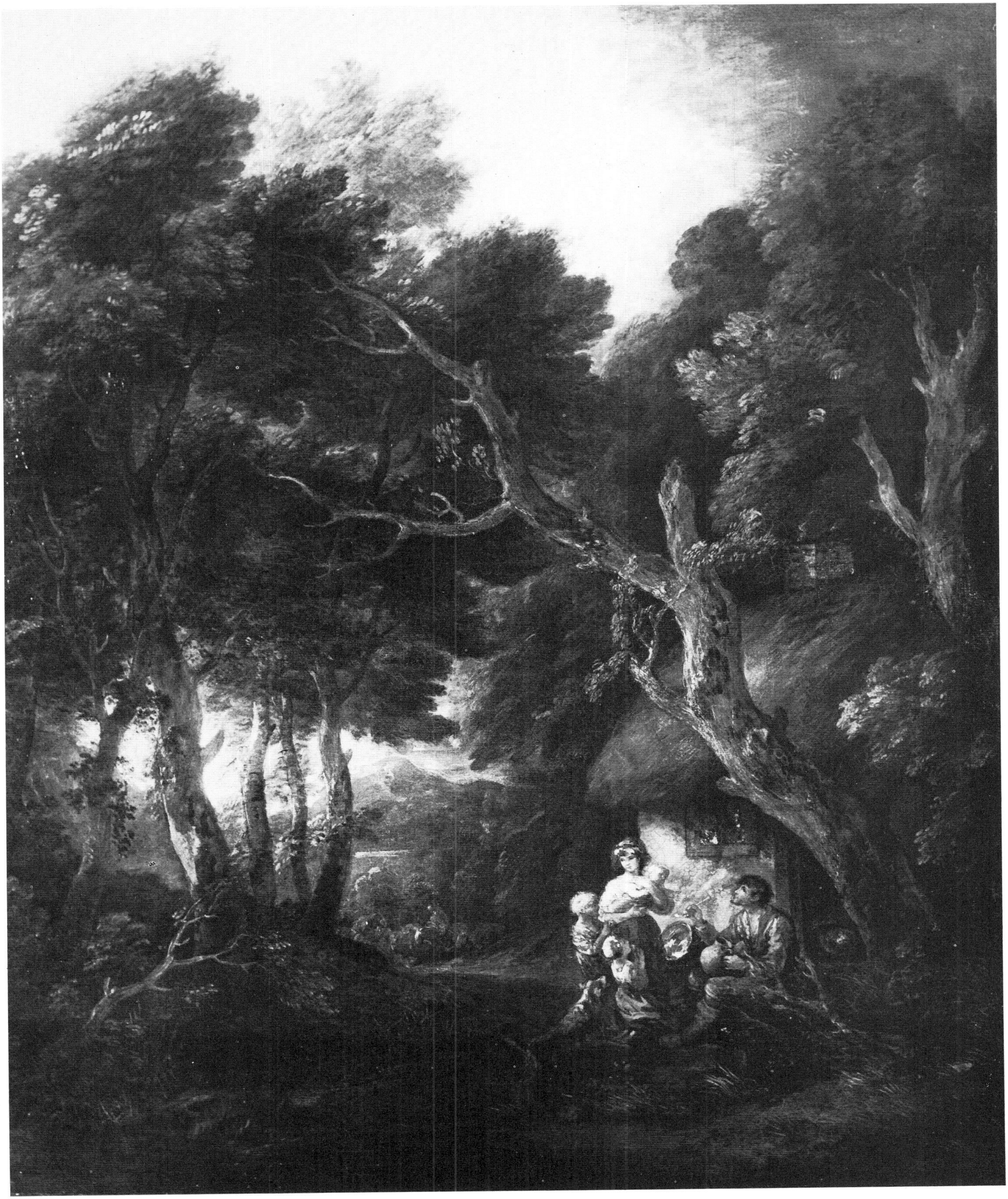

164. *Peasant smoking at a cottage door*. Canvas, 77 × 62 in. Painted spring 1788. Los Angeles, University of California (Note 138)

163. *The Marsham children, Charles, later 2nd Earl of Romney* (1777–1845), *and his three younger sisters*. Canvas, 94½ × 71 in. Painted July 1787. Paris, Baroness Elie de Rothschild (Note 131)

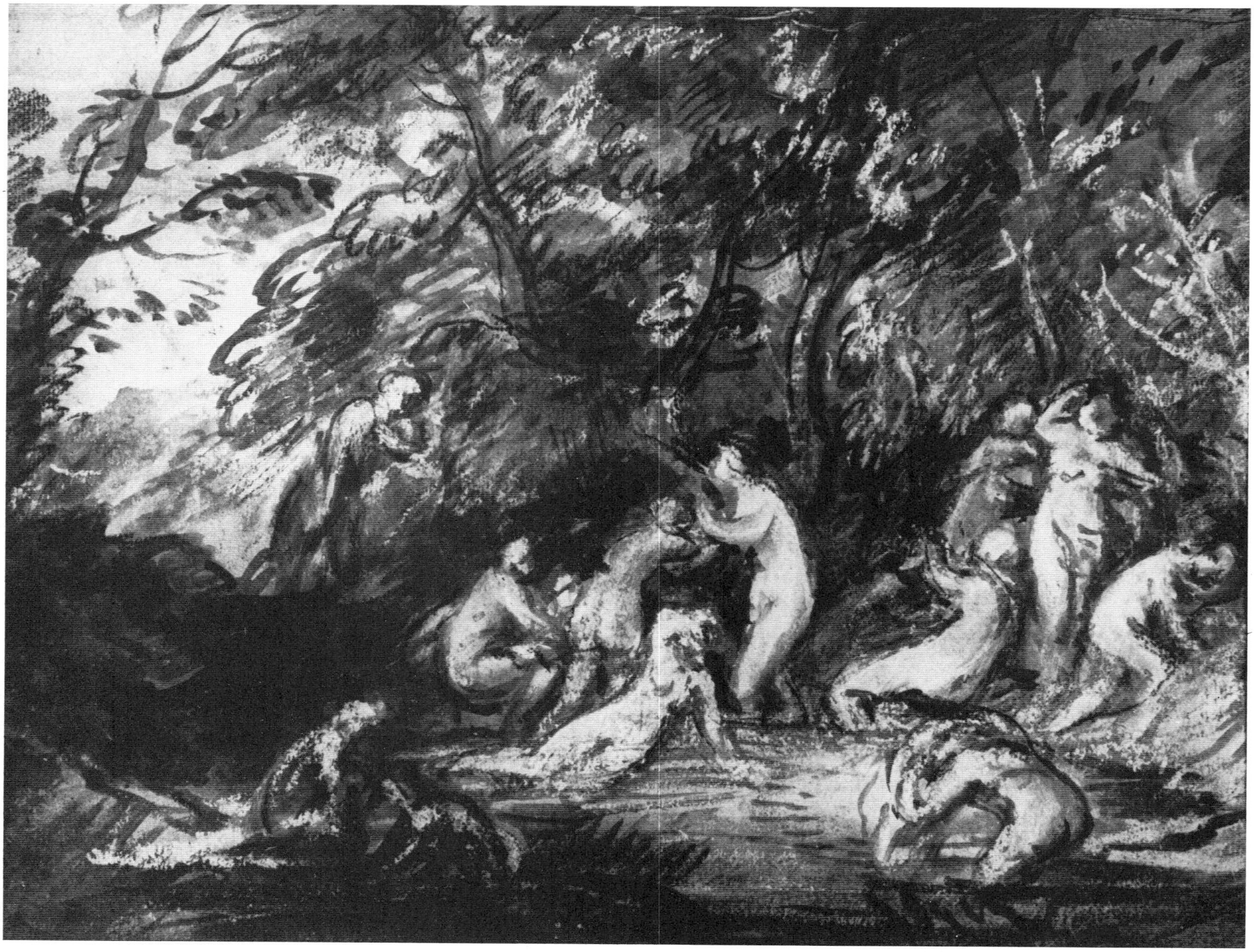

165. First of three studies for '*Diana and Actaeon*'. Black and white chalks and grey and grey-black washes on buff paper, $10\frac{1}{16} \times 13\frac{1}{8}$ in. About 1784–5. Plâs Newydd, Marchioness of Anglesey (Note 118)

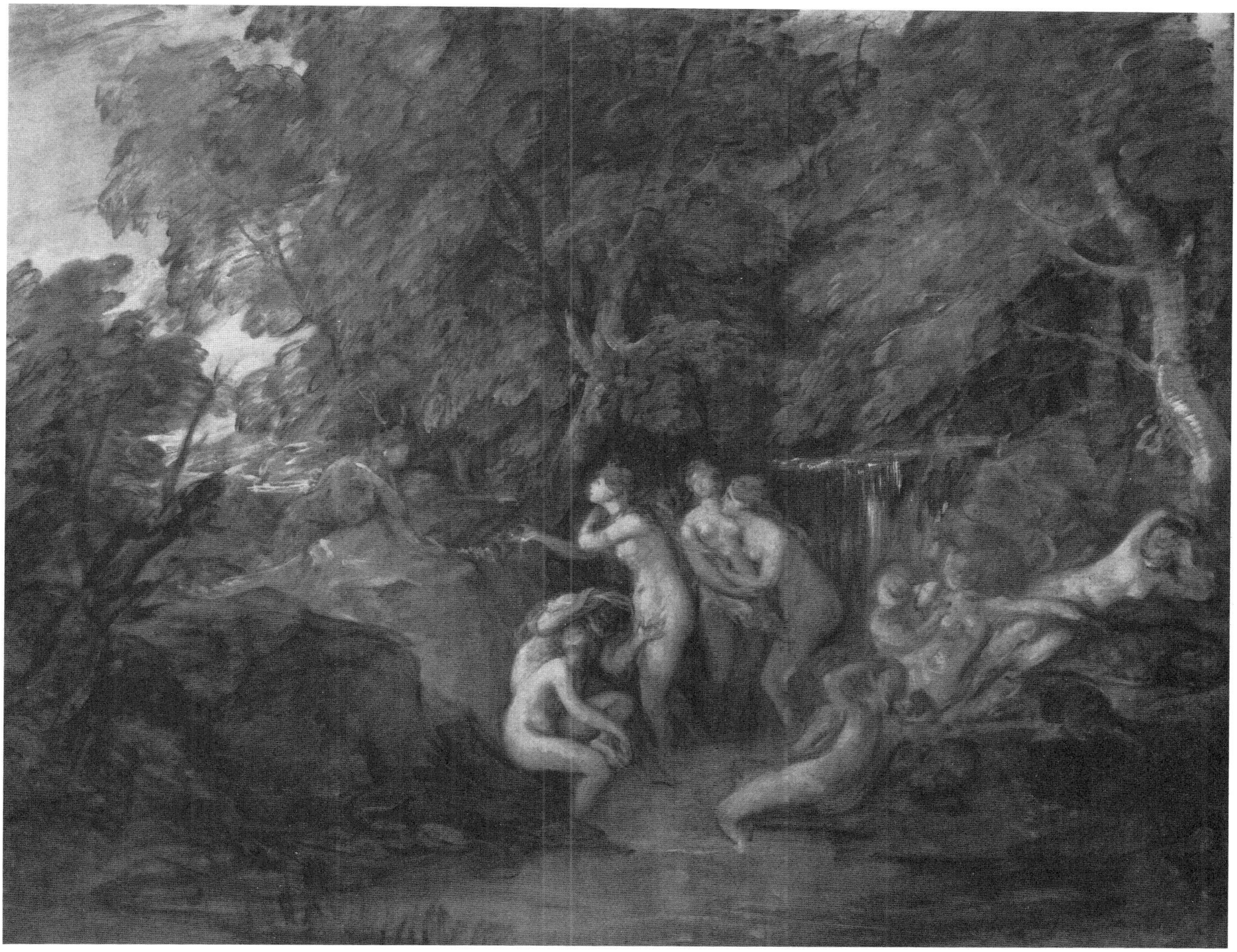

166. *Diana and Actaeon*. Canvas, $62\frac{1}{4} \times 74$ in. About 1784–5. London, Buckingham Palace (Note 118) (reproduced by gracious permission of Her Majesty The Queen)

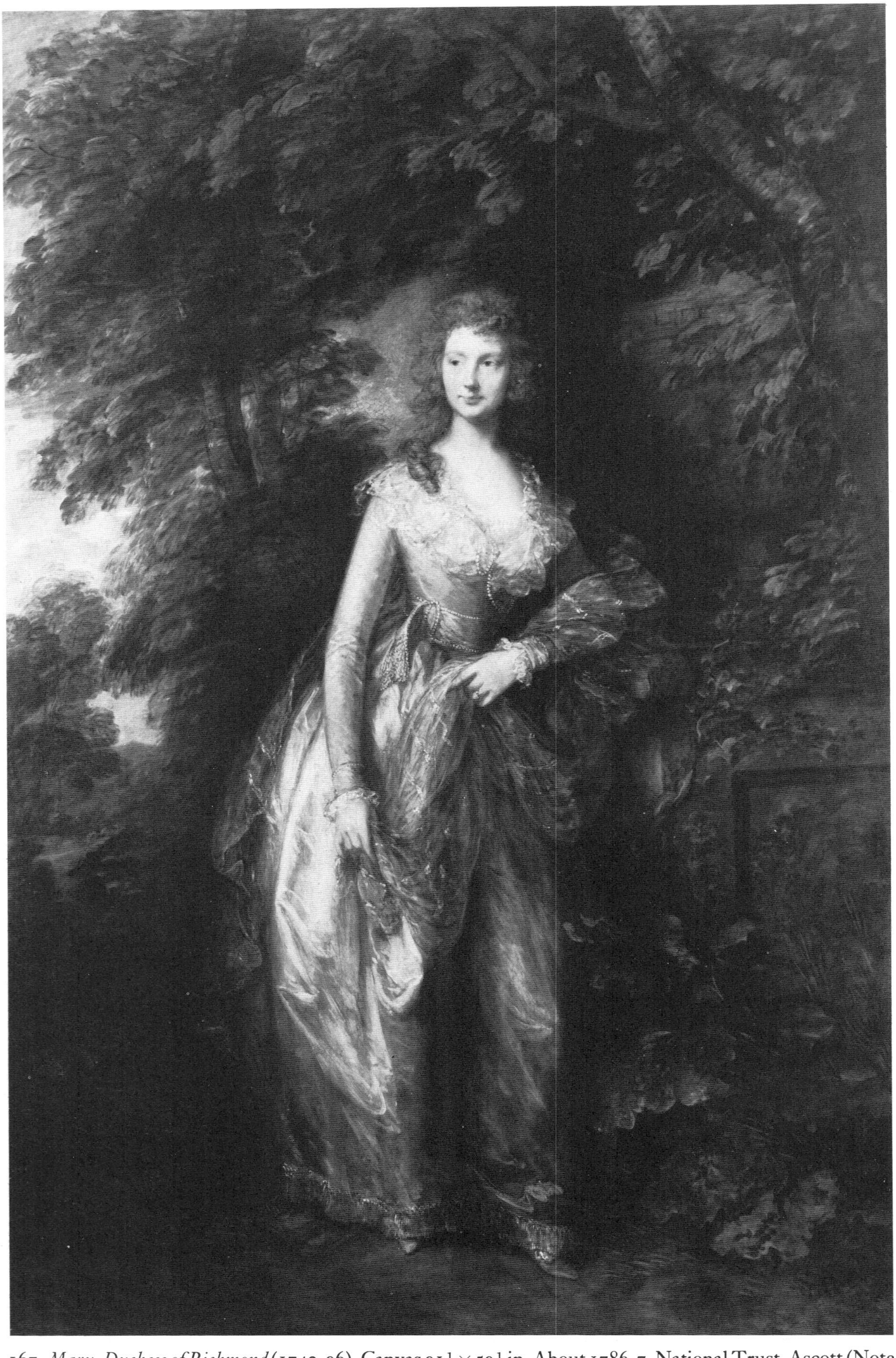

167. *Mary, Duchess of Richmond* (1740–96). Canvas $91\frac{1}{2} \times 59\frac{1}{2}$ in. About 1786–7. National Trust, Ascott (Note 130)

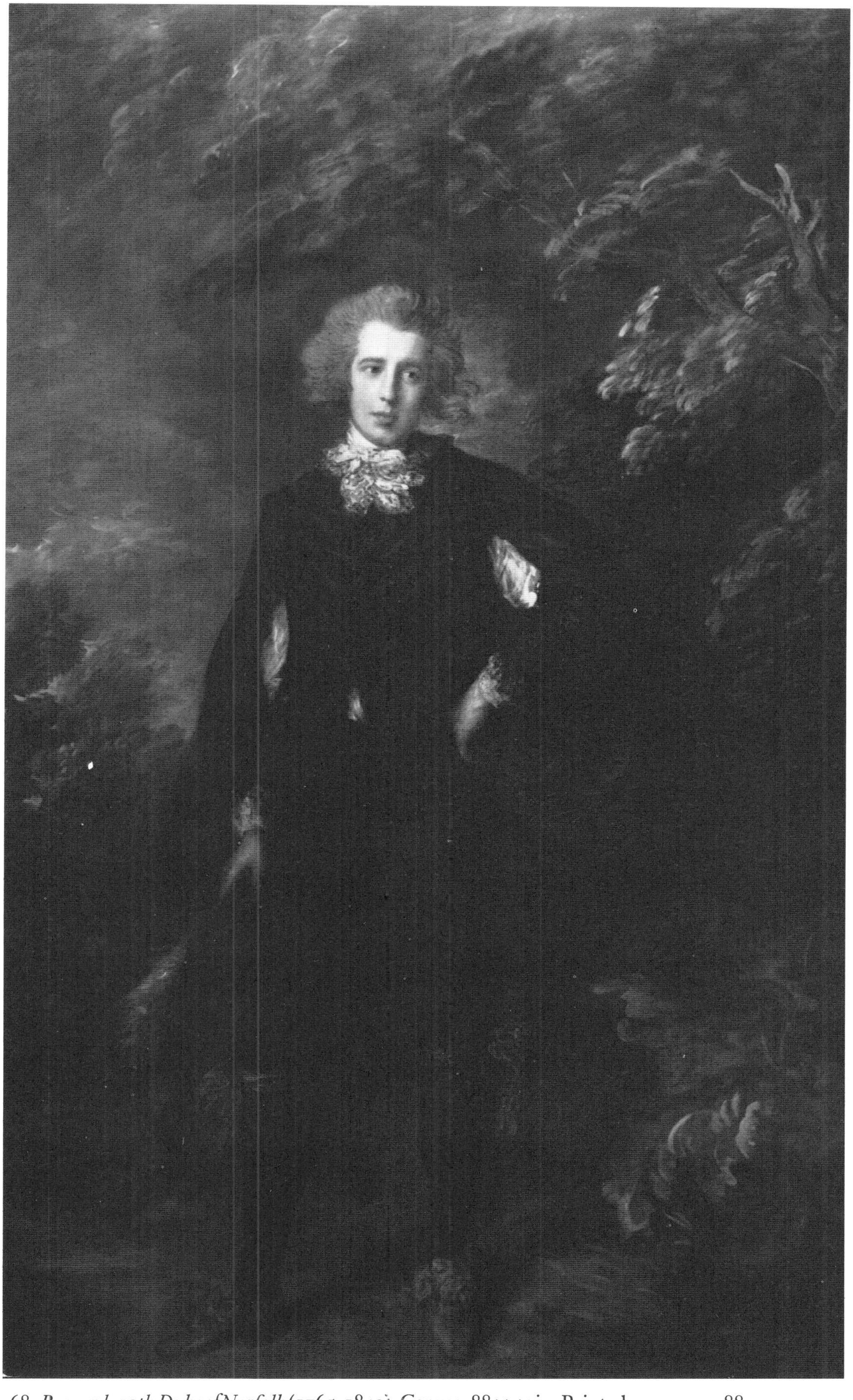

168. *Bernard, 12th Duke of Norfolk* (1765–1842). Canvas, 88 × 54 in. Painted summer 1788. Arundel Castle, Duke of Norfolk (Note 136)

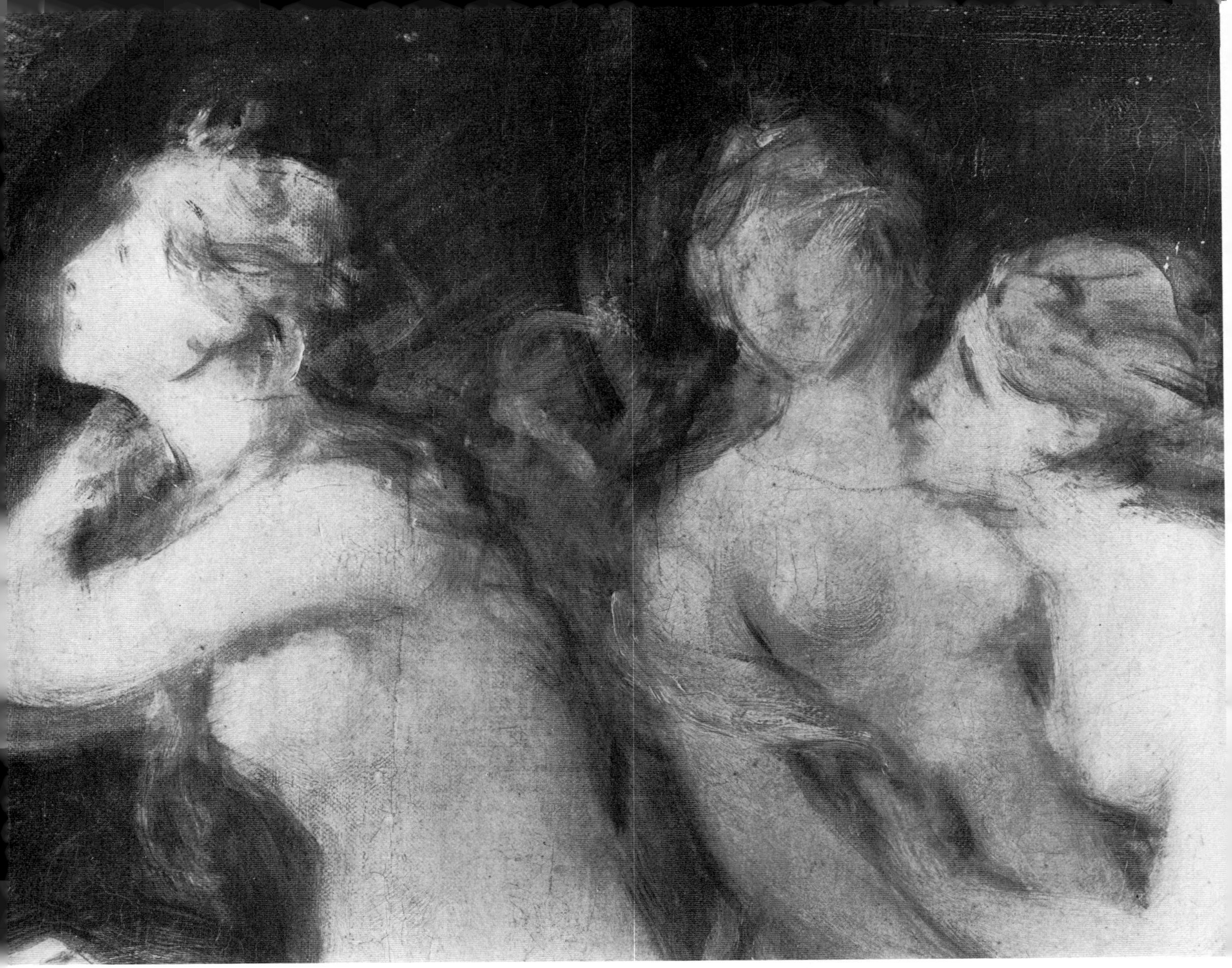

169. Detail from Pl. 166 (Note 118)

170. Detail from Pl. 167 (Note 130)

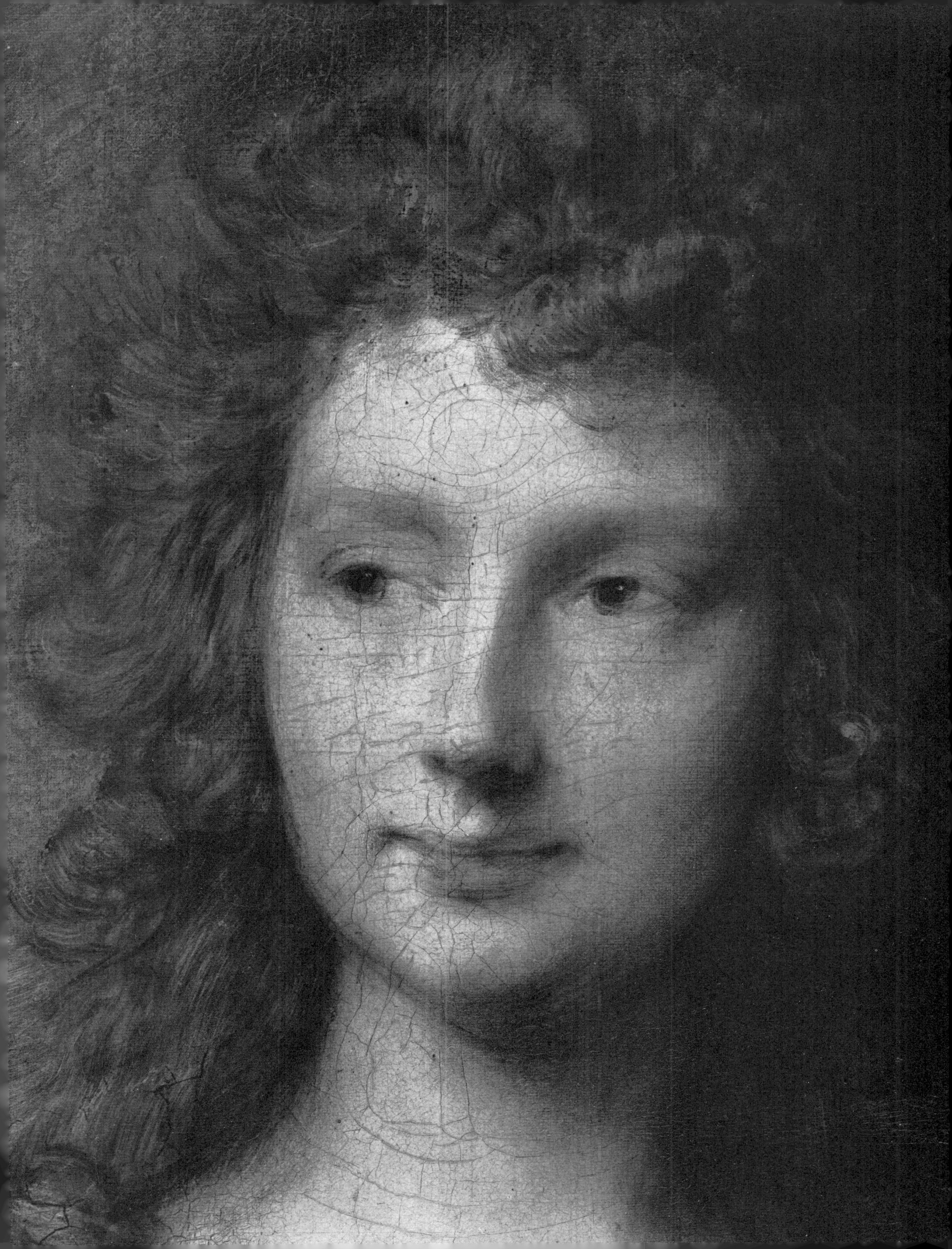

172. Detail from '*The Housemaid*'. Canvas, $92\frac{1}{2} \times 58\frac{1}{2}$ in. Mid 1780s. London, Tate Gallery (Note 126)

171. *Wooded landscape with cow standing beside a pool.* Black and brown chalks, with grey and grey-black washes, heightened with white, $9\frac{1}{2} \times 14\frac{11}{16}$ in. About 1787-8. Berlin, Staatliche Museen (Note 140)

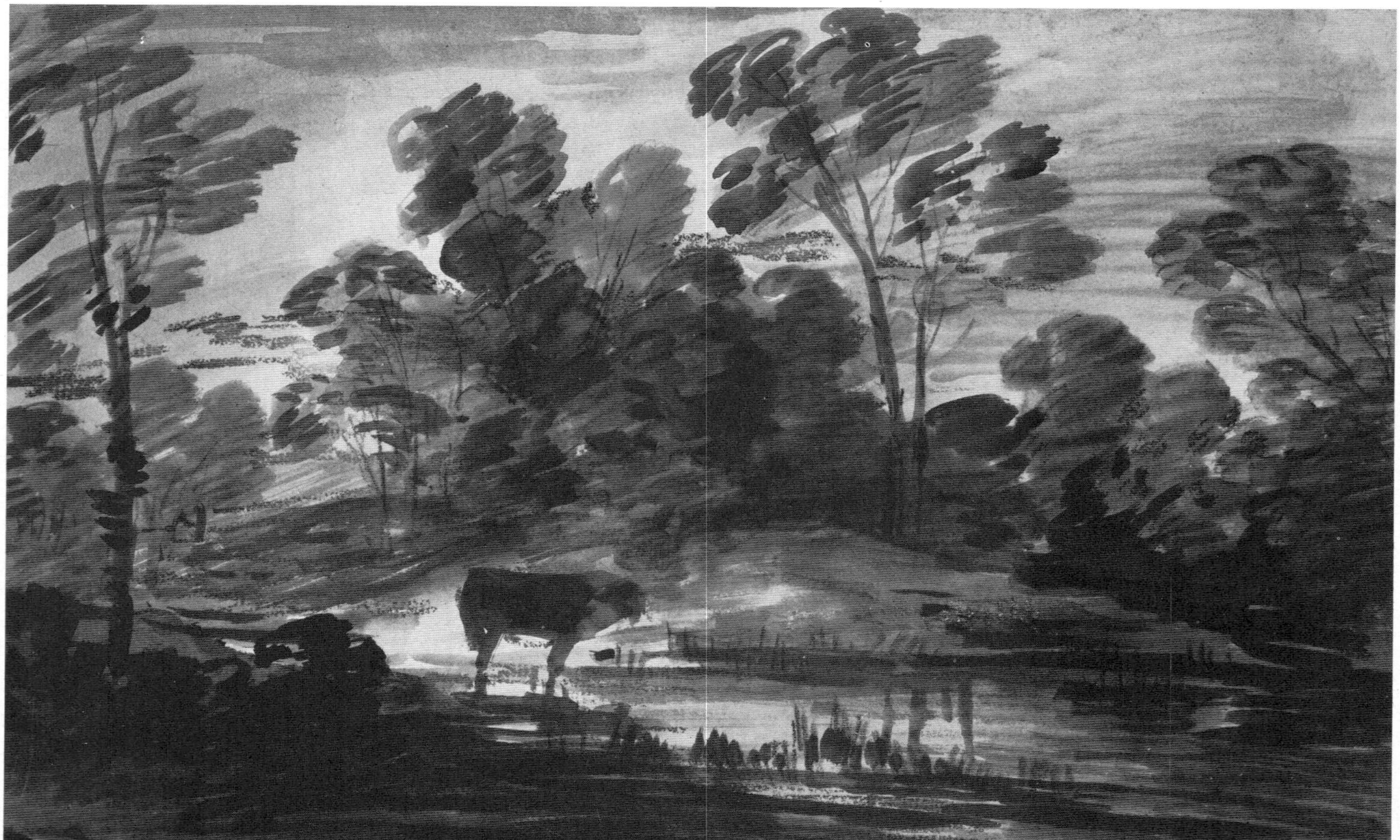

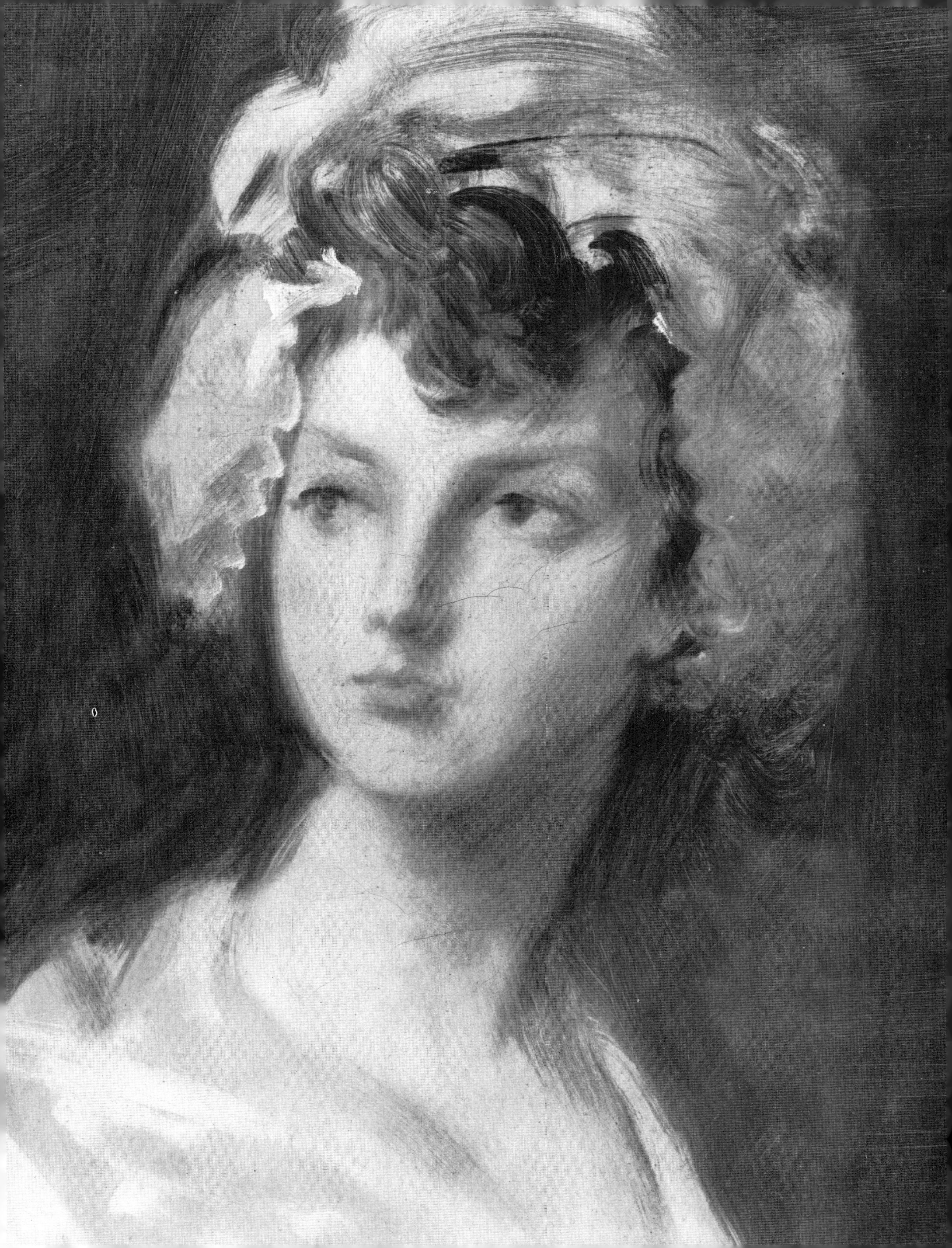

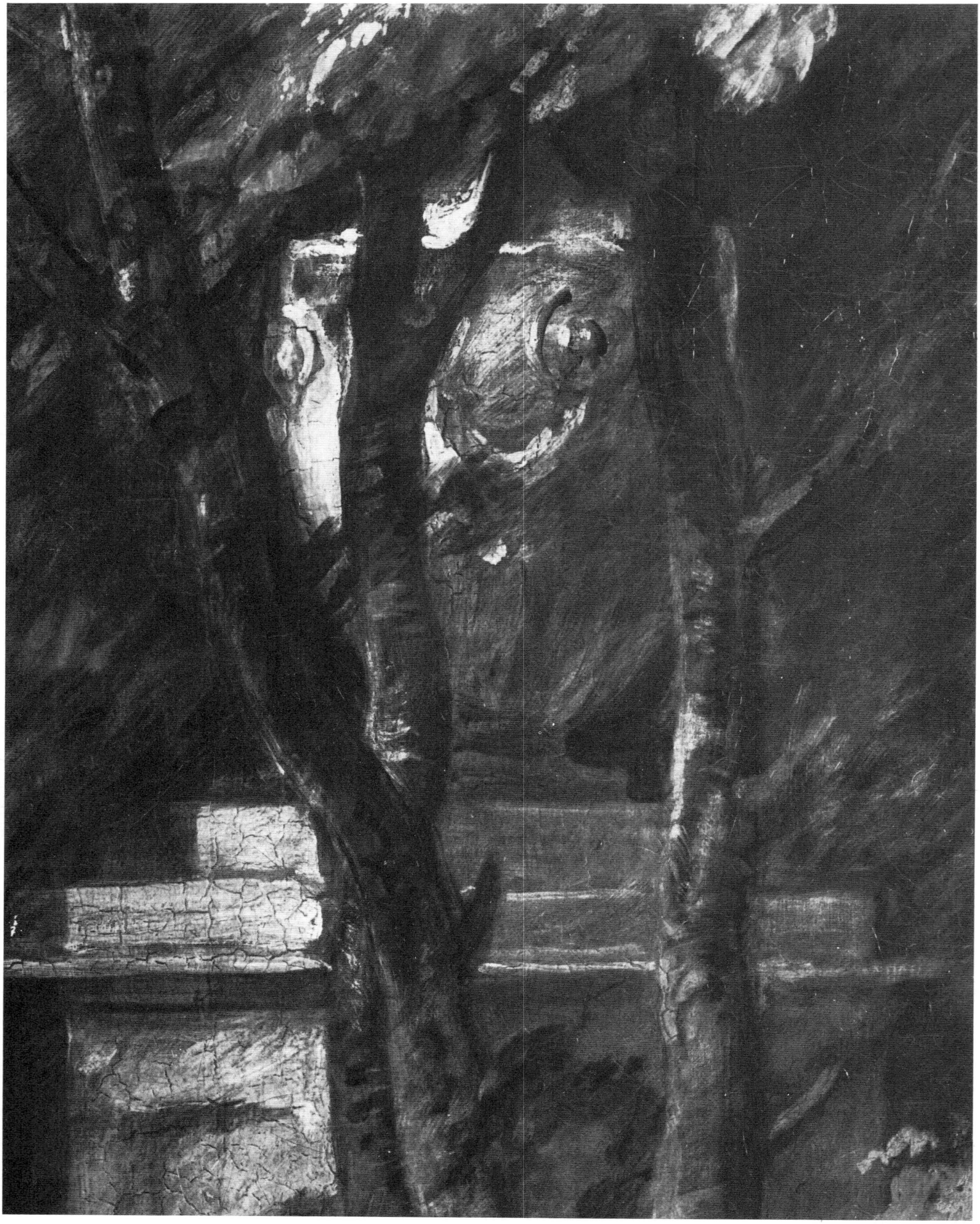

173. Detail from Pl. 159 (Note 110)

NOTES TO THE PLATES

Gainsborough's Development as an Artist

Further details of the paintings and drawings reproduced are given in the captions to the illustrations.

1. 'Bumper'. 1745. Pl. 1

Both Gainsborough's intuitive powers of characterization and his miraculous handling of paint, innate responses of heart and hand, are fully evident already in this superb portrait of a dog, his very earliest dated work, done at the age of eighteen. He adored animals, and the alert intelligence which attracted him to '*Bumper*' (who is described on the back of the canvas as 'A most Remarkable Sagacious/Cur') is revealed in every muscle and sinew of the portrait, notably in the head, ears and forelegs. The background, however, is less convincing. Gainsborough's originality, disregard of convention, natural simplicity, call it what you will, is seen in his introduction of a realistic woodland setting, something one would never expect to find in the work of contemporary painters such as Wootton, but the problem of effecting a satisfactory transition from foreground to middleground is scamped and the tree on the right, which is in any case somewhat stiffly rendered, unbalances the composition; this framing tree was a device which Gainsborough found it difficult, in his subsequent work, either to discard or to turn to good account. His attractive portrait of the dog's owner, Mrs Henry Hill, hangs at Montacute House, Somerset.

2. Landscape. About 1744–6. Pl. 2

One of Gainsborough's very early landscapes, small in size, and without figures or incident. Both the tree trunks and the sandy bank are more convincingly modelled than in '*Bumper*', and the composition is a little less flat, with some suggestion of the depth and recesses of the wood. The winding path is swept in with one broad and vigorous stroke of the brush, and the handling is fresh and fluent, so close indeed to such masterpieces by Watteau as *Le Mezzetin*, now in the Metropolitan Museum, reproduced below, that one is left in no doubt that Gainsborough had been studying, with profit and enthusiasm, such contemporary French pictures as were finding their way onto the London art market.

3. Landscape drawing. About 1746–7. Pl. 6

Gainsborough's early drawing style, in landscape, was formed on a study of Dutch seventeenth-century prints and drawings. The crisp touch, the lively zig-zag technique used for modelling foliage and foreground detail, and the constantly changing pattern of light and shade, which are the most marked characteristics of this drawing, are all to be found in Anthonie Waterloo, the Dutch etcher and draughtsman who was probably best known to the eighteenth-century connoisseur. The motifs of the cottage half hidden among the trees, the cow on a rising bank, and the herdsman resting by the wayside, without which the composition would disintegrate, are Gainsborough's own, and so, too, is the diagonal emphasis of the design.

4. Landscape. About 1746–7. Pl. 5

One of Gainsborough's most exquisite and harmonious early landscapes, neatly, almost painstakingly, constructed on Dutch principles of design, yet entirely rococo in feeling (comparison should be made, however, with his fully developed rococo of the mid 1750s, exemplified by the portrait of John Plampin, Pl. 55). The prominence given to the sky, the way in which the clouds follow the silhouette of the landscape, and the organization of the whole scene in clearly distinct planes, with a rutted path uniting these planes visually and little figures to plot the distance – all these are ideas which Gainsborough absorbed from the Dutch; while the crispness of touch and the complicated pattern of light and shade may be compared with his drawings of this period. On the other hand, the winding of the country track as it disappears into the distance, the slow curve of the horizon, the way in which the clouds cascade across the painting as they might in Fragonard, and the fitful quality of the light indicate plainly enough that, even at this early stage, Gainsborough was no imitator of Ruisdael or Van Goyen and that he was already capable of fusing Dutch and French elements into a style that was recognizably personal, and most obviously characterized at this time by a delicate, pale tonality.

5. Landscape. About 1746–7. Pl. 4

An exceptionally brilliant and effective early composition, dominated by a diamond-shaped patch of bright sunlight in the foreground, which acts as a fulcrum for the whole scene. This way of treating light, and the broad massing of the shadows, Gainsborough must have learnt from Ruisdael, but to point this out does nothing to lessen the imaginative quality of Gainsborough's transcription. The scene on the right is also Dutch in character and might be a vignette from Jan Both: a shepherd is reclining against a tree which, as in '*Bumper*', frames the composition, with a sandy bank behind, and nearby are groups of burdocks, plants of which we know that Gainsborough made careful studies. In freshness and fluency of handling, however, the comparison is still with Watteau. The recession of the middleground is a trifle awkward, if we compare the scale of the three sheep in the centre with that of the animals on the far side of the field, but the panorama beyond, where sunlight is passing fitfully over the distant landscape, is beautifully observed and anticipates similar passages in Constable.

6. Landscape. About 1747. Pls 13 and 135

Comparison with the smaller landscape in the West collection (Pl. 4) is instructive. This is quite a large-scale work, evidently, to judge by the unusual shape, painted to occupy a particular space, probably an overmantel (seven and a half inches were added to the top of the canvas at a later date, and have been removed during restoration). The fundamentally decorative intent explains the boldness with which Gainsborough has treated certain ideas which we have watched him develop, notably the massing together of his forms, the serpentine lines of path and river mapping out space, the low horizon and the compositional use of clouds, which are effectively tied in with the design and roll across the landscape in unashamedly rococo formation. The fact that this is a commissioned picture also helps to explain why Gainsborough has filled the landscape with incident: even the space on the hillside to the left has been occupied with sheep. This tendency to business, and usually quite unconnected business, was a fault which Gainsborough only slowly learnt to eradicate from his larger landscapes. But then turn to the masterly handling of the distance, where a church tower and bridge stand out in bright sunlight and the moisture-laden air blurs the line between fields and sky – atmospheric effects which go well beyond Ruisdael and reveal the uncanny perception and correlation of hand and eye that seemed to come so easily to Gainsborough; and, in the detail (Pl. 135), enjoy the luscious application of paint in the figures, mannered in its rococo rhythms (the way in which the girl's skirt is blown about reminds us of similar arbitrary effects in international Gothic), impressionistic in touch, yet extraordinarily descriptive. The softness of handling throughout is French rather than Dutch in character.

7. Landscape. About 1747. Pl. 8

In handling and tone this little landscape is similar to the Dublin picture (Pl. 5), and the track winding through the wood is dotted with figures in much the same way. But in this case the design is clear and simple, without distracting detail. The trees in different planes are linked together to form a continuous silhouette, and between them the sunlight falling on the cornfields and distant church tower, much as in compositions by Ruisdael, forms a single focus of attention. The motif of the figure seated prominently in the foreground can be paralleled in Gaspard Dughet.

8. Landscape drawing. About 1747. Pl. 15

Gainsborough's largest drawing of this period, executed in black and white chalks rather than the more usual pencil, is in fact a straight copy of a Ruisdael, the painting known as *La Forêt* now in the Louvre, of which several copies exist that may have been accessible to the eighteenth-century art student. The zig-zag technique he had absorbed from Dutch drawings is much in evidence in the foreground, and the elaborate interplay of carefully organized space and surface pattern was a compositional device he employed to good effect in the Dublin and Tate landscapes (Pls 5 and 8) as well as in the slightly later 'Gainsborough's Forest', illustrated opposite. The composition itself he used, in reverse, as the basis for his large landscape now in São Paulo.

9. Drawing, probably of the artist and his wife.
About 1746–7. Pl. 9

This rough sketch of a courting couple, an anglicized equivalent of the French *scène galante*, is wholly, and unusually for the period, free of artifice except for the hand popped inside the waistcoat, a recognized sartorial convention of the day (similar in nature to the more recent custom of leaving the bottom button of one's waistcoat undone). The girl seems to be concentrating on keeping her fashionable *bergère* hat on, but her intimacy with the man is suggested visually by the upward thrust of her pannier hoop, while the man's ardour is indicated by his downward glance and the forward motion of his right leg. The sketch is inscribed as representing Paul Sandby and his wife, but they were not married until 1757, some ten years after the drawing was made; identification of the couple with the sitters in the portrait reproduced beneath is entirely plausible, and there is an early tradition, supported by comparison with the known portraits, that these represent the artist and his wife, who were married in 1746.

10. The artist and his wife (probably).
About 1746–7. Pl. 10

If the drawing illustrated above obviously represents courtship, this picture seems to suggest marriage; the bench, upon which the couple are now seated, is left unoccupied in the drawing. The man, almost certainly a self-portrait, is motioning to the woman with a gesture of the hand, and she, dressed in a ravishing and exquisitely painted pink dress, is looking proudly out at the spectator; part of a temple building, possibly intended to symbolize the Temple of Hymen, is seen in the background. The portrait is elegant in conception, crisp in handling, and pale in tonality.

11. The Gravenor family. About 1747. Pl. 11

The 'conversation' piece was a genre of painting first developed in this country by Hogarth, and it was he who hit upon the happy notion of disposing his 'conversations' and family groups in a suitable landscape or parkland setting. In both his work, however, and, later, that of Hayman and Devis, these settings tended to be somewhat artificial in character, backdrops more than true landscapes; it was left to Gainsborough to assert the vitality of the landscape element. Though the sitters in the *Gravenor family* form a rather stilted group in the front plane, the landscape really envelops the figures as it does not in his earlier portraits-in-little; symptomatic of this is the cornfield which comes right into the foreground, and the ears of corn waving about in front of the elder girl's skirt. The heads, strongly lit, are artfully placed against dark areas of foliage or cloud, and the trees form a vigorous backbone to the whole portrait. The costumes are deliciously handled, and the dress of the girl in the foreground is modelled as though it were some splendid piece of rococo silver or plaster-work decoration. Comparison with Hayman's slightly earlier portrait of the Jacob family (Pl. 12) is instructive.

12. Mr and Mrs Robert Andrews.
About 1748–9. Pls 21, 23 and 161

In this group the landscape assumes equal proportions with the portrait itself. The broad acres of the young squire's estate, Auberies, a couple of miles outside Sudbury, extend far into the distance, where typically rococo clouds hang over the horizon; Gainsborough still found it difficult to effect an easy transition from foreground to middleground, but the hillside is superbly rendered, as freely brushed and as atmospherically true as the background of the Edinburgh landscape. In the foreground the sheaves of stooked corn, traditional symbol of fertility, suggest that the picture is a marriage portrait, and Robert Andrews and Frances Carter were indeed married at All Saints, Sudbury, in November 1748 (the approximate date of the canvas on stylistic evidence) when they were aged about twenty-two and sixteen respectively. The couple are posed against an oak as sturdy and as timeless as a Greek column; Robert is standing cross-legged, a familiar pose in informal British portraiture of the eighteenth century, and Frances is sitting pertly in her best blue satin dress, the folds of which are loosely and exquisitely modelled in luscious highlights contrasting with the rather scratchy touch in his earliest portraits-in-little. Gainsborough may have intended to paint a pheasant shot by her husband in Frances's lap: this part of the picture is unfinished, only a shape being outlined. The group portrait Gainsborough executed of Frances's parents, Mr and Mrs William Carter, has not been traced.

13. Landscape. About 1748. Pl. 7

The most rococo of all Gainsborough's early landscapes in the Dutch manner. Not only the winding track, the clouds and the silhouette formed by the trees but the very tree trunks and branches are twisting themselves into rococo shapes. Strong sunlight is falling across the scene, producing a richly varied pattern of light and shade, as in the early drawing reproduced opposite, and enabling Gainsborough to demonstrate both his richness of *facture* in the chalky banks which link the two halves of the landscape, and the sensitivity of his handling in the reflections in the pool. The little figures and animals are more discreetly managed than in the Edinburgh landscape (Pl. 13), though artfully disposed to form a series of necessary accents, with the cottage in the centre closing the carefully restricted space.

14. The Charterhouse. 1748. Pls 19 and 20

In 1748 Gainsborough presented a small circular view of the Charterhouse to the Foundling Hospital for the embellishment of its Court Room, where the Governors held their meetings; similar views of London hospitals were given by Haytley, Wale and Wilson. The pictures are still *in situ* and form part of one of the most important surviving rococo decorative schemes in England. Gainsborough's composition, which is based on powerful perspective lines drawing the eye into the distance, derives from Hogarth, but, for the rest, the picture is in the Dutch rococo style of the Vienna landscape; the detail shows the crisp, nervous touch in the highlights of tree trunk and foliage, and the contrast between thinly painted shadows and richly encrusted lights in the architecture. Gainsborough painted hardly any topographical views, rightly claiming that this was a field in which Paul Sandby excelled, and even when he did relent, was far more interested in problems of design and the fall of light than he was in the building itself.

15. 'Gainsborough's Forest.' 1748. Pls 16 and 17

Gainsborough himself referred to this famous landscape, in a letter written towards the end of his life, as 'painted at SUDBURY in the year 1748 . . . though there is very little idea of composition in the picture, the touch and closeness to nature in the study of the parts and *minutiae*, are equal to any of my latter productions.' The complexity of design and the number of unrelated figures and incidents on the one hand, and the sensitivity and descriptive accuracy of his nervous, flickering touch on the other, amply bear out the artist's own estimate of this youthful performance. Comparison with the Tate landscape (Pl. 8), so very similar in many respects, demonstrates Gainsborough's inability, at this stage in his career, to work on a large scale with the assurance he could bring to a smaller canvas. The trees both demarcate space and form a pattern across the surface of the picture as in the Whitworth drawing, illustrated opposite, but the clouds do not echo the silhouette of the foliage in quite the self-conscious way characteristic of the Dublin landscape (Pl. 5). The distant village and church tower provide a psychologically essential glimpse of countryside beyond the confines of the wood.

16. Landscape. About 1748–50. Pl. 26

The Claudean character of this composition, with tall trees dominating one side of the picture, a clump of smaller ones on the other, and a view between with a church tower centrally placed, reminds one of Constable's early *Dedham Vale*, similarly influenced by Claude. The two halves of the composition are linked by an uncomfortably artificial device, the inclusion of two great tree trunks which span the foreground, and between which Gainsborough has placed his figures and cows. The highlights are brushed in with that delicious feeling for paint characteristic of the animals in the Edinburgh landscape (Pl. 13), but the handling throughout is much more generalized, even perfunctory, and the foreground is painted in the warm reddish-brown tones which were to become typical of his artificial pastoral style of the mid and later 1750s.

17. The artist with his wife and elder daughter, Mary. About 1751–2. Fig. 7

An informal group-in-a-landscape characteristic of Gainsborough's work of the early 1750s, and comparable with the *Mr and Mrs Joshua Kirby* in the National Portrait Gallery. It was executed some five years later than the self-portrait with his wife in the Louvre, and shows Mary aged about three or four. The background, which is totally different in style from any of the Suffolk pictures, seems to have been added later.

18. John Gainsborough. Early 1750s. Pl. 32

Gainsborough's eldest brother, Jack, passed the whole of his life in Sudbury, engaged in producing mechanical inventions, none of which proved of any practical use. He was supported by other members of the family. This portrait shows him at about the age of forty; the precisely delineated features may be compared with Gainsborough's early portraits-in-little, and the head is painted in the crisp, fresh style of this period.

19. Admiral Vernon. About 1753. Pl. 34

Philip Thicknesse first met Gainsborough in the spring or summer of 1753. 'Mr. Gainsborough received me in his painting room,' he afterwards recalled, 'in which stood several portraits truly drawn, perfectly like, but stiffly painted, and worse coloured; among which was the late Admiral Vernon's . . .' The pose of this early three-quarter length of the Victor of Portobello, then M.P. for Ipswich, which, with the left hand gripping the sword hilt and the right hand tucked inside the coat, relates to the Hudson-early Reynolds tradition of portraiture, is indeed somewhat stiff, and the relationship between the figure and the associational trappings, cannon, rocks and ships, which derives from the formula adopted by Hudson for his series of admirals (see

Pl. 35), is rudimentary. The muted colouring and soft, smooth modelling of the head are influenced by Ramsay, for whom Gainsborough had a greater regard than he had for Hudson.

20. Philip Bowes Broke (?). About 1753–5. Pl. 33

Most of Gainsborough's early portraits on the scale of life are simple head-and-shoulders compositions, either set in feigned ovals or with plain backgrounds; the *Admiral Vernon* was clearly an important commission for Gainsborough in 1753, and one involving a more distinguished sitter. This portrait of a youngster in a smart navy-blue suit with red facings is exceptional in being given a landscape background, albeit very broadly treated. The horizon is beautifully placed, and the glow in the sky above serves as a foil to the bright studio lighting of the head. Though the cuff is roughly high-lit (compare the cravat in *John Gainsborough*), the features are modelled with a soft smoothness of touch comparable to that in *Admiral Vernon.*

21. Heneage Lloyd and his sister (probably).
Early 1750s. Pls 24 and 25

Even when Gainsborough does introduce an artificial romanticized landscape as a setting for one of his portraits-in-little, the naturalism and sheer beauty of the lighting prevent it from deteriorating into the category of a photographer's backdrop. Here the two children are posed in front of a flight of steps, with a stone balustrade, leading to a garden pavilion which provides an excuse for some attractive rococo scroll-work; on the left is a small lake, with behind it a church which has no iconographical connection with the portrait but serves as an essential accent in the composition. The bright patch of sky at the horizon opens up the distance in the same way as the cornfield glimpsed between the trees in the Tate landscape. The boy's coat and waistcoat are beautifully painted in fresh, fluent brushstrokes, and the slight turn of the girl's head emphasizes the sweetness of her expression.

22. John Plampin. About 1753–4. Pl. 55

In this portrait of John Plampin, the squire of Chadacre Park, near Hartest, half-way between Sudbury and Bury St Edmunds, the features are as crisply delineated, the head as enamelled in finish, and the costume as carefully painted, as in the portrait of Mr and Mrs Andrews; but as far as the landscape and the composition are concerned Gainsborough's intentions had radically altered in the space of five or six years. For this is a wholly rococo performance. All the forms radiate outwards from the waist of the sitter as though they were spokes in a wheel, but elegant, serpentine spokes which closely reflect the theories advanced in Hogarth's *Analysis of Beauty*, published in 1753, at just about the date of this picture. Even the dog is absorbed into these predominating rhythms, the sinuous branches on which the sitter is resting his gloved hand fit snugly into the shapes of the clouds, and the handling is appropriately loose, rapid and generalized throughout (compare the broadly brushed distance with the background in *Mr and Mrs Andrews*). In key with this conception, and no doubt also with his image of the fashionable gentleman rather than the squire, John Plampin is reclining in a relaxed pose, partly inspired by Watteau (which Gainsborough had already used, incidentally, for a figure in the foreground of his view of Landguard Fort), with his hand tucked firmly into his expensive braided and betasselled waistcoat in the manner approved by the etiquette books. Hayman's portrait of Philip Thicknesse is clearly influenced by Gainsborough: the pose derives from *John Plampin*, and the background is similar to the handling of the Vienna landscape. The pose also reappears in Devis's portrait of Viscount Boyle.

23. Self-portrait. 1754. Fig. 2

An unfinished sketch of Gainsborough aged twenty-six or seven. The head is painted in the soft, creamy highlights and reddish shadows characteristic of the early 1750s; the tricorne hat, worn at a rakish angle, has been fully modelled but, with the exception of the cravat, the costume has only been outlined in the sketchiest of brushwork over the brown priming.

24. Etching ('The Gipsies'). About 1753–4. Pl. 113

In the early to mid 1750s Gainsborough produced a number of etchings. Though he was impatient when it came to the delicate processes of biting and printing, and had to be helped by friends who were more experienced, his manipulation of the needle on the copper-plate was as skilled and sensitive as his handling of paint or pencil. This is most apparent in his large plate entitled *The Suffolk Plough*, formerly known only from a description but of which an impression has now come to light, and in the first state of *The*

Gipsies, that is to say before the plate was engraved and finished by Wood. In both these compositions the modulations of tone are beautifully handled. There is an earlier, unfinished painting of *The Gipsies* in the Tate Gallery, lacking the rococo development of the branches and in which the figure grouping is quite different and more simply organized.

25. Landscape. About 1754–5. Pl. 14

In certain respects this picture is remarkably similar to the Edinburgh landscape (Pl. 13), and must also have been intended for a particular position in a room, probably, from the size, an overdoor rather than an overmantel. This positioning would account for the breadth of massing and the slow, undulating rhythms. But the contrasts with the Edinburgh landscape are revealing. Detail is less obtrusive. The clouds are equally contrived, but less obviously compositional. Depth is suggested more by a naturalistic fall of light and shadow than through linear means. The foreground is warm, even reddish, in tonality, sounding a note of artificiality in the rural scene. And this note is strengthened by the inclusion of favourite motifs: donkeys, a windmill on a hill, and most particularly, a pollarded tree with the stripped bark strongly highlit. Nowhere more clearly than in this mature and beautiful landscape can one watch Gainsborough attempting to compromise at the cross-roads of naturalism and style.

26. Landscape. 1755. Pl. 27

This canvas was bought from the artist by the Duke of Bedford in May 1755 for twenty-one guineas, 'A Landscape for a Chimneypiece'. The position for which it was intended has now been identified with some certainty as an overmantel in one of the ground-floor rooms at Woburn. Though the picture contains genuinely rural scenes and some finely observed detail, the decorative intent is more overt than in the Minneapolis or Arundel landscapes (Pls 26 and 14). The sky is now tinctured with pink so that the tonality is more artificial throughout; the hollow, pollarded tree trunk has been twisted into elegant, rococo shapes as though it were pottery from the kiln; and the compositional lines radiate from the woodcutter's head in a similar rococo way to those in the portrait of John Plampin. To cap all this, the principal incident is an anglicized, rustic equivalent of a *scène galante*, in which a milkmaid turning coyly away from a woodcutter asking for a bowl of milk has been substituted for an elegantly dressed shepherd and shepherdess; the highlights on the back of the magnificent cow which completes this scene are handled with a succulence worthy of Fragonard (compare the less mature handling of the cows in the Minneapolis landscape, Pl. 26).

27. Landscape. 1755. Pl. 45

A slightly smaller canvas bought by the Duke of Bedford, probably also, from its proportions, intended as an overmantel, for which he paid fifteen guineas in July 1755. The foliage of the great oak tree on the left arches over the composition and links the horses in the foreground (for one of which Gainsborough used an oil sketch he had made from the life) with the haymaking scene in the middle distance. Both the latter and the generalized distance may usefully be contrasted with the Hogarthian rustic subject-matter occasionally employed by, and the infinitely detailed groundplan characteristic of, the *doyen* of contemporary landscape painters, George Lambert (see Pl. 46).

28. Drawing and landscape. About 1755. Pls 28 and 29

This rough notation of a pond and farm buildings is typical of Gainsborough's surviving drawings of the 1750s. The composition was evidently one which attracted him, for he used it as the basis for the landscape now in the Mellon collection; apart from the inclusion of *staffage*, the main additions are the trees on the left and right and the distance opening up the view towards the centre. No doubt detailed studies, similar to the cow from the Oppé collection (Pl. 31), would have intervened between the first rough outline of this subject and the finished painting. The use of clouds to echo the silhouette of the trees, and the warm orange tones in the lights in the foreground, are characteristic of Gainsborough's work of the mid 1750s.

29. Cow and landscape drawings.
About 1755–7. Pls 30 and 31

This careful, detailed drawing of a reclining cow, evidently done from the life, falls into the same category as the study of mallows in the Torbock collection (Pl. 18) and, in this case, it is possible to point to its use, for it was incorporated without alteration into the large finished drawing of a herdsman and cattle, with village scene behind, which was one of the works

Gainsborough later gave to his friend Goodenough Earle, of Barton Grange, in Somerset. It is of interest to note, because it is characteristic of his procedure, that, in an elaborate composition of this kind, Gainsborough has not taken particular trouble over the accuracy of such details as the Suffolk type wheel plough on the left. Shortly afterwards the whole composition was used in reverse, with minor variations and the addition of another cow and a milkmaid climbing over the stile, for the left side of the landscape executed for Handel's friend Charles Jennens. This method of composing is similar to the way in which Watteau worked.

30. Samuel Kilderbee. About 1755. Pl. 57

This bold and vigorous portrait of his life-long friend Samuel Kilderbee (whom he asked to assist his wife and daughter in the execution of his will) is more successful as a composition than the *Admiral Vernon*. The figure is framed by the trees which climb up the left side of the canvas and the head supported by the dark clouds, while the device of the dog looking up at its master goes back to Titian; but there is still no relationship between the sitter, who is placed in limbo in the front plane of the canvas, and the background, which is far sketchier than in the portraits-in-little of this period, such as *John Plampin*. The smooth modelling, long brushstroke flattening the bridge of the nose, and crisp delineation of the features, characteristic of Gainsborough's portraiture of the mid 1750s, are close in style to the work of Van Loo, the French painter fashionable in England around 1740, as interpreted by Ramsay.

31. The artist's daughters chasing a butterfly.
About 1756. Fig. 12

Gainsborough always held that likeness was 'the principal beauty and intention of a Portrait', but here he has gone beyond likeness to capture, with an effectiveness anticipating the snapshot, the eager and intent expressions on the faces of his two little daughters, Margaret, then aged about four, and Mary, who was about eight, as they chase after a butterfly. This charming little incident has dictated the informality, indeed novelty, of the composition, but even in so natural a portrait Gainsborough cannot wholly forget style and he has deliberately folded back Margaret's apron in order to indulge in some bravura painting. The plants on the left, unfinished, like most of the picture, would no doubt have been painted from a detailed pencil study similar to the drawing in the Torbock collection (Pl. 18).

32. Rev. Richard Canning. About 1757. Pl. 40

Though he was patronized by members of the aristocracy as well as the local gentry, much of Gainsborough's clientele in his Ipswich years came from the modestly well-off professional classes: lawyers, clergymen, or musicians like Joseph Gibbs. The pictures these people commissioned were usually face painting of the most ordinary kind, head-and-shoulders portraits with plain background and possibly a feigned oval, presumably the extent of what they wished to pay for. This portrait of the curate of St Lawrence's, Ipswich (who was also the editor of Gainsborough's friend Kirby's *The Suffolk Traveller*), which is one of the best of these simple pictures, was presented by the sitter to his friend the Reverend Henry Hubbard, who reciprocated the gift. In his search for a livelier but acceptable alternative to the smooth, bland finish which was Hudson's formula for face painting, Gainsborough developed an elaborate system of hatching derived from the practice of the French pastellists, La Tour and Perroneau; this gives a new fullness to the flesh, lacking in earlier portraits, as well as the vitality of surface he was striving to achieve. The wig is still executed with a neat, crisp touch, and the background is a plain, undifferentiated brown.

33. Mrs Samuel Kilderbee. About 1757. Pl. 37

Though the head in this portrait is modelled in the same hatching technique characteristic of Gainsborough's work of about 1757, and the features are delineated in the crisp manner found in all Gainsborough's early pictures, the loose handling of the costume and the fashions depicted, notably the high-piled hair with tresses falling over the left shoulder, belong to the late 1770s. Mary Kilderbee was the wife of one of Gainsborough's closest friends, and the most probable explanation of the discrepancies in style is that Gainsborough was asked, twenty years later, to repaint the picture in the current fashion. The head of this high-spirited girl is painted *con amore*, and one can well imagine why the Kilderbees should have wished to retain this likeness rather than to order a fresh portrait.

34. Lady Innes. About 1757. Pl. 107

This portrait of the first wife of Captain Sir William Innes, a sitter more elevated in the social scale than the Reverend Canning, is correspondingly more elaborate in composition, though the head is modelled in precisely the same tight, hatching technique. The sitter is framed by a mass of foliage, as in certain of the earlier portraits-in-a-landscape, and set off by the sparkle of the passages of light beyond, breaking through the stormy sky. Gainsborough has devoted loving care to the delineation of the lace and the modelling of the satin folds, and this crisp handling of detail in the costume is extended to the roses which fill out the left of the picture; the wrists and hands are more loosely painted, fluently rather than with the broken touch of a Manet or a Renoir but suggesting form with the same intuitive brilliance. Though the portrait as a whole is slightly stiff in character, handling, colour and the motif of the hand holding a rose all indicate that Gainsborough was already conscious of Van Dyck.

35. The Hon. Richard Savage Nassau.
About 1757. Pls 42 and 43

Very few sketches exist for any of Gainsborough's portraits, and it is clear that his method of proceeding was totally different, for example, from that of Ramsay. He seems never to have made studies of his sitters' heads, preferring to start directly upon the canvas; and the same applies to the designs of most of his routine portraits (*pentimenti* are consequently commonly to be found, and X-rays of Gainsborough's pictures usually produce interesting results). It was only in the case of his more complex designs that he made preparatory drawings; these were nearly always full composition studies, only rarely studies of detail. This drawing for the pose of Richard Savage Nassau, a bold chalk drawing unusual for the date, was closely followed in the finished portrait, though slight variations in contour are to be detected here and there. Nassau was an aristocratic sitter, related to the Duke of Hamilton, but the pose is nevertheless relaxed and informal to a degree never quite found in Hogarth's portraiture on the scale of life. The dramatic and sketchy handling in the landscape hanging on the wall behind the sitter anticipates Gainsborough's landscape style of the early 1760s.

36. Mrs Nathaniel Acton. About 1757–8. Pl. 38

This half-length of Mrs Nathaniel Acton, a member of the Lee-Acton family of Livermere, is still in the traditional style of English portraiture, set against a plain, dark background, with a head distinctly reminiscent of Cornelius Johnson. The rough modelling of the features, however, is characteristic of Gainsborough's technique as it evolved in the late 1750s, more painterly than the stylized hatching of the *Rev. Richard Canning*, but less bold than the *Mrs Kirby* (Pl. 39).

37. Joshua Kirby. About 1757–8. Fig. 8

Joshua Kirby, son of the author of *The Suffolk Traveller*, was one of Gainsborough's closest friends, and is supposed to have been responsible for bringing him before the notice of George III. Gainsborough particularly requested that he should be buried near his friend's grave in Kew churchyard. The rough modelling of the features is very close to the handling in *Mrs Acton*, though the portrait is unfinished, the costume and background only being sketched in.

38. William Wollaston. About 1758. Pl. 44

This is the earliest surviving full-length by Gainsborough; the sitter was one of the artist's Suffolk friends and, although no other full-lengths can be attributed to the Suffolk period, this is clearly insufficient reason for supposing that the picture was painted at Bath rather than at Ipswich. Wollaston is posed informally, in a manner favoured by Devis, with his head turned away from the spectator, and a view of his country mansion glimpsed between the bars of the gate. However, though the sitter is framed by the trees, which correctly leave his right arm in shadow, and the dog at his feet is well integrated with the design, one is uncomfortably aware that the arm is not really resting upon the gate, and this weakness, of a kind not uncommon in Gainsborough's work, produces an effect of slight imbalance, giving the impression that the figure is unrelated to the landscape behind him.

39. William Wollaston. About 1758–9. Pl. 49

This is undoubtedly the most rococo in its principles of design of all Gainsborough's portraits on the scale of life; the sitter is twisted round so that his body is on three different axes, his coat is fluttering about in a wholly unnaturalistic way so as to reveal a sinuous length of white satin lining, the curtain on the left is spiralling down to join the diagonal of the right arm and the braided hem opposite, and there is a scatter of highlights across the surface of the picture. It is these rococo features in the composition which produce such a lively sense of movement, reinforcing the effect of the sitter having just turned away from his music to listen to someone on his left, and the sense of immediacy created by cutting the canvas just below the knee, which brings the spectator into such close contact with the picture. Wollaston gives the impression of being a shade older than in the full-length, where, incidentally, he is shown with his natural hair and not in a wig.

40. Self-portrait. About 1758–9. Fig. 1

Gainsborough aged about thirty or thirty-one. The features are firmly modelled in rough, thick brushstrokes, and only traces of the hatching style of the previous year or two remain in the half-tones in the left cheek. The head is strongly lit, and stands out above the brownish-plum suit and against the broadly painted foliage, characteristic of the late 1750s, which encircles the composition.

41. Unknown girl. About 1759. Pl. 36

In this appealing portrait of an unknown young girl in a riding habit Gainsborough has avoided the obviousness of the background to *Lady Innes* and the pitfalls of the background to *William Wollaston* by setting the sitter well forward in the canvas and the trees correspondingly back. The result is a much more sophisticated and successful composition. Broken lights are used in the sky to enliven the canvas as in the two earlier portraits, a castle is included in the distance, though less obviously related to the sitter than the country house in the *William Wollaston*, and the pose has the assurance and easy naturalism of Gainsborough's late Ipswich style, still lacking in the *Lady Innes*.

42. Mrs John Kirby. About 1759. Pl. 39

In this extraordinarily direct portrait of the mother of his lifelong friend, Joshua Kirby, the old lady is sitting bolt upright in a feigned oval surround, with her white cap silhouetted against a plain, brown background. Her toothless mouth is suggested by the dexterous placing of the shadows, and the kindly expression is caught to perfection. The rough modelling, leaving the marks of the brush clearly visible, Gainsborough was now prepared to defend, as we know from a letter to a client in Colchester dated March 1758 in which he argued that it was 'of use in giving force to the effect at a proper distance, and what a judge of painting knows an original from a copy by; in short being the touch of the pencil, which is harder to preserve than smoothness.' Although this portrait is usually placed among Gainsborough's earliest works, it is not in fact a companion to the picture of her husband, probably painted about 1752–3, and the maturity of the handling argues against an early dating.

43. The artist's daughters holding a cat. About 1759. Pl. 41

The only part of this brilliant sketch of his two daughters holding a cat which Gainsborough has carried to completion is the heads. There is still some trace of the hatching technique characteristic of the period 1757–8 in the direction of the brushstrokes in Mary's left cheek, but for the rest the handling is deliberately rough and imprecise: the passages of solid pigment in Mary's forehead are built up with very little transition from the priming, which indicates the areas of shadow, the ears are left out of focus, and the modelling of the lips is blurred by apparently misplaced touches – the misplaced touches of a supreme master of the craft of painting. For who would deny that these heads of his little girls are among the most lifelike and the most touchingly moving that Gainsborough ever painted?

44. Study of mallows. Later 1750s. Pl. 18

Gainsborough's landscape drawings of the Suffolk period fall into three classes: notations of scenes that appealed to him either as motifs or as ideas for compositions, finished drawings that were compositions in their own right and not necessarily intended for translation into paint, and detailed studies from nature which could be incorporated into pictures and might even be directly preparatory. This sensitive study of mallows, executed, like most of his Suffolk-period drawings, in pencil, is one of the rare surviving examples from the last category.

45. Study of a tree trunk. Later 1750s. Pl. 59

A powerful study of a tree trunk, done from nature, in which the foliage is indicated in loose scallops and the strong, pervasive hatching (counterpart to the technique adopted in the portraits of this date) imparts a rhythmical urgency to the whole drawing. Gainsborough was later to use trees of this kind as the principal compositional stresses in such portraits as his *General James Johnston* (Pl. 60) and *Viscount Kilmorey* (Pl. 53), both painted in the 1760s.

46. Landscape drawing. About 1758–9. Pl. 47

The rhythmical energy generated by the trees in this drawing seems to extend to the whole landscape, which pivots compositionally round the bank in the centre, into the shade of which the herdsman, his dog and the cow so snugly fit. Highly wrought drawings of this sort Gainsborough is known to have sent up to London for sale in his Ipswich days (in later life he never sold but always gave away his drawings), and the size and technique suggest that it may have formed part of a series dating from about 1759 which was intended for engraving.

47. **Landscape.** About 1760. Pl. 48

One of the earliest landscapes Gainsborough produced at Bath, a remarkable fusion of his Ipswich style with the grand manner which demonstrates his continuing capacity for assimilating new ideas and for absorbing them, without any sense of strain, into his own vision. The design, with its careful placing of a large mass on one side of the canvas and a smaller on the other, and the motif of a vista between closed by mountains and glowing in the evening sunlight, is typical of Claude, and must have been inspired by landscapes by that artist Gainsborough was now in a position to see in West Country collections; but the swing of the composition and the rhythmical treatment of the foliage are still entirely rococo, while the subject-matter, unaffectedly rustic, is far removed from seventeenth-century mythologizing or arcadianism: the peasant boy on horseback is almost identical with the figure in the Woburn landscape of five years earlier (Pl. 45), and the labourer on the left marks the first appearance of one of Gainsborough's most personal images of country life, that of the woodcutter returning home after the day's work.

48. **Mrs Philip Thicknesse.** 1760. Pls 51 and 54

Just as he turned to Claude for the framework of the first large-scale landscape he painted at Bath, so for the first elaborate portrait composition executed in his new studio, a full-length of the wife of one of his closest friends, Gainsborough looked to Van Dyck. The pose as he sketched it out in his preliminary drawing is broadly that of Van Dyck's *Lady Digby*, the most significant change being the placing of the left arm, a motif also derived from Van Dyck. The finished picture is more curvilinear. Gainsborough has broadened the folds of the lovely white dress so that they cascade downwards in such a way as to emphasize the serpentine twist of the pose, which is itself a brilliant re-statement of the idea he had first tried out in the portrait of William Wollaston; this spiralling movement, taken up in the curtain above, is counterbalanced by the verticals of the table leg and the 'cello (which replaces the window and landscape background seen in the drawing). Much of the detail is treated in a rococo manner, and the brushwork displays characteristic rococo surface animation, but the breadth and grandeur go well beyond the limits of what one understands as rococo art.

49. **Uvedale Tomkyns Price.** About 1760. Pl. 50

One of the earliest portraits Gainsborough painted at Bath. The dramatic lighting, which gives a special emphasis to head and hands comparable to Reynolds's practice at the same date, was the result of working by candlelight. The sitter, father of the writer on 'the Picturesque', who became one of Gainsborough's close friends in the 1760s, was evidently proud of his abilities as an amateur landscape draughtsman. The pencil drawing on the wall is a Gainsborough similar in finish to Sir John Witt's (Pl. 47), and shows that large drawings of this type were framed and hung rather than being kept in portfolio.

50. **William Poyntz.** S.A. 1762. Pl. 56

Gainsborough firmly established the informal character of his portrait style with the public when he sent his full-length of William Poyntz to the Society of Artists in 1762. The sitter is leaning nonchalantly against a gnarled tree stump of a type familiar from Gainsborough's landscapes of the mid 1750s, and which, with the diagonal of the gun, provides an effective counterpoise to the figure. The sharp foreshortening of the foreground may be due to Gainsborough's expectation that the picture would be hung at a height but it gives an uncomfortable feeling that the figure is slipping, though the lack of organic relationship to the background, similar to the earlier full-length of William Wollaston, is more than compensated for by the unified and exquisite silvery tonality. Next year Gainsborough followed up with another informal full-length, of Thomas Medlycott reclining on a stile, while Reynolds, in his portrait of Philip Gell, riposted with an idealized transcription of Gainsborough's theme of the sportsman at ease in a landscape.

51. **Landscape.** S.A. 1763 (probably). Pls 70 and 136

It is instructive to compare this canvas, which may have been

Gainsborough's first exhibited landscape, with the large landscape, painted only a year or two before (Pl. 48). The composition is still recognizably Claudean, and has a very similar swing to it; but it is a good deal more complex both in derivation and arrangement. The heavy, dominating trees and dramatically contrasted areas of light and shadow, effects stimulated by his practice of painting by candlelight, look back to Ruisdael, whom he never ceased to admire; while the exceptional vigour and looseness of touch in the handling, notably such lively passages as the pink, yellow and reddish tints suggesting reflected light in the tree stumps in the middle distance, are a first hint of Gainsborough's love for Rubens. Indeed the arrangement of the masses, the use of brilliant clouds to act as a foil to the dark green foliage, the highlighting of the leaves and the pose of the horse drinking all suggest that Rubens's *The Watering Place* (Pl. 112) may already have been known to Gainsborough.

52. The Descent from the Cross (after Rubens).
Early to mid 1760s. Pl. 79

A large-scale, but only partially finished, copy of the central panel of Rubens's great altarpiece for Antwerp Cathedral, executed in reverse, from Vorsterman's engraving, but probably inspired by the *modello* now in the Courtauld Institute Galleries, which in the eighteenth century was at Corsham Court, where Gainsborough would have seen it. What seems to have fascinated Gainsborough in the Rubens was the composition, the movement and interlocking of the figures which sustained the powerful diagonal; and there can be very little doubt that it was this picture which inspired the extraordinary pyramid of figures in *The Harvest Waggon* (Pl. 80), a group so contrived in disposition, and so much at variance with his declared belief of precisely this date (see Note 60) that the figures in a landscape should be strictly subordinate. Although painted on canvas, Gainsborough's copy retains the highly luminous quality characteristic of a Rubens panel.

53. Lords John and Bernard Stuart (after Van Dyck).
Early to mid 1760s. Pl. 93

If Rubens provided the impetus for Gainsborough's mature style in landscape, it was Van Dyck who exerted the most profound and enduring influence on his art, and Gainsborough's captivation by the greatest of Flemish portrait painters is made abundantly clear by the copies he painted of pictures which especially excited him, some of them highly finished and at full scale, and most of which seem to have been executed during his early years at Bath. These copies were done for his own pleasure, and remained in the studio, only appearing in the sale held after his death at Schomberg House in 1789. A large copy of the Pembroke family was described in the sale catalogue as 'Painted by Memory, after having seen the original at Wilton', a full-scale copy of the Duke of Richmond and Lennox was done from the original then at Corsham Court, and the original of Lords John and Bernard Stuart was in the possession of Lord Darnley. What drew Gainsborough to Van Dyck was not only the effortless distinction of his poses (from which he had much to learn), but the refinement of his colour, the sensuousness of his touch, and the brilliance with which he painted materials of every description: the deliberate opportunity Van Dyck gave himself for the bravura handling of costume in this picture, by folding back the cape over Lord Bernard's shoulder, can be compared with the descending folds of Mrs Thicknesse's dress (Pl. 51).

54. Landscape drawing. Mid 1760s. Pl. 69

Gainsborough seems also to have been aware of the landscape sketches of Van Dyck, for the loose handling of the foliage and the fresh, pale tone of this beautiful composition are remarkably close to his gouache drawings of English scenes. The arrangement of the trees, with the cluster of highlit buildings nestling in the distant woods between, redolent of the countryside around Bath, provides an informal and wholly English answer to Claude; and the lyrical summertime mood which pervades the whole scene reminds one of nothing so much as the gay and sensuous landscapes of Renoir.

55. Countess Howe. About 1763–4. Frontispiece and Pl. 61

Lady Howe, wife of the future naval hero, was in her early thirties when Gainsborough painted this ravishing portrait of her; no artist was more deeply moved by feminine grace and vitality, and his imaginative responses to his emotion produced in this canvas a picture which can lay fair claim to be his masterpiece. In its simple distinction of pose, the noble bearing and demeanour of the sitter, the accomplished arrangement of the folds of the dress so that one can almost hear the rustle of the silks and satins, and its exquisite delicacy of colour, it is the very quintessence of Gainsborough's transmutation of Van Dyck. More personal to Gainsborough, however, are the stormy clouds and patch of sunlight breaking through beneath, effects of chiaroscuro which set off the sitter to perfection, and such homely details in the background as the wooden fence; the silver birch on the right is a rather unsatisfactory prop, and evidently a *pentimento*, as the forms of the distant landscape can be detected beneath.

56. General James Johnston. About 1763–4. Pl. 60

Where Reynolds would have painted a general with some indication, in the background, of his profession and valour, Gainsborough has chosen to set General Johnston against the type of dark, wooded landscape enlivened by flashes of light at the horizon which he was using continually in his full-lengths at this period. The nonchalance of the pose, legs planted firmly apart, and the debonair expression, though clearly indicative of the character of a man who was reputed to be the finest swordsman in the army, are also at some remove from Reynolds's canon of portraiture. In this original and lively composition the silver birch, though as contrived in placing as the tree beside Lady Howe, is an integral and brilliantly successful part of the design, spiralling upwards in a serpentine rhythm which echoes and continues the line of the general's scarlet coat.

57. The Byam family. About 1764. Pls 62 and 68

This is the most elaborate portrait Gainsborough had painted thus far in his career. George Byam is shown walking out in his smartest waistcoat, into which his hand is tucked in the approved manner, apparently pointing out some feature in the view to his wife Louisa, who is also dressed at the height of fashion, and whom he is leading by the arm; their small daughter, Sarah, is preoccupied with something nearer at hand, and looks out at the spectator in an engaging manner. The motif of the promenade with the figures linked by joint concentration on the distant prospect, which goes back to Dürer, was later taken up with great success by both Reynolds and Raeburn. The dark and stormy landscape, painted with a breadth and roughness of touch only to be found in Gainsborough's pure landscapes of a decade and more later, seems rather out of key with the refined and elegant figure group.

58. Anne Horton. 1766. Pl. 63

Anne Horton was described by Horace Walpole five years after this portrait was painted, when she married the Duke of Cumberland, as 'a young widow of twenty-four [actually she was twenty-eight], extremely pretty, not handsome, very well made, with the most amorous eyes in the world, and eyelashes a yard long. Coquette beyond measure, artful as Cleopatra, and completely mistress of all her passions and projects.' Both Reynolds and Wright of Derby had trouble in pleasing this capricious sitter, but Gainsborough painted her successfully on several occasions, and this head-and-shoulders, a masterpiece of the portraitist's art, not only captures her beauty in a way of which only Gainsborough was capable but suggests both her seductiveness and her early mastery of the ways of the world: there is, indeed, a strong element of hardness and control in the languish of her expression.

59. Lady Eardley. About 1766. Pl. 85

This full-length shows Lady Eardley at the time of her marriage in 1766, aged twenty-three, formally posed against a landscape background. The costume is very generalized in character, and the brilliant highlights in the satin dress, together with the motifs of plucking up the folds over the arm and of the flower held in the opposite hand, deliberately awaken echoes of Van Dyck: compare his portrait of Lady Peterborough (Pl. 86).

60. Landscape. S.A. 1766. Pl. 71

A shaft of bright sunlight is breaking through the foliage and spotlights the incident which constitutes the subject-matter of this picture, a drover who has deserted his waggon to pay court to a pretty milkmaid, who is seen looking downwards with bashful expression. The picture admirably illustrates Gainsborough's belief at this time, which was expressed in a letter written the following year, that a landscape should never 'be filled with History, or any figures but such as fill a place (I won't say stop a Gap) or to create a little business for the Eye to be drawn from the Trees in order to return to them with more glee.' The theme harks back to the Ipswich pastorals, while the heavy, dark, dominating trees are inspired by Ruisdael. The mood, tonality and touch still have much in common with the Worcester picture, but this was the last great landscape Gainsborough executed in this sombre style. It was purchased by Sir William St Quintin, whose portrait, and those of several members of his family, Gainsborough had painted not many years before.

61. The Harvest Waggon. S.A. 1767. Pls 77 and 80

Apart from the presence of a waggon, the strong shaft of light and the massive trees which fill up the left side of the picture, there is very little in common between *The Harvest Waggon* and Gainsborough's exhibited landscape of the year before. The arrangement of the background owes nothing to Dutch example and is in fact broadly Claudean in character, the tonality is lighter and warmer, deriving from a priming of lead white mixed with a yellow pigment, and the handling is brilliantly free and sketchy: the sky has faded somewhat, as in many of Gainsborough's pictures, owing to his use of indigo rather than ultramarine. There is also an element of drama in the subject-matter – the men struggling over the water bottle, the impatient horse – which is quite new in Gainsborough's pastorals. His style was about to undergo a radical transformation under the influence of Rubens, and in 1768 we find him writing enthusiastically to Garrick, 'I could wish to you to call *upon any pretence* any day after next Wednesday at the Duke of Montagu, because you'd see the Duke & Dutchess in my *last* manner; but not as if you thought anything of mine worth that trouble, only to see his Grace's Landskip of Rubens . . .' Gainsborough did not sell *The Harvest Waggon* and gave it to his friend Walter Wiltshire, the owner of a firm of carriers which had always arranged the transport of his pictures (in return for the present of a grey horse, reputedly the one shown in the picture), when he left Bath for London in 1774.

62. Landscape. About 1767–8. Pls 72 and 73

This superb landscape is the key picture of Gainsborough's new style. It was almost certainly a commissioned work, painted for Lord Shelburne, and together with a Barret and Wilson's *Apollo and the Seasons*, one of the three pictures for the decoration of Shelburne's Wiltshire home, Bowood, 'intended to lay the *foundation of a school of British landscapes*'. The motif of rustic dalliance has now been incorporated into the broader theme of peasants going to market, and the composition forms a majestic arc over the group of horses and figures winding into the distance, while the handling, fresh and brilliant and wholly different from the comparatively laboured technique of the St Quintin picture, is even bolder and more adventurous than in the slightly earlier *The Harvest Waggon*. The figures and horses are hardly more than sketched; the panorama on the left is suggested in a few rapid brush strokes; and the tree trunks are roughly modelled, partially in reflected lights, with rich hues of red, yellow, orange, blue and violet predominating. Above all, a brilliant morning sky is painted in tones of pink and yellow, put on with a thickly loaded brush, so that the light glints through the foliage and between the trees, giving the entire composition a tremendous vitality and sparkle. In the whole conception and handling of this picture, Gainsborough's intense excitement by Rubens, the Rubens of the broad, vigorous, high-keyed landscapes of the 1630s rather than the Rubens of *The Watering Place*, is abundantly apparent.

63. Landscape. About 1768–70. Pl. 74

This is the most complex of Gainsborough's landscapes of this period, and the only landscape he ever produced which has anything like the panoramic extent of a mature Rubens. As in the latter's later landscapes, such as the *Château de Steen* in Vienna, which also contains the motif of the footbridge and of the path winding through the wood, the emphasis is entirely on movement laterally across the picture: the eye is led from the foreground tree stumps on the left through the main subject of the picnic party to the rustic crossing over the bridge, and back again in a further plane through the diagonals of the tree trunk on the right and the group of cattle drinking. There is a tremendous sense of recession in the landscape and the eye is finally lost in the sketchily painted background, where dragged, white brushstrokes envelope the distance in a kind of daze. No less Rubensian than the composition are the sturdy forms of the trees, their roots almost tearing at the ground, and the brilliant effects of light: the beautiful reflections in the water, the shaft of sunlight piercing the wooded glade, and the richly varied sky. As in the Toledo landscape, and as in Rubens, there is more than one source of light: Gainsborough's feeling for the dramatic possibilities of light was always stronger than his respect for naturalism.

64. John, 4th Duke of Argyll. S.A. 1767. Pls 75 and 97

Gainsborough sent three full-lengths to the Society of Artists in 1767 which, in their lightness of key and richness of handling, manifest the influence of Rubens quite as strongly as the landscapes of this period. The rough slabs of impasto suggesting the sunset glow in the background of the *Argyll* are handled with an impressionistic daring that caused raised eyebrows amongst contemporary critics, but the effect is as brilliantly successful as the painting of the finery of the Duke's costume and the management of the fall of the robes. The extraordinary beauty of the handling, however, cannot disguise the failure to achieve a suitable grandeur in the pose: compared with Reynolds's *Earl of Carlisle* in Garter robes the composition is as Mytens to Van Dyck.

65. Countess Grosvenor. S.A. 1767. Pl. 64

Lady Grosvenor has unfortunately been cut down from the original full-length, and the head and shoulders are all that survive, but the treatment of the head is instructive. For the intensity of the expression, the dilation of the nostrils and the sharp turn of the head all demonstrate a new force and power in Gainsborough's portraiture which was at the other end of the spectrum from the nuances of characterization displayed in *Anne Horton*; from now on Gainsborough was capable, when he needed, of adding a new dimension to his Van Dyck manner, and it is tempting to believe that this ability, too, was the result of his enthusiasm for Rubens.

66. Viscount Kilmorey. About 1768. Pls 53 and 105

In this portrait, probably painted very soon after his three exhibited full-lengths of 1767, Gainsborough has re-introduced the motif of the tree trunk spiralling upwards which he had employed in *General James Johnston*. In this case, however, he has not attempted to integrate figure and tree, though the tree does serve as a rustic equivalent of the baroque column and curtain, but has placed his sitter firmly in the front plane of the canvas and square to the spectator; the deep blues, scarlet and gold of the suit stand out vividly against the silvery background, and enhance the impact of the solid 'no-nonsense' pose. The conception again suggests the force of Rubens rather than the sophisticated reticence of Van Dyck, but the tension is relieved by the twinkle of good humour about the eyes and mouth, reminding us that Gainsborough's business was with a person, not simply with an image of a bluff country squire.

67. Duchess of Montagu. About 1768. Pl. 65

This serene and haunting portrait ranks with the small oval of Mrs Kirby as one of the most compelling and deeply sympathetic of Gainsborough's studies of older women with character. The quiet dignity of the expression is matched by the aristocratic erectness of posture, in turn pictorially supported by the upright of the picture frame; but these elements of severity in the design are softened by the broad highlit curve which forms the basic structure of the composition, by the rough texturing of the crinkled satin cape which lies at the centre of this curve, and by such details as the fingers of the right hand, relaxed and natural in pose. Gainsborough referred to this portrait in a letter to Garrick written in the summer of 1768 as 'in my *last* manner'; the picture on the wall evidently represents a landscape also in Gainsborough's latest manner, conceivably an actual landscape bought by the Montagus.

68. Studies of a cat. Mid to later 1760s. Pl. 83

A sheet of studies from life of a cat, vividly portrayed in a number of typically feline positions, alert and watchful, gently licking itself, and curled up on the hearth-rug, half-asleep and purring in self-satisfaction. The drawing is traditionally supposed to have been sketched in a country house and presented to his hostess. Some support to this is lent by the fact that it is one of the rare cases when Gainsborough signed a drawing in full.

69. Landscape drawing. Later 1760s. Pl. 81

Another brilliant sketch *ad vivum*, of a boy reclining at the back of a cart, cheerily whistling as he returns home at the end of the day's work. The loose, bold but wonderfully descriptive penwork is almost Rembrandtesque in quality; the rough scallops outlining the foliage should be contrasted with the zig-zag touch in the early drawings. The sunlight which pours across the scene, and the reassuring spire of the village church, are features reflecting the nostalgic mood characteristic of so many of Gainsborough's pastorals.

70. 'The Pitminster Boy'. Later 1760s. Pl. 82

During the summer months, when the Academy was open and the press of business had receded, Gainsborough devoted more of his time to landscape and to travel. He seems to have been a welcome guest at Barton Grange, the Somersetshire home of Goodenough Earle (about whom, unfortunately, nothing is known), and presented a number of drawings to his host on different occasions in the course of the 1760s. This brilliant portrait study is of a local lad who carried his paints for him on sketching trips when he was staying in Somerset. The eager intentness of the boy's expression – conveyed partly through the fixed gaze of the eyes and partly through the lips, parted in concentration – is beautifully caught, and emphasized by the exaggerated lighting.

71. Countess of Dartmouth. 1769 and about 1771. Pls 89 and 90

Gainsborough's first portrait of Lady Dartmouth was executed, apparently at the sitter's request, in the Reynolds manner. The head is idealized and sculptured in quality, the dress is generalized, and the figure is set against a backdrop landscape. Her husband was evidently unimpressed by the likeness, for he sent the picture back to be altered in 1771. Gainsborough thereupon reminded him of his dislike of the 'ridiculous use of fancied Dresses in Portraits', asserted that 'had I painted Lady Dartmouths Picture, dressed as Her Ladyship goes, no fault . . . would have been found with it', and offered, if he could be permitted to treat the offending canvas as 'a cast off Picture' and alter it to show the effect of modern dress on the production of a good likeness, to begin a new portrait. It is clear, from the survival of the original canvas, that Gainsborough was not allowed to carry out his suggestion; but, following his experiment with '*The Blue Boy*', he did execute a smaller portrait of the Countess in Van Dyck costume, holding a rose, in which the likeness is a good deal more apparent.

72. Viscountess Molyneux. R.A. 1769. Pls 91 and 92

Lady Molyneux was married at St Martin-in-the-Fields a few weeks before Christmas 1768, and the picture was clearly commissioned in celebration. This portrait of the twenty-year-old bride is one of Gainsborough's grandest female full-lengths, painted for the first Royal Academy exhibition in 1769. As one might expect for so important an occasion, he returned very consciously to Van Dyck and the pose is far closer to the spirit of the seventeenth century than is the case, for example, in *Lady Howe*, which is more an inspired interpretation of the Van Dyck tradition; the placing of the left arm over the breast is a characteristic Van Dyck motif, and the landscape has been generalized to an extent rare in Gainsborough, so that the eye is undistracted from the grace of the slightly turned head and the dignity of the figure. The modelling of the features is exceptionally soft and atmospheric, expressive of a gentler, more reflective nature than that of the ebullient Lady Grosvenor; but the highlights in the satin dress are handled with a verve and brilliance unmatched in Gainsborough's previous work.

73. 'The Blue Boy'. R.A. 1770. Pl. 94

Gainsborough's most famous portrait was not a commissioned work at all: X-rays have revealed the beginnings of the portrait of an older man under the paint surface, and thus the fact that '*The Blue Boy*' was painted on a discarded canvas. The picture was clearly done for Gainsborough's own pleasure. Jonathan Buttall, son of a prosperous Soho ironmonger, was a young man of musical tastes whose family had property in Ipswich, and who became a close friend of the artist's (he was one of the few people whom Gainsborough desired to attend his funeral). Gainsborough must have wanted to try out the Van Dyck dress, which we know he kept in his studio in the 1770s for the benefit of those clients who wanted to be painted in 'fancy dress' – and created a masterpiece. The pose is closely derived from Van Dyck, but charged with a force and directness quite foreign to that master which remind us, as does the intensity of expression, of *Viscount Kilmorey*. The figure is skilfully related to the landscape background through its setting against a patch of brilliant light, and through the diagonal of the left forearm, which echoes the rising terrain.

74. Henry, 3rd Duke of Buccleuch. 1770. Pls 66 and 67

This portrait of a twenty-four-year-old grandee is at the opposite pole from '*The Blue Boy*'. The sweetness of the expression, the tilt of the head, the appeal of the pet dog, all add up to an image which lies on the borders of sentiment. The star of the Thistle seems distinctly out of key, except as a pictorial accent, and was no doubt included at the request of the sitter. The conception is unusual in male portraiture of the period, and the formal parallels are with such portraits of motherly affection as Reynolds's enchanting *Lady Spencer and her Daughter* of 1760–1.

75. Viscount Ligonier. 1770. Pl. 95

'Ever since the receipt of your last *un*deserv'd favor,' Gainsborough wrote to his friend James Unwin, 'I have been toss'd about like a ship in a storm; I went by appointment only to spend two or three Days at Mr George Pitt's Country House, by way of taking leave of him, as a staunch Friend of mine before his going to Spain, and behold he had got two whole length Canvasses, & his son [in-law] & Daughter Ld. & Lady Ligonier in readiness to take me prisoner for a months work.' The occasion for this commission was the son-in-law's succession to his uncle's title. The portraits are conceived as a pair compositionally, and neither quite makes sense on its own; they were presumably intended to be hung on either side of a fireplace. Ironically, however, Lady Ligonier was already unfaithful to her husband, whose preoccupations in life may be hinted at in the way in which the horse dominates the canvas, a feature of the composition for which Gainsborough was rightly taken to task in reviews of the Exhibition. Compare the *George, Prince of Wales* at Waddesdon, exhibited eleven years later, for a more assured pose, a less obtrusive horse, and an altogether more balanced design.

76. Viscountess Ligonier. 1770. Pl. 96

Penelope Pitt at the age of twenty or twenty-one. She is seen as Reynolds might have portrayed her, wearing the sort of 'timeless' costume he advocated in portraiture – clothes so generalized as to be unrecognizable as fashionable dress – with her left arm resting on a tall plinth, and curtains rising behind; the cast and sheets of drawings on the chair, and the porte-crayon she holds in her hand, allude to her ambitions as an amateur artist. But the comparison with Reynolds only serves to underline the difference. There is something of a swagger about the right arm and the expression is intense and hard, characteristics totally at odds with the conception of a Reynolds female full-length, while Reynolds would never have painted an accessory like the bronze figurine so *con amore*. Hardly a year after the picture was exhibited the scandal of Lady Ligonier's love life, which included an affair with her husband's postillion, emerged in the gossip-columns; she was divorced, and remarried a cavalry trooper. Gainsborough, who had 'a pretty good knowledge of Mankind', must have been well aware of her propensities, the dancing Bacchante may be a touch of wit, and it is not entirely fanciful to suspect something of Miss Julie about her from the portrait.

77. Elizabeth and Mary Linley. R.A. 1772. Pl. 102

The setting of this enchanting picture, so often taken for granted, is almost unique in Gainsborough's oeuvre, though interestingly there is a precedent in '*Bumper*', painted over a quarter of a century before – and it heralds the late romantic style. For there is hardly a suggestion of distance, and only a glimmer of light on the left to relieve the dark mass of the trees. The dense and richly painted foliage envelops the figures, throwing into relief the two heads, which are strongly lit. It is the faces that are everything in this portrait. Elizabeth and Mary Linley, renowned alike for their beauty and their voices, had been close friends of Gainsborough's since childhood; their father, Thomas Linley, was a composer, and Ozias Humphry, who lodged in the Linleys' house at Bath for some years, tells us that Gainsborough 'lived in great intimacy with this family'. Gainsborough has caught to perfection, in his frontal pose, the liveliness and sparkle of Mary, and the head of Elizabeth is one of the most ravishing studies of feminine beauty he ever painted. 'Her nose . . . Grecian; fine luxurious, easy-sitting hair, a charming forehead, pretty mouth, and most bewitching eyes. With all this her carriage is modest and unassuming, and her countenance indicates diffidence, and a strong desire of pleasing.' So wrote Fanny Burney, about a year after this portrait was painted.

78. Study of a music party. Early 1770s. Pl. 101

A rough sketch, very French in character, this quality emphasized by the use of red chalk, only rarely employed by Gainsborough. The artist's miraculous ability to convey weight, posture and expression with a few swiftly drawn lines is nowhere more splendidly revealed than in this sketch. The musicians have never been identified, but it is tempting to suppose that the scene is at the Linleys: the lady seated at the harpsichord is difficult to identify (conceivably she is Mrs Linley), but comparison with existing portraits does not preclude the possibility that the other sitters are Thomas Linley, Elizabeth Linley and, playing the violin, Felice de Giardini.

79. Sir Benjamin Truman. Early 1770s. Pl. 76

This four-square full-length of the son of the founder of the Truman Brewery in Spitalfields is again close to Reynolds – the hand clasping the stick, which sets the tone for the portrait, is comparable to Burgoyne's resting on his sword – but the features of the bluff old tradesman have not been idealized in the very least, and where in Reynolds would one find the maker's name recorded in the lining of a hat? Nevertheless, the grandeur of the trees on the left, the stormy sky and the castellated building in the background all emphasize the simple nobility of the design, and the sitter must have been well pleased: a few years later Gainsborough was asked to paint full-lengths of his two grand-daughters.

80. Landscape. 1773. Pl. 115

This landscape was purchased by Henry Hoare, who was Gainsborough's banker, and is presumably to be identified with 'Gainsborough's picture' for which he paid eighty guineas on 6 July 1773. It was seen and admired at Stourhead in the summer of 1775 by the Rev. William Gilpin, the writer on 'the Picturesque', who commented that 'both the figures and the effect of this picture are pleasing'. The principal figures are more highly finished than in the canvas of peasants travelling to market at Toledo, and the sentimental intentions of the piece are emphasized by the sophisticated elegance of the beautiful redhead, who is clearly no country girl. Hazlitt later criticized such idealized figures when he wrote that Gainsborough gave 'the air of an Adonis to the driver of a hay-cart, and models the features of a milk-maid on the principles of the antique', but Gainsborough's idyllic view of the countryside and its activities was shared by many of his contemporaries who were troubled by, and wished to forget, the changes caused by the agrarian and industrial revolutions. The ravishing effect of dawn light, also admired by Gilpin, may have been inspired by similar beauties in some such landscape by Rubens as *The Birdcatchers* in the Louvre.

81. The Woodcutter's Return. About 1773. Pl. 114

This picture was bought by the young Charles Manners, later 4th Duke of Rutland, an avid and knowledgeable collector who was advised by Reynolds. It is very probably the landscape by Gainsborough for which he paid sixty pounds, and almost certainly the landscape with a cottage, a 'scene of beauty, and domestic love', purchased by a noble lord, mentioned in a poem of 1773. The subject of the 'Cottage Door', which was praised by Mary Hartley in a letter to Gilpin for its human and affecting qualities, and became one of Gainsborough's most obsessional themes, was the perfect vehicle for the expression of his attitude towards country life: the remote and peaceful cottage, the happy domestic scene, the beautiful daughter, the woodcutter returning home after the day's work, were all symbols of the Gainsborough myth. In the Rutland picture, the effect of evening tranquillity is heightened by the glorious sunset, painted in a rich broken impasto, and by the warm glow of the fire; the spotlit figure group is an example of Gainsborough's unnaturalistic 'double' lighting.

82. Landscape drawing. Early 1770s. Pl. 118

In many respects this is a typical mature Gainsborough landscape drawing. The use of black and white chalks, with stump to suggest the masses, the scatter of lights across the composition, the motif of the pollarded trees, all these are to be found in countless late drawings. But the subject-matter, the figure seated beneath a ruined building difficult to identify except as a ruin, is exceptional. The mood is one of melancholy, close to certain types of Wilson. Gainsborough was not only lively and ebullient, but deeply introspective; with him, sadness was never far away from gaiety. Thus there recur in his imagery bleak and inhospitable views of upland scenery, dark and densely wooded dells. The ruin, symbol of what has passed, as well as an object of 'picturesque' beauty, emerged from this dark side of his imagination.

83. Landscape. Early 1770s. Pl. 109

Though Gainsborough has included his usual rustic lovers, a prominent group of cows and other typical subject-matter in this landscape, the composition is entirely in the manner of Claude; the mass of trees framing the scene on the right, the bridge in the middleground, the carefully mapped out distance (rare in a mature Gainsborough landscape), the mountains and the glowing horizon, all these elements can be compared with such Claudes as the *Jacob and Laban* at Petworth (Pl. 110). It is tempting to think that the picture may have been specially commissioned to hang with a Claude, but unfortunately nothing is known about the circumstances of its painting. A study for the picture was originally in the possession of Sir Thomas Lawrence, and may actually have been given to him by Gainsborough.

84. Mrs William Lowndes-Stone. About 1775. Pls 103 and 104

This full-length was probably done at the time of the sitter's marriage in 1775. The design is broadly reminiscent of Van Dyck, with a fairly generalized robe enlivened with broken highlights and the left hand holding up a gauze shawl; but the prettily smiling face belies the grandeur and the hair curling round the neck echoes the rough treatment of the background foliage. In Gainsborough's development the picture stands half-way between the stateliness of *Lady Eardley*, done ten years earlier, and the romanticism of *Mrs Sheridan*, of ten years later (Pl. 153).

85. Johann Christian Bach. About 1776. Fig. 10

Bach's teacher, Giovanni Battista Martini, did his pupil the signal honour of asking for a portrait of him for display in the Liceo Musicale in Bologna; completed by May 1776, it was not actually dispatched until 1778, 'an excellent portrait of myself by one of our best painters'. This fine replica (an example of Gainsborough's executing two versions of the same portrait with his own hand) Gainsborough painted for Bach himself, and it forms one of a group of simple but deeply sympathetic portraits Gainsborough did of close personal friends such as Garrick and de Loutherbourg. The strength of the sitter's personality is conveyed partly through the kindly but assured and firm expression, and partly through the weight of the arms resting on the table. The uneasy transitions of the right forearm (Gainsborough often scamped anatomical precision) are hidden by the music-paper.

86. Lord Abingdon. Mid 1770s. Pl. 125

This unfinished, informal full-length of Lord Abingdon, an outspoken radical peer, supporter of Wilkes, the American colonists and the French Revolution, who was also a musical amateur, friend of both Abel and J.C.Bach, amply demonstrates Gainsborough's normal procedure in his approach to a portrait. The composition, pose and arrangement of the accessories would all be blocked out before serious work was started on the head itself, which was then carried to a high degree of finish. No more sittings would be needed after this, and in the press of business many canvases would fail to reach completion. The half-length of Lord Cathcart, the handsome brother of the beautiful Mrs Graham, another surviving unfinished canvas, was, rather surprisingly, actually exhibited in its unfinished state at Gainsborough's first exhibition of his pictures at Schomberg House in July 1784.

87. The Watering Place. R.A. 1777. Pl. 111

Horace Walpole described this landscape, when he saw it at the Academy, as 'in the Style of Rubens, and by far the finest Landscape ever painted in England, & equal to the great Masters.' His opinion was a just one, and has been fully confirmed by time. The dark and massive trees are clearly reminiscent of Rubens's own painting of this subject (Pl. 112), which Gainsborough had seen at the Duke of Montagu's so many years before, and the composition, ultimately derived, like Lord Crawford's landscape, from Claude, is of monumental grandeur. Indeed, a comparison between this picture, the most important landscape of the early London period, and the landscapes painted ten years earlier, is extraordinarily revealing. For all the elements in its design – tree trunks, foliage, banks, cows, figures – are much more broadly and roughly handled; the composition is more unified and concentrated; and the effect is more compelling. In many ways it is the heroic style of Titian that is brought to mind rather than the landscapes of Rubens or of Claude – Titian, who was revered throughout the eighteenth century as the very fount of the grand manner in landscape painting and directly influential, in just these years, on the practice of Reynolds in his landscape backgrounds.

88. The Hon. Mrs Thomas Graham. R.A. 1777. Pl. 108

Mrs Graham is the grandest of all Gainsborough's full-lengths in the Van Dyck tradition. The regal pose and slight but majestic turn of the head are matched by the mighty plinth and columns (though who but Gainsborough would have straggled a branch and leaves across them), and these dominate the canvas in a way characteristic of the baroque that Gainsborough had never sought before nor was to seek again. In these respects the picture is the counterpart in portraiture of *The Watering Place*, and it was with these great canvases that Gainsborough heralded his return to the Academy exhibition after four years absence due to a quarrel with the hanging committee. But the portrait is also of a beautiful nineteen-year-old, painted soon after her marriage to the dashing Thomas Graham. The delicacy of the softly modelled head, the lovely Van Dyck dress, the richly impasted brushwork in the highlights of the overskirt and the impressionistic handling in the robe beneath, a welter of pinks and lakes and crimsons, which miraculously assumes form at a distance of twelve feet – all these are part of a sustained hymn of praise to feminine grace and beauty. Gainsborough never excelled the beauty of his *facture* in this painting and, as in the case of '*The Blue Boy*', also a chocolate-box favourite, confrontation with the original produces the most overwhelming effect upon the spectator. The motif of the hand fingering the satin folds derives from Van Dyck, and the drooping right arm and firmly modelled fingers may be directly compared with the latter's work.

89. Carl Friedrich Abel. R.A. 1777. Pl. 126

Another powerful full-length Gainsborough sent to the Academy in this *annus mirabilis* of his achievement was the portrait of his intimate friend, Carl Friedrich Abel, the partner of J.C.Bach. The portrait is an affectionate characterization of the gentle musician, who is seen informally at his writing table in the act of composition; as in the dress of Mrs Graham the flowered waistcoat provided an opportunity for some ravishing bravura handling. One can imagine this conception on the scale of the *William Wollaston*, with an elegant interior setting, deliciously French in feeling. In fact it is grand. Gainsborough has painted the sitter leaning forward towards the focal point of two broad and powerful diagonals, that of the curtain and the viol da gamba, and included on the left a conventional column to stabilize this thrusting movement. If *Mrs Graham* is Gainsborough's most complete statement of Van Dyck grandeur, this is the nearest he approached to the full Italian baroque. After Abel's death the portrait was acquired by Queen Charlotte, to whom the composer had been chamber musician.

90. Viscount Gage. R.A. 1777. Pl. 106

A more conventional Gainsborough full-length, in which the sitter's left arm is resting on a branch of a tree and the sturdy tree trunk replaces the classical column as a means of enhancing the grandeur of the composition. The loose flecks of paint round the eyes and mouth, which give life to the countenance, are typical of Gainsborough's technique at this date.

91. Philip James de Loutherbourg. R.A. 1778. Fig. 11

This is a more intense and rather more rapidly handled variation on the type of portrait represented by the *J.C.Bach*. The sitter is leaning earnestly forward, nostrils dilated and expression set; the head is strongly lit, and the waistcoat is indicated summarily in rough touches of yellow over the pink priming.

92. The Hon. Frances Duncombe. About 1778. Pl. 99

One of Gainsborough's most ravishing portraits of the late 1770s. The sitter, who brought a considerable fortune to her husband, John Bowater, whom she married in 1778, is wearing a similar Van Dyck dress to Mrs Graham, and is depicted with the high-piled hair fashionable at the period. Instead of standing beside baroque columns, however, and resting her arm upon the conventional plinth, she is seen walking happily through an arcadian landscape, her head turned sharply to the left, her lips parted and her eyes sparkling. This image of the twenty-one-year-old, upper-class eighteenth-century girl, dressed as for an evening's gaiety at Ranelagh or Vauxhall, gives the impression of being close to the life.

93. Mrs Thomas Gainsborough. About 1778. Fig. 6

Gainsborough married in 1746, and there was a tradition in his wife's family that for many years he painted Margaret on the anniversary of their wedding day. Certainly he must have painted his wife many times, as he did his daughters, but few portraits survive. The portrait now in Berlin shows her at the age of thirty; this canvas represents her about twenty years later, at fifty, and it is tempting to think that it was her fiftieth-birthday portrait. The composition is lively and unusual. A strong sense of movement is created by the play of the satin and lace of the black mantle, and this is reinforced by the positioning of the hands. The whole effect is of a loose oval – a highly sophisticated development of the device of the feigned oval – within which the head is frontally set, immediately engaging the spectator's attention. The portrait is immensely sympathetic, and affords the surest possible evidence of Gainsborough's deep affection for his wife, with whom we know he found it difficult to get on; not long before this picture was painted he wrote to his sister, Mrs Gibbon: 'If I tell you my wife is weak but good, and never much formed to humour my Happiness, what can you do to alter her?'

94. Sir Henry Bate-Dudley. R.A. 1780. Pl. 58

The Rev. Henry Bate, later Sir Henry Bate-Dudley, proprietor and editor first of *The Morning Post*, then, after 1780, of *The Morning Herald*, was the most consistent supporter of Gainsborough in the daily press. He devoted much of his time to agricultural improvement and to country pursuits on his estate at Bradwell in the remote north-east of Essex, and it seems to have been here that Gainsborough had his country cottage (Rowlandson drew it in 1783). Although, in this full-length, Bate-Dudley is dressed simply and soberly, with neither fancy waistcoat nor flashy accoutrements, the firm stance, the slightly aggressive arc of the right arm and cane, and the set expression, all combine to produce something of a military air entirely in keeping with his reputation as 'the fighting parson'.

95. Johann Christian Fischer. R.A. 1780. Pl. 127

This portrait of Johann Christian Fischer, the most celebrated oboeist of his day and a member of the Queen's Band, was exhibited a couple of months after his short-lived marriage to Gainsborough's daughter Margaret – a match of which the artist disapproved, though, as he wrote to his sister: 'I can't say I have any reason to doubt the man's honesty or goodness of heart, as I never heard any one speak anything amiss of him.' The gentle, artistic character of the sitter is perfectly conveyed by the happy concentration of the expression, the softly modulated flesh tones, the relaxed pose, and the rippling undulation of the coat; while the composition, much subtler in its use of diagonal stresses than the *Carl Friedrich Abel*, and the muted harmonies of the colour scheme, crimson against a background of greens and browns, emphasize this interpretation. Recent cleaning has revealed numerous alterations underlying the present design, but these are so extensive that it is possible the canvas had been used for a previous sitter and then discarded.

96. Mrs Henry Beaufoy. R.A. 1780. Pl. 87

In this full-length the comparison is less with Van Dyck than with Reynolds. The comparatively idealized head and the broad loops of costume, generalized rather than fashionable, are as close as Gainsborough ever approached to the portrait style of his great rival. Yet the contrasts are even greater. In Reynolds's *Lady Bamfylde* (Pl. 88) the head is far more abstracted, the costume and background more generalized, and the lighting broader: studio-controlled rather than naturalistic or even dramatic. The Reynolds retains overtones of the antique where the Gainsborough could never be mistaken for anyone but a fashionable, though perhaps rather vapid, lady of the late eighteenth century.

97. Mark Beaufoy. About 1780–1. Pl. 138

Mark Beaufoy was a Quaker who established a vinegar distillery in Lambeth, and this portrait of him at the age of sixty-two must have been painted by Gainsborough at the same time as the full-length of his daughter-in-law, Mrs Henry Beaufoy, which was exhibited at the Academy of 1780. The pose is relaxed but has the same 'no-nonsense' quality as the *Benjamin Truman*: the sitter, who is dressed in a perfectly plain suit, is firmly ensconced in the studio chair (seen also in the *Carl Friedrich Abel*), no attempt has been made to conceal his embonpoint, and the hat and gloved hand suggest that Beaufoy thought of sitting for his portrait as only a brief interlude in his busy working day.

98. The Cottage Door. R.A. 1780. Pl. 116

This variation on the theme of the 'Cottage Door' is the most concentrated and perhaps the most successful of all Gainsborough's endeavours to perfect this subject. Sir John Leicester, the distinguished nineteenth-century collector and connoisseur, who once owned it, was reported in 1818 as having allotted the picture an entire room, with mirrors placed round to exhibit it to advantage. Familiar are the group of half-ragged but perfectly healthy children, the beautiful mother with her fashionable hair style, the remote thatched cottage nestling amongst trees, the picturesque motifs of the rough surfaces of brick and stone and gnarled tree trunk, and the strong spotlight playing on the scene of idyllic contentment. But whereas Gainsborough's treatment of the subject is normally more diffuse, in this case the figure group has been arranged as a loosely composed pyramid, a pyramid strongly echoed by the interlocking diagonal formed by the silhouettes of the trees and the near-dead tree on the right.

99. The Country Churchyard. 1780. Pls. 117 and 119

Only two fragments of *The Country Churchyard* are known today but the whole composition is recorded, in reverse, in

Maria C. Prestal's aquatint of 1790, beneath which are printed the opening lines of Gray's *Elegy*. Gainsborough was not much of a reading man nor was he an artist particularly concerned with illustrating literary subjects, but the overtones of the theme of *Et in Arcadia Ego*, as developed by Poussin, are unmistakable. He was certainly aware of Gray's work, and it has been pointed out that the peasant leaning on a stick to make out the inscription on the tombstone in the soft-ground etching may echo the figure in Bentley's illustration to the *Elegy*, etched by Gainsborough's old friend Grignion; the couple on the other side of the churchyard represent the innocent and happy acceptance of an idyllic present. In the early to mid 1770s Gainsborough had become fascinated first by the possibilities of aquatint, then by those of soft-ground etching, as a means of reproducing his drawings, and the subjects he chose to reproduce are obviously a key to what lay at the heart of his imagination. *The Country Churchyard* is a more overt statement of the melancholy which is to be found in the drawing of a ruin beside a river, dating from a few years previously.

100. Seascape. R.A. 1781. Pl. 121

Although the two seascapes Gainsborough sent to the Academy of 1781, one of them a calm, the other a storm, were his first efforts in this genre, they were brilliantly successful, and Horace Walpole praised them as being 'so free and natural that one steps back for fear of being splashed'. The storm was painted for the 1st Earl Grosvenor, one of the foremost patrons of British art, who commissioned a companion to it, *Fishermen launching their Boat*, from de Loutherbourg in 1784. The picture is totally dominated by the gale that is blowing up and by the superb effects of light and shade resulting. Clouds are scudding rapidly across the sky, the sails of the boats at sea are heavily weighted down, and the girls on the beach clutch desperately at their clothes. The tonality is as low in key as the weather, and there is a fine sense of recession in the iron-grey sea, created by modulations in tone. The brushwork is rough and free, the painting of the foam, in rich and broken impasto, being handled magnificently; while the composition is no less vigorous, sweeping up to the right – where a shepherd is seen on the cliff-top with his flock of sheep – in a tremendous baroque diagonal. This is the nearest British eighteenth-century marine painting ever approached to the ferocity, grandeur and incredible naturalism of Turner.

101. The Girl with Pigs. R.A. 1782. Pl. 146

At the beginning of the 1780s Gainsborough began to produce a type of picture in which the little figures from his pastoral landscapes took on the scale of life, were sentimentalized, and were depicted in the process of a simple everyday domestic or country activity. These not only proved popular, reflecting the mood of the times, and sold well, but earned the praise of Sir Joshua Reynolds. *The Girl with Pigs* was actually bought by Reynolds, who said it was 'by far the best picture he ever painted, or perhaps ever will'. It was presumably the simplicity and concentration of the picture which appealed to the President's mind; the composition is based on a broad arc, the landscape is neither extensive nor varied, and the wistful little figure is generalized and strongly lit. The three pigs were done from the life, as they were seen in Gainsborough's studio when the picture was on the easel. The history of the painting's ownership is unusually distinguished for a Gainsborough: it was sold by Reynolds about 1789 to the great French collector Calonne, was bought in at the Calonne sale in 1795 and shortly afterwards purchased through the dealer Bryan by the Earl of Carlisle, from whom it has descended.

102. Giovanna Baccelli. R.A. 1782. Pls 128 and 131

The enchanting ballet dancer Giovanna Baccelli was the mistress of the Duke of Dorset, who commissioned this full-length from Gainsborough. An extraordinary effect of lightness and grace of movement is produced by the loop of the design, which ripples along the folds of the skirt, sweeps upwards through the gauze over-skirt and ends in the foliage of the unnaturally tall trees. The mood of ease and grace and delicacy is sustained by the sweetness of the expression and the fluency of the handling, rich in the lights but almost transparent in the shadows. The rich pinks, yellows and oranges at the horizon serve as a dramatic foil to the lovely blue dress. Gainsborough may have been envious of Reynolds's range of invention but, in portraits of this kind, exquisite and fresh in colour, light as gossamer, Reynolds was unable to touch Gainsborough. A small oil sketch exists, in which neither the tambourine nor the tall trees on the right have been introduced.

103. Grace Dalrymple. R.A. 1782 (probably). Pl. 149

This splendid detail, taken long before the picture was lined and restored, demonstrates admirably the flickering touch and the rapidity but incredible sureness of Gainsborough's modelling in his late work. The sitter, one of the best-known *demi-mondaines* of the period, and referred to in the press as 'Dally the Tall', was described by her niece, who only saw her once and then when she was already fifty, as 'the most beautiful woman I had ever beheld'. Gainsborough has captured both her physical charms and the secret of her irresistible appeal in the sensuous nostrils and alluring half-smile of her eyes and lips. This small oval canvas was painted four years after the full-length commissioned by her lover, Lord Cholmondeley, which Gainsborough sent to the Academy of 1778 and is now in the Metropolitan Museum.

104. Landscape. R.A. 1782. Pl. 122

This landscape combines the sentiment of the 'Cottage Door' with the drama of Rubens. A group of figures are seen outside a woodland cottage with, focal point of the composition, a mother and her two children this side of the pool looking at the cows, and some sheep grazing on the far bank. To this extent the picture is a typical Gainsborough pastoral. But the silhouetting of the dark trees against a glowing sunset, the reflections in the water, and the outlining of the cow against the reflected light, are all elements which derive from Rubens's moonlight landscape (Pl. 123) which, by 1778, had come into Reynolds's possession, and was used by him as an object-lesson in his Discourse to the Academy students that December. Gainsborough carried the dramatic chiaroscuro of this landscape still further in his transparencies, inspired partly by his previous experience of painting on glass and partly by the experiments of Thomas Jervais and of his friend Philip James de Loutherbourg (see Pl. 124).

105. Transparency. About 1782. Pl. 124

The eighteenth-century equivalent of a 'happening' was the 'Eidophusikon', an entertainment devised by Gainsborough's friend de Loutherbourg, the celebrated scene-painter, and which was the hit of the town in 1781. Illusionistic effects were created on a miniature stage with the aid of moving scenery, dramatic lighting and sound. Gainsborough, who, under the influence of Rubens, had for some years been trying to force his effects beyond the capacities of oil paint, was so captivated by the 'Eidophusikon' and by contemporary exhibitions of glass painting (a medium to which he was no stranger) that he invented his own show-box, for which he produced transparencies derived from his landscapes. Ten of these transparencies still survive, together with the box, in the Victoria and Albert Museum. Edward Edwards described how they were seen: 'They are lighted by candles at the back, and are viewed through a magnifying lens, by which means the effect produced is truly captivating, especially in the moon-light pieces, which exhibit the most perfect resemblance of nature.'

106. Child asleep. Early 1780s. Pl. 84

One of those miraculous drawings, like *The Music Party*, in which Gainsborough has suggested the weight of the body, movement and expression, with a few rapid touches, chiefly in stump. The variations in tone are beautifully controlled.

107. Princess Elizabeth. 1782. Pl. 132

In September 1782 Gainsborough was at Windsor Castle, occupied with painting small oval portraits of all the members of the Royal Family. The *Princess Elizabeth*, one of the most vivacious of the series, admirably displays the facility of Gainsborough's modelling characteristic of his late portraits, and the inimitable looseness of his brushwork in the hair and dress. The fifteen portraits were exhibited at the Academy in three rows of five, their frames touching (a state to which they were returned at the wish of King George VI); Gainsborough had given the hanging committee a sketch showing the order in which he wanted them hung and begged leave 'to *hint* to Them, that if The Royal Family, which he has sent for this Exhibition (*being smaller than three quarters*) are hung above the line along with full lengths, he never more, whilst he breaths, will send another Picture to the Exhibition. This he swears by God.'

108. Two shepherd boys with dogs fighting. R.A. 1783. Pl. 154

One of the strangest and most difficult to explain of all Gainsborough's pictures. Gainsborough hated suffering and cruelty, and although as a painter he must have admired the brilliance of Snyders, from whom the dogs are taken, the fighting animals are painted with incredible realism and the inclusion of the boy looking on with pleasure and trying to restrain his angry companion seems out of key. Without the second boy, however, there would be no interaction of character and the subject would degenerate into anecdote. In fact, Gainsborough was particularly concerned at this stage in his life about the content in his work, though equally aware of his intellectual shortcomings. He wrote to Sir William Chambers, Treasurer of the Academy: 'I sent my fighting Dogs to divert you, I believe next Exhibition I shall make the Boys fighting and the Dogs looking on—you know my cunning way of avoiding great subjects in Painting and of concealing my Ignorance with a flash in the pan.' The picture was bought by Wilbraham Tollemache, and a copy was painted for Lord Bateman, who had patronized Gainsborough since 1770 or so.

109. The Mall. 1783. Pl. 148

In October 1783, immediately after his return from the Lakes, Gainsborough was reported as 'working on a magnificent picture in a style new to his hand . . . To the connoisseur the most compendious information is to say that it comes nearest to the manner of Watteau, but to say no more it is Watteau far outdone.' Ladies of fashion and pleasure, and their beaux, are promenading in a park intended to evoke the Mall in St James's Park without in any way being a view of it; it was perhaps this latter fact which accounts for the picture not entering the royal collection, for which it was supposed to have been painted, as George III would doubtless have required a map-reference for the scene. The soft, feathery foliage of the trees which tower over the figures, evocative of a Watteau *fête galante*, sets the mood of the scene; the cows on the left and the near-dead tree trunk on the right seem to have strayed out of a different kind of Gainsborough landscape, though the latter contributes to the gentle arc which is the principal compositional stress. According to the catalogue of the Dupont sale held at Christie's in 1797 'the figures are probably known portraits of the times'; on the analogy of Rowlandson's *Vauxhall Gardens*, exhibited 1784, this is not impossible, though none has been identified, but they were apparently executed from one of Gainsborough's dressed-up dolls, as Jackson said that 'all the female figures in his Park-scene he drew from a doll of his own creation.'

110. The Duke and Duchess of Cumberland.
About 1783–5. Pls 156, 158, 159 and 173

Gainsborough's portrait of the Duke and Duchess of Cumberland strolling in the grounds of Cumberland Lodge, Windsor Great Park, with the Duchess's sister, Lady Elizabeth Luttrell, sketching in the background, is one of his most original and subtly balanced compositions. It is of superlative quality throughout, and survives in a perfect state of preservation. The design began simply enough, as a conversation piece with a flat, decorative background, very similar to Zoffany, as can be seen from Gainsborough's first sketch. In the second drawing (Pl. 158), the trees, now more romantic in character, are integrated with the figures rather than being just a setting, and the pattern of light and shade is more complex. The finished picture is neither horizontal nor vertical in format, but oval; the trees, towering over the figures, have now taken on a vigorous life of their own, the Duke's pose has reverted to that adopted in the initial sketch, and the garden urn, also seen in this drawing, has been effectively disposed as a pictorial link between the Cumberlands and Lady Elizabeth. The costumes, notably the elaborate polonese dress and the hats, are those of 1783–5, and similar to those which appear in *The Mall*; it has recently been pointed out that, like *The Mall*, the picture is Watteauesque in inspiration and has its roots in such pictures of couples strolling in a garden as *La Cascade* (where even the relationship of Lady Elizabeth is anticipated in the seated musician).

111. Peasant family receiving charity. 1784. Pl. 141

In this picture, which has been somewhat cut down (the full composition being known from a copy), a servant girl at a country house is supplying food to a peasant family in need. To Gainsborough, as to Wheatley, who executed subjects of a similar nature (see Pl. 143), this kind of charity was the natural corollary of the current structure of society and the representation of it uplifting rather than the reverse. Bate-Dudley's description of the picture when it was shown at Gainsborough's first exhibition at his studio in Pall Mall underlines this point: 'A very fine summer sky is introduced. A vine is represented against the side of the house; several pigeons, also, are descried fluttering about the building. The whole of which forms a beautiful assemblage of an interesting nature.' As in the case of the Huntington *Cottage Door*, the design is based on interlocking diagonals, with the highlit pan held by the servant girl at their centre.

112. George, Prince of Wales. 1784. Pl. 98

In 1784 a splendid new uniform was designed for the Tenth (Prince of Wales's Own) Light Dragoons, of which George,

Prince of Wales, was Colonel Commandant. The Prince, who adored uniforms and dressing up, immediately commissioned a full-length from Gainsborough, which was intended to form part of the magnificent portrait gallery of members of the royal family and of his own circle, 'the ministers of his serious business, and the companions of his looser hours', planned for the state rooms of Carlton House. The scheme never materialized, as the Prince plunged into an abyss of debt, and several works by Gainsborough were amongst the pictures left unfinished or unpaid for: the ravishing group of *The Three Princesses* was still in the artist's studio in 1787, waiting 'till the Picture Saloon at Carlton House is fitted for their reception'. Of the full-length in dragoon uniform Gainsborough had done the head and shoulders, and the magnificent helmet – silver, orange and black, with a soft brown plume – is one of his finest pieces of bravura painting. In 1810 the picture was given by the Prince to Lord Heathfield, and the canvas was then comple‘ l by another artist, possibly Agasse.

113. Landscape. About 1784. Pls 134 and 137

It is significant that, when Gainsborough made a wash drawing of Langdale Pikes during his visit to the Lakes in the late summer of 1783, he unconsciously softened the outline of the peaks. The grandeur and ruggedness of mountain scenery did not stir him, any more than it did Constable; his concern was with rhythm and flowing movement. These qualities are the keynote of the Washington landscape. The lateral movement of the group crossing the bridge is stressed by the lighting, which picks out the track behind it and the bank in front, and the undulating line formed by this progression is echoed in the dark trees in the middle distance and the mountains beyond. The picture may be unfinished, but the effect has been fully achieved; forms might be more clearly defined, but it is difficult, for example, to see how the rough brushstrokes suggesting the figures could be modified without loss of vitality.

114. The Harvest Waggon. 1784–5. Pl. 78

Superficially, this picture is very close in style and composition to the better-known *The Harvest Waggon* painted nearly twenty years before: the *placement*, the lighting and such motifs as the girl being helped over the side of the waggon are identical. But whereas in the earlier painting it was the figures and horses that were in movement, here it is the landscape. The Claudean background of the Birmingham picture has been replaced by a vigorous *mis-en-scène* inspired by Rubens which envelops the entire composition: a wiry, twisting tree trunk acts as a *repoussoir* on the left, intermingled trees and rocks form a cavernous semicircle enclosing the figure group, and the swing of the country track is echoed in the treatment of the clouds, as in Rubens's *Summer* at Windsor Castle. The handling is both vigorous and fluent. The child at the back of the waggon is astonishingly close to Rembrandt in technique, and the girl in shadow is based on Hogarth's *Shrimp Girl*. Recognized at the time as a masterpiece, it was bought from the studio by the Prince of Wales, who later gave it to Mrs Fitzherbert.

115. Greyhounds coursing a fox. About 1784–5. Pl. 155

The emphasis in this sporting painting is less upon the seizure of the fox than on the bounding movement of the hounds as they leap across the foreground. This vigorous motion is echoed in the tree trunks on the right, which snake upwards towards the top of the canvas, carried on in the banks and lines of the landscape on the left, emphasized by the thin, fluent brushwork and counterbalanced by the main mass of trees in the centre. The lateral stress and dynamism, characteristic of so many of Gainsborough's compositions of this period, is clearly influenced by Rubens. Gainsborough owned two large canvases by Snyders, one of them *A Boar Hunting*, and these may well have provided the initial impetus for this picture and its companion, now lost, *A Landscape with Deer*.

116. Landscape drawing. Mid 1780s. Pl. 150

A somewhat similar effect is achieved in this drawing, where the waggon and the track along which it is travelling are strongly lit from a light source on the right. The diagonal movement across the landscape, emphasized by the undulation of the terrain, is given further impetus by the counter-diagonal of the rococo tree trunk. The trees and foreground are roughly handled, in coarse black chalk enriched by stump, and the whole scene seems to be in vigorous motion, as though it were a landscape by Van Gogh. Paradoxically, a Claudean distance, building and mountain seen between trees, still forms a feature of the composition.

117. Cattle ferry. Mid to later 1780s. Pl. 120

A late sketch which gives the impression of being based on a drawing from life. The cows entering the boat are brilliantly outlined in dabs of thick oil paint, and the movement of the cattle is emphasized by the clouds, linked carefully with the diagonal of the sail, which are moving in the opposite direction. The treatment of the clouds and the extraordinary vigour of handling are comparable with the Grosvenor seascape (Pl. 121).

118. Diana and Actaeon.
About 1784–5. Pls 165, 166 and 169

The *Diana and Actaeon* is one of the most beautiful and idyllic of all Gainsborough's works, the only subject drawn from classical mythology he ever attempted. It is also one of the few canvases for which he made more than one preliminary drawing, so that the development of his ideas can be followed stage by stage. The story, taken from Ovid's *Metamorphoses*, tells how Actaeon, hunting in the sacred valley of Gargaphe, stumbled unwittingly on the bathing place of Diana and her attendants; Diana at once threw a handful of water at his face and turned him into a stag, whereupon he was torn to pieces by his own hounds. The first sketch (Pl. 165), brilliant and dramatic in concept, concentrates on the embarrassment caused by the intruding huntsman; the sense of confusion is heightened by the vigorously sketched tree trunks, spiralling in different directions above the figures. In the second sketch Diana has been moved to the left, there are fewer bathers and the nymphs have been grouped broadly in a semicircle, where they are partially sheltered by the foliage, now a protective mass bearing down on the figure of Actaeon. The third sketch shows Actaeon silhouetted against the sky and a largely different arrangement of the figures; neither the attitudes of the nymphs nor the massing of the trees any longer suggest agitation. This calmer design was substantially that used by Gainsborough for the painting itself, though the posture of Actaeon has been changed again and there are alterations in the background, notably the inclusion of a waterfall linking the two groups of figures; these were possibly evolved on the canvas itself, since numerous *pentimenti* can be detected. The picture was never finished in the strict sense of the word; most of the figures and much of the landscape are only sketched in. But, like the Washington landscape, it is complete as a work of art. The figures, one of them certainly based on a classical model, are beautifully grouped and demonstrate the loss we have sustained by Gainsborough's not having emulated his French contemporaries as a painter of the nude; the nymph on the right, reclining on the bank like a Matisse odalisque, emphasizes the mood of *poesie* successfully created by the fresh silvery harmonies of the colour.

119. Mrs Richard Brinsley Sheridan. 1785. Pl. 153

In this full-length of Mrs Sheridan, done thirteen years later than the double portrait at Dulwich, where she was portrayed just before her marriage, Gainsborough has produced a masterpiece in a wholly new style, the beginnings in English painting of that romantic approach to portraiture which Lawrence was to take to its furthest lengths. The abandon of the hair, which curls right down to the waist, and of the gauze wrap that is intertwined with it, is matched by the sketchiness of the brushwork throughout the dress. More important, however, the character of the brushwork in the hair and costume is taken up in the foliage of the trees, so that trees and figure form a natural compositional flow and the sitter really seems to be enveloped by the landscape in which she is seated so much at her ease. It is significant that Bate-Dudley thought it worthwhile mentioning that the lambs in the background, not included in the design when the painting was exhibited, were added by Gainsborough to give the picture 'an air more pastoral than it at present possesses'.

120. Mrs Sarah Siddons. 1785. Pl. 139

This is probably Gainsborough's most famous portrait. Though he has lavished his painterly skill on the silks and satins and furs of Mrs Siddons's dress, attention is firmly concentrated on the beautiful and delicately modelled head, which is the principal light in the picture, and stands out against the broad red curtain that closes the background. The likeness was an unusually striking one, according to contemporaries, and in this respect as well as in every other the portrait contrasted sharply with Reynolds's *Mrs Siddons as the Tragic Muse*, exhibited at the previous Academy, which Lawrence, in his enthusiasm for the Grand Manner in portraiture, was later to describe as 'indisputably the finest female portrait in the world'. It is not known whether Reynolds's *Lady Cornewall*, a far less successful essay in the same pose, and executed at about this time, was painted before or after Gainsborough's masterpiece.

121. Lady Sheffield. 1785. Pl. 100

This full-length of Lady Sheffield was painted in the spring following her marriage in 1784. She is seen walking gently forward towards the spectator, rather than being posed, as Mrs Sheridan is, and the impression which this creates of her being part of the landscape is reinforced not only by the tree on the left which arches over her head, but by the evenly distributed lighting. The face itself is rather generalized and empty in characterization, but the slight turn of the head and the dreaminess in the expression are the keynote, evocative of the poetic mood suffusing the whole canvas, the most original characteristic of Gainsborough's late style in portraiture. It is significant that the pose was later used for one of the figures in his idyll, *The Richmond Water-walk*. The costume accessories and folds of the dress are handled in Gainsborough's most brilliant sketchy technique.

122. Study for 'The Richmond Water-Walk'. About 1785. Pl. 151

One of a superb series of figure drawings, for long erroneously believed to be portraits of the Duchess of Devonshire, but actually studies for an important subject picture, apparently never completed, the idea for which was described by Bate-Dudley in *The Morning Herald* in October 1785: 'Gainsborough is to be employed, as we hear, for Buckingham-house, on a companion to his beautiful *Watteau-like* picture of the Park-scene, the landscape, Richmond water-walk, or Windsor – the figures all portraits.' A note relating to the British Museum study by Gainsborough's friend William Pearce recounts that 'While sketching one morning in the Park for this picture, he [Gainsborough] was much struck with what he called 'the fascinating leer' of the Lady who is the subject of the drawing. He never knew her name, but she was that evening in company with Lady N...field, & observing that he was sketching she walked to & fro' two or three times, evidently to allow him to make a likeness'. The sitter is shown dressed at the height of fashion, the stiff folds of her gown brilliantly modelled in bold highlights, strolling in a romantic landscape in which the trees play almost as important a role as the figure. The finished composition might well have proved to be Gainsborough's masterpiece.

123. Beggar Boys. 1785. Pl. 144

The model Gainsborough used for his *Beggar Boys* was the same boy he had included in his first fancy picture, *A Shepherd* – a street urchin he had found begging in St James's Street. In this picture there are conscious overtones of Murillo, in the tousled hair, the clothes and the water-jug; but, for the playful or cheeky expressions of Murillo's peasant children, Gainsborough has substituted the sentiment of the late eighteenth century, a gentle wistfulness in one case, the head half in shadow, and an upward gaze in the other as though he were an adoring saint in an *Assumption of the Virgin*, strongly spotlit as in the case of *Jack Hill* (the boy who was Gainsborough's favourite model for his fancy pictures, and who lived in Richmond, where the artist had a house). The contrast with a picture of the directness of his daughters chasing a butterfly is complete.

124. The Cottage Girl with Dog and Pitcher. 1785. Pl. 147

The *Cottage Girl with Dog and Pitcher* is the epitome of Gainsborough's sentiment, and perhaps the finest of all his fancy pictures; the expression is wistful, but neither cloying nor unnaturalistic, and the figure is posed with perfect aplomb between the cottage hidden amongst trees on the left and the bright cloud on the right. The picture was universally admired, and was promptly purchased by Sir Francis Basset, who sat to Gainsborough in the following year. A contemporary praised the pose of the dog as 'extremely natural and pleasing', and called the distance 'a charming landscape, with sheep and pastoral objects'; C.R.Leslie, the biographer of Constable, said it was 'unequalled by anything of the kind in the world. I recollect it at the British Gallery, forming part of a very noble assemblage of pictures, and I could scarcely look at or think of anything else in the rooms.' The model was the same as Gainsborough had used for *The Girl with Pigs*; he had met her near Richmond Hill, carrying under her arm the puppy he has painted her with here.

125. Haymaker and sleeping girl. About 1785. Pl. 129

The *Haymaker and sleeping girl* is in a different vein from the rest of Gainsborough's fancy pictures; the sentiment is no longer of an abstract nature, and the theme derives from those rustic lovers who had played a prominent role in so many of his landscapes from the 1750s onwards. The haymaker, prototype of the Victorian love-sick rustic, is gazing adoringly at the beautiful features and half-revealed breast of the sleeping girl, posed, deliberately, like a Correggio goddess, and the relationship between the two figures, with which the spectator feels an instant rapport, is beautifully sustained by the interplay of interlocking diagonals. The high key and fluent handling are emphasized by the delicious patch of sunlit landscape which opens up between the figures. It was this picture which was selected by Gainsborough Dupont, the artist's nephew and studio assistant, when Gainsborough offered him the choice of anything in his studio.

126. The Housemaid. Mid 1780s. Pl. 172

The close similarity in the features and pose of the head and neck between this unfinished sketch of a housemaid sweeping out a doorway and the portrait of Mrs Graham have prompted the tradition that Mrs Graham was the model for this fancy composition. If the head could be established as a portrait, the subject might be interpreted in terms of aristocratic longing for the simple life, something analogous to Marie Antoinette's absorption in her *laiterie*, but the resemblances are probably accidental. Gainsborough's extraordinary ability to create form with a few rapid strokes of the brush is marvellously displayed in the mob cap and the tousle of hair at the forehead.

127. 'The Morning Walk'. 1785. Pls 157 and 160

The Halletts were married in July 1785 and this marriage portrait makes a perfect stylistic contrast with that of Mr and Mrs Andrews, enabling visitors to the National Gallery to see at a glance, and to assess for themselves, the nature of the road upon which Gainsborough had travelled between 1748 and the mid 1780s. The picture is an extension of the type of mood portrait created in *Lady Sheffield*, as much a portrait of the romance of young love as it is a likeness of the two individuals; Mrs Hallett's costume, with its apple-green ribbons and bows, diaphanous wrap and sketchiness of handling, links as closely with the sylvan landscape as that of Mrs Sheridan. The French poet Gautier said that, in front of it, he felt 'a strange retrospective sensation, so intense is the illusion it produces of the spirit of the eighteenth century. We really fancy we see the young couple walking arm in arm along a garden avenue.' A more down-to-earth note is struck by the lively and superbly painted Spitz dog, compositionally the starting point of one of the two crossing diagonals that form the framework of the design, and which meet, appropriately, in Mrs Hallett's left hand.

128. Landscape. 1786. Pl. 145

The design of this beautiful landscape is based on the broad and relaxed compositional arc Gainsborough so often favoured, but within this slow curve into which all the figures and animals fit perfectly he has returned to Claude for the framework: a large mass on the left, with a lighter tree linking it to the background, a smaller mass on the right, and a panoramic distance closed by mountains – a distance much more carefully mapped out than in most of Gainsborough's later landscapes. The housemaid sweeping the steps and the girl with pigs have been borrowed from his fancy pictures of these subjects: at this stage of his development, when he was concerned principally with mood, in this case the sentiment associated with the theme of the 'Cottage Door', he evidently regarded his fancy subjects and the little figures which peopled his landscapes as interchangeable. The picture was bought almost as soon as it was finished by Wilbraham Tollemache, who had purchased the *Two shepherd boys with dogs fighting*.

129. The Market Cart. 1786. Pl. 162

This is perhaps the most famous of all Gainsborough's landscape idylls, and it was bought soon after completion, for three hundred and fifty guineas, by Sir Peter Burrell. The motifs which make up the picture are familiar to us from earlier works, but the force of the statement is new. A peasant family returning contentedly home after a successful day's marketing is gently spotlit by a shaft of light which penetrates the foliage on the right; luxuriant trees, painted in a variety of hues suggestive of early autumn, tower magnificently over the scene; and a boy in a red jacket gathering faggots, added by Gainsborough as an afterthought, provides a necessary accent of bright colour at the edge of the wood. The nobility of the trees, the bright clouds above, the easy naturalism of the scene, and such motifs as the boy in the red jacket, remind us of Constable; and it is only the conventional blue hill and generalized distance, still influenced by Claude, that persuade us we are looking at a picture of the 1780s rather than a Constable of forty years later. The monumental design contrasts sharply with the flowing, Rubensian compositions of a few years before.

130. Duchess of Richmond. About 1786–7. Pls 167 and 170

This full-length of Mary, wife of the third Duke of Richmond, a leading protagonist of parliamentary reform, is one of the most ravishing of Gainsborough's late romantic portraits. She is depicted wearing a blue satin dress, with a blue gauze scarf, her beautiful red hair falling over her shoulders, and set against a richly wooded landscape, her left arm resting on a pedestal. The enigmatic smile, and slightly distant expression, heighten the poetic mood of the canvas. It is a portrait of youthful beauty and hauteur, in the Van Dyck tradition, yet the sitter was forty-five when she was painted. Notice the long, thin right arm, an idiosyncrasy, seen in many of Gainsborough's late works, suggestive of the use of a lay-figure.

131. The Marsham children. 1787. Pl. 163

Although the children in this group are ostensibly gathering cherries, the scene is not very much like an orchard and the background is similar to that in most of Gainsborough's late portraits. The composition is based on a broad, swinging curve, starting with the movement of the boy on the right, passing through the arms of the girl with cherries in her apron, and ending in the tree on the left; this dominant curve is echoed in the broken branches in the foreground, and stabilized by two crossing diagonals similar to those in *The Morning Walk*. As in many of Gainsborough's groups, the relationship between the figures has not been fully resolved.

132. Self-portrait. About 1787. Fig. 5

Gainsborough painted this picture towards the end of his life, aged sixty. In this lively late self-portrait the head itself is very thinly painted, and the blues of the coat and greys of the background are loosely brushed in over the brown priming; touches of blue, yellow, brown and orange enliven the modelling of the cravat. The portrait is almost certainly unfinished and, if it is the canvas intended for Abel (Pl. 126), which is not certain, was presumably put aside after June 1787, the date of his friend's sudden death. The portrait Gainsborough painted for Abel is the one by which he wished to be remembered by posterity: 'It is my strict charge that after my decease no plaster cast, model, or likeness whatever be permitted to be taken: But that if Mr. Sharp . . . should choose to make a print from the $\frac{3}{4}$ sketch, which I intended for Mr. Abel, painted by myself, I give free consent.'

133. Landscape aquatint. About 1787. Pl. 133

One of Gainsborough's most powerful late prints, executed purely in aquatint. Towards the end of his life he had begun to experiment once again with this medium, using soft-ground etching only for secondary purposes within a design, because nothing but aquatint could satisfactorily render the brilliant light effects, dramatic silhouettes and turbulent skies of his late wash drawings and oil sketches. The lyrical swing of this composition, achieved partly through the trees and partly through the skilfully disposed patches of sunlight in the foreground, is directly comparable with *The Marsham children* and reflects one of Gainsborough's basic compulsions as a designer. The technique used for blocking out the foliage is identical to the rapid notation he employed in his late wash drawing now in Berlin (Pl. 171), but the effect, which is to give the features in the landscape a certain ruggedness unusual in his prints, is entirely different. Even in this original and very personal late work Gainsborough has opened up a Claudean vista between the trees.

134. Lady Bate-Dudley. 1787. Pl. 130

This canvas, painted the year before Gainsborough's death, represents the mood portrait taken to its extreme. The sitter is leaning on a pedestal surmounted by an urn, and is set against a sylvan background of soft, feathery foliage; the strong light playing over the figure throws the profile of the head into relief and emphasizes the downward gaze, principal element in the falling diagonals of the design. The expression is seemingly vapid and empty of character, but since the sitter was the wife of one of Gainsborough's closest friends and supporters, and the picture is supposed to have been executed at Bradwell, the Bate-Dudleys' home, this was clearly not the result of failure on the painter's part. The expression is in fact intended to represent 'poetry' or 'sensibility' or some other feminine intellectual ideal, and is the nearest Gainsborough ever approached to Reynolds's idealized portraiture; in his own work it is close in concept to the intentions of his fancy pictures.

135. Lady Petre. 1788. Pl. 52

This powerful full-length was begun shortly after the sitter's return from her honeymoon, and was completed within a month. Though the pose is a little forced – the motif of holding up the shawl does not ring true as an integral part of the design as it does in *Lady Molyneux* – the conception is vigorous and dramatic, and more closely anticipates Lawrence's romantic portraiture than does *Mrs Sheridan*. The brilliance of the background, with its stormy clouds and patches of fitful light, mysterious shadows and windswept trees, is matched by the force of Gainsborough's extraordinary treatment of the costume, deeply sculptural and highlit by a welter of rapidly applied brushstrokes which would not discredit an abstract expressionist. This roughness of handling extends to the modelling of the head. The right arm is somewhat spindly, as in the case of the *Duchess of Richmond*, and the enormous black hat appears either to be an afterthought or to have been added by a later hand.

136. Bernard, 12th Duke of Norfolk. 1788. Pl. 168

One of the last full-lengths Gainsborough painted before the onset of his fatal illness in the early summer of 1788. The sitter (Lady Petre's brother), who was painted as 'Mr. Howard', succeeded his father as 12th Duke of Norfolk in 1815. The composition is based on the crossing diagonals so often favoured by Gainsborough, and the sitter is closely integrated with the landscape background. The head, turned slightly to the right with an expression of gentle humour, is strongly spotlit, and the abandon of the hair, which harmonizes with the roughly massed foliage, emphasizes the informality of the pose and the romantic intent of the portrait. In this last inventive phase of his portraiture Gainsborough was at least the equal of Reynolds.

137. Young Hobbinol and Ganderetta. 1788. Pl. 140

Macklin's 'Poet's Gallery', which opened in April 1788, contained two works by Gainsborough. One of them, *The Cottage Girl with a Bowl of Milk*, painted in 1786, was described by Bate-Dudley as 'oddly perverted by Macklin to the *Lavinia* of Thomson'; the other, *Young Hobbinol and Ganderetta*, from William Somerville, was executed specifically for Macklin. The figures, typical of the roughly clad but healthy and good-looking children Gainsborough habitually used as models for his fancy pictures, and strongly spotlit, happily represent the cousins in the poem who grew up together 'to mutual fondness', and they are posed in a closely knit diagonal counterbalanced by that of the cat gazing upwards towards the sunset on the right. Of this picture Bate-Dudley said, Gainsborough 'always paints to the heart; Truth and Simplicity are his unerring guides, and by their aid he has expressed all that the rustic muse of *Somerville* could wish.'

138. Peasant smoking at a cottage door.
1788. Pl. 164

This was the last landscape of any size by Gainsborough, and the most majestic of all his pastorals. Unsold because the price, five hundred guineas, was too high, it was acquired after the artist's death by Bate-Dudley, and later passed to Sir George Beaumont. Designed as a companion to *The Market Cart*, it is rich and romantic in conception where the former is serene; the foliage is dramatically massed, the spotlight more theatrical, the sunset glow breaking through the trees more vivid than Claude, the paint at the horizon thick and encrusted. The composition is dominated by the near-dead tree trunk, distinctly reminiscent of the similar tree in *The Cottage Door* of 1780, which links together the two tree masses; beneath this the peasant family are grouped on the steps of their cottage in a pyramid rather looser in arrangement than was the case in the Huntington picture. A large composition study for this canvas contains most of the elements included in the finished work except for the cottage and the man smoking: at this stage Gainsborough had conceived the principal figure as a woodman seated on a pile of faggots, using for the pose one of his studies taken from the model, 'a poor smith worn out by labour', he had employed for his famous picture of *The Woodman*, now destroyed.

139. Landscape drawing. About 1787–8. Pl. 152

Gainsborough found relaxation from the strains and sheer hard work of portrait painting in two pleasures which gave him happiness his whole life through, music and drawing: this superb late drawing is dominated by the powerful swinging movement and dramatic sunset effect so personal to Gainsborough, but in which the mountains have been treated atmospherically rather than being outlined in flowing black chalk. The ruined castle gateway on the right is a characteristic Picturesque motif, part of the repertoire of a movement which was rapidly to become fashionable among the landscape painters and draughtsmen of the period.

140. Landscape drawing. About 1787–8. Pl. 171

One of Gainsborough's most dazzling late drawings. T
beauty of the effect of light in the water and the extraord
sureness of tone in the relations of the trees are achi
spite of the obvious rapidity of execution, and blin
to the lumpishness of the cow and the fact that Gai
has used the merest notation for the foliage.

LIST OF COLLECTIONS (works by Gainsborough only)

INDEX OF PERSONS